D0859369

WILDERNESS
WATERWAYS

Wilderness Waterways

The Whole Water Reference for Paddlers

Ronald Ziegler

For BIRGIT and CHRISTOPHER

My daughter and my son (in alphabetical order)

Printed in United States of America
Design and Production by Weisgerber Design

Wilderness Waterways, The Whole Water Reference For Paddlers is published by Canoe America Associates, 10526 NE 68th St, Suite 2, PO Box 3146, Kirkland, Wash. 98083.

Library of Congress Catalog Card Number: 91-90735

ISBN 0-9631595-0-X (hardcover); ISBN 0-9631595-1-8 (paperback)

Foreword

Paddlesport has changed dramatically since I bought my first canoe nearly two decades ago: there has been a renaissance of sorts. People from all walks of life are discovering that a wilderness waterway is a glorious medium, a liquid trail that can lead to serenity, adventure, natural beauty, and insight about ourselves and the planet on which we live. In virtually every part of North America — of the world — there is a river, lake, or stretch of coastline that beckons to be explored.

Commensurate with the boom in canoeing, kayaking and rafting have enjoyed healthy growth in paddling-related literature and reference material. There is a tremendous array of guidebooks, trip accounts, specialized periodicals, and videocassettes which can be particularly bewildering to people just entering the sport of paddling. Now, with the updated, second edition of WILDERNESS WATERWAYS, paddlers, historians, biographers, conservationists, and adventurers can sift through a cornucopia of knowledge with a maximum of organization and a minimum of trouble. Everything you always wanted to know about paddlesport literature — where to go, how to get there, technique and instructions, competition, maps and charts — is contained in this greatly expanded edition of Ronald Ziegler's exhaustive compendium.

One of the beauties of paddlesport is that it doesn't require vast acreages or exotic, faraway places to impart the feeling that you're really out there when aboard a canoe, kayak, or raft. Just reading WILDERNESS WATERWAYS can inspire one to appreciate the crooked creek that's probably only a few miles from home. Yet, whose heart does not race at the thought of paddling the stormy Beagle Channel south of Tierra Del Fuego, or poking down the bear-infested Aniakchak River in Alaska? This volume is a great companion during the quiet hours of a winter evening when the first paddling junket of spring always comes to mind. Whether you ponder an extended canoe trip, or want to discover a new place via a good book, you will find what you are looking for while perusing the literary reference pages of WILDERNESS WATERWAYS.

Today, people who want to get into paddling — and there are more of them than ever before — will find a mind boggling assortment of boats from which to choose. There are tough-as-nails expedition canoes, sleek Kevlar solos, whitewater kayaks, sea kayaks, folding boats, playboats, squirtboats, inflatables, surf skis, and self-bailing rafts. Wood and aluminum are still in use, but taking the center stage are high-tech materials whose composition only a ploymer chemist could understand. Ziegler helps you begin your own research as you start to ponder the purchase of your first boat.

Technology may have changed, but the essence of paddlesport has not. Strip away the veneer, and an elemental desire to seek out watery horizons remains. Whether a dugout canoe or computer-designed flatwater cruiser, a self-propelled craft offers the user satisfaction, challenge, fitness and just plain fun. Through the medium of print (and to a growing extent, videotape), we share our experiences, ideas and instruction, and define the way we think about our sport, each other and the wilderness waterways that make it all happen.

As a writer who has covered the paddling scene for more than a decade, I thought I knew most of what was available in print and video. I was wrong. A quick thumb-through of WILDERNESS WATERWAYS opened my eyes to a treasure-trove of literary productions that I had missed — reference that would have aided me while researching an article or planning a trip, selecting a canoe school, purchasing equipment, or just choosing a book to enjoy on a lazy day indoors. Like an encyclopedia, WILDERNESS WATERWAYS is a repository of derived knowledge, facts, notes and results pertaining to paddlesports, a useful tool that I plan to use often in the years ahead.

A free-flowing river is much more than its individual components, and Wilderness Waterways is much more than a list of books. It is a guide through a maze of information, a celebration of where paddlesport has been, and a glimpse of where it's going.

Larry Rice

Table of Contents

Introduction

Paddlesports — canoeing, kayaking, and rafting — are more popular than ever. More people than ever are discovering that moving under your own power on a lake, river, or stretch of coastline is just plain fun to do, and that serenity, exhilaration, natural beauty, friendship, fitness, and competition are just a few paddle strokes away. You don't have to be a certain age, nor are there many physical requirements. There is a craft and place for anyone willing to climb aboard and go.

Little wonder, then, that as canoeing, kayaking, and rafting grew, people wanted more information about where to go, how to get there, what equipment to take, and how to use it. I first compiled a listing of paddlesports literature in 1979 to provide people with the most comprehensive guide to information about North American waterways and their recreational use. This listing filled an entire book, called WILDERNESS WATERWAYS (Detroit, Mich.: Gale Research, 1979). The mass of guidebooks, trip accounts, technique books, histories, pictorial works, philosophical articles, conservation polemics, fiction, periodicals, videos, and maps produced since reflects the rapid growth of the sport and the need for more information. It prompted this revised edition of WILDERNESS WATERWAYS.

This new edition lists hundreds of paddlers' resources published or reprinted in North America between 1978 and Spring 1990, and includes many of the works listed in the first edition. I have worked to make this resource as complete and accurate as I know how, examining most of the literature personally. I have tried to describe the contents of each item in a straightforward, non-evaluative way, offering praise or criticism when it seems necessary. What I could not examine is cited fully, but without descriptive annotations. Such books are identified by three asterisks (***) located at the end of a citation.

Entries are arranged alphabetically in a letter-by-letter style. "Mc," "M'" and "Mac" are alphabetized as if spelled as "Mac." Compound names are considered as one name. Common abbreviations are listed as though they were spelled out. Non-directory entries are consecutively numbered throughout the book for easy access by cross-reference and from the indexes at the end of the book.

Your Guide to Each Chapter

CHAPTER 1 Guidebooks and Articles

This is the book's largest chapter. It is has five sections: 1) national and regional guidebooks; 2) provincial guidebooks; 3) state guidebooks; 4) guide articles published in CANOE magazine; and 5) maps that contain advise or descriptions regarding a waterway.

Most books in sections 1-3 were published after 1978 and are available in most bookstores, outdoors stores, through paddling clubs, or directly from the publisher. I do not describe guidebooks listed in the first edition of WILDERNESS WATERWAYS, except to specify which waterways they cover, when this is known. Books listed in the first edition carry the concluding citation note: (WW-1st ed).

Whenever possible, the waterways covered in the guidebook are listed within the annotation to facilitate index access. The entries are arranged geographically, by province, territory, or state; then by author or main entry.

Two-letter provincial and state postal abbreviations are used to aid geographic identification of the waterways described in the guides which have either broad regional coverage or non-specific titles. These location codes are at the end of citations. Virtually all the annotations indicate publisher/distributor addresses.

National and regional guidebooks are cited and annotated in Section 1. Any guidebook covering rivers in three or more provinces or states is fully annotated here with cross references from the relevant citations in the province/state sections. In sections 2 and 3 are the provincial and state guides. With 309 entries, these two sections constitute the major part of the chapter.

Section 4 lists articles published by CANOE magazine during 1980-1989. As with the guidebooks, arrangement is geographic and further access is afforded through the Waterways Index. Maps and "map-guides" (my term for the hybrids which may be either are cited in Section 5. This listing is also geographical as in the sections above. No attempt was made to be comprehensive since a large number of these items are of an ephemeral nature.

CHAPTER 2 Technique and Instruction

This chapter lists books about learning and perfecting paddlesports techniques, and the associated fundamentals of safety and rescue. Excluded are the many general works on camping, camp cooking, map reading, survival skills, first aid, and so forth. Instructional books emphasizing racing techniques are listed in Chapter 3.

CHAPTER 3 Competition

These books deal largely with racing technique and related information about competitive paddling. Some books listed in Chapter 2 contain information about competitive paddling, and the paddlesports periodicals in Chapter 7 also may be valuable, especially for timely items such as race dates and results.

CHAPTER 4 Trip Accounts

Trip accounts document extended trips made by modern-day paddlers. These adventurer-authors provide engrossing reading for the fireside adventurer, and they usually provide enormous detail about the waterways they traveled. If you read only guidebooks when you're planning a trip, you're missing an important resource by overlooking the trip account genre.

CHAPTER 5 History and Biography

These are books about early and contemporary travels, accounts, biographies, diaries, and journals that are by and about people who have close associations with North American waterways. Accounts of explorations are listed here. A number of these books are out of print, but larger libraries are likely to have most of them. Recent reprints of older works are cited whenever possible.

CHAPTER 6 Pictorial Works

Pictorial works feature visual images that have waterways or paddlesports as their principal theme. Often, these are large-format or "coffee table" books with exquisite color photographs. There are many books that could be included here, but this listing is selective and meant to be only a representative glimpse of this broad genre.

CHAPTER 7 Periodicals

You can keep current in the world of canoeing, kayaking, and rafting by reading the magazines and newsletters dedicated to paddlesports. This chapter has four sections: 1) paddlesports magazines (newsletters or magazines that focus mostly on canoeing, kayaking, or rafting); 2) a selective listing of club newsletters; 3) watersports and boating magazines that are not specific to paddlesports; and 4) general sports, conservation, and nature magazines that have regular or occasional paddlesports or wilderness waterways articles.

CHAPTER 8 Videotapes

The first edition of WILDERNESS WATERWAYS contained a listing of about 100 motion pictures, filmstrips, slide sets, and slide-audio tape presentations in a section called "visual media." Not a video among them. A decade later, this edition has no "old style" media listings, only videocassettes. Some older paddling films have been transferred to video and are listed among the newer title filmed on videotape. Further, these videorecordings are not exclusively North American in origin or content.

CHAPTER 9 Printed Indexes and Computerized Databases

Printed indexes and computerized databases are efficient tools for finding paddling information. This chapter lists seven sources — both general and single-purpose, print and electronic — which you can use for paddlesports and wilderness recreation research.

CHAPTER 10 Maps and Charts

Maps are as indispensable as matches to the touring paddler, and required reading for the trip planner. This chapter has four sections regarding where to find maps and charts: 1) federal government sources (public mapmakers or distributors); 2) provincial, territorial, and state government sources (geological survey and highway/transportation agencies); 3) commercial mapmakers and distributors; and 4) bibliographies and sales lists.

CHAPTER 11 Government Agencies and Private Organizations

This chapter lists the most current addresses and telephone numbers obtainable. The chapter has four sections: 1) federal agencies; 2) provincial and state agencies appropriate for inquiries about wilderness waterways; 3) national non-government organizations; 4) provincial and state non-government organizations; and 5) paddlesports clubs.

INDEXES

The author/title and waterways indexes assure comprehensive access to the numbered citations in this book, with the exception of guide articles and map-guides from Chapter 1 which are indexed in the waterways index only. Information from the directory chapters is not indexed (Chapter 10, Sections 1-3; and Chapter 11). The numbers given in the indexes refer to citation numbers, **not to page numbers.**

Acknowledgements

Many publishers supplied review copies of books listed in this volume. I am in their debt; good annotated bibliographies citing contemporary sources do not get written unless publishers help. Many books came to me on loan, thanks to the very efficient Holland Library Inter-Library Loan Office at Washington State University in Pullman, Washington. Last, I was permitted access to the considerable riches of the book collection located at CANOE magazine in Kirkland, Washington. I thank Judy and Dave Harrison and Deanna Jagla for their assistance.

Pullman, Washington
August 1990

Chapter 1, Section 1

Guidebooks and Articles for Canada and the United States

National and by Region

1. AMC RIVER GUIDE: MASSACHUSETTS, CONNECTICUT, RHODE ISLAND. Boston: Appalachian Mountain Club, 1985. 192 p. Illus. Maps. Index. Softcover. MA CT RI

For a general description of the AMC guidebooks, see entry 283. Publisher/distributor: Appalachian Mountain Club, 5 Joy St., Boston, MA 02108.

2. Anderson, Fletcher, and Hopkinson, Ann. RIVERS OF THE SOUTHWEST: A BOATERS GUIDE TO THE RIVERS OF COLORADO, NEW MEXICO, UTAH AND ARIZONA. 2d ed. Boulder, CO: Pruett Publishing, 1987. 129 p. Illus. Maps. Softcover. AZ CO NM UT.

"This is a guidebook for whitewater kayakers, rafters, and canoeists," states the book's introduction. The book covers a large number of rivers and does not provide mile-by-mile, rapid-by-rapid descriptions or detailed examinations of riverside attractions. Anderson and Hopkinson list maps, water flow information, and give an overview of the rivers which will help planners make prudent trip choices. The narrative descriptions of the runs are arranged first by drainage, then river/route, with varying amounts of information depending upon paddling suitability. Sketch maps and photographs illustrate this material. Appendixes categorize the runs: 1) multi-day trips (e.g., San Juan River, Flaming Gorge of the Green River, Chama River, Salt River); 2) "hair" runs, including the four Southwestern U.S. Class V "classics," (Pine Creek Rapids of the Arkansas, Narrows Rapids of the Cache la Poudre, Gore Canyon of the Colorado, and Cross Mountain Canyon of the Yampa); and 3) easy runs (e.g., the Blue, Roaring Fork, Verde, and Rio Grande rivers). Publisher/distributor: Pruett Publishing Co., 2928 Pearl St., Boulder, CO 80301-9922.

3. APPALACHIAN WHITEWATER: VOLUME I, THE SOUTHERN MOUNTAINS. Compiled by Bob Sehlinger and others. Birmingham, AL: Menasha Ridge Press, 1986. 159 p. Illus. Maps. Index. Paper. AL GA KY NC SC TN

Three volumes comprise this series (volumes II, THE CENTRAL MOUNTAINS, and III, THE NORTHERN MOUNTAINS, are cited below.) While the authors differ, all have the same general arrangement and format. Over 100 streams in the Appalachians are comprehensively covered in the series, each described by the compilers in several paragraphs with information on river setting, topography, pollution, gauges, best season, difficulties, and put-in/take-out. An "at-a-glance" data table listing runnable water levels, gradient, volume, USGS quads, hazards, scenery, etc., and a detailed map (some with insets of notable rapids), indicating access points, river and shuttle mileage, complete the river information package. Introductory pages provide an overview on river and paddler rating, hazards, safety, and stream dynamics. The states and a sampling of rivers covered in this volume: KY (Cumberland), TN (Tellico, Ocoee, Hiwassee), AL (Little), GA (Chattooga, Upper Chattahoochee), NC (French Broad, Nantahala, New), SC (Chauga). Publisher/ distributor: Menasha Ridge Press, P.O. Box 59257, Birmingham, AL 35259-9257.

4. APPALACHIAN WHITEWATER: VOLUME II, THE CENTRAL MOUNTAINS. Compiled by Ed Grove and others. Birmingham, AL: Menasha Ridge Press, 1987. 207 p. Illus. Maps. Index. Paper. DE MD PA WV

Second volume in a series of three describing canoeing and kayaking on rivers of the Appalachian Range (see citation for VOLUME I, above, for a general description). The states and a sampling of rivers covered in this volume: PA (Lower Youghiogheny, Lehigh), WV (Gauley, New, Cheat, Cacapon), MD and DE (Upper Youghiogheny, Savage, Prime Hook), VA (Potomac,

Maury, James). Publisher/distributor: Menasha Ridge Press, P.O. Box 59257, Birmingham, AL 35259-9257.

5. APPALACHIAN WHITEWATER: VOLUME III, THE NORTHERN MOUNTAINS. Compiled by John Connelly and John Porterfield. Birmingham, AL: Menasha Ridge Press, 1987. 141 p. Illus. Maps. Index. Paper. CT ME MA NH VT

Third volume in a series of three describing canoeing and kayaking on rivers of the Appalachian Range (see citation for VOLUME I, above, for a general description). The states and a sampling of rivers covered in this volume: CT (Husatonic, Farmington), MA (Westfield, Quaboag), VT (West, Ottaquechee), NH (Contoocook, Merrimack, Pemigewasset), ME (Sheepscot, Dead, Kennebec, Penobscot). Publisher/distributor: Menasha Ridge Press, P.O. Box 59257, Birmingham, AL 35259-9257.

6. Armstead, Lloyd D. WHITEWATER RAFTING IN EASTERN NORTH AMERICA: A GUIDE TO RIVERS AND PROFESSIONAL OUTFITTERS. 2d ed. Chester, CT: Globe Pequot Press, East Woods Book, 1989. 155 p. Illus. Maps. Index. Paper. CAN USA

A general introduction to rafting on 40 eastern U.S. streams, and nine in eastern Canada. In the introductory material in Chapter 1, Armstead gives the novice rafter tips on gear, cost, trip organization, safety, and other related information. The river guide sections (chapters 2-5), present for each river: a tabular overview of the run, location, distance, difficulty, season, and commercial outfitters. The table is followed by several short paragraphs of descriptive narrative. Armstead recommends that most river rafters seek the services of professional guides. Chapters 6 and 7 comprise an extensive river-by-river directory of outfitters and riverside accommodations. Publisher/distributor: Globe Pequot Press, P.O. Box Q, Chester, CT 06412.

7. Burmeister, Walter F. THE DELAWARE AND ITS TRIBUTARIES. Appalachian Waters, no. 1. Oakton, VA: Appalachian Books, 1974. 274 p. Map. Bibl. Paper. DE NJ NY PA River(s): upper, central and lower Delaware River system.

8. Burmeister, Walter F. THE HUDSON RIVER AND ITS TRIBUTARIES. Appalachian Waters, no. 2. Oakton, VA: Appalachian Books, 1974. 496 p. Maps. Bibl. Index. Paper. CT MA NJ NY VT (WW-1st ed.) River(s): upper, central and lower Hudson tributaries.

9. Burmeister, Walter F. THE SOUTHEASTERN RIVERS. Appalachian Waters, no. 4. Oakton, VA: Appalachian Books, 1976. 850 p. Bibl. Index. Paper. FL GA NC SC VA (WW-1st ed.)

10. Burmeister, Walter F. THE SUSQUEHANNA RIVER AND ITS TRIBUTARIES. Appalachian Waters, no. 3. Oakton, VA: Appalachian Books, 1975. 600 p. Bibl. Index. Paper. NY MD PA (WW-1st ed.)

11. Burmeister, Walter F. THE UPPER OHIO & ITS TRIBUTARIES. Appalachian Waters, no. 5. Oakton, VA: Appalachian Books, 1978. 948 p. Bibl. Index. Paper. KY NY OH PA VA WV

The Ohio River system is so complex that the task of describing the paddling possibilities on the 200-odd streams in this drainage must have been a daunting one. However, Burmeister, seemingly unintimidated by any chore of guidebook compilation, has produced yet another detailed book in his extensive series (as usual, over-long, and physically unappealing). In addition to the Ohio, the larger rivers covered are the Allegheny, Monongahela, and Kanawha; the renown whitewater streams in the drainage include the Cheat, Youghiogheny, New, and Gauley. Publisher/distributor: Appalachian Books, P.O. Box 248, Oakton, VA 22124.

12.CANOEING AND FISHING GUIDE TO THE UPPER DELAWARE RIVER. Madison, NJ: Pathfinder Publications, 198? 88 p. Illus. Maps. Paper. NJ NY PA

A poorly-conceived, semi-literate guidebook containing a minimum of canoeing information on the upper 135 miles of the Delaware. (There is somewhat more information on how to fish the river.) Display advertisements for canoe rental agents, sporting goods stores, commercial campsites, etc., are sprinkled throughout. A few sketch maps show access points. Publisher/distributor: Pathfinder Publications Inc., 210 Central Ave., Madison, NJ 07940.

13. Canter, Ron, and Canter, Kathy. NEARBY CANOEING STREAMS. 4th ed. Hyattsville, MD: 1979. 62 p. Illus. Maps. Paper. DE MD PA VA WV

Describes over 150 canoe runs within 100 miles of Washington, D.C. Each run is sketch-mapped in the first section. Notes about gauge locations, put-in, take-out, scenery, rapids, obstacles, etc., are on the maps. In the second part of the booklet, the Canters list river sections in tabular format giving: name, class, difficult rapids, section, state, length, size

January 27, 1992

Wilderness Waterways is missing reference headings 18 through 55 in Chapter 1, Section 1. An insert containing the missing information has been added to rectify this unfortunate production error.

To author Ronald Ziegler and all of you who have purchased Wilderness Waterways, I offer my sincere apology.

I hope that you do not find the valuable information within the covers of Wilderness Waterways diluted in any way due to this oversight.

Les Johnson

CANOE AMERICA ASSOCIATES

18. Corbett, H. Roger, Jr., and Matacia, Louis J., Jr. ONE & TWO DAY RIVER CRUISES: MARYLAND, VIRGINIA, WEST VIRGINIA. Blue Ridge Voyages, vol. 2, 2d ed. Oakton, VA: Appalachian Books, 1972. 88 p. Pref. Illus. Maps. Bibl. Paper. MD VA WV (WW-1st ed.) River(s): Potomac and its south branch, Cedar Creek, Catoctin Creek, Cacapon, Monocacy, and Antietam.

19. Dickerman, Pat. ADVENTURE TRAVEL NORTH AMERICA. 15th ed. New York: Adventure Guides; Henry Holt, Owl Book, 1986. 256 p. Illus. Index. Paper. CAN USA

A directory/guide to commercial outfitters for active travelers on foot, horseback, wheels, water, snow, and in the air: Paddling enthusiasts will perhaps be most interested in the 70 pages entitled "On or in Waters a chapter in which Dickerman presents access sources on canoeing, kayaking, river running and scuba diving. The information given in all listings is fairly standard and includes: name, address, phone, area of operation, group size, duration of trip, cost, and a few sentences describing the service. Material is grouped by province/state. There are separate indexes listing river runs and outfitters. Publisher/distributor: Adventure Guides, Inc., 36 E. 57th St., New York, NY 10022.

20. Dirksen, D. J., and Reeves, R. A. RECREATION ON THE COLORADO RIVER. Aptos, CA: Sail Sales Publishing, 1985. 112 p. Illus. Maps. Index. Paper. AZ CA CO NV UT

The guide is organized into four sections in which the authors map and briefly describe recreational possibilities on, along (and above) the river from its source to the Sea of Cortez, Each page has a map, descriptive text, and tabular information giving: location, elevation, size, campsites, boating/fishing/other recreation, and local contact addresses. Government agency and outfitter directory. The power boat emphasis of the book renders it only marginally useful to self-propellers. Publisher/distributor: Recreation Sales Publishing, Inc., P.O. Box 4024, Burbank, CA: 91503-4024.

21. Esslen, Rainer. BACK TO NATURE IN CANOES: A GUIDE TO AMERICAN WATERS. Frenchtown, NJ: Columbia Publishing, 1976. 345 p. Maps. Bibl. Paper. USA (WW-1st ed.)

22. Estes, Chuck; Carter, Liz; and Almquist, Byron. CANOE TRAILS OF THE DEEP SOUTH: THE RIVERS OF LOUISIANA, ALABAMA, AND MISSISSIPPI. Birmingham, AL: Menasha Ridge Press, 1990. 304 p. Illus. Maps. Paper. AL LA MS ***

23. Evans, Laura, and Belknap, Buzz. FLAMING GORGE DINOSAUR NATIONAL MONUMENT: DINOSAUR RIVER GUIDE. Boulder City, NV: Westwater Books, 1973. 63 p. Illus. Maps. Paper. CO UT WY

The Yampa and Green as they flow through Dinosaur and Flaming Gorge, are the subject rivers of this guide. The book consists of a series of strip maps drawn to scale by Belknap from various maps of the U.S. Geological Survey and Forest Service. The first map is of Flaming Gorge Reservoir showing campgrounds, distances, and access roads. Succeeding maps show the rivers by section: Red Canyon, Browns Park, Canyon of Lodore, Whirlpool Canyon, Split Mountain Canyon, and the lower Yampa River. Material alongside the maps includes elevation and topographic detail, rapids, mileage, photographs, and quotations from John Wesley Powell's 1875 report, EXPLORATION OF THE COLORADO RIVER OF THE WEST AND ITS TRIBUTARIES. Publisher/distributor: Westwater Books, P.O. Box 2560, Evergreen, CO 80439.

24. Fixler, Alvin. FAMILY RIVER RAFTING GUIDE. Chicago: Caroline House, 1979. 320 p. Illus. Maps. Bibl. Index. Paper. USA ***

25. Gabler, Ray. NEW ENGLAND WHITE WATER RIVER GUIDE. Boston, MA: Appalachian Mountain Club, 1981. 376 p. Illus. Maps. Bibl. Paper. CT MA ME NH NY VT

Whitewater trips of a day or less in the Northeast. Gabler rates the "toughest" rivers (Boreas, Contoocook, Hudson, Pemigewasset, Rapid, and Swift), the most scenic (Boreas, Dead, Green, Hudson, Rapid, and White), and those best for open boats (Green, White, Piscataquog, Suncook, Westfield, Shepaug, and Salmon). In Part I, the author defines and instructs on the topics of degree of difficulty, river level, gradients gauge use, safety, hypothermia, scouting, and hand signals. The river descriptions, based on on-the-water notes, comprise the second part. Several score of possible runs are given for fifty-eight rivers, each accompanied by a clearly-drawn sketch map and other material: put-in, take-out, difficulties, gauge locations, and a paragraph or so imparting the overall character of the river. This general work is now largely superseded by AMC "s river guide series (see entries 1 or 283). Publisher/distributor: Appalachian Mountain club, 5 Joy St., Boston, MA 02108.

26. Gilbert, David T. RIVERS & TRAILS: BICYCLE TOURING, BACKPACKING, AND CANOEING IN THE MID-ATLANTIC STATES. Drawings by Laura L. Marzloff. Knoxville, MD: Outdoor Press, 1978. 112 P. Illus. Maps. Bibl. Index. Paper. DE MD VA WV

Self-propelled travel in Virginia, West Virginia, Maryland and Delaware. Gilbert's guide is organized by region and travel method. In his canoeing chapter, the author gives a superficial overview of the Potomac, Monongahela, Kanawha, James, York, and Rappahannock Rivers. Specific river guidebooks are cited in the bibliography. The totality of canoeing information in this book is rather sparse.

27. Hamblin, W. Kenneth, and Rigby, J. Keith. GUIDEBOOK TO THE COLORADO RIVER, PART I: LEES FERRY TO PHANTOM RANCH IN GRAND CANYON NATIONAL PARK. PART II: PHANTOM RANCH IN GRAND CANYON NATIONAL PARK TO LAKE MEAD, ARIZONA-NEVADA. Brigham Young University Geology Studies, Studies for students nos. 4 and 5. Provo, UT: Brigham Young University, 1969. 2 vols. Illus. Paper. AZ NV UT (WW-1st ed.) Part III of this series is cited under Rigby, J. Keith, (see entry 402). River(s): Colorado, from Lees Ferry to Lake Mead.

28. HELLS CANYON OF THE SNAKE RIVER. Quinn Map. Redmond, OR: Educational Adventures, 198? [20 p.] Illus. Maps. Paper. ID OR WA

A strip-map/guide on coated paper describing the seventy-eight miles of the Snake from Hells Canyon Dam to Heller Bar at the confluence of the Grande Ronde. Side streams, rapids, campsites, mileage, and road and trail access are indicated on the maps. On parallel text, Quinn gives information on rapids, and human and natural history. A concluding table lists campsite setting and facilities. Publisher/distributor: Educational Adventures, P.O. Box. 4190, Sunriver, OR 97707.

29. Jackson, Bart. WHITE WATER: RUNNING THE WILD RIVERS OF NORTH AMERICA. New York: Walker, 1979. 126 p. Illus. Bibl. Index. Paper. CAN USA

"This volume presents a trip-planning guide to 72 whitewater streams throughout America [U.S.A. only]," (introduction). Jackson's intended audience ranges from the beginner to experienced paddlers in all types of self-propelled craft. River descriptions are very brief narratives introduced with a standardized abstract giving class, description, standard run, location, and running season arranged by region and state. Over 130 photographs in color and black-and-white illustrate the work.

30. Jenkinson, Michael. WILD RIVERS OF NORTH AMERICA. 2d ed. New York: E.P. Dutton, 1981. 409 p. Illus. Bibl. Index. Paper. CAN USA *** Waterway(s): Rogue, Salmon, Urique, Colorado, Suwannee, Yukon, Buffalo, Rio Grande, and the Voyageurs route.

31. Jennings, Alan K. WHITEWATER, WILDWATER. Oak Hill, WV: Royal Oak Press, 1981. 35 p. Illus. Paper. CAN USA

Chiefly a directory of rafting outfitters working the rivers of the eastern U.S. Jennings supplies brief information about the more popular runs. Publisher/distributor: Odyssey River Treks, 142-5 Lively St., Fayetteville, WV 25840.

32. Jones, Charles, and Knab, Klaus. AMERICAN WILDERNESS: A GOUSHA WEEKEND GUIDE: WHERE TO GO IN THE NATION'S WILDERNESS, ON WILD AND SCENIC RIVERS AND ALONG SCENIC TRAILS. San Jose, CA: Gousha Publications, 1973. 212 p. Paper. USA (WW-1st ed.) River(s): Allagash, Clearwater, Lochsa, Selway, Eleven Point, Feather Middle Fork, Rio Grande, Rogues St. Croix, Salmon Middle Fork, and Wolf.

33. Kemmer, Rick. A GUIDE TO PADDLE ADVENTURE: HOW TO BUY CANOES, KAYAKS, AND INFLATABLES, WHERE TO TRAVEL, AND WHAT TO PACK ALONG. New York: Vanguard Press, 1975. 316 p. Illus. Maps. CAN USA (WW-1st ed.)

34. Kissner, Jakob, ed. FABULOUS FOLBOT HOLIDAYS. 4th ed. Charleston, SC: Creative Holiday Guides, 1976? 308 p. Illus. Maps. Paper. CAN USA (WW-1st ed.) Waterway(s): Ottawa River, Rideau Canal (ON), Connecticut River, Delaware River, upper Hudson River, New River (WV), Dan River (NC), Four Hole Swamp (SC), Suwannee River, Econfina Creek (FL), Grand Padre Island, Rio Grande, Wind River (WY), Mokelumne River (CA), Columbia River, North Saskatchewan River (AB), Prince William Sound, and Bering Sea.

35. Letcher, Gary. CANOEING THE DELAWARE RIVER: A GUIDE TO THE RIVER AND SHORE. New Brunswick, NJ: Rutgers University Press, 1985. 244 P. Illus. Maps. Bibl. DE NJ NY PA

A guide to ten day-trips on almost 195 miles of the Delaware from Hancock, NY to Trenton, NJ. Letcher's trip descriptions each have a general introduction, mile-by-mile guide with strip maps (from the Delaware River Basin Commission), and information on special features, camping, and other services. An appendix gives topical access to points of special interest. Publisher/distributor: Rutgers University Press, 109 Church St., New Brunswick, NJ 08901.

36. LOWER SALMON RIVER GUIDE. Rev. ed. Washington, DC: U.S. Dept. of the Interior, Bureau of Land Management, 1983. 18 p. Maps. Paper. ID OR WA

Adapted by the BLM from Scott and Margaret Arighi's, WILDWATER TOURING. Coverage by strip map and parallel log description is from mile eighty-four of the Lower Salmon (Riggins, ID), to its confluence with the Snake River, then down the Snake twenty miles to take-out at the Grande Ronde River confluence. Maps show access, rapids class (International Scale), river miles, public lands, and campsites. Publisher/distributor: Bureau of Land Management, Resource Area Headquarters, Route 39 Cottonwood, ID 83522.

37. Makens, James C. CANOE TRAILS DIRECTORY. Garden City, NY: Doubleday, Dolphin Book, 1979. 360 p. Bibl. Paper. USA Published in 1971 under the title: MAKIN'S GUIDE TO U.S. CANOE TRAILS, Irving, TX: Le Voyageur Publishing Co.

Makens gives concise descriptions of nearly 19000 waterways throughout the fifty United States, which he organizes by state, region, and river. Information given: location, access, portages, mileage, fishing, best season, history, surroundings, difficulty, and the kind of trip one can expect. Publisher/distributor: Doubleday & Co., Inc., 666 Fifth Ave. New York, NY 10103.

38. Malo, John W. MIDWEST CANOE TRAILS. Chicago: Contemporary Books, 1978. 186 p. Illus. Bibl. Index. Paper. CAN USA ***

39. Medes, Elizabeth. EXCITING RIVER RUNNING IN THE U.S. Chicago: Contemporary Books, 1979. 192 p. Illus. Maps. Bibl. Index. Paper. USA

Twenty-eight "classic" rivers, Class III and above, are presented in Medes' book, which seems best suited for the thrill-seeking novice shopping for a river and a guide/ outfitter. Descriptions give rating, put-in/take-out, trip length, outfitters, maps, general observations, suggested reading, and appropriate agencies. Some less renowned rivers are briefly acknowledged in the concluding chapter. This title is out of print, but the loss is not great since much of the information is either dated or easily found elsewhere. Publisher/distributor: Contemporary Books, Inc., 180 No. Michigan Ave., Chicago, IL 60601.

40. Miskimins, Ray W. GUIDE TO FLOATING WHITEWATER RIVERS. Portland, Or: Frank Amato Publications, 1967. 180 p. Illus. Maps. Bibl. Index. Paper. USA

An all-in-one basic river running handbook, and brief introduction to over sixty popular runs throughout the United States. The first nine chapters are a primer covering watercraft, "reading" the water, paddle technique, camping, safety and fishing. Chapter ten, "Our Whitewater Rivers," is a "skeleton" guide—a starting point from which the new paddler may begin researching a river to run. River description data: river name, location, run, distance, season, difficulty, rapids, environment, and a paragraph of comment. Publisher/distributor: Frank Amato Publications, P.O. Box 021129 Portland, OR 97202.

41. Nealy, William. WHITEWATER HOME COMPANION: SOUTHEASTERN RIVERS, VOLUME I. Hillsborough, NC: Menasha Ridge Press, 1981. 156 p. Illus. Maps. Paper. AL GA NC PA SC TN WV

The first in a two-volume work (see the entry for Volume II, below). Cartoonist-kayaker Nealy tries a new approach to presenting river guide information with his strip-map comic book about classic whitewater runs on thirteen southeastern rivers. I was unable to examine the revised edition of Volume I which has a Savage River map and a revision of the Cheat Canyon map. However, the 1981 edition is, above all, an original package of river information containing easy-to-visualize drawings (with "magnified" insets of Class IV+ rapids), and death-by-kayak black humor. Moreover, Nealy gives us an understandable primer on kayak technique, the language and customs of the indigenous kayak peoples, and river hydrodynamics. The thirteen rivers: Chattahoochee, Chattooga, Cheat,

French Broad, Gauley, Haw, Hiwassee, Locust Fork of the Warrior, Nantahala, New, Nolichucky, Ocoee, and the Youghiogheny. Publisher/distributor: Menasha Ridge Press, P.O. Box 59257, Birmingham, AL 35259-9257.

42. Nealy, William. WHITEWATER HOME COMPANION: SOUTHEASTERN RIVERS, VOLUME II. Hillsborough, NC: Menasha Ridge Press, 1984. 165 p. Illus. Maps. Paper. GA KY MD NC TN VA WV

See the annotation for Volume I (above), for a general description of this two-volume set. In this book, after introductory pages with material on technique and safety, Nealy cartoons (in the same inimitable style of Volume I), his way down runs on ten more Southeastern rivers: Chattahoochee, North Fork of the Cumberland, Big South Fork of the Cumberland, James, Maury, New, South Fork of the New, Potomac, Shenandoah, and Wilson (Creek). "Riverese," a glossary of kayaking terms concludes the book. Publisher/distributor: Menasha Ridge Press, P.O. Box 59257, Birmingham, AL 35259-9257.

43. Nichols, Gary. RIVER RUNNERS' GUIDE TO UTAH AND ADJACENT AREAS. Rev. ed. Salt Lake City: University of Utah Press, 1986. 168 p. Illus. Maps. Paper. AZ CO ID UT WY

Sixty trips in and around Utah for river runners of all experience levels using all types of craft (kayak emphasis). Nichols' trip descriptions are concise and contain river name, trip, difficulty, length, seasons gradient, flow, topo map, access, date of first run, and a paragraph or so of narrative (concluding with a suggested guidebook or two). Maps show access roads. The many action photographs in color are stunning. Some of the Utah rivers: Colorado, Logan, Jordan, Provo, Uinta, Green, San Rafael, Sevier, Dirty Devil, North Fork of the Virgin, and the San Juan. Publisher/distributor: University of Utah Press, 101 USB, Salt Lake City, UT 84112

44. Nickels, Nick. NICK NICKELS' CANOE CANADA. Toronto; New York: Van Nostrand Reinhold, 1976. 278 p. Illus. Bibl. Paper. CAN (WW-1st ed.)

45. NORTHEASTERN COASTAL PADDLING GUIDE. Edited by Chuck Sutherland. Tuckahoe, NY: Association of North Atlantic Kayakers, 1984. 39 p. Illus. Maps. Paper. CT MA ME NJ NY RI

Offprints of trip notes first appearing in the newsletters: ANORAK, and MESSING ABOUT IN BOATS. The articles recount kayak trips taken in fourteen coastal areas between Maine and New Jersey. In some cases it is difficult to extricate the guide information from the verbal baggage. However, most of the charts (reproduced from NOAA originals) are clear and contain some helpful notes. Overall, Sutherland's compilation is a convenient source for seldom described trips. Charted trips: Monhegan Island (ME), Down East Coastal Canoe & Kayak Trail (ME), Cape Ann (MA), Plum Island (MA), Salem Sound (MA), Osterville Grand Island (MA), Rhode Island Sound, Lord Cove (CT), Falkner Island (CT), Thimble Islands (CT), Southwest Connecticut coast, Long Islands New York City area, and the North Jersey Marshes. This material may be out of print, but one might write: MESSING ABOUT IN BOATS, 29 Burley St., Wenham, MA 01984.

46. Palzer, Bob, and Palzer, Jody. WHITEWATER, QUIETWATER: A GUIDE TO THE WILD RIVERS OF WISCONSIN, UPPER MICHIGAN, AND N.E. MINNESOTA. 5th ed. Two Rivers, WI: Evergreen Paddleways, 1983. 160 p. Illus. Maps. Bibl. Paper. MI MN WI

"This edition has been revised and updated from an original version prepared in cooperation with the Wisconsin Hoofers Outing Club of the Wisconsin Unions Madison, Wisconsin" (title page). (A virtually identical edition to the one now marketed by Menasha Ridge Press.) Some 750 miles of rivers have been mapped and described. Trips are presented as one-day runs between automobile access points; in this ways trips of many days may be planned by linking a number of runs. Thirty-three rivers are mapped and described; an additional ten are briefly mentioned. The two-color maps are drawn in sufficient detail to show rapids, access, campsites, and other information. Trip descriptions provide data on access, mileage, time, river width, gradient, difficulty, and flow. For perhaps one-fifth of the book, the Palzers discuss equipment, technique, safety, organizations, competition, and other canoe-related issues. A selection of the rivers: Bad, Black, Bois Brule, Cloquet, Kettle, Flambeau, Ford, Little Wolf, Menominee, Namekagon, Oconto, Peshtigo, Pine, St. Croix, Tomahawk, White, Wisconsin, and Wolf. Publisher/distributor: Menasha Ridge Press, P.O. Box 592579 Birmingham, AL 35259-9257.

47. Parks Canada. WILD RIVERS. Ottawa, ON: Parks Canada, 1974-. 10 vols. Illus. Maps. Bibl. Paper. CAN

The first volume in a ten(?)-volume series of river guides is WILD RIVERS: SASKATCHEWAN. Five trips of varying length down the Clearwater, Fon du Lac, Churchill, and Sturgeon-Weir are described. Amply illustrated with photographs and maps, the guide provides a reliable description of rapids, portages, native plants and animals, fishing tips, and geography. Only about half the remaining titles were examined, however uniformity of information presented, and reliability of a high degree may be assumed for all books in the series since it is the product of an official Parks Canada program (Wild Rivers Survey, Planning Division). Other series titles: YUKON TERRITORY (Yukon, Nisutlin, Teslin, Big Salmon, Ross, Pelly, MacMillan, White, Stewart, Sixty Mile, Klondike, Bell, and Porcupine rivers); JAMES BAY AND HUDSON BAY (Fawn, Severn, Attawapiskat, Ogoki, Albany, Missinaibi, Moose, Rupert, and L'Eau Claire rivers); THE BARRENLANDS (Hare Indian, Snare, Coppermine, Hanbury, and Thelon rivers); SOUTHWESTERN QUEBEC AND EASTERN ONTARIO (French, Kipewa, Dumoine, Perch, Chef, and Chamouchouane rivers); QUEBEC NORTH SHORE (Natashquan, Romaine, Manitou, Moisie rivers); CENTRAL BRITISH COLUMBIA; ALBERTA; LABRADOR AND NEWFOUNDLAND; and NORTHWEST MOUNTAINS. (This final survey may not yet be published.) Many of the surveys of individual rivers within the regions may be purchased in mimeographed form. A number of these are listed in chapter 12 of WILD RIVERS: SASKATCHEWAN. Publisher/distributor: Environment Canada, Parks. Les Terrasses de la Chaudiere, Hull, PQ (Mailing address: Ottawa, ON K1A OH3).

48. Penny, Richard. THE WHITEWATER SOURCEBOOK: A DIRECTORY OF INFORMATION ON AMERICAN WHITEWATER RIVERS. Birmingham, AL: Menasha Ridge Press, 1969. 329 p. Illus. Maps. Index. Paper. USA

A directory and information guide to circa 300 U.S. rivers. Penny's idea of publishing a "little black book" of names, addresses, phone numbers and measurements is impressive because of the number of rivers and the quantity of compressed information given for each. Arrangement is by state, with information on each river in a standardized format: name, runnable sections (including class), length of run (number of days, miles), location, maps needed, times runnable, permit, reservations, restrictions, gauge (location), source for water levels (name, telephone), how reported (in cfs, or feet), interpretation of levels (description of min/max in cfs and feet), source of more information (name, address, telephone of local contact), and, the best guidebooks to read. At the end of each state section is a list of general sources of information.

In Parts II—VI, the user will find descriptions and/or lists of wild and scenic rivers, map sources, organizations, published materials, and "tools" (river volume calculation; International Scale of River Difficulty). Reproductions of various permit and reservation forms comprise the appendices. Penny promises subsequent editions of his book—always advisable since directory-type information ages quickly. Publisher/distributor: Menasha Ridge Press, P.O. Box 59257, Birmingham, AL 35259-9257.

49. Pierce, Don. EXPLORING MISSOURI RIVER COUNTRY. Jefferson City, MO: Missouri Department of Natural Resources, 198? 276 p. Illus. Maps. Paper. KS MO NE

The lower Missouri River, 383 miles from Nebraska City, NE, to the Mississippi River confluence in St. Louis, is mapped and described in this combined canoeing/boating guide. The main section of the guide, Part II, is composed of detailed strip maps with mile-by-mile descriptive text on the facing pages. Pierce intersperses "inventories of places of interest," which include campsites. In Part I, he describes the recreational, natural, and historic features to be found on or near the Big Muddy. Publisher/distributor: Missouri Dept. of Natural Resources. Div. of Parks and Historic Preservation. P.O. Box 176, Jefferson City, MO 65102.

50. Pyle, Sara. CANOEING AND RAFTING: THE COMPLETE WHERE-TO-GO GUIDE TO AMERICA'S BEST TAME AND WILD WATERS. Americans Discover America Series. New York: Morrow, 1979. 363 p. Illus. Index. Paper. USA

Five hundred waterways in forty-nine states (where's Hawaii?). Pyle's coverage, shoehorned into 350 pages, leaves scant room for descriptive detail, but the notes are adequate: location, brief description, access, scenery, camping, difficulty rating, best season, and fishing. State sections conclude with a list of outfitters/liveries, and information sources. Some of America's classic streams NOT to be found: Gauley, New, Youghiogheny, Chatooga, Tuolumne, and Rogue! This guide is out of print. Publisher/distributor: W. Morrow & Co., 105 Madison Ave., New York, NY 10016.

51. RIVER INFORMATION DIGEST, 1985: FOR POPULAR WESTERN WHITEWATER BOATING RIVERS MANAGED BY FEDERAL AGENCIES. 3d ed. Washington, DC: Interagency Whitewater Committee, et al, 1985. 70 p. Illus. Maps. Paper. USA

This is not a guidebook containing detailed descriptions of a few selected runs. Rather, it is an attempt by the IWC (National Park Service, Bureau of Land Management, and Forest Service) to condense information about 143 rivers or stretches of rivers in the twelve western states in their jurisdiction into a handy reference directory. The data are general in nature and by no means comprehensive, but they may help people in the early stages of trip planning. States are grouped as follows: OR-WA, ID. CO-MT-WY, CA, and AZ-NV-NM-TX-UT. "Each section begins with a sketch map showing the approximate location and identification number for each river. Next comes a matrix listing general information for each river. Finally, a narrative provides more detailed information including addresses and telephone numbers of the responsible river manager," (introduction). Further editions are planned. Publisher/distributor: U.S. Forest Service (Hells Canyon National Recreation Area), 3620-B Snake River Ave., Lewiston, ID 83501.

52. Schafer, Ann. CANOEING WESTERN WATERWAYS: THE COASTAL STATES. New York: Harper & Row, 1976. 272 p. Maps. Bibl. Index. CA HI OR WA

Waterways are described for the states of CA OR, WA, and HI. The rest of the west is addressed in a companion volume, CANOEING WESTERN WATERWAYS: THE MOUNTAIN STATES (see citation below). Schafer's introductory material (getting started, equipments river camping, safety, arranging trips and classifying rivers) is identical for each volume. Given the scope of the task, the author is understandably selective in her inclusions. Classic trips, e.g., the Rogue, get more of her attention, but a surprising number of "lesser" runs are included. Descriptions are written in an informal, often anecdotal style ("Mercer Slough. Prettier than it sounds"). However, the necessities of content are unevenly included (gradients, flow, put-in/take-out, etc.), while the total package suffers from having simply too much territory to cover. Publisher/distributor: Harper & Row, 10 E. 53rd St., New York, NY 10022.

53. Schafer, Ann. CANOEING WESTERN WATERWAYS: THE MOUNTAIN STATES. New York: Harper & Row, 1978. 279 p. Maps. Bibl. Index. AZ CO ID MT NV NM UT WY

Waterways are described for the states of AZ, CO, ID, MT, NV, NM, UT, and WY. The rest of the west is addressed in a companion volume, CANOEING WESTERN WATERWAYS: THE COASTAL STATES (see citation, and general annotation for both volumes above).

54. Weber, Ken. CANOEING MASSACHUSETTS, RHODE ISLAND, AND CONNECTICUT. Somersworth, NH: New Hampshire Publishing Co., 1980. 159 p. Illus. Maps. Paper. CT MA RI

Twenty-one rivers, an island circumnavigation, a swamp—in all, twenty-two day trips in three states. Tables precede each of Weber's trip descriptions, and concisely show: put-in, take-out, distance, trip time, water condition, and portages. His text describing practical and aesthetic attributes of each run is illustrated with photographs by Lawrence S. Millard. Sketch maps conclude the information. MA rivers: Deerfield, Ware, Quaboag, Concord, Shawsheen, Ipswich, Charles, North, Taunton. RI rivers: Blackstone, Pettaquamscutt, Wood, Pawcatuck. CT rivers: Moosup, Quinebaug, Shetucket, Willimantic, Salmon, Farmington, Shepaug, Housatonic. Publisher/distributor: Backcountry Publications, P.O. Box 175, Woodstock, VT 05091.

55. Wood, Peter. RUNNING THE RIVERS OF NORTH AMERICA. Barre, MA: Barre Publishing, 1976. 296 p. Illus. Maps. USA/CAN

Wood's book is in two parts; the first section deals with the river environment and some introductory pointers on canoe, kayak and raft technique. The second half is a very general descriptive guide to 61 paddling rivers in the U.S. and Canada with undetailed sketch maps of the 25 more popular ones. This work has been long out of print. The best tactic would be to borrow from a library. Original distributor: Crown Publishers, 225 Park Ave. S., New York, NY 10003.

and notes. This title is no longer in print, but certainly available for consultation in libraries in the Virginia-Maryland area.

14. Carter, Randy. CANOEING WHITE WATER RIVER GUIDE. 8th ed. Oakton, VA: Appalachian Books, 1974. 275 p. Illus. Maps. Index. Paper. NC VA WV (WW-1st ed.)

15. Colwell, Robert. INTRODUCTION TO WATER TRAILS IN AMERICA. Harrisburg, PA: Stackpole Books, 1973. 221 p. Illus. Maps. Bibl. Paper. USA (WW-1st ed.)

16. CONNECTICUT RIVER GUIDE. Rev. ed. Easthampton, MA: Connecticut River Watershed Council, 1971. 87 p. Paper. CT MA NH VT (WW-1st ed.) River(s): Connecticut, and its tributaries, the White, West, Millers, Westfield, Salmon.

17. Corbett, H. Roger, Jr., and Matacia, Louis J., Jr. ONE & TWO DAY RIVER CRUISES: MARYLAND, VIRGINIA, WEST VIRGINIA. Blue Ridge Voyages, vol. 1, 4th ed. Oakton, VA: Blue Ridge Voyageurs, 1973. p. Illus. Maps. Bibl. Paper. MD VA WV (WW1st ed.) River(s): Rappahannock, Antietam, Thornton, Potomac, Shenandoah, and Cedar.

18. Corbett, H. Roger, Jr., and Matacia, Louis J., Jr. ONE & TWO DAY RIVER CRUISES: MARYLAND, VIRGINIA, WEST VIRGINIA. Blue Ridge Voyages, vol. 2, 2d ed. Oakton, VA: Appalachian Books, 1972. 88 p. Pref. Illus. Maps. Bibl. Paper. MD VA WV (WW-1st ed.) River(s): Potomac and its south branch, Cedar Creek, Catoctin

Chapter 1, Section 2

Guidebooks and Articles for Canada

Listed by Province or Territory

Alberta (AB)

56.Buhrmann, Hans, and Young, David. CANOEING CHINOOK COUNTRY RIVERS. Lethbridge?, AB: 1980. 154 p. Illus. Maps. Bibl. Paper. AB

"Chinook Country" is the southern part of Alberta where the rivers flush roughly east out of the Rockies, then out through the foothills to the prairies. The authors present canoeing opportunities in the two major drainages of the region: South Saskatchewan River (South Saskatchewan, Oldman, St. Mary, Belly, Waterton, Castle, Crowsnest, Little Bow rivers, and Willow Creek); and, the Milk River system. Streams are described in general terms before trip sections are analyzed according to a standard format: rating, characteristics, scenery, camping, flora, fauna, pollution, obstructions, and recreational potential. Annotated sketch maps support the text. No imprint is given, therefore check availability with: Lethbridge Canoe Club, P.O. Box 655, Lethbridge, AB T1J 3Z4, or the Alberta Canoe Association, P.O. Box 4571, Edmonton, AB T6E 5G4.

57.CANOEING ALBERTA. Compiled and edited by Janice E. MacDonald. Edmonton, AB: Lone Pine Publishing, 1985. 240 p. Illus. Maps. Index. Paper. AB

Compiled from the Travel Alberta Reach Reports, Alberta Wild Rivers Inventory, individual canoeist reports, and supplementary research. MacDonald groups her rivers into six systems: South Saskatchewan (includes Milk River), Red Deer, North Saskatchewan, Churchill, Athabasca, and the Hay-Peace-Slave. Information on the streams within the systems is standardized: a few paragraphs with general overview/comment, sketch map, river notes, and "canoe runs" (duration, distance, gradient, classification, access, and maps required). Publisher possibly defunct, however the guidebook should be obtainable through: Alberta Canoe Association, P.O. Box 4571, Edmonton, AB T6E 5G4.

58.THE CLEARWATER RIVER: A MAP/GUIDE FOR RIVER TRAVEL. Edmonton: Alberta Energy and Natural Resources, Alberta Forest Service, 1980. 35 p. Illus. Maps. Paper. AB

The Clearwater is in northeastern Alberta where put-in access is by float plane; take-out at Ft. McMurray. This booklet is the prototype of a series on the province's recreational waterways. The strip maps are skillfully drawn and show rapids, portages, distance, natural and historical points of interest, obstructions, and campsites. Corresponding narrative explanations are placed with the maps on facing pages. Publisher/ distributor: Alberta Energy and Natural Resources. Alberta Forest Service. 9915-108 St., Edmonton, AB T5K 2C9.

British Columbia (BC)

59.Carey, Neil G. A GUIDE TO THE QUEEN CHARLOTTE ISLANDS. Anchorage, AK: Alaska Northwest Publishing, 1975-. Annual. ***

60.Horwood, Dennis, and Parkin, Tom. ISLANDS FOR DISCOVERY: AN OUTDOOR GUIDE TO BC'S QUEEN CHARLOTTE ISLANDS. Victoria, BC: Orca Book Publishers, 1989. 200 p. Illus. Maps. Paper. BC ***

61.Ince, John, and Kottner, Heidi. SEA KAYAKING CANADA'S WEST COAST. Vancouver, BC: Raxas Books, 1982. 240 p. Illus. Maps. Index. Paper. BC

"This book is divided into two parts. Part I outlines the west coast paddling environment: the weather, the sea, the flora and fauna, and the cultural setting of the coast. Part I also describes the equipment you will need to outfit a paddling cruise. Part II is a region-by-region examination of the length of the west coast from a paddler's perspective" (introduction). The nine regions (Vancouver, Gulf Islands, Sechelt, central coast, north coast, west coast of Vancouver Island, and the Queen Charlotte Islands), are further sub-divided into the twenty best kayaking areas. Trips range from easy paddles of short duration to month-long expeditions on exposed coastal areas. Sketch maps, data page (attractions, access, seascape, hazards, season, length, camping, charts), and a narrative are the standardized components of the trip descriptions. Publisher/distributor (possibly defunct): Raxas Books, Inc., 1103-207 West Hastings St., Vancouver, BC V6B 1H7.

62.Obee, Bruce. THE GULF ISLANDS EXPLORER: THE COMPLETE GUIDE. 4th ed. North Vancouver, BC: Whitecap Books, 1988. 199 p. Illus. Maps. Bibl. Index. Paper. BC ***

63.Obee, Bruce. THE PACIFIC RIM EXPLORER: THE COMPLETE GUIDE. Maps by Janet Barwell-Clarke. North Vancouver, BC: Whitecap Books, 1986. 185 p. Illus. Bibl. Index. Paper. BC ***

64.Pratt-Johnson, Betty. WHITEWATER TRIPS AND HOT SPRINGS IN THE KOOTENAYS OF BRITISH COLUMBIA: FOR KAYAKERS, CANOEISTS AND RAFTERS. Vancouver, BC, Seattle, WA: Adventure Publishing, 1989. 185 p. Illus. Maps. Paper. BC

"The third in a series of five guidebooks covering 157 whitewater trips in British Columbia and Washington" (title page). The southeast corner of British Columbia (Kootenay and Rocky Mountain ranges) is a relatively undiscovered whitewater paddling region. Pratt-Johnson's third BC/WA guidebook describes twenty-eight runs or play spots on twenty-two waterways draining this beautiful area. Her descriptions of the runs are in a standardized arrangement giving: name, locator map, ablility required, rapids class, length, shuttle, "why go" (appraisal of features), riverflow profile, topographic map name, facilities, description of run, access directions, and a reproduced portion of the applicable topo. Like a soak taken at day's end, the hot spring information follows the paddle information. Pratt-Johnson describes a dozen springs—from primitive skinny-dippers to giant commercial thermal tubs. In a pocket on the inside of the endcovers is a set of ten "infocards," mini-directories of paddling data. The rivers: Granby, Columbia, Salmo, Slocan, Little Slocan, Wilson (Creek), Lardeau, Duncan, Bush, Blaeberry, Kiking Horse, Vermilion, Cross, Kootenay, White, Bull, Elk, St. Mary, Findlay (Creek), Toby (Creek), Bobbie Burns (Creek)-Spillimacheen River. Publisher/distributor: Adventure Publishing Ltd., P.O. Box 46545, Sta. G Vancouver, BC V6R 4G8; or, Adventure Publishing Ltd., 1916 Pike Place, Suite 73, Seattle, WA 98101.

65.Pratt-Johnson, Betty. WHITEWATER TRIPS FOR KAYAKERS, CANOEISTS AND RAFTERS IN BRITISH COLUMBIA: GREATER VANCOUVER THROUGH WHISTLER, OKANAGAN AND THOMPSON RIVER REGIONS. Vancouver, BC: Adventure Publishing; Seattle, WA: Pacific Search Press, 1986. 215 p. Illus. Maps. Index. Paper. BC

"The second in a series of five guidebooks covering 157 whitewater trips in British Columbia and Washington," (title page). The trips described are on thirty-seven waterways and one tidal rapid in southwest BC. Trips are presented in a standard format, and incorporate maps with easily-read graphics indicating appropriate craft, put-in, take-out, road access, and campsites. Descriptive chapters on the waterways have detailed narrative sections titled: "why go," "topographic map," "facilities," "guidelines," "shuttle," "season," and, "access to take-outs and put-ins." A "river profile" graphically shows river flow rates over time. Pratt-Johnson offers sensible advice about the experience required to tackle a recommended run. There is an exhaustive subject index. A sampling of the rivers: Capilano, Cheakamus, Lillooet, Chilliwack, Adams, Thompson, and Nahatlatch. Publisher/distributor: Adventure Publishing Ltd., P.O. Box 46545, Sta. G Vancouver, BC V6R 4G8; or, Adventure Publishing Ltd., 1916 Pike Place, Suite 73, Seattle, WA 98101.

66.Pratt-Johnson, Betty. WHITEWATER TRIPS FOR KAYAKERS, CANOEISTS, AND RAFTERS ON VANCOUVER ISLAND. Vancouver, BC: Gordon Soules Book Publishers; Seattle, WA: Pacific Search Press, 1984. 127 p. Illus. Maps. Bibl. Index. Paper. BC

"The first in a series of five guidebooks covering 157 whitewater trips in British Columbia and Washington" (title page). Pratt-Johnson's guidebooks for the southern British Columbia mainland are currently available (see above); others in the series are in preparation. The twenty-two Vancouver Island trips she describes take place on twelve rivers and five ocean surfing sites. They are presented in a standard format incorporating maps with easily-read graphics. Information given: name of waterway/run; experience and/or craft needed; classification (I-VI); length; shuttle; topos; best season, and average flow. This is followed by a trip narrative with sections titled: "Why go," "Facilities," "Guidelines," and "Access to put-in and take-out." River list: Koksilah, Cowichan,

Chemainus, Nanaimo, Campbell, White, Adam, Eve, Davie, Nimpkish, Marble, and Gold. Publisher/distributor: Gordon Soules Book Publishers Ltd., 1352-B Marine Dr., West Vancouver, BC V7T 1B5; or, Pacific Search Press, 222 Dexter Ave N, Seattle, WA 98109.

67.Rue, Roger L. CIRCUMNAVIGATING VANCOUVER ISLAND. Seattle?, WA: Evergreen Pacific Marine Publications, 1982. 128 p. Illus. BC ***

68.Serup, Sheila. WHITEWATER KAYAKING ON VANCOUVER ISLAND: A COMPREHENSIVE, ILLUSTRATED GUIDE TO 25 RIVER TRIPS. Prince George, BC: Sheila Serup, 1982. 31 p. Illus. Maps. BC

Describes "all the major rivers on Vancouver Island that are popular with kayakers," (preface). Short pieces on safety, equipment preparation, rescue, and river classification precede Serup's trip information. She describes fifteen rivers (25 trips) using a standard format occupying a page or two. An access sketch map concludes each description. The rivers: Sookie, Cowichan, Koksilah, Chemainus, Nanaimo, Englishman, Puntledge, Campbell, Elk, Gold, Davie, Nimpkish, Marble, White, and Adam. Publisher/distributor: (c/o the author), R.R. 6, R.M.D. 11, Prince George, BC V2N 2J4.

69.Snowden, Mary Ann. ISLAND PADDLING: A PADDLER'S GUIDE TO THE GULF ISLANDS AND BARKLEY SOUND. Victoria, BC: Orca Publishers, 1990. 200 p. Illus. Paper. BC ***

70.Stewart, Dave. EXPLORING BRITISH COLUMBIA WATERWAYS. Illustrated by Nelson Dewey. Sidney, BC: Saltaire Publishing, 1976. 159 p. Illus. Maps. Paper. BC ***

71.VanDine, Doug, and Fandrich, Bernard. RAFTING IN BRITISH COLUMBIA, FEATURING THE LOWER THOMPSON RIVER. Surrey, BC, Blaine, WA: Hancock House, 1984. 70 p. Illus. Maps. Index. Paper. BC

Covers eighty kilometers of the Thompson, from Ashcroft to Lytton, a trip of one to three days depending on watercraft. Emphasis is on floating with a commercial rafting outfitter. Twelve strip-maps are keyed by mileage to descriptive data on facing pages. Publisher/distributor: Hancock House Publishers, 19313 Zero Ave., Surrey, BC V3S 5J9; or, 1431 Harrison Ave., Blaine, WA 98230.

72.Washburne, Randel. THE COASTAL KAYAKER: KAYAK CAMPING ON THE ALASKA AND B.C. COAST. Seattle, WA: Pacific Search Press, 1983. 214 p. Illus. Maps. Bibl. Index. Paper. AK BC

Suggests seven trips along the Pacific coast between Seattle and Glacier Bay. Washburne's intended audience is the beginning and intermediate kayaker. Two-thirds of the book is a primer on paddling, camping, safety, the sights, trip planning, bears, etc. The author's trip descriptions comprise chapters of a few pages giving general overview, access, supply points, charts needed, and a sketch map. The trips: Puget Sound area, Wrangell Narrows, Hoonah to Tenakee, Sitka area, Glacier Bay, North Prince of Wales Island, and Central BC coast. Publisher/distributor: Pacific Search Press, 222 Dexter Ave. N, Seattle, WA 98109.

73.Washburne, Randel. KAYAKING PUGET SOUND, THE SAN JUANS, AND GULF ISLANDS: 45 TRIPS ON THE NORTHWEST'S INLAND WATERS. Seattle, WA: Mountaineers, 1990. 224 p. Illus. Bibl. Paper. BC WA ***

74.Wright, Richard. THE BOWRON LAKES: A YEAR-ROUND GUIDE. BC Outdoors Discovery Series, Vol. 7. Vancouver, BC: Special Interest Publications; Maclean Hunter, 1985. 130 p. Illus. Maps. Index. Paper. BC

"Bowron Lake Provincial Park is a geological oddity, a liquid parallelogram, described in the park brochure as a 'magnificent wilderness of more than 121,600 hectares,'" (introduction). Wright qualifies this wilderness designation, since the park has boardwalks, shelters, signs, designated camping, and picnic tables. Not untouched wilderness certainly, but magnificent. This is not just a canoe guide to the chain, although paddling information predominates. The author covers X-country skiing, hiking, and mountain biking, plus the natural and human history of the region. The lakes circuit totals 116 km, with six portages totalling 8 km. Sketch maps and a descriptive log provide all the necessary information for the trip. Publisher/distributor: Special Interest Publications, 202-1132 Hamilton St., Vancouver, BC V6B 2S2.

75.Wright, Richard, and Wright, Rochelle. CANOE ROUTES: BRITISH COLUMBIA. Vancouver, BC: Douglas & McIntyre, 1980. 176 p. Illus. Maps. Bibl. Index. Paper. BC

A comprehensive guide to waterways in B.C. Arrangement is by region: Vancouver Island, Lower Mainland, Thompson-Okanagan, Kootenay,

Cariboo, Skeena, and Omineca-Peace. Although the Wrights have written this for canoeists, the 100 routes examined naturally contain much data useful to rafters and kayakers. Route information is standardized: name, grade of difficulty (international scale), length, width, drop, time needed, emergency communication, camping or accommodation, maps, hazards, directions, and a paragraph of description. Prefacing the route material is a section on first aid, equipment, safety, river classification, and history. Publisher/distributor: Douglas & McIntyre, Ltd., 1615 Venables St., Vancouver, BC V5L 2H1.

Nova Scotia (NS)

76.CANOE ROUTES OF NOVA SCOTIA. Halifax, NS: Canoe Nova Scotia Association; Camping Association of Nova Scotia, 1983. 95 p. Illus. Maps. Bibl. Index. Paper. NS

Updates and expands (from 43 to 94 trips) the first edition published by the Camping Association in 1967. Arrangement is by region: Fundy, Highland, Cape Breton, Central, Valley, and South Shore. Regional index maps show the locations of waterways. Each trip description begins with a table on which is listed route name, type (river, lake, etc.), rating, length, portages, main bodies of water, put-in, intermediate put-in, and take-out. Several paragraphs of additional information expand the tabular data. Topo map numbers and additional printed information sources are given. Numerous sketch maps indicate access routes. Publisher/distributor: Canoe Nova Scotia, P.O. Box 3010 S, Halifax, NS B3J 3G6.

77.HIKING TRAILS AND CANOE ROUTES IN HALIFAX COUNTY. Edited by Howard Morris. Halifax, NS: Canadian Hostelling Association, Maritime Region, 1977. 44 p. Maps. Paper. NS

Six canoe routes within an easy drive of Halifax, Nova Scotia. Routes are indicated on fold-out topographic maps, varying in distance from about two miles to thirty. Morris' descriptions, keyed to the map, are on a facing page, showing distance from Halifax, length, access, put-in, take-out, and trip narrative. The routes: Kelly Lake-Moser River, Birch Cove, Scraggy Lake-Ship Harbour, Essen Lakes, Mushaboom-Grand Lake, and Lake Panuke. The other part of the guidebook is a similarly-arranged discussion of hiking trails. Publisher/distributor: Canadian Hostelling Assn., Maritime Region, P.O. Box 3010 South, Halifax, NS B3J 3G6.

78.Leefe, John, et al. KEJIMKUJIK NATIONAL PARK: A GUIDE. Maps by Goldie Gibson. Tantallon, NS: Four East Publications, 1981. 111 p. Illus. Maps. Index. NS ***

Ontario (ON)

79.Baxter, Thomas S.H. QUIET COVES AND ROCKY HIGHLANDS: EXPLORING LAKE SUPERIOR. Wawa, ON: Superior Lore, 1983. 212 p. Illus. Bibl. Index. Paper. ON ***

80.Beymer, Robert. A PADDLER'S GUIDE TO QUETICO PROVINCIAL PARK. Virginia, MN: W.A. Fisher, 1985. 167 p. Illus. Map. Index. Paper. ON

"Spanning a region of almost eighteen hundred square miles in western Ontario, Quetico is laced with hundreds of miles of interconnected waterways through some of the most beautiful country in the world" (page 11). Beymer has been been paddling and guiding in this area since 1967. Chapters 1 and 2 of his guidebook cover natural and human history, trip planning, fishing, camping tips, etc. Chapters 3 through 6 are organized by regional entry points (18), and routes (31). Entry point information includes name, daily quota, use level, location, and narrative summary. Route information: name, duration, distance, lakes, rivers, creeks, portages, difficulty, Fisher map number, highlights, and a day-by-day descriptive log. There is an index of routes by duration and a separate color Fisher map of Quetico and the Boundary Waters Canoe Area. Publisher/distributor: W.A. Fisher, P.O. Box 1107, Virginia, MN 55792-1107.

81.CANOEING ON THE GRAND RIVER: A CANOEISTS' GUIDE FOR A TRIP DOWN ONTARIO'S SCENIC GRAND RIVER. Cambridge, ON: Grand River Conservation Authority, 1982. 23 p. Illus. Maps. Paper. ON

"Canoeing is possible on the entire stretch of the Grand River from Elora Gorge [north of Guelph, ON] right to Lake Erie" (introduction). Fold-out maps (in 10 river sections) are of professional quality. Descriptive logs are brief, giving relevant information in a few paragraphs, and concluding with a list of points of interest. Publisher/distributor: Grand River Conservation Authority, Box 729, Cambridge, ON N1R 5W6.

82.CANOE ROUTES OF ONTARIO. Toronto, ON: Ministry of Natural Resources, Parks and Recreational Areas Branch; in cooperation with McClelland and Stewart, 1981. 110 p. Illus. Maps. Bibl. Index. Paper. ON

Intended primarily as a route selection source, hence there is minimal detailed guidebook-style information. Arranges within area, over one hundred routes giving in a standardized format: route name, type, rating, length, portages, main bodies of water, put-in, take-out, intermediate access, and source(s) for detailed information. A paragraph or so of text completes the description. Quickest subject access is through a waterway index and removable index-map of the province. Publisher/distributor: McClelland and Stewart Ltd., 481 University Ave., Suite 900, Toronto, ON M5G 2E9.

83.Denis, Keith. CANOE TRAILS THROUGH QUETICO. Quetico Foundation Series no. 3. Toronto: Quetico Foundation, 1959. 93 p. Illus. Map. Paper. ON (WW-1st ed.) Waterway(s): Quetico Provincial Park.

84.Kates, Joanne. EXPLORING ALGONQUIN PARK. Vancouver, BC; Toronto: Douglas & McIntyre, 1983. 160 p. Illus. Maps. Bibl. Index. Paper. ON

Within a three-hour drive of Toronto is Algonquin Provincial Park, containing a 1600-kilometer network of canoeing waterways. The park has some of the feel of the wilderness, but with amenities such as picnic tables and pit toilets. Canoeists can be as thick as blackflies during the high summer Algonquin season). Therefore, Kates, a lifelong resident of the area, steers the backcountry canoer along six routes in the northern, less-traveled section of the park: Canoe Lake-Big Trout Circuit; Canoe Lake-Porcupine-Louisa Circuit; Barron Canyon, Nipissing River, Opeongo-Laveille Circuit; and, the Petawawa River. In other parts of her guide she covers the park's extensive hiking trails, and the natural and human history of the region. Publisher/distributor: Douglas & McIntyre, 1615 Venables St. Vancouver, BC V5L 2H1.

85.ONTARIO VOYAGEURS RIVER GUIDE. Toronto: Ontario Voyageurs Kayak Club, 1970. 150 p. Paper. ON (WW-1st ed.)

86.Reid, Ron, and Grand, Janet. CANOEING ONTARIO'S RIVERS: GREAT CANOE TRIPS IN CANADA'S NORTHERN WILDERNESS. Vancouver, BC: Douglas & McIntyre; San Francisco: Sierra Club Books, 1986. 320 p. Illus. Maps. Bibl. Index. Paper. ON

"...We are able to present only a few of the hundreds of canoeing rivers encompassed by Ontario's vast expanse. So in the 16 rivers described, we have tried to be as representative as possible. Some of our rivers are easy enough for beginners; others involve difficult portages and advanced whitewater" (introduction to section 1). The guide is arranged into five regions within which Reid and Grand present three or four selected rivers cut into trips outlined in a page or two of text. Strip maps contain extensive marginal notes about the waterway and its surroundings. River list: Credit, Saugeen, Rankin, Skootamatta-Moira, Magnetawan, Black, Lady Evelyn, Spanish, Mississagi, Temagami, French, Mattawa, Missinaibi, Chapleau-Nemegosenda, Misehkow, and Kesagami. Publishers/distributors: Douglas & McIntyre, 1615 Venables St., Vancouver, BC V5L 2H1; Random House, 201 E. 50th St., New York, NY 10022 (dist. for Sierra Club Books).

87.Scott, Ian, and Kerr, Mavis. CANOEING IN ONTARIO. Toronto: Greey de Pencier Publications, 1975. 80 p. Illus. Maps. Bibl. Paper. ON (WW-1st ed.)

88.Wilson, Hap. TEMAGAMI CANOE ROUTES. Rev. ed. Temagami, ON: Northern Concepts, 1988. 144 p. Maps. ON ***

Quebec (PQ)

89.Federation quebecoise de canot-kayak. GUIDE DES RIVIERES DU QUEBEC. Montreal: Messageries du Jour, 1973. 228 p. Illus. Maps. Paper. PQ (WW-1st ed.)

90.Fortin, Guilles. GUIDE DES RIVIERES SPORTIVES AU QUEBEC. La Prairie, PQ: M. Broquet, 1980. 445 p. Illus. Maps. PQ ***

91.RIVIERES ET LACS CANOTABLES DU QUEBEC. Edited by Federation quebecoise du canot-camping inc. Collection Sport. Montreal, PQ: Editions de l'Homme, 1982. 375 p. Illus. PQ ***

92.Wilson, Hap. RIVIERE DUMOINE: A COMPREHENSIVE GUIDE FOR THE ADVENTURING CANOEIST. Temagami, ON: Northern Concepts, 1987. 32 p. Illus. Paper. PQ ***

Yukon Territory (YT)

93.Batchelor, Bruce T. YUKON CHANNEL CHARTS: STERNWHEELER-STYLE STRIP MAPS OF THE HISTORIC YUKON RIVER. Whitehorse, YT: B. Batchelor, 1980. 56 p. Illus. Maps. AK YT (WW-1st ed.) River(s): Yukon.

94.A BOATER'S GUIDE TO THE UPPER YUKON RIVER. Rev. ed. Anchorage, AK: Alaska Northwest Publishing, 1976. 87 p. Maps. Paper. YT (WW-1st ed.) Waterway(s): Yukon, Pelly, Teslin rivers, Bennett Lake.

95.DeHart, Don, and DeHart Vangie. A GUIDE OF THE YUKON RIVER. Cheyenne, WY: Cheyenne Litho, 1971. 47 p. Illus. Maps. Paper. AK YT (WW-1st ed.) River(s): Yukon.

96.Rourke, Mike. BIG SALMON RIVER. Rivers of the Yukon Territory. Faro, YT: Rivers North Publications, 1983. 27 p. Illus. Maps. Bibl. Paper. YT For a general description of the contents of all books in the series, see entry 97.

97.Rourke, Mike. NISUTLIN RIVER. Rev. ed. Rivers of the Yukon Territory. Watson Lake, YT: Rivers North Publications, 1985. 23 p. Illus. Maps. Bibl. Paper. YT

Part of a series of guides (typescript pamphlets, really) for six major Yukon rivers. Rourke's five other publications: BIG SALMON RIVER (1983), PELLY RIVER (1983), ROSS RIVER (1985), TESLIN RIVER (1983), and YUKON RIVER: MARSH LAKE, YUKON TO CIRCLE, ALASKA (1985). The content, arrangement and format of each book appear to be very similar, based on my inspection of the Nesutlin, Teslin, and Yukon guides. (For some added observations on the Yukon River book, see entry 101.) Strip-maps comprise the main section of each pamphlet, and Rourke provides running annotations on features, history and mileage. The maps are preceded by a short narrative history, river description, monthly cfs flow averages, and a key to map symbols. A list of equipment and menu suggestions conclude the work. Publisher/ distributor: Rivers North Publications, Box 403, Watson Lake, YT Y0A 1C0.

98.Rourke, Mike. PELLY RIVER. Rivers of the Yukon Territory. Faro, YT: Rivers North Publications, 1983. 55 p. Illus. Maps. Bibl. Paper. YT For a general description of the contents of all books in the series. see entry 97.

99.Rourke, Mike. ROSS RIVER. Rivers of the Yukon Territory. Watson Lake, YT: Rivers North Publications, 1985. 32 p. Illus. Maps. Bibl. Paper. YT For a general description of the contents of all books in the series, see entry 97.

100.Rourke, Mike. TESLIN RIVER. Rivers of the Yukon Territory. Faro, YT: Rivers North Publications, 1985. 29 p. Illus. Maps. Bibl. Paper. YT For a general description of the contents of all books in the series, see entry 97.

101.Rourke, Mike. YUKON RIVER: MARSH LAKE, YUKON TO CIRCLE, ALASKA. Rivers of the Yukon Territory. Watson Lake, YT: Rivers North Publications, 1985. 157 p. Illus. Maps. Bibl. Paper. AK YT

For a general description of the contents of all books in the series, see entry 97. This particular work in the series is an exceptional guide to the upper Yukon; the best I have seen. It differs significantly from Rourke's other guidebooks in qualtity of production values and quantity of information. The author has arranged numerous photographs of historical note opposite relevant locations on the strip-maps. This section is followed by a narrative trip log keyed to the map pages. There is an extensive bibliography.

102.Satterfield, Archie. EXPLORING THE YUKON RIVER. Seattle, WA: The Mountaineers, 1979. 129 p. Illus. Maps. Bibl. Index. Paper. YT

While Satterfield never specifically mentions THE YUKON RIVER TRAIL GUIDE, (see entry 103), this volume appears to be an updated edition of that earlier work; he describes the same 600-mile water route from Lake Bennett-Lake Atlin to Dawson City, YT. It contains descriptions of the trip with digressions on the people and history of the region. None of the many strip maps are to scale, but mileage numbers are said to be accurate. (There is a listing of all the topographic maps available from The Canada Map Office.) Other trip planning advice is given. The photographs from the gold-rush era are reproduced from those in the Asahel Curtis Collection at the Washington State Historical Society Museum. Contemporary photographs are by the author. The concluding section contains a brief description of tributary streams suitable for canoe and kayak: Teslin River, Big Salmon River, Pelly River, Macmillan River, White River, Stewart River, and Sixtymile River. Possibly out of print. Publisher/distributor: Mountaineers Books, 306 Second Ave. W, Seattle, WA 98119.

103.Satterfield, Archie. THE YUKON RIVER TRAIL GUIDE. Harrisburg, PA: Stackpole Books, 1975. 159 p. Illus. Maps. Paper. YT (WW-1st ed.) Waterway(s): Yukon River route from Lake Bennett-Lake Atlin to Dawson City.

104.THE UPPER YUKON RIVER, WHITEHORSE TO CARMACKS, YUKON. Written and published by Karpes and Pugh Company. Whitehorse, YT: The Company, 1985. 54 p. Maps. Bibl. YT ***

105.Wright, Richard, and Wright, Rochelle. CANOE ROUTES: YUKON TERRITORY. Vancouver, BC: Douglas & McIntyre, 1980. 112 p. Illus. Maps. Bibl. Paper. YT

Companion volume to the Wright's CANOE ROUTES BRITISH COLUMBIA (see entry 75). This source describes trips in the Yukon with experience levels ranging from novice to expert. Enough information is given "...to make the trip comfortable, safe and interesting." Each route listing is prefaced with basic data: put-in, take-out; rating (international 1-6); length; width; gradient; time required; nearest emergency communication; camping/accommodation; maps (Geological Survey of Canada, or U.S.G.S. topos); and, hazards. Trip narratives cover from two to ten pages. Illustrated with photographs and large-scale maps. An introduction contains information on safety, history, equipment, clothing, hypothermia, food, first aid, etc. Routes are on Frances and Kluane Lakes and the following rivers: Yukon, Wolf, Nisutlin, Teslin, Big Salmon, Ross, MacMillan, Pelly, White, Stewart, Sixtymile, Klondike, Fortymile, Bell-Porcupine, Blow, Ogilvie-Peel, Frances-Liard, Hyland and Alsek. Publisher/ distributor: Douglas & McIntyre, Ltd., 1615 Venables St., Vancouver, BC V5L 2H1.

Chapter 1, Section 3

Guidebooks and Articles

United States

Listed By State

Alabama (AL)

106.APPALACHIAN WHITEWATER: VOLUME I, THE SOUTHERN MOUNTAINS. Compiled by Bob Sehlinger and others. Birmingham, AL: Menasha Ridge Press, 1986. 159 p. Illus. Maps. Index. Paper. AL GA KY NC SC TN See entry 3 for a full description.

107.Estes, Chuck; Carter, Liz; and Almquist, Byron. CANOE TRAILS OF THE DEEP SOUTH: THE RIVERS OF LOUISIANA, ALABAMA, AND MISSISSIPPI. Birmingham, AL: Menasha Ridge Press, 1990. 304 p. Illus. Maps. Paper. AL LA MS ***

108.Foshee, John H.; ALABAMA CANOE RIDES AND FLOAT TRIPS: A DETAILED GUIDE TO THE CAHABA AND OTHER CREEKS AND RIVERS OF ALABAMA PLUS PUT-INS, TAKE-OUTS, AND GENERAL INFORMATION ABOUT NUMEROUS OTHER STREAMS OF THE STATE. 1975. Reprint. University, AL: University of Alabama Press, Strode Book, 1986. 263 p. Illus. Maps. Paper. AL

Contains maps and descriptions of fifty-two day trips on twenty-five of Alabama's smaller rivers. Each river is mapped and described mile-by-mile: access, trip length, dangers, shoals, rapids, and difficulty (class I-IV). The rivers: Cahaba, Little Cahaba (Purdy), Six-Mile Creek, Locust Fork of the Warrior, Blackburn Fork, Mulberry Fork of the Warrior, West Fork Sipsey, Blackwater Creek, Tallapoosa River, Hatchet and Weogufka Creeks, and Little River. Fifteen additional rivers (fifty trips) which the author has never paddled are briefly mentioned in the appendix. There is a section presenting information on clothing, equipment and safety. Publisher/distributor: University of Alabama Press, P.O. Box 2877, Tuscaloosa, AL, 35487.

109.Nealy, William. WHITEWATER HOME COMPANION: SOUTHEASTERN RIVERS, VOLUME I. Hillsborough, NC: Menasha Ridge Press, 1981. 156 p. Illus. Maps. Paper. AL GA NC PA SC TN WV See entry 41 for a full description.

Alaska (AK)

110.Batchelor, Bruce T. YUKON CHANNEL CHARTS: STERNWHEELER-STYLE STRIP MAPS OF THE HISTORIC YUKON RIVER. Whitehorse, YT: B. Batchelor, 1980. 56 p. Illus. Maps. AK YT (WW-1st ed.) River(s): Yukon.

111.Carter, Marilyn. ALASKA'S BACK TRAILS: HIKING AND CANOE. Palmer, AK: Aladdin Publishing, 1982. 74 p. Illus. AK ***

112. Carter, Marilyn. FLOATING ALASKAN RIVERS: WHITEWATER & FAMILY FLOATS. Palmer, AK: Aladdin Publishing, 1982. 111 p. Illus. Maps. Paper. AK ***

113.DeHart, Don, and DeHart Vangie. A GUIDE OF THE YUKON RIVER. Cheyenne, WY: Cheyenne Litho, 1971. 47 p. Illus. Maps. Paper. AK YT (WW-1st ed.) River(s): Yukon.

114.DuFresne, Jim. GLACIER BAY NATIONAL PARK: A BACKCOUNTRY GUIDE TO THE GLACIERS AND BEYOND. Seattle, WA: The Mountaineers, 1987. 152 p. Illus. Maps. Index. Paper. AK

Glacier Bay is viewed by thousands of visitors yearly from the decks of cruise ships and the windows of "flightseeing" charter planes. While this guide can provide information for these visitors, it is of primary use to the hiker and paddler—the two ways to really get "into" the park. The book has a general introduction followed by: "Glacier Bay by Paddle" (18 routes), and "Glacier Bay on Foot" (17 routes). Paddle information includes time, distance, scenery, drop-off and pick-up points, wildlife, suggestions for hikes, and more. All routes are shown on sketch maps. Publisher/distributor: Mountaineers Books, 306 Second Ave. W, Seattle, WA 98119.

115.Lethcoe, Nancy R. AN OBSERVER'S GUIDE TO THE GLACIERS OF PRINCE WILLIAM SOUND, ALASKA. Valdez, AK: Prince William Sound Books, 1987. 151 p. Illus. Maps. Paper. AK ***

116.Miller, David William. A GUIDE TO ALASKA'S KENAI FJORDS. 2d ed. Cordova, AK: Wilderness Images, 1987. 116 p. Illus. Bibl. Index. Paper. AK

The Kenai Fjords is a 750-mile coastline area in the southwestern part of the Kenai Peninsula best explored by sea in one's own powered vessel or kayak. Miller has spent sixteen years exploring and photographing the Fjords. His guide aids the waterborne or hiking visitor to this rugged, glaciated place with knowledgeable descriptions of the terrain and natural history of the fjords, islands, and inland areas. Fishing advice abounds. Each regional description is accompanied by a sketch map. Sadly, in order to guide a paddler AWAY from oil smeared areas, a post Exxon Valdez edition may now be required. Publisher/ distributor: Wilderness Images, P.O. Box 1455, Cordova, AK 99574.

117.Mosby, Jack, and Dapkus, David. ALASKA PADDLING GUIDE. 3d ed. Anchorage, AK: J & R Enterprises, 1986. 113 p. Maps. Paper. AK

No-frills descriptions of 111 trips on streams and lakes throughout Alaska. The descriptions include an introductory paragraph, followed by data on suitable watercraft, trip length, access points, topo maps, land management agency, and a sketch map. The authors provide a centerfold map number-keying each waterway. These waterways are also conveniently summarized on a separate chart. Selected kayak streams are ranked by their difficulty and then compared to some well-known streams in the "Lower 48."

118.Piggott, Margaret H. DISCOVER SOUTHEAST ALASKA WITH PACK AND PADDLE. Seattle, WA: The Mountaineers, 1974. 268 p. Illus. Maps. Bibl. Index. AK (WW-1st ed.) Waterway(s): tidal waters of southeastern Alaska.

119.Rourke, Mike. YUKON RIVER: MARSH LAKE, YUKON TO CIRCLE, ALASKA. Rivers of the Yukon Territory. Watson Lake, YT: Rivers North Publications, 1985. 157 p. Illus. Maps. Bibl. Paper. AK YT See entry 101 for a full description.

120.Washburne, Randel. THE COASTAL KAYAKER: KAYAK CAMPING ON THE ALASKA AND B.C. COAST. Seattle, WA: Pacific Search Press, 1983. 214 p. Illus. Maps. Bibl. Index. Paper. AK BC See entry 72 for a full description.

121.Weber, Sepp. WILD RIVERS OF ALASKA. Anchorage: Alaska Northwest Publishing Co., 1976. 169 p. Illus. Maps. Paper. AK (WW-1st ed.) River(s): (those chosen for detailed description): Noatak, Aniak, Porcupine, Copper, and Chilikadrotna.

Arizona (AZ)

122.Anderson, Fletcher, and Hopkinson, Ann. RIVERS OF THE SOUTHWEST: A BOATERS GUIDE TO THE RIVERS OF COLORADO, NEW MEXICO, UTAH AND ARIZONA. 2d ed. Boulder, CO: Pruett Publishing, 1987. 129 p. Illus. Maps. Paper. AZ CO NM UT See entry 2 for a full description.

123.Belknap, Buzz. GRAND CANYON RIVER GUIDE. 2d ed. Boulder City, NV: Westwater Books, 1989. 98 p. Illus. Maps. Paper. AZ

In this full-color waterproof revision of the classic 1969 guidebook, Belknap covers the section of the Colorado lying within the Grand Canyon from Lees Ferry to Lake Mead. His strip maps are based on U.S.G.S. topographicals. Adjacent to the maps are: river miles (from Lees Ferry); names of major rapids with ratings (one to ten scale); river elevation; timely photographs of people, places and things; and, often, a brief John Wesley Powell quote about the river and its surroundings. Sections on geology, natural history, archaeology are new to this edition as are those on photography and river hydraulics. Publisher/distributor: Westwater Books, P.O. Box 2560, Evergreen, CO 80439.

124.Crumbo, Kim. A RIVER RUNNER'S GUIDE TO THE HISTORY OF THE GRAND CANYON. Boulder, CO: Johnson Books, 1981. [89] p. Illus. Maps. Bibl. Paper. AZ Crumbo, a professional river runner, writes about "...humanity's encounter with the wild Colorado River in Grand Canyon. Events are tied to places in a mile-by-mile sequence for reference while running the river. The text is keyed to the [26 strip maps] that follow. Miles below Lee's Ferry are marked on the maps and in the margin of the text" (introduction). The foreword is by Edward Abbey who recommended this work as a companion and supplement to Buzz Belknap's,

GRAND CANYON RIVER GUIDE (see above). Publisher/distributor: Johnson Publishing Co., 1880 S. 57th Ct., Boulder, CO 80301.

125.Dirksen, D. J., and Reeves, R. A. RECREATION ON THE COLORADO RIVER. Aptos, CA: Sail Sales Publishing, 1985. 112 p. Illus. Maps. Index. Paper. AZ CA CO NV UT See entry 20 for a full description.

126.Hamblin, W. Kenneth, and Rigby, J. Keith. GUIDEBOOK TO THE COLORADO RIVER, PART I: LEES FERRY TO PHANTOM RANCH IN GRAND CANYON NATIONAL PARK. PART II: PHANTOM RANCH IN GRAND CANYON NATIONAL PARK TO LAKE MEAD, ARIZONA-NEVADA. Brigham Young University Geology Studies, Studies for students nos. 4 and 5. Provo, UT: Brigham Young University, 1969. 2 vols. Illus. Paper. AZ NV UT (WW-1st ed.) Part III of this series is cited below under entry 402. River(s): Colorado, from Lees Ferry to Lake Mead.

127.Nichols, Gary. RIVER RUNNERS' GUIDE TO UTAH AND ADJACENT AREAS. Rev. ed. Salt Lake City: University of Utah Press, 1986. 168 p. Illus. Maps. Paper. AZ CO ID UT WY See entry 43 for a full description.

128.Pewe, Troy Lewis. COLORADO RIVER GUIDEBOOK: A GEOLOGIC AND GEOGRAPHIC GUIDE FROM LEES FERRY TO PHANTOM RANCH, ARIZONA. Tempe: Arizona State University Press, 1969. 78 p. Illus. Paper. AZ (WW-1st ed.) River(s): Colorado.

129.Schafer, Ann. CANOEING WESTERN WATERWAYS: THE MOUNTAIN STATES. New York: Harper & Row, 1978. 279 p. Maps. Bibl. Index. AZ CO ID MT NV NM UT WY See entry 53 for a full description.

130.Simmons, George C., and Gaskill, David L. MARBLE GORGE AND GRAND CANYON. River Runners' Guides, vol. 3. Denver, CO: Powell Society, 1969. 132 p. Illus. Maps. Diag. Paper. AZ UT (WW-1st ed.) River(s): Colorado from Lees Ferry to Pierces Ferry at Lake Mead.

131.Stevens, Larry. THE COLORADO RIVER IN GRAND CANYON: A COMPREHENSIVE GUIDE TO ITS NATURAL AND HUMAN HISTORY. 3d ed. Flagstaff, AZ: Red Lake Books, 1987. 115 p. Illus. Maps. Bibl. Index. Paper. AZ

The author is a commercial boatman and biologist intimately familiar with the river and the canyon. His guide is a presentation of the climate, geology, human history, dams, and biology, along with detailed, updated strip maps of the Grand Canyon run. The maps and arrangement of material are reminiscent of Buzz Belknap's, GRAND CANYON RIVER GUIDE. Stevens' guide is one of few in this genre having numbered references keyed to a detailed chapter bibliography. There are several comprehensive lists giving species of flora and fauna, and historical chronologies. Small photographs and drawings abound. Mile-by-mile strip maps illustrate the run by means of symbols, place names, and photographs. The guide is sold in a waterproof edition. Publisher/distributor: Red Lake Books, P.O. Box 1315 Flagstaff, AZ 86002.

Arkansas (AR)

132.Clark, Fogle C. BUFFALO NATIONAL RIVER GUIDE. University, MS: Recreational Publications, 1976. Map. AR (WW-1st ed.) River(s): Buffalo.

133.Hedges, Harold, and Hedges, Margaret. BUFFALO RIVER CANOEING GUIDE. Rev. ed. Little Rock, AR: Ozark Society, 1983? 15 p. Illus. Map. Paper. AR

The Buffalo rises in the Boston Mountains of northwest Arkansas and flows 150 miles to its White River confluence. Approximately 133 miles are navigable by canoe or kayak (put-in at Boxley, AR). The authors segment the river into fourteen runs, the longest being the twenty-four miles from Rush Creek to Buffalo City. Descriptions of the trips are in narrative form and include information on access, rapids, mileage, gradient, flow, and the sights and history of the surroundings. Paddler's services (canoe rentals, shuttle service, supplies) and appropriate U.S.G.S. maps are listed on the concluding page. Illustrated with (outdated) photographs. Publisher/distributor: Ozark Society Books, P.O. Box 3503, Little Rock, AR 72203.

134.Hedges, Harold, and Hedges, Margaret. THE MIGHTY MULBERRY: A CANOEING GUIDE. Rev. ed. Little Rock, AR: Ozark Society, 1983? 16 p. Illus. Map. Paper. AR

Describes the most canoeable fifty miles of the swift (average drop, 12 feet to the mile) Mulberry River of northwestern Arkansas. Since only one large-scale map is provided, prospective river runners should note the appropriate quadrangle maps (Watalula, and Mountainburg SE) cited in the introduction. River description is in narrative form. Illustrated with (outdated) photographs. Publisher/distributor: Ozark Society Books, P.O. Box 3503, Little Rock, AR 72203.

135.Kennon, Tom. ARKANSAS WHITEWATER RIVERS. Bartlett, TN: 1978. 43 p. Illus. Maps. Paper. AR

"...A guide to some of the more popular rivers in the state of Arkansas" (introduction). An unexamined expansion of this guidebook is Kennon's OZARK WHITEWATER (1989), below. The author describes runs on 12 streams using a standard format of brief textual information followed by access maps. The descriptions contain a general river overview, name of run, location, difficulty, distance, time, scenery, water quality, gauge location, difficulties, and campsites. The streams (ranked from least to most difficult): Spring River, South Fork Spring River, Big Creek, Saldo Creek, Cadron Creek, Buffalo River, Illinois Bayou, Middle Fork of the Little Red River, Mulberry River, Big Piney Creek, Little Missouri River, and the Cassatot River. Publisher/distributor (of rev. ed.): Menasha Ridge Press, P.O. Box 59257, Birmingham, AL 35259-9257.

136.Kennon, Tom. OZARK WHITEWATER: A PADDLER'S GUIDE TO THE MOUNTAIN STREAMS OF ARKANSAS AND MISSOURI. Birmingham, AL: Menasha Ridge Press, 1989. 300? p. Illus. Maps. Paper. AR MO ***

California (CA)

137.Cassady, Jim, and Calhoun, Fryar. CALIFORNIA WHITE WATER: A GUIDE TO THE RIVERS. Richmond, CA: The authors, 1984. 283 p. Illus. Maps. Bibl. Index. Paper. CA

"For 45 of the state's best runs we provide maps, mile-by-mile guides, and other information most boaters like to have before they set out for the river" (preface). The information about the runs is substantial, given the large number covered: name of run, difficulty, season, runnable levels, length, gradient, narrative mile-by-mile log, and strip map. Preceding these data is a river overview: drainage, elevation, flow information telephone number, scenery, solitude, appropriate watercraft, permits, commercial raft trips, drinking water, campsites, maps needed and shuttle access. Concluding chapters address, river geology, flora, fishing, water politics, and access regulation. A selection of rivers: Kern, Kaweah, Kings, Merced, Tuolumne, Stanislaus, Mokelumne, Cosumnes, American, Truckee, Yuba, Russian, Eel, Sacramento, Trinity, Klamath, and Smith. Publisher/distributor: (self-published, write c/o authors): P.O. Box 5372, Richmond, CA 94805. (Later note: A second edition was published in June, 1990, available through Friends of the River, Guidebook Sales, Ft. Mason Center, Bldg. C, San Francisco, CA 94123.)

138.Center, Robert M., ed. INTERPRETIVE GUIDE OF THE AMERICAN, STANISLAUS, AND TUOLUMNE RIVERS. Oakland, CA: American River Touring Association, 1975. 89p. Maps. Paper. CA (WW-1st ed.) River(s): American, Stanislaus, Tuolumne.

139.Dirksen, D. J., and Reeves, R. A. RECREATION LAKES OF CALIFORNIA. 8th ed. Burbank, CA: Recreation Sales Publishing, 1988. 196 p. Illus. Maps. Index. Paper. CA

Concisely presents the location, facilities, and recreational opportunities of over 300 California lakes. Each page has a map, descriptive text, and tabular information giving: location, elevation, size, campsites, boating/fishing/other recreation, and local contact addresses. The power boat emphasis of the book renders it only marginally useful to self-propellers. Publisher/distributor: Recreation Sales Publishing, Inc., P.O. Box 4024, Burbank, CA: 91503-4024.

140.Dirksen, D. J., and Reeves, R. A. RECREATION ON THE COLORADO RIVER. Aptos, CA: Sail Sales Publishing, 1985. 112 p. Illus. Maps. Index. Paper. AZ CA CO NV UT See entry 20 for a full description.

141.Dwyer, Ann. CANOEING WATERS OF CALIFORNIA. Kentfield, CA: GBH Press, 1973. 95 p. Illus. Maps. Paper. CA (WW-1st ed.) River(s): Merced, Kings, Kern, and lower Colorado rivers, thirty-eight lakes, and several tidewater possibilities.

142.Harris, Thomas. DOWN THE WILD RIVERS: A GUIDE TO THE STREAMS OF CALIFORNIA. 2d ed. San Francisco: Chronicle Books, 1973. 219 p. Illus. Maps. Index. Paper. CA (WW-1st ed.) River(s): Trinity, Eel, American, Consumnes, Merced, Mokelumne, Stanislaus, Tuolumne, Owens, Feather, Sacramento, Yuba, Salmon, Scott, Big, Mad, Mattole, Navarro, Noyo, Russian, and Cache Creek.

143.HELL'S CORNER GORGE OF THE UPPER KLAMATH. Quinn Map. Medford, OR: Educational Adventures, 198? [10 p.] Illus. Maps. Paper. CA OR See entry 331 for a full description.

144.Margulis, Rena K. THE COMPLETE GUIDE TO WHITEWATER RAFTING TOURS: 1986 CALIFORNIA EDITION. Palo Alto, CA: Aquatic Adventure Publications, 1986. 287 p. Illus. Maps. Bibl. Paper. CA

A comprehensive guide in which Margulis compares more than 600 tours offered by 67 outfitters on all of the 29 comercially rafted rivers in California. The author introduces each of the rivers with short paragraphs on difficulty, water level/flow, permit system, commercial outfitters, gear, safety, distinctive river features, access, environment, fishing, river rapids summary between put-ins, wild and scenic status, motels/lodges, private/public campgrounds. This narrative is followed by detailed tables showing: number of days, outfitter, dates run, craft type, mileage, facilities, wetsuit requirement, age requirement, cost, discount, transportation, and comments. Preceding all this is a lengthy trip preview aimed at the novice. Appendices: what to bring, safety, etiquette, boat types, preparation, equipment sources, and a glossary. The cumulative result is a big package of timely data for anyone shopping for a commercial California trip in a raft (paddle, oar, you-oar) or inflatable kayak. Publisher/distributor: Aquatic Adventure Publications, P.O. Box 60494, Palo Alto, CA 94306.

145.Martin, Charles. SIERRA WHITEWATER: A PADDLER'S GUIDE TO THE RIVERS OF CALIFORNIA'S SIERRA NEVADA. Sunnyvale, CA: Fiddleneck Press, 1974. 192 p. Illus. Maps. Bibl. Paper. CA (WW-1st ed.) River(s): Pit, Feather, Yuba, Bear, American, Consumnes, Mokelumne, Stanislaus, Tuolumne, Merced, Kings, Kaweah, Kern, Truckee, East Fork Carson, and West Walker Rivers, plus Mill and Deer Creeks.

146.Meloche, Ernie. QUIET WATERS—A CARTOP PADDLER'S GUIDE TO THE LAKES AND BAYS OF NORTHWESTERN CALIFORNIA. Trinidad, CA: E. Meloche, 198? 88 p. Paper. CA ***

147.Quinn, James W., and Quinn, James M. HANDBOOK TO THE KLAMATH RIVER CANYON. Redmond, OR: Educational Adventures, 1983. 180 p. Illus. Maps. Paper. CA OR

"The Klamath flows out of Oregon southwesterly through the Cascades into California, then west through the Coast Range to the Pacific. The Upper Klamath is interrupted by dams, most notably Iron Gate. However, a seventeen-mile section above Copco Lake (strip-mapped and described), contains two class V rapids, two class IV's, and many class III's, making it a very attractive whitewater venue. The 180 miles below Iron Gate flow unobstructed to the sea; the Quinns have logged and mapped the 148 miles to the Trinity confluence. There are five books in this "HANDBOOK TO..." series on running western rivers, each of which aims to combine adventure and education through sharing "...the knowledge of professional guides who make their livelihoods from the rivers." See the entry under IDAHO, Quinn, James M., HANDBOOK TO THE MIDDLE FORK OF THE SALMON RIVER CANYON, for a general description of the contents. Publisher/distributor: Educational Adventures, P.O. Box 4190, Sunriver, OR 97707.

148.Schafer, Ann. CANOEING WESTERN WATERWAYS: THE COASTAL STATES. New York: Harper & Row, 1978. 272 p. Maps. Bibl. Index. CA HI OR WA See entry 52 for a full description.

149.Schwind, Dick. WEST COAST RIVER TOURING: ROUGE RIVER CANYON AND SOUTH. Beaverton OR: Touchstone Press, 1974. 224 p. Illus. Maps. Bibl. Paper. CA OR (WW-1st ed.) River(s): west coast rivers from the Rogue to the Salinas, with sources in the coastal mountains.

150.SOGGY SNEAKERS: GUIDE TO OREGON RIVERS. 2d ed. Edited by Willamette Kayak and Canoe Club. Corvallis, Or: The Club, 1986. 208 p. Illus. Maps. Bibl. Index. Paper. OR WA CA See entry 341 for a full description.

151.Stanley, Chuck, and Holbek, Lars. A GUIDE TO THE BEST WHITEWATER IN THE STATE OF CALIFORNIA. Limited ed. Stanford, CA: Friends of the River Books, 1984. 217 p. Illus. Maps. Index. Paper. CA

A guide for advanced intermediate and expert kayakers. In the Stanley/Holbek lexicon, "best" whitewater is defined as very large and/or technically demanding. The descriptions of 124 runs are concise yet informative; written in a give-a-hoot, Class IV-V+ style. These narratives are preceded by a standardized heading giving: river and run, difficulty, flow range, optimum flow, miles, portages, put-in, take out, shuttle, possibliity for rafting, average gradient, gauge, season, water source, and topos. A second edition (not inspected) presents seventeen doubtlessly hair-raising new runs. The rivers: San Lorenzo, Russian, Eel, Mad, Redwood (Creek), Trinity, Salmon, Klamath, Scott, Smith, Grindstone (Creek), Stony (Creek), Cache (Creek), Putah (Creek), Sacramento, Feather, Yuba, American, Cosumnes, Mokelumne, Stanislaus, Tuolumne, Merced, San Joaquin, King, Kaweah, Kern, Walker, Carson, and Truckee. Publisher/distributor (1st ed.): Friends of the River, Ft. Mason Center, Bldg. C, San Francisco, CA 94123.

152.Wright, Terry. ROCKS AND RAPIDS OF THE TUOLUMNE RIVER: A GUIDE TO NATURAL AND HUMAN HISTORY. Contributions by Peter

Pressley, Pat Carr, John Amodio, and Greg Thomas. Forestville, CA: Wilderness Interpretation Publications, 1983. 88 p. Illus. Map. Bibl. Paper. CA

Wilderness Interpretation is a natural history-adventure travel company. The first thirty-eight pages of Wright's book consist of a mile-keyed river log of the popular run between Lumsden Camp and Wards Ferry Bridge in which he describes all the named rapids, including vantage points for scouting, plus locations for best exploration of the canyon's geology and biology. In the remaining half of the book are chapters by experts on Tuolumne biology, fishing and conservation issues. Publisher/distributor: Box 279, Forestville, CA 95436.

Colorado (CO)

153.Anderson, Fletcher, and Hopkinson, Ann. RIVERS OF THE SOUTHWEST: A BOATERS GUIDE TO THE RIVERS OF COLORADO, NEW MEXICO, UTAH AND ARIZONA. 2d ed. Boulder, CO: Pruett Publishing, 1987. 129 p. Illus. Maps. Paper. AZ CO NM UT See entry 2 for a full description.

154.Dirksen, D. J., and Reeves, R. A. RECREATION ON THE COLORADO RIVER. Aptos, CA: Sail Sales Publishing, 1985. 112 p. Illus. Maps. Index. Paper. AZ CA CO NV UT See entry 20 for a full description.

155.Evans, Laura, and Belknap, Buzz. DINOSAUR RIVER GUIDE. Boulder City, NV: Westwater Books, 1973. 64 p. Illus. Maps. Paper. CO UT (WW-1st ed.) River(s): Green, Yampa.

156.Evans, Laura, and Belknap, Buzz. FLAMING GORGE DINOSAUR NATIONAL MONUMENT: DINOSAUR RIVER GUIDE. Boulder City, NV: Westwater Books, 1973. 63 p. Illus. Maps. Paper. CO UT WY See entry 23 for a full description.

157.Hayes, Philip T., and Simmons, George C. RIVER RUNNERS' GUIDE TO DINOSAUR NATIONAL MONUMENT AND VICINITY, WITH EMPHASIS ON GEOLOGIC FEATURES. Rev. ed. River Runners' Guides, vol. 1. Denver, CO: Powell Society, 1973. 78 p. Illus. Maps. Diag. Bibl. Paper. CO UT (WW-1st ed.) Revision of FROM FLAMING GORGE DAM THROUGH DINOSAUR CANYON TO OURAY, by Philip T. Hayes and E.S. Santos (1969), and the YAMPA RIVER SUPPLEMENT, by Philip T. Hayes (1971). River(s): Green (Flaming Gorge Dam to Ouray), and Yampa (Deerlodge Park to Echo Park).

158.McCaffrey, Mark Stanislaus. THE DELORES: A RIVER RUNNING GUIDE. Boulder, CO: Pruett Publishing, 1981. CO UT *** 159.Nichols, Gary. RIVER RUNNERS' GUIDE TO UTAH AND ADJACENT AREAS. Rev. ed. Salt Lake City: University of Utah Press, 1986. 168 p. Illus. Maps. Paper. AZ CO ID UT WY See entry 43 for a full description.

160.Perry, Earl. RIVERS OF COLORADO: TEN EASY RIVER TRIPS IN THE MOUNTAINS, CANYONS AND PLAINS OF COLORADO. Denver, CO: American Canoe Association, 1978. 60 p. Illus. Maps. Paper. CO

"This pamphlet provides information on ten river trips in Colorado for beginners. ... Nowhere is Mutability's reign in the sublunary sphere more obvious than on a river" (this invitation and admonition quoted from the introduction). Perry gives the following information on each river: length, boating time, gradient, rating, width, boating history, geomorphology, wildlife, hazards, gage, flows, season, access, log and maps. All this is accompanied by topo strip maps, and photographs. Six pages of preliminary material cover a rapid rating system (A, B, C, I - VI), and "River Navigation in Colorado." Trips are on the following rivers: South Platte, Yampa, Colorado, Gunnison, Arkansas, Animas, Rio Grande, and Dolores. Publisher/distributor: American Canoe Assn., P.O. Box 1190, Newington, VA 22122-1190.

161.Rampton, Thomas G. RIVER RUNNER'S GUIDE TO BROWN'S CANYON. 1987. 57 p. Paper. CO ***

162.Schafer, Ann. CANOEING WESTERN WATERWAYS: THE MOUNTAIN STATES. New York: Harper & Row, 1978. 279 p. Maps. Bibl. Index. AZ CO ID MT NV NM UT WY See entry 53 for a full description.

163.Staub, Frank. THE UPPER ARKANSAS RIVER; RAPIDS, HISTORY & NATURE MILE BY MILE: FROM GRANITE TO THE PUEBLO RESERVOIR. Contributions by Peter Anderson. Golden, CO: Fulcrum, 1988. 265 p. Illus. Maps. Bibl. Paper. CO

The upper Arkansas has many of the qualities of big western wilderness rivers plus proximity to the urbanized Front Range region, a combination that makes it Colorado's favorite whitewater run. With this guidebook, Staub intends to inform and educate the prospective Arkansas traveller. Included with the expected practicalities of running the river is information about the river's history, geology, and biology. In the guide section, principal access points, major rapids, bridges, dams, etc. are described in a mile-by-mile log. Strip maps are keyed to the log data. The book is designed to fit inside a ziplock sandwich bag or a normal pocket. Publisher/distributor: Fulcrum, Inc., Indiana St., Suite 510, Golden, CO 80401.

164.Stohlquist, Jim. COLORADO WHITEWATER: A GUIDE TO THE DIFFICULT RIVERS AND STREAMS OF THE ROCKY MOUNTAIN STATE REGION. Buena Vista, CO: Colorado Kayak Supply, 1982. 156 p. Illus. Maps. Paper. CO

Stohlquist presents Colorado runs for skilled kayakers using a succinct, standardized format: stream name, run name, class, volume, gradient, scenery, time, miles, optimum volume, character, put-in, take-out, description, flow-rate chart, and map. More than forty photographs, most in color, illustrate this awsome paddling environment. Streams covered: Lake Creek, Arkansas, Colorado, Blue, Eagle, Roaring Fork, Crystal, Fryingpan, Gunnison, Taylor, Yampa, Rio Grande, Conejos, Animas, Piedra, North Platte, North Fork South Platte, South Fork South Platte, South Platte, Boulder Creek, Cache La Poudre, and South Fork Poudre. Publisher/distributor: Colorado Kayak Supply, P.O. Box 291, Buena Vista, CO 81211.

165.Wheat, Doug. THE FLOATER'S GUIDE TO COLORADO. Billings, MT, Helena, MT: Falcon Press, 1983. 296 p. Illus. Maps. Bibl. Index. Paper. CO

Wheat organizes his Colorado guide into thirteen river basins; four on the east side of the continental divide, nine on the west. A map of each basin begins its chapter, with larger-scale sketch maps of the rivers and runs on suceeding pages. There is an impressive amount of information given—the "necessaries" of length, drop, gradient, flow, quad maps, land ownership, etc., are considerably augmented with informed comment on geology, conservation, wildlife, plantlife, and human interaction with the rivers, past and present. River basins: Upper Colorado, Lower Colorado, Gunnison, Dolores, San Juan, Upper Green, Lower Green, White, Yampa, North Platte, South Platte, Arkansas, and Rio Grande. For a final dam statement, read the "Afterword." Publisher/distributor: Falcon Press, P.O. Box 731, Helena, MT 59624.

Connecticut (CT)

166.AMC RIVER GUIDE: MASSACHUSETTS, CONNECTICUT, RHODE ISLAND. Boston: Appalachian Mountain Club, 1985. 192 p. Illus. Maps. Index. Paper. MA CT RI See entry 283 for a full description.

167.APPALACHIAN WHITEWATER: VOLUME III, THE NORTHERN MOUNTAINS. Compiled by John Connelly and John Porterfield. Birmingham, AL: Menasha Ridge Press, 1987. 141 p. Illus. Maps. Index. Paper. CT ME MA NH VT See entry 5 for a full description.

168.Burmeister, Walter F. THE HUDSON RIVER AND ITS TRIBUTARIES. Appalachian Waters, no. 2. Oakton, VA: Appalachian Books, 1974. 496 p. Maps. Bibl. Index. Paper. CT MA NJ NY VT (WW-1st ed.) River(s): upper, central and lower Hudson tributaries.

169.Cawley, James S., and Cawley, Margaret. EXPLORING THE HOUSATONIC RIVER AND VALLEY. South Brunswick, NJ: A.S. Barnes, 1978. 128 p. Illus. Bibl. Index. Paper. CT MA (WW-1st ed.) River(s): Housatonic.

170.THE COMPLETE BOATING GUIDE TO THE CONNECTICUT RIVER. Rev. ed. Edited by Mark C. Borton. Easthampton, MA: Connecticut River Watershed Council, 1986. 245 p. Maps. Paper. CT MA NH VT ***

171.CONNECTICUT RIVER GUIDE. Rev. ed. Easthampton, MA: Connecticut River Watershed Council, 1971. 87 p. Paper. CT MA NH VT (WW-1st ed.) River(s): Connecticut, and its tributaries: the White, West, Millers, Westfield, Salmon.

172.Detels, Pamela, and Harris, Janet. CANOEING: TRIPS IN CONNECTICUT, THE LONG AND SHORT OF IT... Madison, CT: Birch Run Press, 1977. 128 p. Illus. Maps. Paper. CT

"The intent of this book is to serve as a guide and suggest areas within Connecticut for canoeing. ...What we present are shared discoveries—discoveries of places we found particularly appealing and enriching" (preface). After seventeen introductory pages ("What's it All About?," "Starting Out!"), the authors go about the business of describing various trips on the Housatonic (3 trips), Farmington (4 trips), Connecticut (4 trips), and Thames rivers (1 trip each on the "feeder" rivers Shetucket, and Quinebaug), and on lakes and coastal areas. Description contents include: access map, put- in and take-out locations, and a narrative of a page or so describing the run. Possibly unobtainable by this time. Publisher/distributor: Globe Pequot Press, P.O. Box Q, Chester, CT 06412.

173.Farmington River Watershed Association. THE FARMINGTON RIVER GUIDE. 1970. Reprint. Avon, CT: The Association, 1984. 56 p. Illus. Map. Paper. CT MA

Almost evenly divided into descriptions of nine canoe runs and other information about the area contained within the watershed—fishing, wildlife, geology, and ornithology. Access, mileage, approximate trip times, portages, and rapids ratings (international scale) are given for each run. Hazards are emphasized. A separate (11x13) map accompanies the guide. Publisher/distributor: Farmington River Watershed Assoc., 749 Hopmeadow St., Simsbury, CT 06070.

174.Gabler, Ray. NEW ENGLAND WHITE WATER RIVER GUIDE. Boston, MA: Appalachian Mountain Club, 1981. 376 p. Illus. Maps. Bibl. Paper. CT ME MA NH NY VT See entry 25 for a full description.

175.NORTHEASTERN COASTAL PADDLING GUIDE. Edited by Chuck Sutherland. Tuckahoe, NY: Association of North Atlantic Kayakers, 1984. 39 p. Illus. Maps. Paper. CT MA ME NJ NY RI See entry 45 for a full description.

176.Weber, Ken. CANOEING MASSACHUSETTS, RHODE ISLAND, AND CONNECTICUT. Somersworth, NH: New Hampshire Publishing Co., 1980. 159 p. Illus. Maps. Paper. CT MA RI See entry 54 for full description.

Delaware (DE)

177.APPALACHIAN WHITEWATER: VOLUME II, THE CENTRAL MOUNTAINS. Compiled by Ed Grove and others. Birmingham, AL: Menasha Ridge Press, 1987. 207 p. Illus. Maps. Index. Paper. DE MD PA WV See entry 4 for a full description.

178.Burmeister, Walter F. THE DELAWARE AND ITS TRIBUTARIES. Appalachian Waters, no. 1. Oakton, VA: Appalachian Books, 1974. 274 p. Map. Bibl. Paper. DE NJ NY PA (WW 1st ed.) River(s): upper, central and lower Delaware River system.

179.Canter, Ron, and Canter, Kathy. NEARBY CANOEING STREAMS. 4th ed. Hyattsville, MD: 1979. 62 p. Illus. Maps. Paper. DE MD PA VA WV See entry 13 for a full description.

180.Gertler, Edward. MARYLAND AND DELAWARE CANOE TRAILS: A PADDLER'S GUIDE TO RIVERS OF THE OLD LINE AND FIRST STATES. 2d ed. Silver Spring, MD Seneca Press, 1983. 221 p. Maps. Index. Paper. DE MD

Several dozen streams in Maryland and Delaware are examined. Overall organization is by drainage, with subdivisions by river/trip. Trip descriptions contain: introduction, tabular data (gradient, difficulty, distance, time, width, scenery and strip map number), narrative description, gauge, and other information. Strip maps show road access. River drainages covered: Youghiogheny, Potomac, West Chesapeake, Susquehanna, Eastern Shore, Christina, and Delaware Bay. Publisher/distributor: Seneca Press, 503 Bonifant St., Silver Spring, MD 20910.

181.Gilbert, David T. RIVERS & TRAILS: BICYCLE TOURING, BACKPACKING, AND CANOEING IN THE MID-ATLANTIC STATES. Drawings by Laura L. Marzloff. Knoxville, MD: Outdoor Press, 1978. 112 p. Illus. Maps. Bibl. Index. Paper. DE MD VA WV See entry 26 for a full description.

182.Letcher, Gary. CANOEING THE DELAWARE RIVER: A GUIDE TO THE RIVER AND SHORE. New Brunswick, NJ: Rutgers University Press, 1985. 244 P. Illus. Maps. Bibl. DE NJ NY PA See entry 35 for a full description.

Florida (FL)

183.Burmeister, Walter F. THE SOUTHEASTERN RIVERS. Appalachian Waters, no. 4. Oakton, VA: Appalachian Books, 1976. 850 p. Bibl. Index. Paper. FL GA NC SC VA (WW-1st ed.)

184.Carter, Elizabeth F., and Pearce, John L. A CANOEING AND KAYAKING GUIDE TO THE STREAMS OF FLORIDA; VOLUME I, THE NORTH CENTRAL PANHANDLE AND PENINSULA. Hillsborough, NC: Menasha Ridge Press, 1985. 190 p. Illus. Maps. Index. FL (Volume II, covering southern Florida, is described below, entry 187.)

"Our intention is to inform the reader about how to go about canoeing in north Florida" (introduction). Every mile described was canoed by Carter or Pearce. Some thirty streams are described—1,000 miles of paddling. Springs, a singular treat for Florida paddlers, are described when they occur along the waterways. Organization is by stream, then by trip. Descriptions are in narrative form, introduced with a short section giving name of run, length, difficulty, scenery, location (county), and access. There is a map of each waterway. The rivers: Perdido, Blackwater, Yellow, Shoal, Choctawhatchee, Chipola, Sopchoppy, New, Little, St. Marks, Wakulla, Aucilla, Wacissa, Withlacoochee, Suwannee, Santa Fe, Ichetucknee, Oklawaha, Wekiva, and St. Mary's. Publisher/distributor: Menasha Ridge Press, P.O. Box 59257, Birmingham, AL 35259-9257.

185.Carter, Elizabeth F. DOWNRIVER CANOEING IN THE BIG BEND. 1985. 24 p. FL ***

186.Council, Clyde C. SUWANNEE COUNTRY. 2d ed. Sarasota, FL: Council Co., 1988. 61 p. Illus. Maps. Paper. FL

"A canoeing, boating and recreational guide to Florida's immortal Suwannee River" (subtitle on cover). The Suwannee rises in the Okefenokee Swamp and meanders 220 miles from Georgia, across Florida to the Gulf of Mexico. The author writes that he has included all the information he "can find and remember" about the river. This information is a product of canoe trips, aircraft over-flight, and other research. Strip maps form the core of the guide. At the edges of the maps are scores of photographs interspersed with informational paragraphs on local history and canoe camping suggestions. The maps show mileage, access, camp and picnic sites, and the locations of the many magnificent stream-side springs. Publisher/distributor: Council Co., P.O. Box 5822, Sarasota, FL 34277.

187.Glaros, Lou, and Sphar, Doug. A CANOEING AND KAYAKING GUIDE TO THE STREAMS OF FLORIDA; VOLUME II: CENTRAL AND SOUTH PENINSULA. Birmingham, AL: Menasha Ridge Press, 1987. 136 p. Illus. Maps. Bibl. Index. FL (See entry 184 for the first volume of this Florida guide written by Elizabeth F. Carter and John L. Pearce, subtitled: THE NORTH CENTRAL PANHANDLE AND PENINSULA.)

The Glaros-Sphar, southern Florida guide is intended for the "...adventurous explorer, the serious naturalist, and the family boater. Twenty-six waterways have been included in this book. They range from the broad, open rivers that flow into tidal marshes to the tight creeks that snake through dense swamp and challenge the paddler's maneuvering skills," (introduction). The authors give difficulty and scenery ratings; county map, topo quad or coastal chart name; and road access. The waterways: (Atlantic coast): Bulow Creek, Tomoka River, Spruce Creek, Turkey Creek, Sebastian Creek, St. Lucie River, Loxahatchee River; (Southwest Gulf coast): Weeki Wachee River, Hillsborough River, Alafia River, Little Manatee River, Manatee River, Braden River, Ding Darling National Wildlife Refuge, Estero River; (Central highlands): Deep Creek, Econlockhatchee River, Reedy Creek, Arbuckle Creek, Peace River; (Everglades): Blackwater River, Evergalades City and Ten Thousand Islands, Wilderness Waterway, Turner River, Everglades National Park, East Everglades. Publisher/distributor: Menasha Ridge Press, P.O. Box 59257, Birmingham, AL 35259-9257.

188.Kalma, Dennis. BOAT AND CANOE CAMPING IN THE EVERGLADES BACKCOUNTRY AND TEN THOUSAND ISLANDS REGION. Miami, FL: Florida Flair Books, 1988. 64 p. Illus. Maps. Bibl. Paper. FL

A guide to planning a canoe trip through the subtropical mangrove forests of the Everglades National Park and Ten Thousand Islands region of southwest Florida. The author covers the basics of planning, route-finding, campsites, emergencies, and diversions (exploring, fishing, blue crabbing, nature study). Eleven popular trips are briefly described and mapped. There are addresses for park headquarters, map sources, canoe liveries and outfitters. Publisher/distributor: Florida Flair Books, 8955 S.W. 93 Ct., Miami, FL 33176.

189.Marks, Henry, and Riggs, Gene Britt. RIVERS OF FLORIDA. Atlanta, GA: Southern Press, 1974. 116 p. Illus. Paper. FL (WW-1st ed.) River(s): Saint Marys, Saint Johns, Miami, Lostman's, Peace, Hillsborough, Weeki Wachee, Withlacooche, Suwanee, Saint Marks, Ochlockonee, and Apalachicola.

190.Toner, Mike, and Toner, Pat. FLORIDA BY PADDLE AND PACK: 45 WILDERNESS TRAILS IN CENTRAL AND SOUTH FLORIDA. Miami, FL: Banyan Books, 1979. 144 p. Illus. Maps. Bibl. Paper. FL

The Toner's guide covers (in a compressed arrangement of two pages per trip) 28 canoe and 17 hiking trails in the Sunshine State. In addition to trip descriptions, the authors provide tips on wilderness ethics, equipment, hazards, snakes, alligators, mosquitoes, family trips, and more. Canoe runs are presented in standardized format: length, time, access, maps, "notes," and further information source. This is followed by a narrative about the run, and a large-scale topographic/access map on the facing page. The waterways: Withlacoochee, Rock Springs, Wekiva, Econlockhatchee, Alafia, Peace, Fisheating Creek, Loxahatchee, Estero, Blackwater, and Turner Rivers; "Ding" Darling Wildlife Refuge, Rookery Bay, Indian Key, Wilderness Waterway (Everglades National Park), East Cape Sable, Hell's Bay, West Lake, and Noble Hammock. This guide is no longer in print.

191.Truesdell, William G. A GUIDE TO THE WILDERNESS WATERWAY OF THE EVERGLADES NATIONAL PARK. 1969. Reprint. Coral Gables, FL: Published in cooperation with the Everglades Natural History Association, University of Miami Press, 1985. 64 p. Illus. Maps. Paper. FL

A guide through the mangroves and sawgrass of the Everglades prepared by an ENP naturalist. There are twenty-seven maps based on charts and aerial photographs. The water route has been marked for its one-hundred-mile length. Both guidebook and waterway trail have been designed for use by novice canoeists. Publisher/distributor: Everglades Natural History Assn., P.O. Box 279, Homestead, FL 33030; or, University of Miami Press, Drawer 9088, Coral Gables, FL 33124.

Georgia (GA)

192.APPALACHIAN WHITEWATER: VOLUME I, THE SOUTHERN MOUNTAINS. Compiled by Bob Sehlinger and others. Birmingham, AL: Menasha Ridge Press, 1986. 159 p. Illus. Maps. Index. Paper. AL GA KY NC SC TN See entry 3 for a full description.

193.BROWN'S GUIDE TO THE GEORGIA OUTDOORS: BIKING, HIKING, AND CANOEING TRIPS, SELECTED FROM BROWN'S GUIDE TO GEORGIA. Edited by John W. English, and Katie Baer. Atlanta, GA: Cherokee Publishing, 1986. Illus. Maps. GA ***

194.Burmeister, Walter F. THE SOUTHEASTERN RIVERS. Appalachian Waters, no. 4. Oakton, VA: Appalachian Books, 1976. 850 p. Bibl. Index. Paper. FL GA NC SC VA (WW-1st ed.)

195.Nealy, William. WHITEWATER HOME COMPANION: SOUTHEASTERN RIVERS, VOLUME I. Hillsborough, NC: Menasha Ridge Press, 1981. 156 p. Illus. Maps. Paper. AL GA NC PA SC TN WV See entry 41 for a full description.

196.Nealy, William. WHITEWATER HOME COMPANION: SOUTHEASTERN RIVERS, VOLUME II. Hillsborough, NC: Menasha Ridge Press, 1984. 165 p. Illus. Maps. Paper. GA KY MD NC TN VA WV See entry 42 for a full description.

197.Rathnow, Ron. CHATTOOGA RIVER, SECTION IV. Great American Rivers Flip Map Series. Birmingham, AL: Menasha Ridge Press, 1986. 34 p. Illus. Maps. Paper. GA SC ***

198.Sehlinger, Bob, and Otey, Don. NORTHERN GEORGIA CANOEING: A CANOEING AND KAYAKING GUIDE TO THE STREAMS OF THE CUMBERLAND PLATEAU, BLUE RIDGE MOUNTAINS, AND EASTERN PIEDMONT. Hillsborough, NC: Menasha Ridge Press, 1980. 184 p. Illus. Maps. Index. Paper. GA

Much of the information in the introduction and appendixes of this guide is duplicated in its southern counterpart below, SOUTHERN GEORGIA CANOEING. No lakes are included in either guide. Descriptive material is standardized: stream description, day or camping trip, skill level required, runnable months, interest highlights, scenery, difficulty average width, velocity, gradient, runnable water levels (min/max), hazards, scouting, portages, rescue, water temperature, additional information sources, access, and quad maps. More than forty streams are examined, some of which are: Chattooga, Tallulah, Hiawassee, Toccoa, Chestatee, Coosawattee, Broad, Savannah, and Oconee. Publisher/distributor: Menasha Ridge Press, P.O. Box 59257, Birmingham, AL 35259-9257.

199.Sehlinger, Bob, and Otey, Don. SOUTHERN GEORGIA CANOEING: A CANOEING AND KAYAKING GUIDE TO THE STREAMS OF THE WESTERN PIEDMONT, COASTAL PLAIN, GEORGIA COAST, AND OKEFENOKEE SWAMP. Hillsborough, NC: Menasha Ridge Press, 1980. 294 p. Illus. Maps. Index. Paper. GA

For a general description of content and arrangement see the authors' NORTHERN GEORGIA CANOEING, above. In this guide, thirty-seven waterways are examined, some of which are: Alcovy, Yellow, Towaliga, Flint, Dog, Chatahoochee, Tallapoosa, Savannah, Ogeechee, Ocmulgee, Satilla, Suwannee, Withlacoochee, and Ochlockonee rivers, the Okefenokee Swamp, and Georgia coast. Publisher/distributor: Menasha Ridge Press, P.O. Box 59257, Birmingham, AL 35259-9257.

Hawaii (HI)

200.Schafer, Ann. CANOEING WESTERN WATERWAYS: THE COASTAL STATES. New York: Harper & Row, 1978. 272 p. Maps. Bibl. Index. CA HI OR WA See entry 52 for a full description.

201.Sutherland, Audrey. PADDLING HAWAII. Seattle, WA: The Mountaineers, 1988. 239 p. Illus. Maps. Bibl. Index. Paper. HI

Sutherland's guide shows paddler-adventurers how to explore the coasts and rivers of Kauai, Oahu, Molokai, Lanai, Maui, and Hawai'i by kayak. In part I of her book, she compares ten different craft one may use (emphasis on inflatables), the gear needed, safety, the water environment, food, and trip preparation. Part II is a trip guide divided by island, and then subdivided by shorline/coast, rivers, and offshore islands. A standard table introduces the narrative part of the descriptions: trip name, rating (special I-VI classification), quad maps, length, time, put-in, take-out, hazards, and best season. The total voyage data cover several pages—each accompanied by a sketch map and illustrated with photographs. Publisher/distributor: Mountaineers Books, 306 Second Ave. W, Seattle, WA 98119.

Idaho (ID)

202.Arighi, Scott, and Arighi, Margaret S. WILDWATER TOURING: TECHNIQUES AND TOURS. New York: Macmillan, 1974. 352 p. Illus. Maps. ID OR (WW-1st ed.) River(s): Rogue, Grande Ronde, John Day, Main and Middle Fork Salmon, and Owyhee.

203.FLOATING THE WILD SELWAY. Washington, DC: U.S. Dept. of Agriculture, Forest Service, 1986. 14 p. Illus. Maps. Paper. ID

"The Selway River is a remnant of primitive America. For 47 roadless miles it flows through the heart of the Selway Bitterroot Wilderness" (page 1). Six strip maps drawn with topographic detail show the run from the launch site at Paradise Guard Station to take-out at the top of Selway Falls. Between these points, the river drops an average of twenty-eight feet per mile. The maps indicate rapids (29 of them) by name and show the shuttle roads. There is a short introductory section about the river but no mile-by-mile logs or other narrative. Publisher/distributor: West Fork Ranger Station, Bitterroot National Forest, Darby, MT 59829.

204.Garren, John. IDAHO RIVER TOURS: A GUIDE TO TOURING IDAHO'S MOST POPULAR WILDERNESS WHITEWATER RIVERS. Portland, OR: Garren Publishing, 1987. 125 p. Illus. Maps. Bibl. Paper. ID

This is a carefully-organized guide to five of the top "overnight" wilderness whitewater trips in the lower United States. Rivers covered: Selway, Middle Fork of the Salmon, Main Salmon, Lower Salmon, and Snake (Hells Canyon). All the rivers except the Lower Salmon are "permit rivers." "The intent of this book is to provide useful information primarily for the boater using these river tours for the first time or those who may use the river infrequently. Each tour includes a river map, a trip narrative, a river discharge curve and a river log with campsites and rapids" (p. 7). In material preceding the guide sections, Garren writes about river slope, discharge, velocity, and drift time. His shuttle tips and maps should be particularly helpful for trip planners. Publisher/distributor: Garren Publishing, 01008 SW Comus, Portland, OR 97219.

205.Geier, Dick, and Graeff, Todd. A RIVER RUNNERS GUIDE TO IDAHO. Boise, ID: Idaho Department of Parks and Recreation; Idaho State Office Bureau of Land Management, 1980. 47 p. Illus. Maps. Paper. ID

"From the canyons of the high desert to the mountains of the Idaho batholith, an intriguing variety of free-flowing rivers are available," (introduction). To ease the selection of a suitable Idaho river, the authors recommend skill level and type of boat. Information on 64 trips on fifteen rivers is standardized in a columnar arrangement: river, put in, take out, quad map, classification, craft, skill level, season, miles, difficulty, portages, permit required, flow information source. A short narrative and sketch map complete the description. The rivers: Blackfoot, Portneuf, Boise, Bruneau, Snake, Clearwater, Coeur d'Alene, Kootenai, Moyie, Salmon, Owyhee, Payette, Priest, Pack, and St. Joe. Publisher/distributor: Idaho Dept. of Parks and Recreation, 2263 Warm Springs Ave., Boise, ID, 83720.

206.HELLS CANYON OF THE SNAKE RIVER. Quinn Map. Redmond, OR: Educational Adventures, 198? [20 p.] Illus. Maps. Paper. ID OR WA See entry 28 for a full description.

207.LOWER SALMON RIVER GUIDE. Rev. ed. Washington, DC: U.S. Dept. of the Interior, Bureau of Land Management, 1983. 18 p. Maps. Paper. ID OR WA See entry 36 for a full description.

208.THE MIDDLE FORK OF THE SALMON, A WILD AND SCENIC RIVER: FOREST VISITOR MAP AND GUIDE. Washington, DC: U.S. Dept. of Agriculture, Forest Service, 1981. 26 p. Illus. Maps. Paper. ID

A series of nine carefully-prepared strip maps containing topographic detail and printed on coated paper, cover the "River of No Return" from put-in at Dagger Falls to take-out at Cache Bar on the Main Salmon. Adjacent to the maps is a running narrative of the journey for its 100-mile length. This is excellent government work. Publisher/distributor: U.S. Forest Service, Middle Fork Ranger District, Challis, ID 83226.

209.Moore, Greg, and McClaran, Don. IDAHO WHITEWATER: THE COMPLETE RIVER GUIDE. McCall, ID: Class VI, 1989. 220 p. Illus. Maps. Bibl. Paper. ID

A comprehensive guide to Idaho's rivers for paddlers of all skill levels. Eighty-one runs are described by Moore and McClaran using standardized data tables (skill level, craft type, put-in, take-out, shuttle length, maps, gradient, etc.). Their tables are augmented by a descriptive narrative, a map showing access, and a flow level graphic. River drainage sections covered: Snake, Salmon, Clearwater, northern Idaho area. The less widely-known runs/rivers described: St. Joe, Priest, Kootenai, Moyie, Pack, Coeur d'Alene, Big Sands (Creek), White Sands (Creek), Fish (Creek), Secesh, Big (Creek), Loon (Creek), Marsh (Creek), Panther (Creek), Bruneau, Jarbidge, Malad, Wilson, Bear, Portneuf, Blackfoot, Teton, Bitch (Creek), Fall, and Henry's Fork. Illustrated with photographs—black and white, and (lush) color. Index map. Publisher/distributor: Class VI, P.O. Box 1794, McCall, ID 83638.

210.Nichols, Gary. RIVER RUNNERS' GUIDE TO UTAH AND ADJACENT AREAS. Rev. ed. Salt Lake City: University of Utah Press, 1986. 168 p. Illus. Maps. Paper. AZ CO ID UT WY See entry 43 for a full description.

211.Quinn, James M., et al. HANDBOOK TO THE MIDDLE FORK OF THE SALMON RIVER CANYON. Medford, OR: Educational Adventures, 1981. 186 p. Illus. Maps. Paper. ID

"If there is such a thing as magic, it is surely found on the Middle Fork" (introduction). This is an Idaho wilderness trip of some ninety-six miles, from Boundary Creek to the confluence with the Main Salmon. There are five books in this series on running western rivers, each of which aims to combine adventure and education through sharing "...the knowledge of professional guides who make their livelihoods from the rivers." Arrangement and format are similar for each book: history of the area, mammals, fish, vegetation, birds, safety, gear needed, commercial guides listing, and river log. In the log section, strip maps show rapids numbered in ascending order from put-in to take-out. These numbers coordinate with parallel descriptive information indicating mileage, class, rapid name (if any), identification, comments, and maneuvering directions—this latter information seldom seen in such detail in guidebooks. Heavily illustrated with many "action" photographs in color and black and white, early photographs of people and activities, and a number of aerial shots of the river. Publisher/distributor: Educational Adventures, P.O. Box 4190, Sunriver, OR 97707.

212.Schafer, Ann. CANOEING WESTERN WATERWAYS: THE MOUNTAIN STATES. New York: Harper & Row, 1978. 279 p. Maps. Bibl. Index. AZ CO ID MT NV NM UT WY See entry 53 for a full description.

213.WHITEWATER PRIMER, INCLUDING SELWAY AND ILLINOIS RIVER LOGS. Portland, OR: Wilderness Public Rights Fund, Northwest Chapter, 198? 86 p. Illus. Maps. Paper. ID OR

There is something for all river paddling activists here—on or off the water—since WHITEWATER PRIMER is almost evenly divided between practical guidebook data on two rivers (Idaho's Selway, and the Illinois in Oregon), and a selection of eight previously published articles expressing opposition to the disproportionate number of trip permits granted commercial operators versus private applicants on "permit rivers." The guidebook section is by John Garren, who provides an introductory narrative on the river trips followed by information on their location, campsites, flow gauge readings, and a detailed log (time, miles, riverside landmarks, rapids, mini-description). Sketch maps are provided. Publisher/distributor: Wilderness Public Rights Fund/Northwest Chapter, P.O. Box 5791, Portland, OR 97228.

214.THE WILD AND SCENIC SNAKE RIVER: HELLS CANYON NATIONAL RECREATION AREA. Washington, DC: U.S. Dept. of Agriculture, Forest Service, 1985. 23 p. Illus. Maps. Paper. ID OR WA

Covers the run down the Snake from Hells Canyon Dam (mile 247 to Heller Bar (mile 168.3). (Reservations and officer-issued permits are required for the portion from the dam to Rush Creek Rapids.) A series of six strip maps with an interspersed mile-by-mile descriptive log is the principal feature of this guide. Other information given: regulations, access, cultural resources, historic sites, hunting, and fishing. Publisher/distributor: Hells Canyon National Recreation Area, Wallowa-Whitman National Forest, 3620-B Snake River Ave., Lewiston, ID 83501.

Illinois (IL)

215.ILLINOIS CANOEING GUIDE. Springfield: Illinois Dept. of Conservation, 1975. 67 p. Maps. Paper. IL (WW-1st ed.)

216.Vierling, Philip E. ILLINOIS COUNTRY CANOE TRAILS. 2d ed. Guidebook—Illinois Country Outdoor Guides, no. 2. Chicago: Illinois Country Outdoor Guides, 1979. 124 p. Illus. Maps. Paper. IL

Contains strip-maps and logs to three of Illinois' most popular canoeing rivers (Fox, Mazon, Vermillion), and best whitewater river—Little Vermillion. Vierling's maps are annotated, with numbers coded to the text. At strategic river points there are blow-up drawings showing rocks, rapids, dams, etc. The author's other canoeing guides in this series are out of print (ILLINOIS COUNTRY CANOE TRAILS: KANKAKEE, DU PAGE, AND DES PLAINES RIVERS, AUX SABLE CREEK; and, ILLINOIS COUNTRY CANOE TRAILS: DES PLAINES RIVER). He is apparently updating or expanding these on a river-by-river basis under a new general title: ILLINOIS COUNTRY LANDINGS. Number 1 (DU PAGE) is available; No. 2 (KISHWAUKEE), and 3 (DES PLAINES) are in preparation. Publisher/distributor: Illinois Country Outdoor Guides, 4400 N. Merrimac Ave., Chicago, IL 60630.

Indiana (IN)

217.INDIANA CANOE GUIDE. Indianapolis: Indiana Dept. of Natural Resources, 1980. 122 p. Illus. Maps. Paper. IN

Produced from information gathered by Indiana Dept. of Natural Resources employees and others knowledgeable about Indiana waterways. Data on 24 canoeing streams are divided into trip segments, then mapped and marked showing access roads, portages, and points of interest. Descriptions of the trips include distance, access, picnic areas, and location of medical facilities. The appropriate U.S.G.S. maps are identified. A sampling of the rivers: Blue, Deep, Driftwood, Eel, Elkhart, Fawn, Flatrock, Iroquois, Kankakee, Little Calumet, Pigeon, St. Joseph, Wabash, White, and Whitewater. Publisher/distributor: Indiana Dept. of Natural Resources, Div. of Outdoor Recreation, 612 State Office Bldg., Indianapolis, IN 46204.

Iowa (IA)

218.Knudson, George E. GUIDE TO THE UPPER IOWA RIVER. Decorah, IA: Luther College, 1970. 57 p. Maps. Paper. IA (WW-1st ed.) River(s): Iowa.

Kansas (KS)

219.Pierce, Don. EXPLORING MISSOURI RIVER COUNTRY. Jefferson City, MO: Missouri Department of Natural Resources, 198? 276 p. Illus. Maps. Paper. KS MO NE See entry 49 for a full description.

Kentucky (KY)

220.Burmeister, Walter F. THE UPPER OHIO & ITS TRIBUTARIES. Appalachian Waters, no. 5. Oakton, VA: Appalachian Books, 1978. 948 p. Bibl. Index. Paper. KY NY OH PA VA WV See entry 11 for a full description.

221.Nealy, William. WHITEWATER HOME COMPANION: SOUTHEASTERN RIVERS, VOLUME II. Hillsborough, NC: Menasha Ridge Press, 1984. 165 p. Illus. Maps. Paper. GA KY MD NC TN VA WV See entry 42 for a full description.

222.Sehlinger, Bob. A CANOEING AND KAYAKING GUIDE TO THE STREAMS OF KENTUCKY. Ann Arbor, MI: Thomas Press, 1978. 320 p. Illus. Maps. Bibl. Index. Paper. KY

This book is available in a revised edition which I was unable to examine. Sehlinger, author of a half dozen southeastern waterways guides, has covered paddling opportunities in all of Kentucky's primary and secondary watersheds. Some seventy streams are described. Runs are outlined on data sheets containing extensive information, including: USGS quads, difficulty, average width, recommended watercraft, gradient, hazards, and portages. A sketch map showing road access is on a facing page. A some of the major rivers: Big Sandy, Licking, Kentucky, Dix, Cumberland, Salt, Green, Tradewater, Little, and Tennessee. Publisher/ distributor: Menasha Ridge Press, P.O. Box 59257, Birmingham, AL 35259-9257.

Louisiana (LA)

223.Estes, Chuck; Carter, Liz; and Almquist, Byron. CANOE TRAILS OF THE DEEP SOUTH: THE RIVERS OF LOUISIANA, ALABAMA, AND MISSISSIPPI. Birmingham, AL: Menasha Ridge Press, 1990. 304 p. Illus. Maps. Paper. AL LA MS ***

224.Williams, Richard, and Williams, Joan. CANOEING IN LOUISIANA. 3d ed. Lafayette, LA: Lafayette Natural History Museum & Planetarium, 1985. 111 p. Illus. Maps. Bibl. Paper. LA

A guide to twenty-five trips on sixteen drainages. The trips: Whiskey Chitto Creek, Calcasieu River, Six Mile Creek, Vermilion River, Bayou Tortue,

Bayou Teche, Lake Fausse Point, Lake Grevenberg, Buffalo Cove, Atchafalaya Basin, Tangipahoa River, Bogue Chitto River, McGees Creek, Amite River, Castor Creek, Chemin-A-Haut Bayou, Bayou de Loutre, Bayou Dorcheat, Lake Bistineau, Saline Bayou, Kisatchie Bayou, Spring Creek, Cocodrie Lake, Anacoco Bayou, and Cypress Creek. Sketch maps show nearby roads and campsites. Reports of the trips (supplied by over twenty contributors) are in narrative form and standardized under headings: location, history, description, access and take-out, and distance. Publisher/distributor: Lafayette Natural History Museum & Planetarium, 637 Girard Park Dr., Lafayette, LA 70503.

Maine (ME)

225.AMC RIVER GUIDE: MAINE. 2d ed. Boston: Appalachian Mountain Club, 1988. 312 p. Maps. Paper. ME See entry 283 for a full description.

226.APPALACHIAN WHITEWATER: VOLUME III, THE NORTHERN MOUNTAINS. Compiled by John Connelly and John Porterfield. Birmingham, AL: Menasha Ridge Press, 1987. 141 p. Illus. Maps. Index. Paper. CT ME MA NH VT See entry 5 for a full description.

227.Gabler, Ray. NEW ENGLAND WHITE WATER RIVER GUIDE. Boston, MA: Appalachian Mountain Club, 1981. 376 p. Illus. Maps. Bibl. Paper. CT ME MA NH NY VT See entry 25 for a full description.

228.Kellog, Zip. CANOEING. Maine Geographic Series. Freeport, ME: DeLorme Publishing, 1983. 3 vols. Illus. Maps. Bibl. Paper. ME

"The waterways of Maine are its lifeblood. Get to know them and you'll really get to know Maine" (introduction). Kellog provides river write-ups on 49 Maine streams. The three regional volumes (Coastal & Eastern Rivers, vol. 1; Western Rivers, vol. 2; Northern Rivers, vol. 3) average 50 pages in length and fit into a shirt pocket. Each description is a downstream narrative on the sights, rapids, obsticles, access, and history. A map showing roads and rapids accompanies the text. Volume 1 waterways: Royal, Cobbosseecontee, Sheepscot, St. George, Passagassawaukeag, Blue Hill Falls, Kenduskeag, Souadabscook, Union, Passadaumkeag, Nicatous, Narraguagus, Machias, East Machias, St. Croix, Dennys, Grand Lake, Orange; Volume 2: Ossipee, Saco, Nezinscot, Crooked, Little Androscoggin, Androscoggin, Swift, Ellis, Sebasticook, Carrabassett, Sandy, Dead (South Branch), Dead (North Branch), Lower Dead, Kennebec, Moose, Piscataquis, Sebec, Pleasant (West Branch),; Volume 3: Nesowadnehunk, Mattawamkeag, Baskahegan, Penobscot (West Branch), Penobscot (East Branch), Seboeis, Webster, Allagash, St. John, St. Francis, Aroostook, Big Machias, and Fish. Publisher/distributor: DeLorme Publishing Co., P.O. Box 298GS, Freeport, ME 04032.

229.NORTHEASTERN COASTAL PADDLING GUIDE. Edited by Chuck Sutherland. Tuckahoe, NY: Association of North Atlantic Kayakers, 1984. 39 p. Illus. Maps. Paper. CT MA ME NJ NY RI See entry 45 for a full description.

230.Rathnow, Ron. WEST BRANCH OF THE PENOBSCOT AND THE KENNEBEC GORGE. Great American Rivers Flip Map Series. Birmingham, AL: Menasha Ridge Press, 1989. 57 p. Illus. Maps. Paper. ME ***

231.Thomas, Eben. CANOEING MAINE #1. Rev. ed. of NO HORNS BLOWING. Thorndike, ME: Thorndike Press, 1979. 134 p. Illus. Maps. Bibl. Paper. ME ***

232.Thomas, Eben. CANOEING MAINE #2. Rev. ed. of THE WEEKENDER. Thorndike, ME: Thorndike Press, 1979. 130 p. Illus. Maps. Paper. ME ***

233.Thomas, Eben. HOT BLOOD AND WET PADDLES: A GUIDE TO CANOE RACING IN MAINE AND NEW HAMPSHIRE. Hallowell, ME: Hallowell Printing Co., 1974. 188 p. Maps. Paper. ME NH (WW-1st ed.)

Maryland (MD)

234.APPALACHIAN WHITEWATER: VOLUME II, THE CENTRAL MOUNTAINS. Compiled by Ed Grove and others. Birmingham, AL: Menasha Ridge Press, 1987. 207 p. Illus. Maps. Index. Paper. DE MD PA WV See entry 4 for a full description.

235.Burmeister, Walter F. THE SUSQUEHANNA RIVER AND ITS TRIBUTARIES. Appalachian Waters, no. 3. Oakton, VA: Appalachian Books, 1975. 600 p. Bibl. Index. Paper. MD NY PA (WW-1st ed.)

236.Canter, Ron, and Canter, Kathy. NEARBY CANOEING STREAMS. 4th ed. Hyattsville, MD: 1979. 62 p. Illus. Maps. Paper. DE MD PA VA WV See entry 13 for a full description.

237.Corbett, H. Roger, Jr., and Matacia, Louis J., Jr. ONE & TWO DAY RIVER CRUISES: MARYLAND, VIRGINIA, WEST VIRGINIA. Blue Ridge Voyages, vol. 1, 4th ed. Oakton, VA: Blue Ridge Voyageurs,

1973. p. Illus. Maps. Bibl. Paper. MD VA WV (WW1st ed.) River(s): Rappahannock, Antietam, Thornton, Potomac, Shenandoah, and Cedar.

238.Corbett, H. Roger, Jr., and Matacia, Louis J., Jr. ONE & TWO DAY RIVER CRUISES: MARYLAND, VIRGINIA, WEST VIRGINIA. Blue Ridge Voyages, vol. 2, 2d ed. Oakton, VA: Appalachian Books, 1972. 88 p. Pref. Illus. Maps. Bibl. Paper. MD VA WV (WW-1st ed.) River(s): Potomac and its south branch, Cedar Creek, Catoctin Creek, Cacapon, Monocacy, and Antietam.

239.Gertler, Edward. MARYLAND AND DELAWARE CANOE TRAILS: A PADDLER'S GUIDE TO RIVERS OF THE OLD LINE AND FIRST STATES. 2d ed. Silver Spring, MD Seneca Press, 1983. 221 p. Maps. Index. Paper. DE MD See entry 180 for a full description.

240.Gilbert, David T. RIVERS & TRAILS: BICYCLE TOURING, BACKPACKING, AND CANOEING IN THE MID-ATLANTIC STATES. Drawings by Laura L. Marzloff. Knoxville, MD: Outdoor Press, 1978. 112 p. Illus. Maps. Bibl. Index. Paper. DE MD VA WV See entry 26 for a full description.

241.Nealy, William. WHITEWATER HOME COMPANION: SOUTHEASTERN RIVERS, VOLUME II. Hillsborough, NC: Menasha Ridge Press, 1984. 165 p. Illus. Maps. Paper. GA KY MD NC TN VA WV See entry 42 for a full description.

242.Robinson, William M., Jr. MARYLAND-PENNSYLVANIA COUNTRYSIDE CANOE TRAILS: CENTRAL MARYLAND TRIPS. Oakton, VA: Appalachian Books, 1974. 34 p. Illus. Bibl. Paper. MD (WW-1st ed.) Waterway(s): Gunpowder and Patapsco rivers, Muddy Creek, and several flatwater trips in the Baltimore area.

243.Thomson, John Seabury. POTOMAC WHITE WATER: A GUIDE TO SAFE CANOEING ABOVE WASHINGTON, SENECA TO LITTLE FALLS. Oakton, VA: Appalachian Books, 1974. 44 p. Illus. Map. Bibl. Paper. MD VA (WW-1st ed.) River(s): Potomac.

Massachusetts (MA)

244.AMC RIVER GUIDE: MASSACHUSETTS, CONNECTICUT, RHODE ISLAND. Boston: Appalachian Mountain Club, 1985. 192 p. Illus. Maps. Index. Paper. MA CT RI See entry 283 for a full description.

245.APPALACHIAN WHITEWATER: VOLUME III, THE NORTHERN MOUNTAINS. Compiled by John Connelly and John Porterfield. Birmingham, AL: Menasha Ridge Press, 1987. 141 p. Illus. Maps. Index. Paper. CT ME MA NH VT See entry 5 for a full description.

246.Burmeister, Walter F. THE HUDSON RIVER AND ITS TRIBUTARIES. Appalachian Waters, no. 2. Oakton, VA: Appalachian Books, 1974. 496 p. Maps. Bibl. Index. Paper. CT MA NJ NY VT (WW-1st ed.) River(s): upper, central and lower Hudson tributaries.

247.Cawley, James S., and Cawley, Margaret. EXPLORING THE HOUSATONIC RIVER AND VALLEY. South Brunswick, NJ: A.S. Barnes, 1978. 128 p. Illus. Bibl. Index. Paper. CT MA (WW-1st ed.) River(s): Housatonic.

248.THE COMPLETE BOATING GUIDE TO THE CONNECTICUT RIVER. Rev. ed. Edited by Mark C. Borton. Easthampton, MA: Connecticut River Watershed Council, 1986. 245 p. Maps. Paper. CT MA NH VT ***

249.CONNECTICUT RIVER GUIDE. Rev. ed. Easthampton, MA: Connecticut River Watershed Council, 1971. 87 p. Paper. CT MA NH VT (WW-1st ed.) River(s): Connecticut, and its tributaries, the White, West, Millers, Westfield, Salmon.

250.Farmington River Watershed Association. THE FARMINGTON RIVER GUIDE. 1970. Reprint. Avon, CT: The Association, 1984. 56 p. Illus. Map. Paper. CT MA See entry 173 for a full description.

251.Gabler, Ray. NEW ENGLAND WHITE WATER RIVER GUIDE. Boston, MA: Appalachian Mountain Club, 1981. 376 p. Illus. Maps. Bibl. Paper. CT ME MA NH NY VT See entry 25 for a full description.

252.NORTHEASTERN COASTAL PADDLING GUIDE. Edited by Chuck Sutherland. Tuckahoe, NY: Association of North Atlantic Kayakers, 1984. 39 p. Illus. Maps. Paper. CT MA ME NJ NY RI See entry 45 for a full description.

253.Thomas, Deborah, and Clauser, Suzanne S. CANOEING: TRIPS IN WESTERN MASSACHUSETTS. Edited by P. Detels. Madison, CT: Birch Run Publishing, 1979. Paper. MA ***

254.Weber, Ken. CANOEING MASSACHUSETTS, RHODE ISLAND, AND CONNECTICUT. Somersworth, NH: New Hampshire Publishing Co., 1980. 159 p. Illus. Maps. Paper. CT MA RI See entry 54 for full description.

Michigan (MI)

255.Dennis, Jerry, and Date, Craig. CANOEING MICHIGAN RIVERS: A COMPREHENSIVE GUIDE TO 45 RIVERS. Davison, MI: Friede Publications, 1986. 139 p. Illus. Maps. Bibl. Paper. MI

Dennis and Date examine 1900 miles of flowing water on Michigan's peninsulas (upper, 28 streams; lower, 17 streams). Textual material, divided by river section, is detailed and keyed by number to a map. The maps are small scale, but sufficient for indicating access roads. The text is preceded by an at-a-glance table: county, start/end, miles, gradient, portages, rapids/falls, campgrounds, liveries, and skill level. Appendices cite additional information sources. Some selected rivers: Au Sable, Brule, Chippewa, Ford, Kalamazoo, Manistee, Michigamme, Muskegon, Ontonagon, Pigeon, Presque Isle, Rifle, Thunder Bay, Two Hearted, and Whitefish. Publisher/distributor: Friede Publications, 2339 Venezia Dr., Davison, MI 48423.

256.DuFresne, Jim. ISLE ROYALE NATIONAL PARK: FOOT TRAILS & WATER ROUTES. Seattle, WA: The Mountaineers, 1984. 136 p. Illus. Maps. Bibl. Index. Paper. MI

A hiking-paddling guidebook to the first island National Park in the United States, and apparent prototype for DuFresne's other national park guides (Glacier Bay, Voyageurs). The book is in three parts: (1) introduction (history, flora, fauna, fishing, access from the mainland, and "Enjoying the Back Country);" (2) hiking (21 trails arranged by location and length), and (3) paddling (19 inland lake and shorline routes by location). Trip information (terrain, campsites, wildlife, fishing, history) is introduced by a brief table giving distance, portages, longest portage, paddling time, and difficulty rating. Publisher/distributor: Mountaineers Books, 306 Second Ave. W, Seattle, WA 98119.

257.Palzer, Bob, and Palzer, Jody. WHITEWATER, QUIETWATER: A GUIDE TO THE WILD RIVERS OF WISCONSIN, UPPER MICHIGAN, AND N.E. MINNESOTA. 5th ed. Two Rivers, WI: Evergreen Paddleways, 1983. 160 p. Illus. Maps. Bibl. Paper. MI MN WI See entry 46 for a full description.

Minnesota (MN)

258.Beymer, Robert. THE BOUNDARY WATERS CANOE AREA, VOLUME 1: THE WESTERN REGION. 4th ed. Berkeley, CA: Wilderness Press, 1988. 119 p. Illus. Maps. Index. Paper. MN

This guide and its regional companion (see Beymer, below), form a set which covers all 1,075,000 watersoaked acres of the BWCA, and "... is written for the canoe camper who is capable of taking care of himself in a wilderness environment" (preface). In volume 1, Beymer describes fifty-two routes starting at twenty-eight entry points from Crane Lake east to Kawishiwi Lake. A typical route description has the following information: name; length in days/miles; number of lakes, rivers, creeks, portages; difficulty (easy, challenging, rugged); appropriate "Fisher" maps; travel zones crossed; introduction; and daily trip log. Sketch maps show waterways and portages. The first three chapters are Beymer's introduction to the BWCA and the 1978 Wilderness Act by which it is administered, plus instructions on using the guidebook. A folding map of the area completes the package. Publisher/distributor: Wilderness Press, 2440 Bancroft Way, Berkeley, CA 94704.

259.Beymer, Robert. BOUNDARY WATERS CANOE AREA, VOLUME 2: THE EASTERN REGION. 2d ed. Berkeley, CA: Wilderness Press, 1986. 132 p. Illus. Maps. Index. Paper. MN

This guide and its regional companion (see Beymer, above), form a set which covers all 1,075,000 watersoaked acres of the BWCA, and "... is written for the canoe camper who is capable of taking care of himself in a wilderness environment" (preface). In volume 2, Beymer describes ninety routes starting at twenty-one entry points from Sawbill Lake east to McFarland Lake. (See the annotation above for an examination of typical route description content, and other material which is duplicated in volume 2). Publisher/distributor: Wilderness Press, 2440 Bancroft Way, Berkeley, CA 94704.

260.Beymer, Robert. SUPERIOR NATIONAL FOREST: A COMPLETE RECREATION GUIDE FOR PADDLERS, HIKERS, ANGLERS, CAMPERS, MOUNTAIN BIKERS, AND SKIERS. Seattle, WA: Mountaineers; Vancouver, BC: Douglas & McIntyre, 1989. 270 p. Illus. Maps. Bibl. Index. Paper. MN

"There is a whole lot more to Superior National Forest than the BWCAW" (preface). This statement notwithstanding, canoeists need not be dismayed, for while this is an all-activities, all-seasons guide to nearly 4 million acres of the great North Woods, over 60 pages contain canoe route information. All the sections of Beymer's guide are organized by forest districts (6), with descriptions in the canoeing portion addressing individual lakes and streams. Two or three-paragraph trip descriptions give access, length, campsites, scenery, terrain, portages, etc. Appropriate Fisher and McKenzie map numbers are provided. Basic data for dozens of other waterways are contained in tables at the end of the canoeing section. Publisher/distributor: The Mountaineers, 306 Second Avenue West, Seattle, WA 98119; Douglas & McIntyre, 1615 Venables St., Vancouver, BC V5L 2H1.

261.Breining, Greg, and Watson, Linda. A GATHERING OF WATERS: A GUIDE TO MINNESOTA'S RIVERS. St. Paul: Minnesota Dept. of Natural Resources, 1977. 106 p. Illus. Maps. Bibl. Paper. MN

A very polished production covering eighteen legislatively- designated Minnesota canoeing rivers in detail (plus twenty-five other waterways in abbreviated form). A narrative text covers the necessary data: rapids, portages, campsites, access, history, flora, fauna, and setting. Maps and color photographs illustrate the descriptions. Featured Rivers: Big Fork, Cannon, Cloquet, Crow Wing, Des Moines, Kettle, Little Fork, Minnesota, Mississippi, North Fork of the Crow, Red Lake, Root, Rum, St. Croix, St. Louis, Snake, Straight, and Zumbro. Watch for any apparently careless (but, in this case potentially dangerous) understatement like the one describing a rapids on the Big Fork River: "Little American Falls (river mile 103), a 10-foot, nearly vertical drop over exposures of mica-schist and granite, SHOULD [emphasis mine] be portaged." This work may be out of print. Publisher/ distributor: Minnesota Dept. of Natural Resources. Div. of Parks and Recreation, Rivers Section. Centennial Bldg., St. Paul, MN 55155.

262.DuFresne, Jim. VOYAGEURS NATIONAL PARK: WATER ROUTES, FOOT PATHS, & SKI TRAILS. Seattle, WA: The Mountaineers, 1986. 176 p. Illus. Maps. Bibl. Index. Paper. MN

Located just west of the Boundary Waters Canoe Area on the Ontario-Minnesota border is a canoeist's eden named after the French Canadian fur trade paddlers who covered the route two centuries ago. The park differs from the BWCA in that it has bigger lakes (fewer portages), and far less use. Guidebook arrangement is in parts: Part I, "Voyageurs: The National Park;" Part II, "Voyageurs by Paddle;" and, Part III, "Voyageurs on Foot: Hiking, Skiing, and Snowshoeing." DuFresne's canoe route descriptions are by area and trip, with data on trip length, time, portages (length and difficulty), and campsites. Sketch maps of the trips. Publisher/distributor: Mountaineers Books, 306 Second Ave. W, Seattle, WA 98119.

263.Duncanson, Michael E. A PADDLER'S GUIDE TO THE BOUNDARY WATERS CANOE AREA. Virginia, MN: W.A. Fisher Co., 1976. 76 p. Illus. Maps. Paper. MN (WW-1st ed.) Waterway(s): B.W.C.A. (31 wilderness canoe routes).

264.Minnesota Department of Natural Resources. MINNESOTA VOYAGEUR TRAILS. 1970. Reprint. St. Paul, MN: 1972. 48 p. Maps. Paper. MN (WW-1st ed.) Waterway(s): the B.W.C.A., and the Big Fork, Cannon, Cloquet, Crow Wing, Des Moines, Kettle, Little Fork, Minnesota, Mississippi, Crow, Red Lake, Root, Rum, Snake, St. Croix, and St. Louis Rivers.

265.Palzer, Bob, and Palzer, Jody. WHITEWATER, QUIETWATER: A GUIDE TO THE WILD RIVERS OF WISCONSIN, UPPER MICHIGAN, AND N.E. MINNESOTA. 5th ed. Two Rivers, WI: Evergreen Paddleways, 1983. 160 p. Illus. Maps. Bibl. Paper. MI MN WI See entry 46 for a full description.

266.Umhoefer, Jim. GUIDE TO MINNESOTA'S PARKS, CANOE ROUTES, AND TRAILS. Madison, WI: Northword, 1984. 104 p. Illus. Maps. Paper. MN ***

Mississippi (MS)

267.Estes, Chuck; Carter, Liz; and Almquist, Byron. CANOE TRAILS OF THE DEEP SOUTH: THE RIVERS OF LOUISIANA, ALABAMA, AND MISSISSIPPI. Birmingham, AL: Menasha Ridge Press, 1990. 304 p. Illus. Maps. Paper. AL LA MS ***

Missouri (MO)

268.Clark, Fogle C. OZARK SCENIC RIVERWAYS GUIDE. University, MS: Recreational Publications, 1977. Map. MO (WW-1st ed.) River(s): Current, Jack's Fork, and Eleven Point.

269.Hawksley, Oscar. MISSOURI OZARK WATERWAYS. Rev. ed. 1976. Reprint? Jefferson City: Missouri Conservation Commission, 1981. 114 p. Maps. Paper. MO

Hawksley has canoed more than 3,500 miles of Ozark waterways. Data collected during these trips document his descriptions of some thirty-seven major paddling streams in the area. Maps are clearly drawn, and in acceptable detail. Mile-by-mile descriptions parallel the map pages. Difficulty ratings are indicated. Topographic map quadrangles are listed in the order of their use, from headwaters to stream mouth. Publisher/ distributor: Missouri Conservation Commission, c/

o Dept. of Conservation, P.O. Box 180, Jefferson City, MO 65101; or, American Canoe Association, P.O. Box 1190, Newington, VA 22122-1190.

270.Kennon, Tom. OZARK WHITEWATER: A PADDLER'S GUIDE TO THE MOUNTAIN STREAMS OF ARKANSAS AND MISSOURI. Birmingham, AL: Menasha Ridge Press, 1989. 300? p. Illus. Maps. Paper. AR MO ***

271.Pemberton, Mary Ann. AN INTRODUCTION TO FLOATABLE STREAMS NORTH OF THE MISSOURI RIVER. Jefferson City, MO: Division of Parks & Historic Preservation. Missouri Department of Natural Resources, 1982. 55 p. Illus. Maps. Paper. MO

"...This booklet is designed to liberate canoeists from the feeling that southern Missouri is the only place to paddle a canoe" (page 6). Each of the 15 river runs Pemberton describes is in a standardized form giving information on put in, take out, quadrangle and county map names, mile-by-mile log, campsites, scenery, and an access map (with numbers keyed to the log). Admonitions in the text notwithstanding, it is disturbing to still find books in which the illustrations show paddlers without life preservers—and going down the Mississippi yet! River runs described: Nodaway, Hundred and Two, Platte, Grindstone, Big Creek, Thompson, Grand, Locust, Chariton, Cedar Creek, Des Moines, Wyaconda, Salt, Loutre, and Cuivre. Publisher/distributor: Division of Parks & Historic Preservation. Missouri Dept. of Natural Resources, P.O. Box 176, Jefferson City, MO 65102.

272.Pierce, Don. EXPLORING MISSOURI RIVER COUNTRY. Jefferson City, MO: Missouri Department of Natural Resources, 198? 276 p. Illus. Maps. Paper. KS MO NE See entry 49 for a full description.

Montana (MT)

273.Burdge, Ray E. FLOATING, FISHING AND HISTORICAL GUIDE TO YELLOWSTONE STATE WATERWAY. Billings, MT: R. E. Burdge, n.d. 55 p. Maps. Paper. MT (WW-1st ed.) River(s): Yellowstone.

274.Fischer, Hank. THE FLOATER'S GUIDE TO MONTANA. 2d ed. Helena, Billings: Falcon Press, 1986. 140 p. Illus. Maps. Bibl. Paper. MT

Not a typical mile-by-mile guide, but an overview of twenty-six of Montana's major floating rivers. Fischer's intent is to provide basic river information needed for a safe trip. Wildlife, history, scenery, and fishing are also covered. Trips are rated by skill level (beginner, intermediate, expert). Maps show road access. A separate whitewater chapter contains runs on the Blackfoot, Clark Fork, Flathead, Gallatin, Madison, Middle Fork of the Flathead, Stillwater, and Yellowstone rivers. Selected rivers from the main section: Beaverhead, Bighorn, Jefferson, Kootenai, Missouri, Swan, and Tongue. Publisher/distributor: Falcon Press Publishing, P.O. Box 279, Billings, MT 59103.

275.Schafer, Ann. CANOEING WESTERN WATERWAYS: THE MOUNTAIN STATES. New York: Harper & Row, 1978. 279 p. Maps. Bibl. Index. AZ CO ID MT NV NM UT WY See entry 53 for a full description.

276.Walcheck, Ken. TREASURE OF GOLD: FLOAT GUIDE TO THE YELLOWSTONE RIVER FROM BILLINGS TO THE MISSOURI CONFLUENCE. Helena: Montana Dept. of Fish, Wildlife and Parks, 1982? 64 p. Illus. Maps. Paper. MT

The Yellowstone "represents one of the last major rivers in the continental United States that still functions as a free-flowing system... ." Walcheck is technically correct, although there are six diversion dams along the 352 miles of the lower river covered by this guide. A carefully-drawn strip map traces the route noting access, state recreation and wildlife management areas, and points of interest and sites of historical significance. Narrative sections cover fishing, regional history, and some paddling and safety basics. Publisher/distributor: Montana Dept. of Fish, Wildlife and Parks, Sam W. Mitchell Bldg., Helena, MT 59601.

Nebraska (NE)

277.LaGreca, Stephen. CANOER'S GUIDE: THE NIOBRARA RIVER, CORNELL DAM TO NORDEN BRIDGE. 4th ed. Omaha, NE: Stephen LaGreca, 1989? 27 p. Illus. Map. Paper. NE

"This booklet was prepared to guide you along the history, nature and preparation for your trip down the Niobrara River [Nebraska]. Your trip will take four to eleven hours depending on the number of stops you make and where you end your adventure" (introduction). There is a removable map. Numbers on the map are keyed to the corresponding page of descriptive text. Publisher/distributor: S. LaGreca, 2809 S. 40th St., Omaha, NE 68105.

278.Pierce, Don. EXPLORING MISSOURI RIVER COUNTRY. Jefferson City, MO: Missouri Department of Natural Resources, 198? 276 p. Illus. Maps. Paper. KS MO NE See entry 49 for a full description.

Nevada (NV)

279.Dirksen, D. J., and Reeves, R. A. RECREATION ON THE COLORADO RIVER. Aptos, CA: Sail Sales Publishing, 1985. 112 p. Illus. Maps. Index. Paper. AZ CA CO NV UT See entry 20 for a full description.

280.Hamblin, W. Kenneth, and Rigby, J. Keith. GUIDEBOOK TO THE COLORADO RIVER, PART I: LEES FERRY TO PHANTOM RANCH IN GRAND CANYON NATIONAL PARK. PART II: PHANTOM RANCH IN GRAND CANYON NATIONAL PARK TO LAKE MEAD, ARIZONA-NEVADA. Brigham Young University Geology Studies, Studies for students nos. 4 and 5. Provo, UT: Brigham Young University, 1969. 2 vols. Illus. Paper. AZ NV UT (WW-1st ed.) Part III of this series is cited below under: UTAH, Rigby, J Keith. River(s): Colorado, from Lees Ferry to Lake Mead.

281.Schafer, Ann. CANOEING WESTERN WATERWAYS: THE MOUNTAIN STATES. New York: Harper & Row, 1978. 279 p. Maps. Bibl. Index. AZ CO ID MT NV NM UT WY See entry 53 for a full description.

282.Simmons, George C., and Gaskill, David L. MARBLE GORGE AND GRAND CANYON. River Runners' Guides, vol. 3. Denver, CO: Powell Society, 1969. 132 p. Illus. Maps. Diag. Paper. AZ UT (WW-1st ed.) River(s): Colorado from Lees Ferry to Pierces Ferry at Lake Mead.

New Hampshire (NH)

283.AMC RIVER GUIDE: NEW HAMPSHIRE, VERMONT. 2d ed. Edited by Victoria Jas. Boston: Appalachian Mountain Club, 1989. 308 p. Illus. Maps. Index. Paper. NH VT

This pocket-size guide, and the others in this series cited under their appropriate states above: AMC RIVER GUIDE: MAINE; and, AMC RIVER GUIDE: MASSACHUSETTS, CONNECTICUT, RHODE ISLAND, are the standard, authoritative sources of paddling information about rivers in the Northeast. A fourth guidebook, AMC RIVER GUIDE: NEW YORK, NEW JERSEY, is in preparation. The runs examined in each book have been tested by experienced AMC canoeists. Jas' New Hampshire/ Vermont work is representative of the general format and arrangement of the others. Arrangement is by watershed, from north to south and west to east. Chapters begin with a list of principal rivers and their tributaries. These streams are broken into "reasonable-length" trips, each concisely described with textual and tabular data—mileage, difficulty, date checked, navigability, scenery, maps needed, portages, campsites, road access and landmarks. A handy table in the introduction lists runs by water condition: "flatwater/quickwater," "easy rapids," "whitewater-Class III," and, "whitewater-Class IV." A river index provides further access to the contents. Publisher/distributor: Appalachian Mountain Club, 5 Joy St., Boston, MA 02108.

284.APPALACHIAN WHITEWATER: VOLUME III, THE NORTHERN MOUNTAINS. Compiled by John Connelly and John Porterfield. Birmingham, AL: Menasha Ridge Press, 1987. 141 p. Illus. Maps. Index. Paper. CT ME MA NH VT See entry 5 for a full description.

285.THE COMPLETE BOATING GUIDE TO THE CONNECTICUT RIVER. Rev. ed. Edited by Mark C. Borton. Easthampton, MA: Connecticut River Watershed Council, 1986. 245 p. Maps. Paper. CT MA NH VT ***

286.CONNECTICUT RIVER GUIDE. Rev. ed. Easthampton, MA: Connecticut River Watershed Council, 1971. 87 p. Paper. CT MA NH VT (WW-1st ed.) River(s): Connecticut, and its tributaries, the White, West, Millers, Westfield, Salmon.

287.Gabler, Ray. NEW ENGLAND WHITE WATER RIVER GUIDE. Boston, MA: Appalachian Mountain Club, 1981. 376 p. Illus. Maps. Bibl. Paper. CT ME MA NH NY VT See entry 25 for a full description.

288.Schweiker, Roioli. CANOE CAMPING, VERMONT & NEW HAMPSHIRE RIVERS: A GUIDE TO 600 MILES OF RIVERS FOR A DAY, WEEKEND, OR WEEK OF CANOEING. 2d ed. Woodstock, VT: Backcountry Publications, 1985. 123 p. Illus. Maps. Paper. NH VT

The chief attraction of the rivers Schweiker describes is their accessibility. The trips, for novice or intermediate paddlers, are grouped by watershed and run from just under twenty to over eighty miles. Each decription gives: table (mileage, break points, rating, difficulties); narrative log (character of the river, access, and other relevant facts); and, sketch map. The streams: Magalloway, Androscoggin, Baker, Pemigewasset, Merrimack, Batten Kill, Otter Creek, Lemon Fair, Winooski, Lamoille, Missisquoi, Connecticut, and White. Publisher/distributor: Backcountry Publications, P.O. Box 175, Woodstock, VT 05091.

289.Thomas, Eben. HOT BLOOD AND WET PADDLES: A GUIDE TO CANOE RACING IN MAINE AND NEW HAMPSHIRE. Hallowell, ME: Hallowell Printing Co., 1974. 188 p. Maps. Paper. ME NH (WW-1st ed.)

New Jersey (NJ)

290.Burmeister, Walter F. THE DELAWARE AND ITS TRIBUTARIES. Appalachian Waters, no. 1. Oakton, VA: Appalachian Books, 1974. 274 p. Map. Bibl. Paper. DE NJ NY PA (WW 1st ed.) River(s): upper, central and lower Delaware River system.

291.Burmeister, Walter F. THE HUDSON RIVER AND ITS TRIBUTARIES. Appalachian Waters, no. 2. Oakton, VA: Appalachian Books, 1974. 496 p. Maps. Bibl. Index. Paper. CT MA NJ NY VT (WW-1st ed.) River(s): upper, central and lower Hudson tributaries.

292.CANOEING AND FISHING GUIDE TO THE UPPER DELAWARE RIVER. Madison, NJ: Pathfinder Publications, 198? 88 p. Illus. Maps. Paper. NJ NY PA See entry 12 for a full description.

293.Cawley, James S., and Cawley, Margaret. EXPLORING THE LITTLE RIVERS OF NEW JERSEY. 3d ed. New Brunswick, NJ: Rutgers University Press, 1971. 262 p. Illus. Maps. Paper. NJ (WW-1st ed.) River(s): Millstone, Rancocas, Mullica, Wading, Maurice, Raritan, Passaic, Ramapo, Paulins Kill, Musconetcong, Toms, Oswego, Batsto, Manasquan, Hackensack, and Delaware.

294.Letcher, Gary. CANOEING THE DELAWARE RIVER: A GUIDE TO THE RIVER AND SHORE. New Brunswick, NJ: Rutgers University Press, 1985. 244 P. Illus. Maps. Bibl. DE NJ NY PA See entry 35 for a full description.

295.Meyer, Joan, and Meyer, Bill. CANOE TRAILS OF THE JERSEY SHORE. New Jersey Recreation Series. Ocean, NJ: Specialty Press, 1974. 73 p. Maps. Paper. NJ (WW-1st ed.) Stream(s): Batsto, Cedar, Great Egg Harbor, Mamasquan, Mullica, Oswego, Tom's, and Wading.

296.NORTHEASTERN COASTAL PADDLING GUIDE. Edited by Chuck Sutherland. Tuckahoe, NY: Association of North Atlantic Kayakers, 1984. 39 p. Illus. Maps. Paper. CT MA ME NJ NY RI See entry 45 for a full description.

297.Parnes, Robert. CANOEING THE JERSEY PINE BARRENS. Rev. ed. Chester, CT: Globe Pequot Press; Fast & McMillan Publishers, 1981. 284 p. Illus. Maps. Bibl. Paper. NJ

Pocket-sized and with a sturdy, waterproof cover, this "revised edition" is identical to the first edition (1978). The Pine Barrens, a sandy, sparsely-settled part of New Jersey, are a network of inky rivers close to the megapopulations of the east coast. About half of Parnes' book is comprised of discourses on geology, human history, pollution, flora, fauna, camping, canoe rentals, and canoe technique. The guidebook half is organized by stream (17 of them), and trip (some 24 days worth). Narrative descriptions give: general observations/information, routes, campgrounds, canoe rental agencies, public transportation, "other amenities," water level, and river details. There is a strip map for each stream: Mullica, Batsto, Wading, Oswego, Toms, Cedar, Oyster, Metedeconk, Manasquan, Mount Misery, Rancocas, Great Egg Harbor, and the Maurice. Publisher/distributor: Globe Pequot Press, P.O. Box Q, Chester, CT 06412.

New Mexico (NM)

298.Anderson, Fletcher, and Hopkinson, Ann. RIVERS OF THE SOUTHWEST: A BOATERS GUIDE TO THE RIVERS OF COLORADO, NEW MEXICO, UTAH AND ARIZONA. 2d ed. Boulder, CO: Pruett Publishing, 1987. 129 p. Illus. Maps. Paper. AZ CO NM UT See entry 2 for a full description.

299.NEW MEXICO WHITEWATER: A GUIDE TO RIVER TRIPS. Santa Fe, NM: New Mexico State Park Division. Natural Resources Deptartment, 1983. 69 p. Illus. Maps. Paper. NM

In arid New Mexico, spring is THE river-running time. Disecting the state from north to south is the most prominent river, the Rio Grande, which offers some of the best whitewater boating in the West. Forty trips on nineteen rivers are described, and sketch maps are included for the more popular streams (Chama, Gila, Pecos, and Rio Grande). Descriptions are contained on one page and give a general overview, land ownership, U.S.G.S. maps, length, rapids, gradient, season, access, hazards, camping, water, firewood, and hiking data. Additional rivers not named above: Animas, Brazos, Canadian, Cimarron, Embudo, Jemez, Los Pinos, Mora, Navajo, Ojo Caliente, Red, Rio Pueblo, San Antonio, San Francisco, and San Juan. Publisher/distributor: New Mexico State Park Division. Natural Resources Dept., P.O. Box 1147, Santa Fe, NM 87503.

300.Schafer, Ann. CANOEING WESTERN WATERWAYS: THE MOUNTAIN STATES. New York: Harper & Row, 1978. 279 p. Maps. Bibl. Index. AZ CO ID MT NV NM UT WY See entry 53 for a full description.

301.Ungnade, Herbert. E. GUIDE TO THE NEW MEXICO MOUNTAINS. 2d ed. Albuquerque: University of New Mexico Press, 1972. 235 p. Illus. Bibl. Paper. NM (WW-1st ed.) River(s): Rio Grande, Pecos, Chama, San Juan, Gila, Canadian.

NEW YORK (NY)

302.Burmeister, Walter F. THE DELAWARE AND ITS TRIBUTARIES. Appalachian Waters, no. 1. Oakton, VA: Appalachian Books, 1974. 274 p. Map. Bibl. Paper. DE NJ NY PA (WW 1st ed.) River(s): upper, central and lower Delaware River system.

303.Burmeister, Walter F. THE HUDSON RIVER AND ITS TRIBUTARIES. Appalachian Waters, no. 2. Oakton, VA: Appalachian Books, 1974. 496 p. Maps. Bibl. Index. Paper. CT MA NJ NY VT (WW-1st ed.) River(s): upper, central and lower Hudson tributaries.

304.Burmeister, Walter F. THE SUSQUEHANNA RIVER AND ITS TRIBUTARIES. Appalachian Waters, no. 3. Oakton, VA: Appalachian Books, 1975. 600 p. Bibl. Index. Paper. MD NY PA (WW-1st ed.)

305.Burmeister, Walter F. THE UPPER OHIO & ITS TRIBUTARIES. Appalachian Waters, no. 5. Oakton, VA: Appalachian Books, 1978. 948 p. Bibl. Index. Paper. KY NY OH PA VA WV See entry 11 for a full description.

306.CANOEING AND FISHING GUIDE TO THE UPPER DELAWARE RIVER. Madison, NJ: Pathfinder Publications, 198? 88 p. Illus. Maps. Paper. NJ NY PA See entry 12 for a full description.

307.Ehling, William P. CANOEING CENTRAL NEW YORK. Woodstock, VT: Backcountry Publications, 1982. 171 p. Illus. Maps. Paper. NY

Twenty-six selected trips on as many waterways, all within a seventy-five mile radius of Syracuse, are presented by Ehling. Waterway notes are standardized giving tabular data: river, run, distance, ability level, access, drop, trip time, water conditions, and obstacles. Additional tabular information enables easy linkage for further mileage on the same waterway. The narrative log, informal and informative, follows the introductory tables. A sketch map accompanies every description. Selected waterways: Susquehanna, Chenango, Oneida, Seneca, Clyde, Oswego, Salmon, and Mohawk Rivers; Catatonk, Fish, Ganargua, Mudge, Sterling, Deer, Black, West Canada, and Oriskany Creeks; Oneida, Onondaga, Ontario, and Delta Lakes; and, Old Erie Canal. Publisher/distributor: Backcountry Publications P.O. Box 175, Woodstock, VT 05091.

308.Gabler, Ray. NEW ENGLAND WHITE WATER RIVER GUIDE. Boston, MA: Appalachian Mountain Club, 1981. 376 p. Illus. Maps. Bibl. Paper. CT ME MA NH NY VT See entry 25 for a full description.

309.Grinnell, Lawrence I. CANOEABLE WATERS OF NEW YORK STATE AND VACINITY. New York: Pageant Press, 1956. 349 p. NY (WW-1st ed.)

310.Jamieson, Paul, and Morris, Donald. ADIRONDACK CANOE WATERS: NORTH FLOW. 3d ed. Glen Falls, NY: Adirondack Mountain Club, 1988. 343 p. Illus. Index. Paper. NY

One of a pair of Adirondack canoe guides. (See also entry 315: Proskine, Alec C., ADIRONDACK CANOE WATERS: SOUTH AND WEST FLOW). Many of the Adirondack Park waters are authentically wild, most are unpolluted, and all are uncrowded. By 1986, 1,238 miles of Adirondack rivers were classified wild, scenic or recreational. The northwest watershed toward the St. Lawrence River Basin affords the most river cruising opportunities in the Park. Rivers in this section: Oswegatchie, Little, Grass, Raquette, Cold, Big Brook, Bog, Jordan, St. Regis, Osgood, Deer, Salmon and Chateaugay. To the northeast, in the Lake Champlain drainage, the rivers are short and steep (except the Saranac). Even half-day trips will include whitewater stretches. The northeast waterways: Great Chazy, Saranac, Ausable, Chubb, and Boquet Rivers; and, Lakes Placid, Champlain, and George. Jamieson and Morris' narrative descriptions of the runs are detailed, yet written in an informal, anecdotal style. The authors offer practical information on rapids, campsites, access, etc., with asides on history, scenery, and man-made points of interest. There is a concluding chapter on camping by Robert N. Bliss. Publisher/distributor: Adirondack Mountain Club, RD 3, Box 3055, Luzerne Rd., Lake George, NY 12845. Glen Falls, NY 12801.

311.Ka-Na-Wa-Ke Canoe Club. CENTRAL NEW YORK CANOE ROUTES. Syracuse, NY: The Club, 1981. 55 p. Maps. Bibl. NY ***

312.Letcher, Gary. CANOEING THE DELAWARE RIVER: A GUIDE TO THE RIVER AND SHORE. New Brunswick, NJ: Rutgers University Press, 1985. 244 P. Illus. Maps. Bibl. DE NJ NY PA See entry 35 for a full description.

313.NORTHEASTERN COASTAL PADDLING GUIDE. Edited by Chuck Sutherland. Tuckahoe, NY: Association of North Atlantic Kayakers, 1984. 39 p. Illus. Maps. Paper. CT MA ME NJ NY RI See entry 45 for a full description.

314.Patterson, Barbara McMartin. WALKS AND WATERWAYS: AN INTRODUCTION TO ADVENTURE IN THE EAST CANADA CREEK AND THE WEST BRANCH OF THE SACANDAGA RIVER SECTIONS OF THE SOUTHERN ADIRONDACKS. Glen Falls, NY: Adirondack Mountain Club, 1974. 171 p. Map. Paper. NY (WW-1st ed.) Waterway(s): East Canada Creek, West Branch of the Sacandaga River.

315.Proskine, Alec C. ADIRONDACK CANOE WATERS: SOUTH AND WEST FLOW. Glen Falls, NY: Adirondack Mountain Club, 1989. 150 p. Maps. Bibl. Index. Paper. NY

One of a pair of books on Adirondack waterways. (See also entry 310: Jamieson, Paul F., and Morris, Donald, ADIRONDACK CANOE WATERS, NORTH FLOW). Proskine's work covers the Black, Mohawk, and upper Hudson River basins within the Adirondack Park and Tug Hill areas of northeastern New York. Trips on fourteen streams and several lakes are described and mapped. Explications of the runs are concise; each is prefaced with a standardized table giving location, U.S.G.S. maps, length, recommended season, campsites, access, elevation, distance, drop, gradient, and rating (I-V). There is informed commentary on the flora and fauna one may encounter along the way. Canoeing safety is emphasized. The waterways: Boreas, Cedar, Hudson, Indian, Kunjamuk, Moose, Sacandaga, Salmon, Schroon, Beaver, and Black Rivers; East Canada, West Canada, and Fish Creeks; Indian, Lewey, Fulton Chain, Big Moose, Sacandaga, Pleasant, Piseco, Vly, Spy, and Schroon Lakes; and, Salmon River Reservoir. Publisher/distributor: Adirondack Mountain Club, RD 3, Box 3055, Luzerne Rd., Lake George, NY 12845.

316.Proskine, Alec C. NO TWO RIVERS ALIKE: 50 CANOEABLE RIVERS IN NEW YORK AND PENNSYLVANIA. Trumansburg, NY: Crossing Press, 1980. 215 p. Illus. Maps. Bibl. NY PA

"No two rivers are alike. Some flow northward, others southward, while still others (like the Allegheny), flow in every direction," (page 15). Proskine has selected the 49 waterways for his guidebook on the basis of personal interest"—they are the ones I would choose to travel." New York streams predominate. Waterways descriptions are standardized under headings: name, character (lazy, dynamic, etc.), data chart (showing county, tributary, U.S.G.S. map, rating, length, distance, scenery rating, season, and campsites), narrative description of stream (1-3 pages long), and, table (river location, elevation, distance, run distance, drop, and gradient). Stream information is preceded by a section on canoeing technique and safety. The rivers (there are 21 "creeks," and "outlets" not mentioned in this list): Allegheny, Beaver Kill, Canisteo, Cedar, Chemung, Chenango, Cohocton, Delaware, Genesee, Hudson, Lackawaxen, Lehigh, Moose, Neversink, Oswegatchie, Otselic, Raquette, Sacandaga, Salmon, Saranac, Susquehanna, Tioga, Tioughnioga, Unadilla, and Youghiogheny. Publisher/distributor: The Crossing Press, Trumansburg, NY 14886.

North Carolina (NC)

317.APPALACHIAN WHITEWATER: VOLUME I, THE SOUTHERN MOUNTAINS. Compiled by Bob Sehlinger and others. Birmingham, AL: Menasha Ridge Press, 1986. 159 p. Illus. Maps. Index. Paper. AL GA KY NC SC TN See entry 3 for a full description.

318.Benner, Bob. CAROLINA WHITEWATER: A CANOEIST'S GUIDE TO THE WESTERN CAROLINAS. 4th ed. Hillsborough, NC: Menasha Ridge Press, 1981. 244 p. Illus. Maps. Bibl. Index. Paper. NC SC

In this latest edition, Benner describes some sixty rivers in western North and South Carolina. (The annotation following describes the 2d ed.): Intended for the open-canoe paddler, with much of the whitewater suitable for the novice. The river guide portion of the book is divided into five sections, four of which describe rivers in neighboring counties of NC; the fifth covers rivers outside this area. A total of fifty-four streams are included. Typical information on a stream includes a general description, location and access, gauge location, and an estimate of the difficulty. The table for each stream gives drop, difficulty rating, distance, time, scenery, and water quality. Other information includes advice about winter canoeing, safety, and the legal rights of canoeists. Publisher/distributor: Menasha Ridge Press, P.O. Box 59257, Birmingham, AL 35259-9257.

319.Benner, Bob, and McCloud, Tom. A PADDLER'S GUIDE TO EASTERN NORTH CAROLINA. Birmingham, AL: Menasha Ridge Press, 1987. 257 p. Illus. Maps. Index. Paper. NC

Intended for the recreational canoeist, from novice to intermediate. The organization of the guidebook is by seven major river basins located primarily in the piedmont and coastal plains areas of the state. Basins are further divided by stream and run. Information given for each run: topos, county location, put-in, drop, difficulty scale, distance, time, scenery, water quality, gauge, hazards, shuttle, and access map. The seven drainages: Yadkin-Pee Dee, Cape Fear, Roanoke, Tar-Pamlico, Neuse, Lumber, and Merchants Mill Pond and Bennetts Creek. Publisher/distributor: Menasha Ridge Press, P.O. Box 59257, Birmingham, AL 35259-9257.

320.Burmeister, Walter F. THE SOUTHEASTERN RIVERS. Appalachian Waters, no. 4. Oakton, VA: Appalachian Books, 1976. 850 p. Bibl. Index. Paper. FL GA NC SC VA (WW-1st ed.)

321.Carter, Randy. CANOEING WHITE WATER RIVER GUIDE. 8th ed. Oakton, VA: Appalachian Books, 1974. 275 p. Illus. Maps. Index. Paper. NC VA WV (WW-1st ed.)

322.Nealy, William. WHITEWATER HOME COMPANION: SOUTHEASTERN RIVERS, VOLUME I. Hillsborough, NC: Menasha Ridge Press, 1981. 156 p. Illus. Maps. Paper. AL GA NC PA SC TN WV See entry 41 for a full description.

323.Nealy, William. WHITEWATER HOME COMPANION: SOUTHEASTERN RIVERS, VOLUME II. Hillsborough, NC: Menasha Ridge Press, 1984. 165 p. Illus. Maps. Paper. GA KY MD NC TN VA WV See entry 42 for a full description.

324.Rathnow, Ron. NANTAHALA RIVER. Great American Rivers Flip Map Series. Birmingham, AL: Menasha Ridge Press, 1986. 34 p. Illus. Maps. Paper. NC ***

Ohio (OH)

325.Burmeister, Walter F. THE UPPER OHIO & ITS TRIBUTARIES. Appalachian Waters, no. 5. Oakton, VA: Appalachian Books, 1978. 948 p. Bibl. Index. Paper. KY NY OH PA VA WV See entry 11 for a full description.

326.Combs, Richard, and Gillen, Stephen E. A CANOEING AND KAYAKING GUIDE TO THE STREAMS OF OHIO. Hillsborough, NC: Menasha Ridge Press, 1983. 2 vols. Illus. Maps. Index. Paper. OH

In volume I, Combs and Gillen examine streams of western Ohio; in volume II, the eastern half. Geography and/or drainage dictate arrangement within the volumes. Information on the waterways is preceded by chapters on stream dynamics, climate and geology, and sundry instruction and information. These chapters repeat in both volumes. Data on the streams are standardized: introductory paragraphs on setting, conditions, and general observations; tabular information (location, USGS quads, rating, season, scenery, width, gradient, hazards, portages, additional information source, access, mileage); and, a map showing road access. Whitewater runs are identified in Appendix A. A selection of streams: Maumee, Tiffin, Sandusky, Great Miami, Whitewater, Scioto, Olentangy, White Oak, Huron, Rocky, Cuyahoga, Ashtabula, Mohican, Tuscarawas, Muskingum, Mahoning, and Hocking. Publisher/distributor: Menasha Ridge Press, P.O. Box 59257, Birmingham, AL 35259-9257.

Oregon (OR)

327.Arighi, Scott, and Arighi, Margaret S. WILDWATER TOURING: TECHNIQUES AND TOURS. New York: Macmillan, 1974. 352 p. Illus. Maps. ID OR (WW-1st ed.) River(s): Rogue, Grande Ronde, John Day, Main and Middle Fork Salmon, and Owyhee.

328.Campbell, Arthur. JOHN DAY RIVER DRIFT AND HISTORICAL GUIDE FOR RAFT, DRIFT BOAT, CANOE, KAYAK. Portland, OR: Frank Amato Publications, 1980. 90 p. Illus. Maps. Index. Paper. OR

A complete "one-river" guidebook containing many practical tips and abundant historical lore on the John Day. This river drains much of northeastern Oregon's Blue Mountains, flows west and north through arid canyons, and then, some 200 miles from its source, into the Columbia. Campbell deals with the most commonly floated section—the 116 miles from Service Creek to Cottonwood Bridge. Sketch maps (1:24,000) give river miles, checkpoints, places of interest, landmarks, rapids, campsites, and access roads. On each map's facing page: drift time, recommended flow rates, and a mile-by-mile narrative on river conditions and history. Publisher/distributor: Frank Amato Publications, P.O. Box 02112, Portland, OR 97202.

329.Garren, John. OREGON RIVER TOURS, INCLUDING ILLINOIS RIVER: A GUIDE TO OREGON'S MOST POPULAR WHITEWATER RIVERS. Rev. ed. Portland, OR: Garren Publications, 198-? 202 p. Illus. Maps. Bibl. Paper. OR

"The rivers selected [12] do have many outstanding characteristics. Hells Canyon on the Snake is the deepest in America. The Owyhee would vie with any rugged, remote river. The Rogue and Deschutes are famous nation-wide. Many are classed as scenic wild rivers [Rogue, Snake, Owyhee, Illinois]" (introduction). Garren's river descriptions are in a standardized format: narrative introduction/ description, c.f.s. discharge/gauge location, strip map (with river miles), river log (mileage, drift time, drop, etc.). Other rivers covered: Clackamas, Upper/Lower Deschutes, Grande Ronde, Upper/ Lower John Day, McKenzie, North/South Santiam, Sandy, and Umpqua. Publisher/distributor: Garren Publishing, 01008 SW Comus, Portland, OR 97219.

330.HELLS CANYON OF THE SNAKE RIVER. Quinn Map. Redmond, OR: Educational Adventures, 198? [20 p.] Illus. Maps. Paper. ID OR WA See entry 28 for a full description.

331.HELL'S CORNER GORGE OF THE UPPER KLAMATH. Quinn Map. Medford, OR: Educational Adventures, 198? [10 p.] Illus. Maps. Paper. CA OR

A strip-map/guide on coated paper covering the challenging Upper Klamath (Class III-IV-V) from the powerhouse below John Boyle Dam (OR) to take-out seventeen miles downstream at Copco Lake (CA). In fact, the "maps" are a series of ten aerial photographs showing rapids and mileage. Rapids descriptions are positioned parallel to the maps. Publisher/distributor: Educational Adventures, P.O. Box 4190, Sunriver, OR 97707.

332.Jones, Philip N. CANOE ROUTES: NORTHWEST OREGON. Seattle, WA: The Mountaineers, 1982. 157 p. Illus. Maps. Bibl. Paper. OR WA

Jones inventories some of the day-trip flatwater canoeing possibilities in northwestern Oregon (and a few trips in southwestern Washington). Arrangement of the book is by area: Willamette River from Eugene north to Portland; the lower Columbia from Portland to the Pacific; and, the coast from Newport north to the Columbia—in all fifty trips. All descriptions give location, distance, time needed, appropriate maps and charts, rating (class A, B, and C), and best season. Accompanying narratives summarize what one may expect aesthetically, biologically, and historically, plus the practicalities of hazards, portages, and access. Well-conceived sketch maps show access roads, put-in, take-out, mileage, bridges, parks, etc. In addition to the Columbia/Willamette trips are those on other rivers: Marys, Calapooia, South Santiam, Santiam, Luckiamute, South Yamhill, Yamhill, Pudding, Mollala, Tualatin, East Fork of the Lewis, Lewis, Youngs, Lewis and Clark, Nehalem, Nestucca, Siletz, and Yaquina. Publisher/distributor: Mountaineers Books, 306 Second Ave. W, Seattle, WA 98119.

333.LOWER SALMON RIVER GUIDE. Rev. ed. Washington, DC: U.S. Dept. of the Interior, Bureau of Land Management, 1983. 18 p. Maps. Paper. ID OR WA See entry 36 for a full description.

334.McLean, Cheryl, and Brown, Clint. OREGON'S QUIET WATERS: A GUIDE TO LAKES FOR CANOEISTS AND OTHER PADDLERS. Corvallis, OR: Jackson Creek Press, 1987. 128 p. Illus. Maps. Index. Paper. OR

A guide for self-propelled boaters to forty of the best of Oregon's 6,500 lakes and reservoirs. Within the detailed descriptions are brief discussions of sixty more lakes. The authors have summarized their information into the following categories: location, including distance from nearest population area; accessibility; size; camping and fishing; hiking trails; points of interest; other recreation opportunities; nearby lakes; nearby supplies; and specific directions. Each description includes a sketch map and a photograph.

335.Quinn, James M.; Quinn, James W.; and King, James G. HANDBOOK TO THE DESCHUTES RIVER CANYON. 3d ed. Bend, OR: Educational Adventures, 1979. 168 p. Illus. Maps. Paper. OR

"The Deschutes drains a watershed larger than the state of Maryland. From its mile-high beginnings the river cuts a path through forests and lava as it flows 252 miles to join the Columbia" (page 20a). With excellent fishing and abundant wildlife, the upper Deschutes is a popular area to canoe. The final 100 miles is entirely free flowing with an average drop of thirteen feet per mile—sufficient to interest rafters, driftboaters, and decked boaters. There are five books in this "HANDBOOK TO..." series on running western rivers, each of which aims to combine adventure and education through sharing "...the knowledge of professional guides who make their livelihoods from the rivers." See entry 211: Quinn, James M., HANDBOOK TO THE MIDDLE FORK OF THE SALMON RIVER CANYON, for a general description of the contents. Publisher/distributor: Educational Adventures, P.O. Box 4190, Sunriver, OR 97707.

336.Quinn, James M.; Quinn, James W.; and King, James G. HANDBOOK TO THE ILLINOIS RIVER CANYON. 2d ed. Medford, OR: Educational Adventures, 1979. 162 p. Illus. Maps. Paper. OR

This is class IV-V river best run by experts at a flow between 600 and 1500 c.f.s. (a rate usually found only during March, April, May). "To the dedicated white water addict, the Illinois may be the ultimate river in the Northwest" (introduction). There are five books in this "HANDBOOK TO..." series on running western rivers, each of which aims to combine adventure and education through sharing "...the knowledge of professional guides who make their livelihoods from the rivers." See entry 211: Quinn, James M., HANDBOOK TO THE MIDDLE FORK OF THE SALMON RIVER CANYON, for a general description of the contents. Publisher/distributor: Educational Adventures, P.O. Box 4190, Sunriver, OR 97707.

337.Quinn, James W., and Quinn, James M. HANDBOOK TO THE KLAMATH RIVER CANYON. Redmond, OR: Educational Adventures, 1983. 180 p. Illus. Maps. Paper. CA OR See entry 147 for a full description.

338.Quinn, James M.; Quinn, James W.; and King, James G. HANDBOOK TO THE ROGUE RIVER CANYON. 2d ed. Waldport, OR: Educational Adventures, 1979. 131 p. Illus. Maps. Bibl. Paper. OR

"The lower Rogue [Grave Creek to Foster Bar, Oregon] offers one of the wildest boat rides in the northwest" (introduction). There are five books in this "HANDBOOK TO..." series on running western rivers, each of which aims to combine adventure and education through sharing "...the knowledge of professional guides who make their livelihoods from the rivers." See entry 211: Quinn, James M., HANDBOOK TO THE MIDDLE FORK OF THE SALMON RIVER CANYON, for a general description of the contents. Publisher/distributor: Educational Adventures, P.O. Box 4190, Sunriver, OR 97707.

339.Schafer, Ann. CANOEING WESTERN WATERWAYS: THE COASTAL STATES. New York: Harper & Row, 1978. 272 p. Maps. Bibl. Index. CA HI OR WA See entry 52 for a full description.

340.Schwind, Dick. WEST COAST RIVER TOURING: ROUGE RIVER CANYON AND SOUTH. Beaverton OR: Touchstone Press, 1974. 224 p. Illus. Maps. Bibl. Paper. CA OR (WW-1st ed.) River(s): west coast rivers from the Rogue to the Salinas, with sources in the coastal mountains.

341.SOGGY SNEAKERS: GUIDE TO OREGON RIVERS. 2d ed. Edited by Willamette Kayak and Canoe Club. Corvallis, Or: The Club, 1986. 208 p. Illus. Maps. Bibl. Index. Paper. OR WA CA

Willamette KCC members collected contributions of trip reports from dozens of paddlers throughout the state preparatory to creating this inclusive guide to (primarily) Oregon waterways. The book is divided into eleven chapters corresponding to nine river regions in Oregon, a region in southern Washington, and an examination of Oregon surf kayaking venues. Rivers are subdivided into runs which are described in a standard form giving name of trip, contributing author, class, flow, gradient, miles, character, and a few paragraphs of comments containing general observations, difficulties, gauge information and shuttles. Sketch maps show access roads. A selection of the rivers: Nehalem, Siletz, Coos, Umpqua, Rogue, Illinois, Klamath, Smith (CA), Willamette, Sandy, Washougal (WA), White Salmon (WA), Klickitat (WA), Deschutes, John Day, Grande Ronde, and Owyhee. Publisher/distributor: Willamette Kayak and Canoe Club, P.O. Box 1062, Corvallis, OR 97339.

342.Sullivan, William L. EXPLORING OREGON'S WILD AREAS: A GUIDE FOR HIKERS, BACKPACKERS, CLIMBERS, XC SKIERS & PADDLERS. Seattle, WA: Mountaineers Books, 1988. 263 p. Illus. Maps. Bibl. Index. Paper. OR

Not so much a guidebook as an activities suggestion book for the outdoor enthusiast. Sullivan briefly describes sixty-five Oregon wild areas and the variety of self-propelled sports they can accommodate. (Look under the heading, "Things to Do," e.g., hiking, climbing, hang-gliding, boating.) For the paddler, there are river runs suggested on the Owyhee, Snake (Hells Canyon), John Day, Rogue, and Deschutes. Publisher/distributor: Mountaineers Books, 306 Second Ave. W, Seattle, WA 98119.

343.WHITEWATER PRIMER, INCLUDING SELWAY AND ILLINOIS RIVER LOGS. Portland, OR: Wilderness Public Rights Fund, Northwest Chapter, 198? 86 p. Illus. Maps. Paper. ID OR See entry 213 for a full description.

344.THE WILD AND SCENIC SNAKE RIVER: HELLS CANYON NATIONAL RECREATION AREA. Washington, DC: U.S. Dept. of Agriculture, Forest Service, 1985. 23 p. Illus. Maps. Paper. ID OR WA See entry 214 for a full description.

Pennsylvania (PA)

345.Acquardo, Chip. CANOEING THE BRANDYWINE: A NATURALIST'S GUIDE. Chadds Ford, PA: Tri-County Conservancy of the Brandywine, 1973. 61 p. Illus. Maps. Paper. PA (WW-1st ed.) River(s): Brandywine.

346.APPALACHIAN WHITEWATER: VOLUME II, THE CENTRAL MOUNTAINS. Compiled by Ed Grove and others. Birmingham, AL: Menasha Ridge Press, 1987. 207 p. Illus. Maps. Index. Paper. DE MD PA WV See entry 4 for a full description.

347.Burmeister, Walter F. THE DELAWARE AND ITS TRIBUTARIES. Appalachian Waters, no. 1. Oakton, VA: Appalachian Books, 1974. 274 p. Map. Bibl. Paper. DE NJ NY PA (WW 1st ed.) River(s): upper, central and lower Delaware River system.

348.Burmeister, Walter F. THE SUSQUEHANNA RIVER AND ITS TRIBUTARIES. Appalachian Waters, no. 3. Oakton, VA: Appalachian Books, 1975. 600 p. Bibl. Index. Paper. MD NY PA (WW-1st ed.)

349.Burmeister, Walter F. THE UPPER OHIO & ITS TRIBUTARIES. Appalachian Waters, no. 5. Oakton, VA: Appalachian Books, 1978. 948 p. Bibl. Index. Paper. KY NY OH PA VA WV See entry 11 for a full description.

350.CANOEING AND FISHING GUIDE TO THE UPPER DELAWARE RIVER. Madison, NJ: Pathfinder Publications, 198? 88 p. Illus. Maps. Paper. NJ NY PA See entry 12 for a full description.

351.CANOEING GUIDE: WESTERN PENNSYLVANIA AND NORTHERN WEST VIRGINIA. 7th ed. Compiled and edited by Roy R. Weil and Mary M. Shaw. Pittsburgh, PA: American Youth Hostels, Pittsburgh Council, 1983. 280 p. Illus. Maps. Index. Paper. PA WV

"The geographic area covered by this guide includes all streams whose waters drain into the Ohio River before it leaves Pennsylvania" (introduction). Focus is on easy rivers suitable for open-canoe paddling; other streams have been included to either challenge the kayaker, or for their scenic beauty. Trip reports originated from throughout the canoeing community. The reports were edited for uniformity to give: name of run, length, class, gradient, volume, scenery/pollution, maps, short narrative description, difficulties, shuttle, gauge, and low water period. Watersheds covered: Ohio/Beaver, Allegheny, and Monongahela. An eighth edition is scheduled for publication in Spring, 1990. Publisher/distributor: Pittsburgh Council, American Youth Hostels, Inc., 6300 Fifth Ave., Pittsburgh, PA 15232.

352.Canter, Ron, and Canter, Kathy. NEARBY CANOEING STREAMS. 4th ed. Hyattsville, MD: 1979. 62 p. Illus. Maps. Paper. DE MD PA VA WV See entry 13 for a full description.

353.Gertler, Edward. KEYSTONE CANOEING: A GUIDE TO CANOEABLE WATERS OF EASTERN PENNSYLVANIA. Silver Spring, MD: Seneca Press, 1985. 401 p. Maps. Index. Paper. PA

Not precisely a guide to eastern Pennsylvania as the subtitle suggests, since Gertler also has a chapter describing thirteen of his favorite streams in the western part of the state. It is an exhaustive piece of work covering over 5,000 miles of runnable waterways. General arrangement is by watershed, then stream. Trip descriptions include a standard table with gradient, difficulty, distance, time, scenery and strip map number. A text describes the trip, and indicates hazards, water conditions and gauge information. Strip maps complete the trip data. River basins covered: Delaware, Susquehanna, North Branch Susquehanna, West Branch Susquehanna, and Potomac. Publisher/distributor: Seneca Press, 503 Bonifant St., Silver Spring, MD 20910.

354.Letcher, Gary. CANOEING THE DELAWARE RIVER: A GUIDE TO THE RIVER AND SHORE. New Brunswick, NJ: Rutgers University Press, 1985. 244 P. Illus. Maps. Bibl. DE NJ NY PA See entry 35 for a full description.

355.Nealy, William. WHITEWATER HOME COMPANION: SOUTHEASTERN RIVERS, VOLUME I. Hillsborough, NC: Menasha Ridge Press, 1981. 156 p. Illus. Maps. Paper. AL GA NC PA SC TN WV See entry 41 for a full description.

356.PADDLE PENNSYLVANIA. Edited by the Pennsylvania Fish Commission. Harrisburg, PA: The Commission, 1984. 36 p. Maps. Paper. PA ***

357.Palmer, Tim. RIVERS OF PENNSYLVANIA. University Park, PA; London: Pennsylvania State University Press, Keystone Books, 1980. 229 p. Illus. Bibl. Paper. PA

An introduction to 45,OOO miles of navigable Pennsylvania streams in which Palmer provides information for the canoeist, kayaker, rafter, hiker and camper, naturalist, history buff, angler, or conservationist. Organization is by three major river basins: Susquehanna (23 stream listings), Ohio (15 stream listings), and Delaware (7 stream listings). In each chapter, Palmer relates specific experiences on streams in these watersheds. The author's practical advice and recommendations about recreation opportunities on the various waterways conclude the work. Publisher/ distributor: Pennsylvania State University Press, 215 Wagner Bldg., University Park, PA 16802.

358.Palmer, Tim. SUSQUEHANNA WATERWAY: THE WEST BRANCH IN LYCOMING COUNTY. Williamsport, PA: Lycoming County Planning Commission, 1975. 56 p. Paper. PA (WW-1st ed.) River(s): Susquehanna.

359.Penn State Outing Club. SELECT RIVERS OF CENTRAL PENNSYLVANIA. 4th ed. University Park, PA: Penn State Outing Club, 1974. Map. Paper. PA ***

360.Proskine, Alec C. NO TWO RIVERS ALIKE: 50 CANOEABLE RIVERS IN NEW YORK AND PENNSYLVANIA. Trumansburg, NY: Crossing Press, 1980. 215 p. Illus. Maps. Bibl. NY PA See entry 316 for a full description.

361.Rathnow, Ron. YOUGHIOGHENY RIVER. Great American Rivers Flip Map Series. Birmingham, AL: Menasha Ridge Press, 1987. 40 p. Illus. Maps. Paper. PA ***

Rhode Island (RI)

362.AMC RIVER GUIDE: MASSACHUSETTS, CONNECTICUT, RHODE ISLAND. Boston: Appalachian Mountain Club, 1985. 192 p. Illus. Maps. Index. Paper. MA CT RI See entry 283 for a full description.

363.NORTHEASTERN COASTAL PADDLING GUIDE. Edited by Chuck Sutherland. Tuckahoe, NY: Association of North Atlantic Kayakers, 1984. 39 p. Illus. Maps. Paper. CT MA ME NJ NY RI See entry 45 for a full description.

364.Weber, Ken. CANOEING MASSACHUSETTS, RHODE ISLAND, AND CONNECTICUT. Somersworth, NH: New Hampshire Publishing Co., 1980. 159 p. Illus. Maps. Paper. CT MA RI See entry 54 for full description.

South Carolina (SC)

365.Able, Gene, and Horan, Jack. PADDLING SOUTH CAROLINA: A GUIDE TO PALMETTO STATE RIVER TRAILS. Columbia, SC: Palmetto Byways Press, 1986. 134 p. Illus. Maps. Bibl. Index. Paper. SC

"The rivers described in the book represent the best in South Carolina for canoeing and kayaking. All told, they make up a system of trails that cover 1,292.8 miles" (introduction). The authors define "trail" as all or part of a free-flowing river which has paddling excitement and/or aesthetic qualities. In the guide portion of their book they describe and map twenty-seven waterways grouped by area (lowcountry, piedmont, mountain), and divided by trip. Information is standardized: general waterway introduction, trip description(s), concluding table giving distance, maps, average flow, gradient, difficulty, hazards, runnable water level, and skill rating. Other parts of the book contain material on trip planning, outdoor hazards, information sources, and a directory of outfitters. Some of the twenty-seven waterways described: Edisto, Little Pee Dee, Four Holes Swamp, Saluda, Tyger, Congaree, Catawba, Chattooga, and Chauga. Publisher/distributor: Palmetto Byways Press, P.O. Box 50465, Columbia, SC 29250.

366.APPALACHIAN WHITEWATER: VOLUME I, THE SOUTHERN MOUNTAINS. Compiled by Bob Sehlinger and others. Birmingham, AL: Menasha Ridge Press, 1986. 159 p. Illus. Maps. Index. Paper. AL GA KY NC SC TN See entry 3 for a full description.

367.Benner, Bob. CAROLINA WHITEWATER: A CANOEIST'S GUIDE TO THE WESTERN CAROLINAS. 4th ed. Hillsborough, NC: Menasha Ridge Press, 1981. 244 p. Illus. Maps. Bibl. Index. Paper. NC SC See entry 318 for a full description.

368.Burmeister, Walter F. THE SOUTHEASTERN RIVERS. Appalachian Waters, no. 4. Oakton, VA: Appalachian Books, 1976. 850 p. Bibl. Index. Paper. FL GA NC SC VA (WW-1st ed.)

369.Nealy, William. WHITEWATER HOME COMPANION: SOUTHEASTERN RIVERS, VOLUME I. Hillsborough, NC: Menasha Ridge Press, 1981. 156 p. Illus. Maps. Paper. AL GA NC PA SC TN WV See entry 41 for a full description.

370.Rathnow, Ron. CHATTOOGA RIVER, SECTION IV. Great American Rivers Flip Map Series. Birmingham, AL: Menasha Ridge Press, 1986. 34 p. Illus. Maps. Paper. GA SC ***

371.SOUTH CAROLINA RIVER TRAILS. Columbia: South Carolina Dept. of Parks, Recreation and Tourism; South Carolina Dept. of Wildlife and Marine Resources, 1978. 30 p. Illus. Maps. Paper. SC

"All the rivers listed [12] have been experienced first hand by a team of expert canoeists. ...The ones selected for inclusion are those which best represent the State's diverse network of whitewater, redwater and blackwater streams, and which are superior with respect to navigability, access, and lack of man-caused disturbance," (introduction). Descriptions of the waterways cover a page or two, each containing: name, introduction, biological aspects, historic attractions, navigability and access, safety factors, and a strip map showing road access and campsites. The rivers: Ashepoo, Black, Congaree, Cooper, Edisto, Enoree, Little Pee Dee, Saluda, Santee, Savannah, Tyger, and Wambaw (Creek).

Tennessee (TN)

372.Nealy, William. WHITEWATER HOME COMPANION: SOUTHEASTERN RIVERS, VOLUME I. Hillsborough, NC: Menasha Ridge Press, 1981. 156 p. Illus. Maps. Paper. AL GA NC PA SC TN WV See entry 41 for a full description.

373.Nealy, William. WHITEWATER HOME COMPANION: SOUTHEASTERN RIVERS, VOLUME II. Hillsborough, NC: Menasha Ridge Press, 1984. 165 p. Illus. Maps. Paper. GA KY MD NC TN VA WV See entry 42 for a full description.

374.Rathnow, Ron. OCOEE RIVER. Great American Rivers Flip Map Series. Birmingham, AL: Menasha Ridge Press, 1985. 32 p. Illus. Maps. Paper. TN ***

375.Sehlinger, Bob, and Lantz, Bob. A CANOEING AND KAYAKING GUIDE TO THE STREAMS OF TENNESSEE. 2d ed. Birmingham, AL: Menasha Ridge Press, 1983. 2 vols. Illus. Maps. Index. Paper. TN

Sehlinger and Lantz cover the thousands of miles of waterways crisscrossing Tennessee, ranging from flatwater through the high class drops. Each volume repeats the general introductory chapters which provide an overview of the state's geology, climate, water quality, and stream dynamics. After these chapters are the river guides, separated into two volumes, roughly by region. Volume I (185 p.): Streams of the Mountains, Ridges, Valleys (8 streams); Streams of the Cumberland Valley (19 streams); and, Streams of the Tennessee Valley (8 streams). Volume II (175 p.): Streams of the Mountains, Ridges, Valleys (9 streams); Streams of the Cumberland Plateau (25 streams); and, Streams of the Mississippi Plain (6 streams). Appendixes contain information on outfitters, map sources, clubs, and printed guides. Publisher/distributor: Menasha Ridge Press, P.O. Box 59257, Birmingham, AL 35259-9257.

376.Smith, Monte. A PADDLER'S GUIDE TO THE OBED-EMORY WATERSHED: DETAILED INFORMATION ON 18 WHITEWATER TRIPS IN THE OBED RIVER SYSTEM. 2d ed. Birmingham, AL: Menasha Ridge Press, 1990. 200? p. Illus. Paper. TN ***

Texas (TX)

377.Aulbach, Louis F., and Butler, Joe. THE LOWER CANYONS OF THE RIO GRANDE: LA LINDA TO DRYDEN CROSSING, MAPS AND NOTES FOR RIVER RUNNERS. Houston, TX: Wilderness Area Map Service, 1988. 90 p. Illus. Maps. Bibl. Paper. TX

Aulbach and Butler write in their introduction that "this is the best river trip in Texas in terms of isolation, scenery, and adventure." The trip they describe covers 83 miles of river flowing through desert canyons. Put in is at La Linda, just downstream from the Big Bend National Park boundary. The run is suitable for experienced canoe campers, kayakers or rafters. Introductory material on shuttles, gear and food planning, side trip hiking possibilities, and the environment, precedes a narrative mile-by-mile log which is accompanied by good topographic maps (24 of them) showing mileage, camp sites, rapids, geologic features, and points of interest. Publisher/distributor: Louis F. Aulbach, 3002 Helberg Rd., Houston, TX 77092.

378.Boy Scouts of America. Sam Houston Area Council. CAMPING AND CANOEING GUIDEBOOK. Houston, TX: 1971. 306 p. Pref. Maps. Paper. TX (WW-1st ed.) River(s): Neches, Angelina, Trinity, Brazos, Colorado, Guadalupe, Rio Grande, Pecos, and Village Creek, and Armand's Bayou.

379.Burmeister, Walter F. THE GRANDIOSE RIO GRANDE. Charleston, SC: Creative Holiday Guides, 1978. 128 p. Illus. Map. Bibl. Paper. TX

A promotional publication of the Folbot Corporation, but also a useful guidebook and a visual banquet of 90 color photographs. Part 3 contains river running information, canyon-by-canyon. Highlighted numbers appearing here and throughout the book are keyed to the photographs. A "statistical outline" (notes, mileage, drop, time, difficulty, scenery) completes part 3. Burmeister presents four other sections which have information about Big Bend morphology, plants and animals, fossils, trails, and river and desert photography. Publisher/distributor: Creative Holiday Guides, P.O. Box 7097, Charleston, SC 29405.

380.Humphrey, Mary E. RUNNING THE RIO GRANDE: A FLOATERS GUIDE TO THE BIG BEND. Austin, TX: AAR/Tantalus, 1981. 66 p. Illus. Bibl. Map. TX

"The Big Bend area is an arid conglomeration of rock, sand, and spiny botanicals; much of it today is within Big Bend National Park" (introduction). Traversing the Park is the Rio Grande, and Humphrey offers a combination river guide and information sourcebook as an introduction to the area. Mile-by-mile river logs: Presidio, TX to Castolon, TX; Castolon to LaLinda, Mexico; and LaLinda to Langtry, TX. The logs note points of interest and rapids. Non-log information includes general characteristics of the region, weather, wildlife, rocks, camping, facilities, gear, and maps. Publisher/distributor: AAR/Tantalus, Inc., P.O. Box 893, Austin, TX 78767.

381.Kirkley, Gene. A GUIDE TO TEXAS RIVERS AND STREAMS. Houston, TX: Gulf Publishing, Lone Star Books, 1983. 107 p. Illus. Maps. Index. Paper. TX

Divided into two sections—thirty-seven major waterways, and forty-six secondary and seasonal streams—each with trip segment maps showing road, pipeline, and rail crossings. Kirkley's trip descriptions contain information on general setting, fishing, water level, obstructions, access, and camping. Some of the rivers he examines: Brazos, Colorado, Devil's, Guadalupe, Pedernales, Rio Grande, Sabine, San Saba, and Trinity. Publisher/distributor: Gulf Publishing Co., P.O. Box 2608, Houston, TX 77001.

382.RIVER GUIDE TO THE RIO GRANDE. Edited by John Pearson. Big Bend National Park, TX: Big Bend Natural History Association, and the National Park Service, 1982. 4 vols. Illus. Maps. Paper. TX

A set of three strip map-guides plus an introductory booklet covering the most popular Rio Grande river runs in the Big Bend region. (Much of the information was provided by Bob Burleson and the Texas Explorers Club.) Pearson's the introductory volume concisely covers regulations, safety, first aid, river ethics, and other general information. The map-guides, on waterproof paper, are topographic strips incorporating a log giving put-in, take-out, access, rapids classification, sights, flora, fauna, and land ownership. The runs: Colorado Canyon through Santa Elena Canyon (43 mi.), Mariscal Canyon through Boquillas Canyon (61 mi.), and the lower canyons (La Linda to Dryden Crossing, 83 mi.). Publisher/distributor: Big Bend Natural History Assoc., Big Bend Nat. Park, TX 79834.

383.Texas Explorers Club. SUGGESTED RIVER TRIPS THROUGH THE RIO GRANDE RIVER CANYONS IN THE BIG BEND REGION OF TEXAS. Rev. ed. Temple, TX: 1979. 33 p. Illus. Maps. Mimeo. TX

A compilation of notes taken during many trips by members of the TEC, and the Chihuahuan Desert Research Institute. The notes begin at Presidio and trace the run downstream, through elevin canyons, to Langtry. Explanations of the main runs, how to get there, and special points of interest in each canyon are given. A few rough sketch maps are provided, however the appropriate U.S.G.S. maps are also identified. The notes contain many practical suggestions on what to do with shuttle cars, vantage points for photographers, and areas of interest near the river. Publisher/distributor: Texas Explorers Club, c/o Bob Burleson, P.O. Box 844, Temple, TX 76501.

384.Texas Parks and Wildlife Department. Trail and Waterways Section. AN ANALYSIS OF TEXAS WATERWAYS: A REPORT ON THE PHYSICAL CHARACTERISTICS OF RIVERS, STREAMS, AND BAYOUS IN TEXAS. Austin, TX: 1972. 240 p. Maps. Paper. TX (WW-1st ed.) River(s): 82 waterways are examined, either fully or in part.

385.TEXAS RIVERS AND RAPIDS. Edited by Ben M. Nolen. Humble, TX: B. Narramore?, 1972-. Illus. Maps. Paper. TX

Published periodically, but on an irregular basis. Although primarily a canoeing guide to Texas waterways, the reader will also find material on the Buffalo and Cossatot Rivers (AR), the Illinois (OK), the Arkansas (CO), and the Rio Concho (Mexico). In all, twenty-nine trips are mapped and described in the 1974 issue inspected. The 1987 edition (unexamined) has descriptions of rivers in TX, AR, OK, LA, CO, NM, and Texas hiking trails. The maps vary in scale and quality; all lack detail, however access points, mileage, camping facilities, and hazards are usually indicated. Also included are paddling tips and items of regional interest, e.g., Texas canoe competition dates. A significant portion of the book is given over to advertising by local canoe liveries and equipment manufacturers. Publisher/distributor: Westwater Books, Box 2560,

Evergreen, CO 80439; American Canoe Association, P.O. Box 1190, Newington, VA 22122-1190.

Utah (UT)

386.Aitchison, Stewart, et al. A NATURALIST'S SAN JUAN RIVER GUIDE. Boulder, CO: Pruett Publishing, 1983. 57 p. Illus. Maps. Bibl. Paper. UT

The San Juan is a major tributary of the Colorado; from Bluff, UT to Grand Gulch, it is still a wild and beautiful river. Primarily intended as a guide to flora and fauna, Aitchison's book also contains information on the area's former inhabitants (Anasazi, Navajo, and "Canyoneers"). His work begins with twenty pages of strip maps adapted from U.S.G.S. topos. Superimposed on the maps are river miles and descriptive information. Available in a waterproof edition. Publisher/distributor: Pruett Publishing Co., 2928 Pearl St., Boulder, CO 80301.

387.Anderson, Fletcher, and Hopkinson, Ann. RIVERS OF THE SOUTHWEST: A BOATERS GUIDE TO THE RIVERS OF COLORADO, NEW MEXICO, UTAH AND ARIZONA. 2d ed. Boulder, CO: Pruett Publishing, 1987. 129 p. Illus. Maps. Paper. AZ CO NM UT See entry 2 for a full description.

388.Baars, Don. CATARACT CANYON VIA THE GREEN OR COLORADO RIVERS: A RIVER RUNNER'S GUIDE AND NATURAL HISTORY OF CANYONLANDS. Waterproof ed. Evergreen, CO: Canon Publishers, 1987. 80 p. Illus. Maps. Paper. UT Cover title: A RIVER RUNNER'S GUIDE TO CATARACT CANYON AND APPROACHES.

The text and strip maps (drawn with good topographic detail by Robin L. Lockhart) cover the Colorado River from Moab, UT to the confluence with the Green (Baars calls this stretch "Meander Canyon"); from the confluence through Cataract Canyon to Hite Marina; and the Green River from Green River, UT to the Colorado confluence—Labyrinth and Stillwater Canyons. There is a great deal of mileage here—120 on the Green, 112 on the Colorado—but the descriptive logs accompanying the maps cover the territory adequately. William L. Chesser's drawings illustrate Baars' knowledgeable text about important aspects of the Canyonlands. If only one guidebook is to be chosen as a primer for this classic river running region, consider this one. Publisher/distributor: Canon Publishers, 29056 Histead Dr. Evergreen, CO 80439.

389.Baars, Don, and Stevenson, Gene. SAN JUAN CANYONS: A RIVER RUNNER'S GUIDE AND NATURAL HISTORY OF SAN JUAN RIVER CANYONS. Waterproof ed. Evergreen, CO: Canon Publishers, 1986. 64 p. Illus. Maps. Paper. UT

The San Juan "...is a fast river, with a rate of drop greater than the Colorado River through Grand Canyon. Its several rapids are small, but rocky and hazardous" (page 4). This guidebook is quality work, and along with Baars' Cataract Canyon guide (see above), establishes a standard for the genre. It is printed on waterproof paper with carefully-drafted strip maps giving topographic detail. Narrative chapters on the geology, flora, fauna, and human history of the region comprise over half the contents. River coverage is from mile 0 near Bluff, UT to mile 83 at Clay Hills Crossing, UT (at the top of a slackwater arm of Lake Powell). A log, interspersed with the strip maps, identifies hazards, points of interest, and other information. The maps are Stevenson's; illustrations are by William L. Chesser. Publisher/distributor: Canon Publishers, 29056 Histead Dr. Evergreen, CO 80439.

390.Belknap, Bill, and Belknap Buzz. CANYONLANDS RIVER GUIDE: WESTWATER, LAKE POWELL, CANYONLANDS NATIONAL PARK. Boulder City, NV: Westwater Books, 1974. 63 p. Illus. Maps. Paper. AZ UT (WW-1st ed.) River(s): Colorado, Green.

391.Dirksen, D. J., and Reeves, R. A. RECREATION ON THE COLORADO RIVER. Aptos, CA: Sail Sales Publishing, 1985. 112 p. Illus. Maps. Index. Paper. AZ CA CO NV UT See entry 20 for a full description.

392.Evans, Laura, and Belknap, Buzz. DESOLATION RIVER GUIDE: GREEN RIVER WILDERNESS. Boulder City, NV: Westwater Books, 1974. 55 p. Illus. Maps. Paper. UT (WW-1st ed.) River(s): Green (from Split Mountain to Green River, UT.

393.Evans, Laura, and Belknap, Buzz. DINOSAUR RIVER GUIDE. Boulder City, NV: Westwater Books, 1973. 64 p. Illus. Maps. Paper. CO UT (WW-1st ed.) River(s): Green, Yampa.

394.Evans, Laura, and Belknap, Buzz. FLAMING GORGE DINOSAUR NATIONAL MONUMENT: DINOSAUR RIVER GUIDE. Boulder City, NV: Westwater Books, 1973. 63 p. Illus. Maps. Paper. CO UT WY See entry 23 for a full description.

395.Hamblin, W. Kenneth, and Rigby, J. Keith. GUIDEBOOK TO THE COLORADO RIVER, PART I: LEES FERRY TO PHANTOM RANCH IN GRAND CANYON NATIONAL PARK. PART II: PHANTOM RANCH IN GRAND CANYON NATIONAL PARK TO LAKE MEAD, ARIZONA-NEVADA. Brigham Young University Geology Studies, Studies for students nos. 4 and 5. Provo, UT: Brigham Young University, 1969. 2 vols. Illus. Paper. AZ NV UT (WW-1st ed.) Part III of this series is cited under entry 402. River(s): Colorado, from Lees Ferry to Lake Mead.

396.Hayes, Philip T., and Simmons, George C. RIVER RUNNERS' GUIDE TO DINOSAUR NATIONAL MONUMENT AND VICINITY, WITH EMPHASIS ON GEOLOGIC FEATURES. Rev. ed. River Runners' Guides, vol. 1. Denver, CO: Powell Society, 1973. 78 p. Illus. Maps. Diag. Bibl. Paper. CO UT (WW-1st ed.) Revision of FROM FLAMING GORGE DAM THROUGH DINOSAUR CANYON TO OURAY, by Philip T. Hayes and E.S. Santos (1969), and the YAMPA RIVER SUPPLEMENT, by Philip T. Hayes (1971). River(s): Green (Flaming Gorge Dam to Ouray), and Yampa (Deerlodge Park to Echo Park).

397.Huser, Verne. CANYON COUNTRY PADDLES: A PRACTICAL, INFORMATIVE AND ENTERTAINING GUIDE TO RIVER RUNNING USING THE KAYAK, CANOE, OR RUBBER RAFT IN SOUTHEASTERN UTAH. Canyon Country Guide Book, no. 12. Salt Lake City, UT: Wasatch Publishers, 1978. 96 p. Illus. Maps. Bibl. UT ***

398.McCaffrey, Mark Stanislaus. THE DELORES: A RIVER RUNNING GUIDE. Boulder, CO: Pruett Publishing, 1981. CO UT ***

399.Mutschler, Felix E. DESOLATION AND GRAY CANYONS. River Runners' Guides, vol. 4. Denver, CO: Powell Society, 1969. 85 p. Illus. Maps. Diag. Paper. UT (WW-1st ed.) River(s): Colorado, from Ouray to Green River, UT.

400.Mutschler, Felix E. RIVER RUNNERS' GUIDE TO CANYONLANDS NATIONAL PARK AND VICINITY, WITH EMPHASIS ON GEOLOGICAL FEATURES. River Runners' Guides, vol 2. Denver, CO: Powell Society, 1977. 99 p. Illus. Maps. Diag. Paper. UT (WW-1st ed.) Replaces Mutchler's LABYRINTH, STILLWATER, AND CATARACT CANYONS (1969). River(s): Colorado from Moab, UT, to the confluence with the Green River.

401.Nichols, Gary. RIVER RUNNERS' GUIDE TO UTAH AND ADJACENT AREAS. Rev. ed. Salt Lake City: University of Utah Press, 1986. 168 p. Illus. Maps. Paper. AZ CO ID UT WY See entry 43 for a full description.

402.Rigby, J. Keith, et. al. GUIDEBOOK TO THE COLORADO RIVER, PART III: MOAB TO HITE, UTAH, THROUGH CANYONLANDS NATIONAL PARK. Brigham Young University Geology Studies, Studies for Students, no. 6. Provo, UT: Brigham Young University, 1971. 91 p. Illus. Paper. UT (WW-1st ed.) Parts I and II of this series are cited under entry 126. River(s): Colorado, from Moab to Hite, Ut.

403.Schafer, Ann. CANOEING WESTERN WATERWAYS: THE MOUNTAIN STATES. New York: Harper & Row, 1978. 279 p. Maps. Bibl. Index. AZ CO ID MT NV NM UT WY See entry 53 for a full description.

404.Simmons, George C., and Gaskill, David L. MARBLE GORGE AND GRAND CANYON. River Runners' Guides, vol. 3. Denver, CO: Powell Society, 1969. 132 p. Illus. Maps. Diag. Paper. AZ UT (WW-1st ed.) River(s): Colorado from Lees Ferry to Pierces Ferry at Lake Mead.

Vermont (VT)

405.AMC RIVER GUIDE: NEW HAMPSHIRE, VERMONT. 2d ed. Edited by Victoria Jas. Boston: Appalachian Mountain Club, 1989. 308 p. Illus. Maps. Index. Paper. NH VT See entry 283 for a full description.

406.APPALACHIAN WHITEWATER: VOLUME III, THE NORTHERN MOUNTAINS. Compiled by John Connelly and John Porterfield. Birmingham, AL: Menasha Ridge Press, 1987. 141 p. Illus. Maps. Index. Paper. CT ME MA NH VT See entry 5 for a full description.

407.Burmeister, Walter F. THE HUDSON RIVER AND ITS TRIBUTARIES. Appalachian Waters, no. 2. Oakton, VA: Appalachian Books, 1974. 496 p. Maps. Bibl. Index. Paper. CT MA NJ NY VT (WW-1st ed.) River(s): upper, central and lower Hudson tributaries.

408.THE COMPLETE BOATING GUIDE TO THE CONNECTICUT RIVER. Rev. ed. Edited by Mark C. Borton. Easthampton, MA: Connecticut River Watershed Council, 1986. 245 p. Maps. Paper. CT MA NH VT ***

409.CONNECTICUT RIVER GUIDE. Rev. ed. Easthampton, MA: Connecticut River Watershed Council, 1971. 87 p. Paper. CT MA NH VT (WW-1st ed.) River(s): Connecticut, and its tributaries, the White, West, Millers, Westfield, Salmon.

410.Gabler, Ray. NEW ENGLAND WHITE WATER RIVER GUIDE. Boston, MA: Appalachian Mountain Club, 1981. 376 p. Illus. Maps. Bibl. Paper. CT ME MA NH NY VT See entry 25 for a full description.

411.Schweiker, Roioli. CANOE CAMPING, VERMONT & NEW HAMPSHIRE RIVERS: A GUIDE TO 600 MILES OF RIVERS FOR A DAY, WEEKEND, OR WEEK OF CANOEING. 2d ed. Woodstock, VT: Backcountry Publications, 1985. 123 p. Illus. Maps. Paper. NH VT See entry 288 for a full description.

Virginia (VA)

412.Burmeister, Walter F. THE SOUTHEASTERN RIVERS. Appalachian Waters, no. 4. Oakton, VA: Appalachian Books, 1976. 850 p. Bibl. Index. Paper. FL GA NC SC VA (WW-1st ed.)

413.Burmeister, Walter F. THE UPPER OHIO & ITS TRIBUTARIES. Appalachian Waters, no. 5. Oakton, VA: Appalachian Books, 1978. 948 p. Bibl. Index. Paper. KY NY OH PA VA WV See entry 11 for a full description.

414.Carter, Randy. CANOEING WHITE WATER RIVER GUIDE. 8th ed. Oakton, VA: Appalachian Books, 1974. 275 p. Illus. Maps. Index. Paper. NC VA WV (WW-1st ed.)

415.Corbett, H. Roger, Jr., and Matacia, Louis J., Jr. ONE & TWO DAY RIVER CRUISES: MARYLAND, VIRGINIA, WEST VIRGINIA. Blue Ridge Voyages, vol. 1, 4th ed. Oakton, VA: Blue Ridge Voyageurs, 1973. p. Illus. Maps. Bibl. Paper. MD VA WV (WW1st ed.) River(s): Rappahannock, Antietam, Thornton, Potomac, Shenandoah, and Cedar.

416.Corbett, H. Roger, Jr., and Matacia, Louis J., Jr. ONE & TWO DAY RIVER CRUISES: MARYLAND, VIRGINIA, WEST VIRGINIA. Blue Ridge Voyages, vol. 2, 2d ed. Oakton, VA: Appalachian Books, 1972. 88 p. Pref. Illus. Maps. Bibl. Paper. MD VA WV (WW-1st ed.) River(s): Potomac and its south branch, Cedar Creek, Catoctin Creek, Cacapon, Monocacy, and Antietam.

417.Corbett, H. Roger, Jr., and Matacia, Louis J., Jr. ONE DAY RIVER CRUISES: VIRGINIA, WEST VIRGINIA. Blue Ridge Voyages, vol. 3. Dunn Loring, VA: L.J. Matacia, 1972. 122 p. Illus. Maps. Bibl. Paper. VA WV (WW-1st ed.) River(s): Virginia rivers: Hughes, Shenandoah, Rappahannock, North and South Anna, Passage Creek, Goose Creek; West Virginia rivers: Upper Lost, and Sleepy Creek.

418.Corbett, H. Roger, Jr. VIRGINIA WHITE WATER: A CANOEING GUIDE TO THE RIVERS OF THE OLD DOMINION. Rockville, MD: Seneca Press, 1977. 287 p. Maps. Paper. VA

"...A compilation of technical data, trip descriptions, maps, and historical facts for eighty-seven rivers, creeks, or runs in Virginia. It is the first volume of a two volume series; it covers the Potomac River, the Shenandoah River, the Rappahannock River, the York River, and the James River watersheds" (preface). Corbett's planned second volume (apparently) has not been published. Watershed chapters begin with a general sketch map and introduction. Waterways within the chapters are mapped and described run by run in a standard format: name, gradient, difficulty, distance, time, width, scenery, map number, trip narrative, hazards, water conditions, history, and "other" information. The introduction has information on geology, hydrology, stream description and classification, gauges and markings. Publisher/distributor: Seneca Press, 512 Monet Dr., Rockville, MD 20850.

419.Gilbert, David T. RIVERS & TRAILS: BICYCLE TOURING, BACKPACKING, AND CANOEING IN THE MID-ATLANTIC STATES. Drawings by Laura L. Marzloff. Knoxville, MD: Outdoor Press, 1978. 112 p. Illus. Maps. Bibl. Index. Paper. DE MD VA WV See entry 26 for a full description.

420.Matacia, Louis J., Jr., and Cecil, Owen S. BLUE RIDGE VOYAGES: AN ILLUSTRATED CANOE LOG OF THE SHENANDOAH RIVER AND ITS SOUTH FORK. Blue Ridge Voyages, vol. 4. Oakton, VA: L.J. Matacia, 1974. 184 p. Illus. Paper. VA WV (WW-1st ed.) River(s): Shenandoah.

421.Matacia, Louis J., and Cecil, Owen S., III. AN ILLUSTRATED CANOE LOG OF THE SHENANDOAH RIVER AND ITS SOUTH FORK. Blue Ridge Voyages, vol. 4. Oakton, VA: Matacia, 1974. 171 p. Illus. Maps. Paper. VA

The Shenandoah, from its headwaters to Harpers Ferry, is thoroughly documented in this guidebook. Water level is critical on this river; the general rule is that low flow dictates trips on the northern portions. Maps giving mileage, obstructions, rapids, and access points are provided. Illustrated with photographs. Suggestions are given for one-week, three-day, and two-day trips. Alternate trips for high water conditions are proposed. Publisher/distributor: Louis J. Matacia, P.O. Box 32, Oakton, VA 22124.

422.Nealy, William. WHITEWATER HOME COMPANION: SOUTHEASTERN RIVERS, VOLUME II. Hillsborough, NC: Menasha Ridge Press, 1984. 165 p. Illus. Maps. Paper. GA KY MD NC TN VA WV See entry 42 for a full description.

423.Thomson, John Seabury. POTOMAC WHITE WATER: A GUIDE TO SAFE CANOEING ABOVE WASHINGTON, SENECA TO LITTLE FALLS. Oakton, VA: Appalachian Books, 1974. 44 p. Illus. Map. Bibl. Paper. MD VA (WW-1st ed.) River(s): Potomac.

Washington (WA)

424.Furrer, Werner. KAYAK AND CANOE TRIPS IN WASHINGTON. Lynnwood, WA: Signpost Publications, 1971. 32 p. Maps. Bibl. Paper. WA (WW-1st ed.) Waterway(s): Quinault, Cedar, Sauk, Skykomish, Stillaguamish, Wenatchee, Cle Elum, and Yakima Rivers, Sucia Island (Puget Sound), Green Lake, Little Kachess Lake, and Lower Crab Creek.

425.Furrer, Werner. WATER TRAILS OF WASHINGTON. Rev. ed. Edmonds, WA: Signpost Books, 1979. 96 p. Illus. Maps. Bibl. Index. Paper. WA

Furrer presents descriptions of thirty-seven trips suitable for beginners in canoes or kayaks. He defines beginner as one who has had some previous qualified instruction. The author prefaces the trip descriptions with introductory material on equipment, craft, river classification, table of navigability (optimal paddling months), paddle pointers, and boat maneuvers. Descriptions are brief (on two facing pages) and consist of a sketch map showing access, mileage, and average gradient, and a descriptive paragraph, topo map name, and a trip log form. Possibly out of print. Publisher/distributor: Signpost Books, 8912 192nd SW, Edmonds, WA 98020.

426.HELLS CANYON OF THE SNAKE RIVER. Quinn Map. Redmond, OR: Educational Adventures, 198? [20 p.] Illus. Maps. Paper. ID OR WA See entry 28 for a full description.

427.Huser, Verne. PADDLE ROUTES OF WESTERN WASHINGTON: 50 FLATWATER TRIPS FOR KAYAK AND CANOE. Seattle, WA: The Mountaineers, 1990. 240 p. Illus. Maps. Bibl. Paper. WA

Huser has written enough paddling books and articles to earn the honorific, "Dean of river writing." In this, his latest work, he describes waters in an area where he has lived the last twelve years. His introduction contains information on choice of craft, power and control techniques (including poling and lining), safety, riverine environment, river etiquette, tides, maps and charts. Trip descriptions are standardized in a paragraph to give name, location, distance, time, maps, season, hazards, shuttle and difficulty rating. Huser follows with a narrative under the headings: overview, access, driving directions and description. I was unable to see the trip maps since I was inspecting a pre-publication galley of this work. The rivers: Dakota (Creek)/California (Creek), Lummi, Nooksack (2 trips), Skagit (3 trips), Sauk (2 trips), Stillaguamish (3 trips), Snoqualmie (4 trips), Sammamish, Issaquah (Creek), Chehalis (5 trips), Hoquiam, Little Hoquiam, Wishkah, Wynoochee, Satsop, Black, Humtulips, Queets, Clearwater, Hoh, Quillayute/Lower Dickey, Bogachiel, Willapa, Grays, Cowlitz (2 trips), and (Lower) Kalama. Publisher/distributor: The Mountaineers, 306 Second Ave. West, Seattle, WA 98119; Douglas & McIntyre, Ltd., 1615 Venables St., Vancouver, BC V5L 2H1.

428.Jones, Philip N. CANOE ROUTES: NORTHWEST OREGON. Seattle, WA: The Mountaineers, 1982. 157 p. Illus. Maps. Bibl. Paper. OR WA See entry 332, for a full description.

429.LaRoux, Dave, and Rudersdorf, Martha. PADDLE WASHINGTON. Seattle, WA: Neah Bay Books, 1984. 163 p. Illus. Maps. Paper. WA

A book for the "...fairweather canoeist." Most of the twenty-eight trips require only basic paddling skills. Arrangement is broadly geographical: salt water, urban, western WA, and eastern WA. (One trip off northwest Vancouver Island somewhat exceeds extablished state and international borders.) A chatty narrative of each trip is preceded by a table: maps, distance, and time), and illustrated by a sketch map. A sample of the trips: Crab Creek, Sucia Island, Willapa Bay, Skagit River, Green River, Yakima River, and Elliot Bay. There are about a dozen pages of non-guidebook lore: safety, river ratings, maps, etc. Publisher/distributor: Neah Bay Books, P.O. Box 58123, Seattle, WA 98118.

430.LOWER SALMON RIVER GUIDE. Rev. ed. Washington, DC: U.S. Dept. of the Interior, Bureau of Land Management, 1983. 18 p. Maps. Paper. ID OR WA See entry 36 for a full description.

431.North, Douglas A. WASHINGTON WHITEWATER 1: A GUIDE TO SEVENTEEN OF WASHINGTON'S MOST POPULAR WHITEWATER RIVERS. 2d ed. Seattle: The Mountaineers, 1988. 175 p. Illus. Maps. Index. Paper. WA

A companion volume to North's WASHINGTON WHITEWATER 2 (below); together, they exemplify the state-of-the-art for guidebooks in which the ideal is giving specific directions and maneuvering details of a run. The author has updated his 1984 edition by adding two more runs, revising put-in/ take-out locations, and augmenting conservation information. This is a detailed and carefully organized regional guide (Cascade Range rivers) intended for rafters or kayakers of intermediate to expert ability. Each river is described (getting there, put-ins and take-outs, water level, special hazards, scenery, camping, rapids), sketch-mapped, and, on a facing page, logged mile-by-mile (using 19 standard symbols). The river runs: Cowlitz, Naches, Upper Middle Fork Snoqualmie, Upper Sauk, Skagit, Suiattle, Wenatchee, Tieton, Nooksack North Fork, Klickitat, White Salmon, Middle Middle Fork Snoqualmie, Methow, Chewuch, Middle Sauk, Green, and Skykomish. Publisher/distributor: Mountaineers Books, 306 Second Ave. W, Seattle, WA 98119.

432.North, Douglas A. WASHINGTON WHITEWATER 2: A GUIDE TO SEVENTEEN OF WASHINGTON'S LESSER KNOWN WHITEWATER TRIPS. Seattle: The Mountaineers, 1987. 183 p. Illus. Maps. Index. Paper. WA

A companion volume to North's WASHINGTON WHITEWATER 1 (above); together, they exemplify the state-of-the-art for guidebooks in which the ideal is giving specific directions and maneuvering details for a run. Eleven of the trips in this book are on rivers draining the Cascade Range, and three each in the Olympic Range and eastern Washington. The guide is divided into level-of-difficulty trips. Each river is described (getting there, put-ins and take-outs, water level, special hazards, scenery, camping, rapids), sketch-mapped, and, on a facing page, logged mile-by-mile (using 19 standard symbols). The river runs: Lower Soleduck, Upper Spokane, Stehekin, Elwha, Grande Ronde, Lewis, Upper Soleduck, Lower Cispus, Entiat, White, Lower Spokane, Chiwawa, Snoqualmie (North Fork), Kalama, Toutle, Upper Cispus, and Skykomish (North Fork). Publisher/ distributor: Mountaineers Books, 306 Second Ave. W, Seattle, WA 98119.

433.Schafer, Ann. CANOEING WESTERN WATERWAYS: THE COASTAL STATES. New York: Harper & Row, 1978. 272 p. Maps. Bibl. Index. CA HI OR WA See entry 52 for a full description.

434.SOGGY SNEAKERS: GUIDE TO OREGON RIVERS. 2d ed. Edited by Willamette Kayak and Canoe Club. Corvallis, Or: The Club, 1986. 208 p. Illus. Maps. Bibl. Index. Paper. OR WA CA See entry 341 for a full description.

435.Washburne, Randel. KAYAKING PUGET SOUND, THE SAN JUANS, AND GULF ISLANDS: 45 TRIPS ON THE NORTHWEST'S INLAND WATERS. Seattle, WA: Mountaineers, 1990. 224 p. Illus. Bibl. Paper. BC WA ***

436.Washburne, Randel. KAYAK TRIPS IN PUGET SOUND AND THE SAN JUAN ISLANDS. Seattle, WA: Pacific Search Press, 1986. 153 p. Illus. Maps. Bibl. Paper. WA

Focus is on loop-trip possibilities in Washington State's watery northwest corner (excluding the Strait of Juan de Fuca and Hood Canal). The loops allow stringing together two or three-day paddles. Routes rated "exposed," "moderate," or "protected." The "Places to Go" section is prefaced with remarks on the paddling environment: weather, water, shipping lanes, tides and currents, going ashore, and going paddling. Trips are bunched by region: San Juan Islands, north and south Puget Sound. Some of the trips: Skagit and Nisqually River deltas; Carr Inlet; Blake, Stuart, Lummi, and Hartstene Islands. Sketch maps and photographs illustrate the book. Publisher/ distributor: Pacific Search Press, 222 Dexter Ave. N, Seattle, WA 98109.

437.THE WILD AND SCENIC SNAKE RIVER: HELLS CANYON NATIONAL RECREATION AREA. Washington, DC: U.S. Dept. of Agriculture, Forest Service, 1985. 23 p. Illus. Maps. Paper. ID OR WA See entry 214 for a full description.

West Virginia (WV)

438.APPALACHIAN WHITEWATER: VOLUME II, THE CENTRAL MOUNTAINS. Compiled by Ed Grove and others. Birmingham, AL: Menasha Ridge Press, 1987. 207 p. Illus. Maps. Index. Paper. DE MD PA WV See entry 4 for a full description.

439.Burmeister, Walter F. THE UPPER OHIO & ITS TRIBUTARIES. Appalachian Waters, no. 5. Oakton, VA: Appalachian Books, 1978. 948 p. Bibl. Index. Paper. KY NY OH PA VA WV See entry 11 for a full description.

440.CANOEING GUIDE: WESTERN PENNSYLVANIA AND NORTHERN WEST VIRGINIA. 7th ed. Compiled and edited by Roy R. Weil and Mary M. Shaw. Pittsburgh, PA: American Youth Hostels, Pittsburgh Council, 1983. 280 p. Illus. Maps. Index. Paper. PA WV See entry 351 for a full description.

441.Canter, Ron, and Canter, Kathy. NEARBY CANOEING STREAMS. 4th ed. Hyattsville, MD: 1979. 62 p. Illus. Maps. Paper. DE MD PA VA WV See entry 13 for a full description.

442.Carter, Randy. CANOEING WHITE WATER RIVER GUIDE. 8th ed. Oakton, VA: Appalachian Books, 1974. 275 p. Illus. Maps. Index. Paper. NC VA WV (WW-1st ed.)

443.Corbett, H. Roger, Jr., and Matacia, Louis J., Jr. ONE & TWO DAY RIVER CRUISES: MARYLAND, VIRGINIA, WEST VIRGINIA. Blue Ridge Voyages, vol. 1, 4th ed. Oakton, VA: Blue Ridge Voyageurs, 1973. p. Illus. Maps. Bibl. Paper. MD VA WV (WW1st ed.) River(s): Rappahannock, Antietam, Thornton, Potomac, Shenandoah, and Cedar.

444.Corbett, H. Roger, Jr., and Matacia, Louis J., Jr. ONE & TWO DAY RIVER CRUISES: MARYLAND, VIRGINIA, WEST VIRGINIA. Blue Ridge Voyages, vol. 2, 2d ed. Oakton, VA: Appalachian Books, 1972. 88 p. Pref. Illus. Maps. Bibl. Paper. MD VA WV (WW-1st ed.) River(s): Potomac and its south branch, Cedar Creek, Catoctin Creek, Cacapon, Monocacy, and Antietam.

445.Corbett, H. Roger, Jr., and Matacia, Louis J., Jr. ONE DAY RIVER CRUISES: VIRGINIA, WEST VIRGINIA. Blue Ridge Voyages, vol. 3. Dunn Loring, VA: L.J. Matacia, 1972. 122 p. Illus. Maps. Bibl. Paper. VA WV (WW-1st ed.) River(s): Virginia rivers: Hughes, Shenandoah, Rappahannock, North and South Anna, Passage Creek, Goose Creek; West Virginia rivers: Upper Lost, and Sleepy Creek.

446.Davidson, Paul; Eister, Ward; and Davidson, Dirk. WILDWATER WEST VIRGINIA. 3rd ed. Hillsborough, NC: Menasha Ridge Press, 1985. 2 vols. Illus. Index. Paper. WV

Intended for West Virginia river paddlers of any skill level using a variety of watercraft. In volume I, the authors cover the northern streams, in volume II, the southern. "In most instances, the description of a section of a river is preceded by the following data: river miles of the section described, river classification, gradient, volume, type of scenery, time needed to travel, and water level [and U.S.G.S. map name]. The descriptions are usually followed by information concerning difficulties, how to set up a shuttle, and the location of a gauge" (introduction). The trip narratives are more readable than many. Maps indicate runs and access roads. West Virginia river tributaries and/or areas covered: Potomac, Cheat, Tygart Sub-basin, Ohio, Greenbriar, Central (includes the Gauley), South (New and Bluestone), and West (Kanawa and Guyandotte). Publisher address: Menasha Ridge Press, P.O. Box 59257, Birmingham, AL 35259-9257.

447.Gilbert, David T. RIVERS & TRAILS: BICYCLE TOURING, BACKPACKING, AND CANOEING IN THE MID-ATLANTIC STATES. Drawings by Laura L. Marzloff. Knoxville, MD: Outdoor Press, 1978. 112 p. Illus. Maps. Bibl. Index. Paper. DE MD VA WV See entry 26 for a full description.

448.Matacia, Louis J., Jr., and Cecil, Owen S. BLUE RIDGE VOYAGES: AN ILLUSTRATED CANOE LOG OF THE SHENANDOAH RIVER AND ITS SOUTH FORK. Blue Ridge Voyages, vol. 4. Oakton, VA: L.J. Matacia, 1974. 184 p. Illus. Paper. VA WV (WW-1st ed.) River(s): Shenandoah.

449.Nealy, William. WHITEWATER HOME COMPANION: SOUTHEASTERN RIVERS, VOLUME I. Hillsborough, NC: Menasha Ridge Press, 1981. 156 p. Illus. Maps. Paper. AL GA NC PA SC TN WV See entry 41 for a full description.

450.Nealy, William. WHITEWATER HOME COMPANION: SOUTHEASTERN RIVERS, VOLUME II. Hillsborough, NC: Menasha Ridge Press, 1984. 165 p. Illus. Maps. Paper. GA KY MD NC TN VA WV See entry 42 for a full description.

451.Rathnow, Ron. NEW RIVER GORGE. Great American Rivers Flip Map Series. Birmingham, AL: Menasha Ridge Press, 1986. 40 p. Illus. Maps. Paper. WV ***

Wisconsin (WI)

452.CANOEING THE WILD RIVERS OF NORTHWESTERN WISCONSIN. 1969. Reprint. Eau Claire, WI: Wisconsin Indian Head Country, 1977. Maps. Paper. WI (WW-1st ed.) River(s): Brule, Eau Claire, Totogatic, Namekagon, St. Croix, Yellow, and Clam rivers.

453.CANOE TRAILS OF NORTH-CENTRAL WISCONSIN. Madison, WI: Wisconsin Tales and Trails, 1973. 64 p. Maps. Paper. WI (WW-1st ed.) River(s): Chippewa, Flambeau, Couderay, Jump, Turtle, Manitowish, Yellow, Thornapple, Deertail, and Main.

454.CANOE TRAILS OF NORTHEASTERN WISCONSIN. Madison, WI: Wisconsin Tales and Trails, 1972. 72 p. Maps. Paper. WI (WW-1st ed.) River(s): Brule, Deerskin, Embarrass, Manitowish, Menominee, Oconto, Pelican, Peshtigo, Pike, Pine, Popple, Prairie, Spirit, Tomahawk, Wisconsin, and Wolf.

455.CANOE TRAILS OF NORTHWESTERN WISCONSIN. Madison, WI: Wisconsin Tales and Trails, 1972. 72 p. Illus. WI ***

456.Duncanson, Michael E. BEST CANOE TRAILS OF SOUTHERN WISCONSIN. Madison, WI: Wisconsin Trails Publications, 1987. 70 p. Paper. WI ***

457.Duncanson, Michael E. A CANOEING GUIDE TO THE INDIAN HEAD RIVERS OF WEST CENTRAL WISCONSIN. Virginia, MN: W.A. Fisher Co., 1976. 61 p. Maps. Paper. WI (WW-1st ed.) River(s): Chippewa, Eau Claire, Red Cedar, Hay, Chetek, Buffalo, Trempealeau, Black, St. Croix, and Mississippi.

458.Duncanson, Michael E. CANOE TRAILS OF SOUTHERN WISCONSIN. Madison, WI: Wisconsin Tales and Trails, 1974. 65 p. Illus. Maps. Paper. WI (WW-1st ed.)

459.Palzer, Bob, and Palzer, Jody. WHITEWATER, QUIETWATER: A GUIDE TO THE WILD RIVERS OF WISCONSIN, UPPER MICHIGAN, AND N.E. MINNESOTA. 5th ed. Two Rivers, WI: Evergreen Paddleways, 1983. 160 p. Illus. Maps. Bibl. Paper. MI MN WI See entry 46 for a full description.

460.WISCONSIN'S NORTH CENTRAL CANOE TRAILS. Rev. ed. Ladysmith, WI: North Central Canoe Trails, 1967. 30 p. Maps. Paper. WI

The Chippewa, Flambeau, South Fork Flambeau, Jump, and Yellow Rivers are featured on twenty-eight strip maps. Marked on these carefully-prepared maps are hazards, rapids, campsites, landmarks, and access points. Difficult stretches of water are shown in enlarged detail. The maps are based on aerial photographs drawn to a four-inch-per-mile scale. No accompanying descriptions of the runs are given. Rapids are rated on a scale of one to four. Publisher/distributor: North Central Canoe Trails, Inc., Ladysmith, WI 54848.

Wyoming (WY)

461.De la Montagne, John. WILDERNESS BOATING ON YELLOWSTONE LAKES. Bozeman: Montana State College, 1961. 31 p. Maps. Paper. WY (WW-1st ed.) Lake(s): Upper Yellowstone, Shoshone, and Lewis.

462.Evans, Laura, and Belknap, Buzz. FLAMING GORGE DINOSAUR NATIONAL MONUMENT: DINOSAUR RIVER GUIDE. Boulder City, NV: Westwater Books, 1973. 63 p. Illus. Maps. Paper. CO UT WY See entry 23 for a full description.

463.Huser, Verne, and Belknap, Buzz. GRAND TETON NATIONAL PARK SNAKE RIVER GUIDE. Boulder City, NV: Westwater Books, 1972. 72 p. Illus. Maps. Paper. WY (WW-1st ed.) Waterway(s): Snake River, and Jenny and Jackson Lakes.

464.Nichols, Gary. RIVER RUNNERS' GUIDE TO UTAH AND ADJACENT AREAS. Rev. ed. Salt Lake City: University of Utah Press, 1986. 168 p. Illus. Maps. Paper. AZ CO ID UT WY See entry 43 for a full description.

465.Schafer, Ann. CANOEING WESTERN WATERWAYS: THE MOUNTAIN STATES. New York: Harper & Row, 1978. 279 p. Maps. Bibl. Index. AZ CO ID MT NV NM UT WY See entry 53 for a full description.

Chapter 1, Section 4

Guidebooks and Articles

Guide Articles From Canoe Magazine

Canada, National and Regional

466. Benda, Chuck. "Shattered Expectations." 9(2), (March, 1981): 44-46, 50-54. (Rivers: Fraser, Crooked, Pack (BC), Peace (BC-AB), Slave (AB-NT), Mackenzie (NT), Lakes: Williston BC), Great Slave (NT).

Canada, By Province and Territory

British Columbia (BC)

467. Keith, Al. "Short Strokes." 15(4), (August, 1987): 42-45. (Wells Gray Provincial Park.)

468. Nordby, Will. "Of Totems, Coves & Kelp." 11(4),(July/August, 1983): 26-34. (Queen Charlotte Islands.)

469. Nordby, Will. "Orca!" 12(4), (July/August, 1984): 50-56,64-65. (Northeastern Vancouver Island.)

470. Parkin, Tom. "In the Wake of the War Canoe." 17(4),(August, 1989): 28-36. (Queen Charlotte Islands, South Moresby Island.)

471. Stalmaster, Mark, and Gladstone, Gail. "Canoeing the Circuit." 13(5), (September/October, 1985): 43-47. Bowron Lake Provincial Park.)

472. Thomas, George. "Short Strokes." 14(5), (October, 1986):43-47. (Vancouver Island, Barkley Sound.)

Labrador (LB)

473. Beebe, Rod. "Of Myths and Mountains." 10(2), (April,1982): 30-35. (Rivers: Korok, Stecker, Nachvak Fjord.)

Manitoba (MB)

474.Grewell, Kevin. "Bissett to the Bay." 14(3), (June,1986): 14-18. (Rivers: Gods, Hayes, Severn.)

Northwest Territories (NT)

475.Davidson, Jim, and Rugge, John. "The Great Canadian Wild Rivers Survey." 8(2), (March, 1980): 28-32. (Hanbury-Thelon rivers.)

476.Jacobson, Cliff. "Thirty-One Days to the Arctic Sea." 11(3), (May/June, 1983): 46-53. (Hood River.)

477.Lentz, John. "Paddling under the Pole." 14(3), (June 1986): 24-29. (Victoria Island, Kuujjua River.)

478.Rice, Larry. "On the Trail of the White Whales of Helluland." 16(4), (August 1988): 39-44. (Baffin Island,Cumberland Sound.)

Nova Scotia (NS)

479.Viehman, John. "On Tour in Nova Scotia." 12(2), (April 1984): 46-47, 50-51. (Rivers: Annapolis, Grand, Hebert, Liscomb,Margaree, Musquodoboit, Napier-Tusket, St. Mary's, Shubenacadie,Silver, Sissiboo, Stewiacke. Lakes: Molega, Ponhook.)

Ontario (ON)

480. Furtman, Michael. "Quetico." 16(5), (October, 1988):37-38, 50-51. (Quetico Provincial Park.)

481. Harrison, Dave. "Algonquin Park." 16(4), (August, 1988):23-27. (Algonquin Provincial Park.)

482. Jacobson, Cliff. "Little Boats and Long River Trips." 10(3), (May/June, 1982): 50-51, 53, 55-57. (Steel River, Lakes:Cairngorm, Santoy, Steel.)

483.Rice, Larry. "Pukaskwa." 15(5), (October, 1987): 36-39,70-71. (Pukaskwa National Park.)

484.Rice, Larry. "Short Strokes." 15(4), (August, 1987):40-42. Killarney Provincial Park.)

485.U'Ren, Janet. "Three Canals: Rideau Canal." 15(1), (March,1987): 15-17, 69.

486.Vickery, Jim dale. "The Wabakimi-Kopka Capers." 12(4),(July/August, 1984): 34-40. (Wabakimi Provincial Park, KopkaRiver.)

Quebec (PQ)

487.Coursey, Bill. "A Month of Mecatina Madness." (13 (1)(February/March, 1985): 46-52. (Petit Mecatina River.)

Saskatchewan (SK)

488.Jacobson, Cliff. "Canoeing for Trophy Fish." 16 (3)(July, 1988): 49-52, 62-63. (Cree River, Cree Lake.)

Yukon Territory (YT)

489.Dappen, Andy. "Spell of the Yukon." 17 (3) (July, 1989):40-45. (Rivers: Yukon, and a score of others in a generaloverview.)

490.Harrison, Dave. "From the Mountains to the Sea." 15 (4)(August, 1987): 14-17. (Rivers: Ogilvie, Peel.)

491.Harrison, Dave. "The Yukon's Hyland River." 17 (3) (July,1989): 28-31, 37-39.

492.Steere, Mike. "Blind Date with a Lake." 17 (3) (July,1989): 24-25, 86. (Delayee Lake.)

United States, National and Regional

493.Evans, Eric. "The Outer Limits." 9(4), (June/ July, 1981):38-44. (Rivers: West Branch Penobscot (ME), Hudson (NY), Gauley (WV), Ocoee (TN), Presque Isle (MI), Arkansas (CO), Bruneau (ID), Klamath (OR-CA), Tuolumne (CA), West Branch Magpie (PQ).

494.Hostetter, Ginny. "Traveling Inn to Inn by Canoe." 13(1),(February/March, 1985): 38-45. (Streams in NH, VT).

495.Howells, James. "Short Strokes." 15(2), (May, 1987):22-24. (Virgin River AZ-UT).

496.Kemmer, Rick. "Short Strokes." 15(6), (December 1987):116-117. (Caddo Lake LA-TX).

497.Lansing, Phil. "Short Strokes." 17(6), (December 1989):127-129. (Owyhee River (ID-NV-OR).

498.Oakley, Glenn. "Rodeo River." 12(1), (February/March,1984): 40-46. (Owyhee River (ID-NV-OR).

499.Ray, Slim. "Classic Rivers" 17(2), (May, 1989): 22-27,93-95. (Rivers: Arkansas (CO), Buffalo (AR), Chattooga(GA-NC-SC), Colorado (Middle) (UT), New (NC-VA-WV), Obed-Emory(TN), Ocoee (TN), Potomac & Shenandoah (VA, MD), Rio Grande (TX),Salmon (ID).

500.Rice, Larry. "After the Siege." 9(5), (August/ September,1981): 38-41. (Rivers: Namekagon (WI), St. Croix (WI-MN).

501.Rice, Larry. "The Land of the Flying Goose: A Paddler'sGuide to Five National Wildlife Refuges." 14(2), (May, 1986):41-46. (Refuges: Havasu, Cibola and Imperial (AZ-CA), Kenai(AK), Mingo (MO), Okefenokee (GA), Upper Mississippi(IL-IA-MN-WI).

502.Rice, Larry. "Winter's Paddling Getaways." 17(5),(October, 1989): 36-39, 51, 70. (Rivers: Colorado (Lower)(AZ-CA), Peace, and a general overview of a dozen other Floridastreams (FL), Suwannee (FL-GA), Rio Grande (Lower) (TX), Coastalareas: Baja California (MX), Gulf Islands National Seashore, Gulfof Mexico (AL, FL, MS), Swamps: Everglades National Park (FL),Okefenokee National Wildlife Refuge (GA).

United States, By State

Alabama (AL)

503.Fears, J. Wayne. "West Fork Sipsey River." 8(2), (March,1980): 20.

504.McCafferty, Jim. "Short Strokes." 14(3), (June, 1986):46-49. (Locust Fork of the Warrior River.)

Alaska (AK)

505.Jacobs, Syd. "Frolic under a Midnight Sun." 13(3), (May/June, 1985): 53-60. (Prince William Sound.)

506.Rennicke, Jeff. "Travels on the Kobuk River." 15(3),(June, 1987): 18-21, 76.

507.Rice, Larry. "Four Alaskas to Paddle." 15(3), (June,1987): 14-17, 83, 87. (Areas: Southeast, Southcentral/Gulf Coast, Interior and Northern, Southwest).

508.Rice, Larry. "Glacier Bay." 9(4), (June/July, 1981):26-31.

509.Rice, Larry. "Katmai!" 11(6), (November/ December, 1983):116-125. (Katmai Peninsula.)

510.Sharrard, Sally. "Wilderness Passage." 8(6), (November,1980): 12-16, 57. (Fortymile River.)

511.Steere, Mike. "Short Strokes." 15(3), (June, 1987):36-39. (Admiralty Island.)

Arizona (AZ)

512.Callanan, Tom. "Short Strokes." 14(6), (December, 1986):10, 101. (Verde River.)

513.Kinkade, Randal S. "Short Strokes." 14(1), (March, 1986):25-27. (Salt River Project Lakes.)

Arkansas (AR)

514.Mills, Mike. "Arkansas' Big Ten Rivers." 8(1), (February1980): 58-61. (Rivers: Big Piney, Buffalo, Caddo, Cossatot,Illinois Bayou, Little Missouri, Mulberry, North Cadron,Ouachita, Spring.)

California (CA)

515.Getchell, Dave. "Short Strokes." 14(1), (March, 1986):20-22. (Salmon River.)

516.Hoobyar, Paul. "Joocin' in the Mother Lode." 11(3),(May/June, 1983): 38-45. (Tuolumne River.)

Colorado (CO)

517.Rennicke, Jeff. "Going the Gorge." 12(3), (May/June,1984): 66-70, 74-75. (Gunnison River.)

518.Rennicke, Jeff. "Short Strokes." 13(3), (May/June, 1985):75-76. (Colorado River-Westwater Canyon.)

519.Rennicke, Jeff. "Short Strokes." 16(4), (August, 1988):53-54. (South Fork South Platte River.)

Connecticut (CT)

520.Beebe, Rod. "The Farmington." 12(1), (February/March,1984): 31-38.

521.Beebe, Rod. "Short Strokes." 14(4), (August, 1986):49-50. (Shepaug River.)

Florida (FL)

522.Gluckman, David. "Short Strokes." 14(5), (October, 1986):39-40. (Big Bend Coast.)

523.Martell, Scott. "The Majestic Everglades." 16(6),(December, 1986): 16, 103-107, 109-110.

524.Wilson, Joyce. "As You Like It." 9(1), January/February,1981): 38-39, 52. (Hillsborough River.)

Georgia (GA)

525.Hulslander, Vic. "Watergate Rescinded." 8(6), (November,1980): 10-11, 58. (Flint River.)

526.Jacobs, Jimmy. "Short Strokes." 15(3), (June, 1987):40-41. (Etowah River.)

527.Pendergrast, Scott. "Canoes on a Golden Coast." 13(3),(May/June, 1985): 62-68. (Islands: Blackbeard, St. Catharine's Sapelo.)

Hawaii (HI)

528.Karasic, Keith. "Short Strokes." 16(1), (March, 1988):14-16. (Molokai Coast.)

Idaho (ID)

529.Shepard, John G. "Short Strokes." 16(2), (May, 1988):48-51. (Big Creek, Middle Fork of the Salmon River.)

Illinois (IL)

530.Rice, Larry. "Enter the Prairie." 8(4), (July, 1980):36-40. (Rivers: Apple, Big Muddy, Cache, Chicago, Des Plaines,Embarras, Fox, Green, Illinois, Iroquois, Kankakee, Kaskaskia,Little Vermillion, Little Wabash, Mackinaw, Middle Fork-SouthVermillion, Pecatonia, Rock, Saline, Salt Creek, Sangamon, ShoalCreek, Skokie Lagoons, Spoon, Vermilion.)531.Rice, Larry. "Paddling to Peoria." 13(2), (April, 1985):40-43, 46. (Illinois River.)

532.Rice, Larry. "Short Strokes." 17(1), (March, 1989):24-25, 63-65. (Middle Fork of the Vermilion River, KickapooState Park.)

Iowa (IA)

533.Rice, Larry. "Canyons in the Iowa Corn." 11(1),(February/March, 1983): 30-35. (Upper Iowa River.)

Maine (ME)

534.Henry, Kathryn. "The Family That Paddles Together." 10(2), (April, 1982): 40-44. (Machias Lakes.)

535.Miller, Dorcas. "Short Strokes." 13(3), (May/June, 1985):76-77. (AMC Coastal Canoe Trail-Kennebec River, Beal Island.)

Maryland (MD)

536.Badger, Curtis. "Short Strokes." 15(6), (December, 1987):118-119, 124, 127-128. (Pocomoke River.)

537.Gertler, Ed, and Metzger, Pat. "All You Can Paddle." 8(6), (November, 1980): 60-63. (Rivers: Antietam Creek, Catoctin,Conocheague Creek, Deer Creek, Gunpowder Falls, Monocacy, NorthBranch

Potomac, Octoraro Creek, Patauxent, Pocomoke, Potomac,Savage, Sideling Hill Creek, Town Creek, Youghiogheny.)538.Stanton, Dick. "Three Canals: C & O Canal." 15(1),(March, 1987): 18-19.

Massachusetts (MA)

539.Scheller, Bill. "Short Strokes." 13(5),(September/October, 1985): 60-61. (Ipswich River.)

Michigan (MI)

540.Dennis, Jerry. "Short Strokes." 14(3), (June, 1986):40-42. (Little Manistee River.)

541.Rice, Larry. "Islands of Magic." 12(3), (May/June, 1984):46-54. (Isle Royal National Park, Lake Superior.)

542.Rice, Larry. "Short Strokes." 13(5), (September/October,1985): 62-63. (Sylvania Recreation Area-Upper Peninsula.)

Minnesota (MN)

543.Breining, Greg, and Sames, Wayne. "Glacial Groovin'." 8(2), (March, 1980): 34-38. (Rivers: Baptism, Big Fork, BlueEarth, Brule, Cannon, Cloquet, Crow Wing, Kettle, Little Fork,Lower Tamarack, Minnesota, Mississippi, Nemadji, Pine, Root, Rum,Sturgeon, St. Croix, St. Louis, Snake, Vermilion, Whiteface,Zumbro.)

544.Shepard, John. "Short Strokes." 14(1), (March, 1986):22-24. (Minehaha Creek.)

545.Vickery, Jim dale. "In a Land of Rocks and Water." 11(2),(April, 1983): 32-38. (Boundary Waters Canoe Area.)

546.Vickery, Jim dale. "Short Strokes." 13(4), (July/August,1985): 34-35. (Big Fork River.)

Missouri (MO)

547.Rice, Larry. "Journey to Owls Bend." 10(5),(September/October, 1982): 30-35. (Ozark National ScenicRiverways. Rivers: Current, Jacks Fork.)

548.Rice, Larry. "Short Strokes." 14(2), (May, 1986): 37-39. (Eleven Point River.)

Montana (MT)

549.Amstutz, Lynn. "Short Strokes." 14(5), (October, 1986):41-43. (North Fork of the Flathead River.)

550.Fischer, Hank. "Yellowstone." 8(5), (September, 1980):22-25. (Yellowstone River.)

551.Poe, Anne. "Short Strokes." 14(2), (May, 1986): 32-33. (Clark Fork River-Alberton Gorge.)

Nebraska (NE)

552.Rice, Larry. "Niobrara River." 15(4), (August, 1987):20-23, 56-58.

New Jersey (NJ)

553.Higgins, Ed. "Three Canals: Delaware & Raritan Canal." 15(1), (March, 1987): 19-22.

554.Scheller, Bill. "Urban Renewal." 13(4), (July/August,1985): 52-57. (Passaic River.)

555.von Dobeneck, Monica. "Short Strokes." 17(1), (March,1989): 22-23, 62-63. (Pine Barrens, Wharton State Forest.)

New York (NY)

556.Gullion, Laurie. "Short Strokes." 13(6),(November/December, 1985): 8. (Raquette River.)

557.LaBastille, Anne. "Jewel of the Adirondacks." 10(2),(April, 1982): 24-29. (St. Regis Canoe Area.)

558.Roberts, Harry. "On Harry's River." 11(5),(September/October, 1983): 42-47. (Mohawk River.)

559.Scheller, Bill "Bobbing for the Big Apple." 14(4),(August, 1986): 20-24. (Manhattan Island.)

560.Tenney, John. "Short Strokes." 15(2), (May, 1987): 24-27. (Oswegatchie River.)

North Carolina (NC)

561.Ray, Slim. "Short Strokes." 13(3), (May/June, 1985):78-79. (Big Laurel Creek.)

North Dakota (ND)

562.Vickery, Jim dale. "Good Medicine in the Badlands." 11(5),(September/October, 1983): 32-40, 61. (Little Missouri River.)

Ohio (OH)

563.Combs, Rick, and Gillen, Steve. "Short Strokes." 13(4),(July/August, 1985): 32-33. (Little Beaver Creek.)

Oklahoma (OK)

564.Lantz, Gary. "Short Strokes." 14(6), (December, 1986):8-10. (Salt Creek.)

Pennsylvania (PA)

565.Palmer, Tim. "The Third Movement." 9(2), (March, 1981):56-58. (West Branch Susquehanna River.)

Tennessee (TN)

566.Morgan, Alan. "Short Strokes." 14(2), (May, 1986): 34-36. (Sequatchie River.)

567.Ray, Slim. "Short Strokes." 14(4), (August, 1986): 54-55. (Tellico River.)

Texas (TX)

568.Rice, Larry. "Canyon Cruising." 10(1), (March, 1982):32-33, 35-38. (Rio Grande.)

569.Rice, Larry. "In the (Big) Thick of It." 17(1), (March,1989): 18-21, 69. (Big Thicket National Preserve.)

Utah (UT)

570.Cross, Bill. "The Grand Canyon of San Juan." 16(6),(December, 1988): 10-12. (San Juan River.)

571.Rennicke, Jeff. "On a Trail of Thieves." 14(1), (March,1986): 63, 66-67. (Colorado River-Horsethief Canyon.)

Vermont (VT)

572.Wass, Stan. "Short Strokes." 16(3), (July, 1988): 46-48. (White River.)

Washington (WA)

573.Huser, Verne. "Two Sides to the Mountains." 8(3),(April/May, 1980): 38-44. (Lakes: Central Basin area, Chelan,Seattle area. Saltwater: Everett Harbor, Sequim Bay, San JuanIslands. Rivers: Cle Elum, Grande Ronde, Hoh, Humptulips,Klickitat, Methow, Nooksack, Okanogan, Queets, Quinault, Satsop,Sauk, Skagit, Skykomish, Snake, Snohomish, Snoqualmie, Spokane,Stillaguamish, Suiattle, Wenatchee, Yakima.)

574.Moyer, Lee. "Short Strokes." 14(3), (June, 1986): 42-43,46. (Winchester Wasteway, Potholes Reservoir.)

575.Rogers, Joel. "Short Strokes." 14(4), (August, 1986):51-53. (San Juan Islands.)

Wisconsin (WI)

576.Rennicke, Jeff. "Wisconsin's Fox River." 15(1), (March,1987): 22-25.

577.Rice, Larry. "Short Strokes." 16(3), (July, 1988): 44-45. (Horicon Marsh.)

578.Rice, Larry. "Where Whitewater and Quietwater Meet." 11(4), (July/August, 1983): 40-47. (Flambeau River.)

579.Shepard, John G. "Short Strokes." 15(1), (March, 1987):73-75. (Lake Superior, Apostle Islands.)

Wyoming (WY)

580.Furbush, Patty. "Short Strokes" 13(6),(November/December, 1985): 6-7. (Grand Teton National Park-SnakeRiver.)

581.Rice, Larry. "Safe in the Arms." 12(5),(September/October, 1984): 62-69. (Yellowstone National Park-Yellowstone Lake.)

Chapter 1, Section 5

Guidebooks and Articles

Maps and Map-Guides

CANADA

Alberta (AB)

582.CANOE ALBERTA. 1978. Single sheet, 96 x 51 cm., scale 1:1,500,000. Relief shown by shading. Gives physical characteristics of rivers, safety, list of clubs, etc. Available from: Travel Alberta; Alberta Canoe Association

British Columbia (BC)

583.BRITISH COLUMBIA CANOE ROUTES. 1974. Single sheet. Shows the top ten canoe routes in the province. Available from: Canadian Recreational Canoeing Association; National Organization for River Sports.

584.BRITISH COLUMBIA RECREATIONAL ATLAS. 19?? May still be available from: Ministry of Municipal Affairs, Recreation & Culture, Victoria, BC.

Labrador (LB)

585.NEWFOUNDLAND CANOEING INFORMATION. 19?? Not a map, but a guide to 17 routes and general canoeing information for Newfoundland and Labrador. Available from: Canadian Recreational Canoeing Association

Manitoba (MB)

586.CANOE TRIPS IN MANITOBA. 19?? Not itself a map, but a listing of how to obtain specific canoe maps for some 25 Manitoba trips. Available from: Canadian Recreational Canoeing Association

587.MANITOBA HISTORIC CANOE MAPS. 19?? Separate sheets. Over 13 maps of Manitoba fur trade routes give lore, legend, and history useful to canoeists. Waterways: Grass River, Kantunigan, Land of Little Sticks, Little Grand Rapids River, Mistik Creek, Winnipeg River, Assiniboine River, Oiseau-Manitotagan, Riviere aux Rats, Sasaginnigak, The Middle Track and Hayes, Waterhen Country, and Whitemouth River. Available from: Canadian Recreational Canoeing Association

New Brunswick (NB)

588.GUIDE TO CANOE RIVERS IN NEW BRUNSWICK. 19?? Outlines 26 canoe trips in the province. Includes information of preparation, access, portages, etc. Available from: Canadian Recreational Canoeing Association

Newfoundland (NF)

589.NEWFOUNDLAND CANOEING INFORMATION. 19?? Not a map, but a guide to 17 routes and general canoeing information for Newfoundland and Labrador. Available from: Canadian Recreational Canoeing Association

Northwest Territories (NT)

590.CANOEING AND BOATING IN THE NORTHWEST TERRITORIES: NAHANNI NATIONAL PARK. 19?? Includes the South Nahanni River. Available from: NT TravelArctic.

591.NWT GENERAL CANOEING INFORMATION. 19?? Materials about canoeing in the NWT including: northern trip planning; maps sources; 36 brief route summaries; and, a scale map of the canoe route areas. Available from: Canadian Recreational Canoeing Association

Nova Scotia (NS)

592.CANOE WATERWAYS OF NOVA SCOTIA, INDEX. 1988. Single sheet. 20 x 30 in. An index map to 44 Nova Scotia waterways which includes information on how to order individual strip maps for 16 of them. Available from: Nova Scotia Sport & Recreation Commission; Canadian Recreational Canoeing Association

Ontario (ON)

593.ALGONQUIN PROVINCIAL PARK CANOE ROUTES. 1987. Single Sheet. 95 x 94 cm. Scale 1:126,720. Includes a descriptive index to canoe routes. Available from: The Friends of Algonquin Park.

594.CANOE ROUTE: SIOUX LOOKOUT TO FORT HOPE ON THE ALBANY RIVER. 19?? A map-guide. Perhaps still available from: Ontario Ministry of Natural Resources.

595.CANOE ROUTES OF ONTARIO. 1981. Single Sheet. 109 x 77 cm. Scale 1:2,100,00. Includes textual material, indexes, illustrations, and a location map. Available from: Ontario Ministry of Natural Resources.

596.CHAPLEAU-NEMEGOSENDA PROVINCIAL WATERWAY PARK. 1983. A map-guide. Available from: Ontario Ministry of Natural Resources.

597.GULL RIVER SYSTEM. 19?? Single sheet. Available from: Canoe Ontario.

598.KILLARNEY PROVINCIAL PARK. 19?? Single sheet. Available from: Canoe Ontario.

599.LAKE TEMAGAMI "MINI MAP." 19?? Single sheet? Three-color map of the Temagami vacinity including campsites, portages, etc. Available from: Canadian Recreational Canoeing Association

600.MAGNETAWAN RIVER CANOE ROUTE. 1983. A map-guide covering the west part of the route. Available from: Ontario Ministry of Natural Resources.

601.MAPS OF NORTHERN MINNESOTA AND ONTARIO. 1990. Single sheet. 10 x 20 in. An index map and list of W.A. Fisher maps for the Superior-Quetico region. Available from: W.A. Fisher Co.

602.MATTAWA PROVINCIAL PARK. 19?? Map-guide. Available from: ON Min. of Natural Resources, Outdoor Recreation, Parks and Recreational Areas Br.

603.MISSINAIBI RIVER CANOE ROUTE. 1983. A map-guide to the section from Missinaibi Lake to Mattice; Mattice to Moosonee. Available from: Ontario Ministry of Natural Resources.

604.MISSISSAGI CANOE ROUTE. 1983. A map-guide covering Biscotasing to Aubrey Falls. Available from: Ontario Ministry of Natural Resources.

605.QUETICO PROVINCIAL PARK. 19?? Single sheet. Waterproof. Available from: Canoe Ontario.

606.RANKIN RIVER CANOE ROUTE. 19?? A map-guide. Perhaps still available from: Ontario Ministry of Natural Resources.

607.SPANISH RIVER CANOE ROUTE. 19?? A map-guide. Available from: Ontario Ministry of Natural Resources.

608.TEMAGAMI CANOE ROUTES. 1983. Single sheet? Map and brief route descriptions. Available from: Ontario Ministry of Natural Resources.

609.TEMAGAMI DISTRICT. 19?? Single sheet. Available from: Canoe Ontario.

Prince Edward Island (PE)

610.PRINCE EDWARD ISLAND CANOEING INFORMATION. 19?? A map-guide outlining 62 rivers, lakes, and coastal areas to paddle on P.E.I. Available from: Canadian Recreational Canoeing Association

Quebec (PQ)

611.QUEBEC CANOE ROUTES. (LES PARCOURS CONSTABLE DE QUEBEC). 19?? Single sheet? A map showing circa 110 canoe routes in the provence, produced by the Federation Quebecoise du Canot-Camping. Includes river classifications, campsites, access, etc. Available from: Canadian Recreational Canoeing Association

Saskatchewan (SK)

612.CANOE SASKATCHEWAN. 19?? Map-guide listing routes. Available from: SK Dept. of Economic Development & Tourism.

613.50 POPULAR CANOE ROUTES IN SASKATCHEWAN. 19?? A map-guide produced by Saskatchewan Parks & Renewable Resources describing over 50 canoe routes. Available from: Canadian Recreational Canoeing Association

614.LAC LA RONGE PROVINCIAL PARK. 19?? Information available from: Lac La Ronge Provincial Park Headquarters, Box 5000, La Ronge, SK S0J 1L0.

615.PRINCE ALBERT NATIONAL PARK. 19?? Information available from: Princ Albert National Park Headquarters, Box 100, Waskesin, SK S0J 2Y0.

616.SASKATCHEWAN CANOE TRIPS. 19?? General title for a series of individual map-guides of some 50 trips. Available from: SK Dept. of Economic Development & Tourism.

617.SASKATCHEWAN OUTDOOR ADVENTURE GUIDE. 19?? A map-guide listing, among other related things, 74 Provincial canoe routes. Possibly available from: SK Dept. of Economic Development & Tourism.

Yukon Territory (YT)

618.RIVER ROUTES OF THE YUKON. 19?? Single sheet? Forty-one paddling routes in the Yukon. Published by the Yukon Voyageurs Paddling Club. Available from: Canadian Recreational Canoeing Association

UNITED STATES

Alabama (AL)

619.Foshee, John H. MAP OF LITTLE RIVER CANYON, GRAND CANYON OF THE SOUTH. 1970. Single sheet. 42 x 55 cm. Scale: 1:20,000. Includes a location map. Availability unknown.

Alaska (AK)

620.ALASKA CANOE TRAILS. 19?? A dozen paddling routes in a map-guide. Available from: Kenai National Moose Range, P.O. Box 500, Kenai, AK 99611.

621.ALASKA'S WILD AND SCENIC RIVERS. 198? A map-guide produced by the Bureau of Land Management. Available from: BLM (Superintendent of Documents).

622.CANOEING IN THE KENAI NATIONAL WILDLIFE REFUGE. 19?? Map-guide. Available from: Kenai National Wildlife Refuge, P.O. Box 2139, Soldatna, AK 99669

623.Weaverling, Charles K. KAYAK ROUTES AND CAMPING BEACHES IN WESTERN AND CENTRAL PRINCE WILLIAM SOUND, ALASKA. 1987. Single sheet. 19 x 19 in. This map marks routes, distances of open-water legs, and camping beaches. Covers the Sound from Valdez to Whittier, and south to Ressurection Bay. Scale 1 in. equals about 6 mi. Available from: Wild Rose Guidebooks.

Arizona (AZ)

624.Stevens, Larry. GRAND CANYON. 19?? Strip-map of the Colorado River in Grand Canyon. Available from: National Organization for River Sports.

625.THE HEART OF THE GRAND CANYON. 19?? Single sheet? A map of the Grand Canyon. Available from: National Geographic Society.

626.LEES FERRY: A RECREATIONAL MAP TO THE LEES FERRY AREA. 19?? Single sheet. 22 x 27 in. Trails, rapids and river miles keyed to descriptions. Availability unknown.

627.COLORADO RIVER GUIDE. 19?? River map-guide. Available from: Grand Canyon Natural History Association

Arkansas (AR)

628.Boyles, F. THE BUFFALO RIVER, ARKANSAS. 1962. Single sheet. 50 x 77 cm. Scale 1:200,000. Produced by the Arkansas Game & Fish Commission. Includes mileage, notes, and location map.

629.BUFFALO NATIONAL RIVER: OFFICIAL MAP AND GUIDE. 1986. Single sheet. 40 x 42 cm. Available from: the National Park Service (Superintendent of Documents).

630.Clark, Fogle C. BUFFALO NATIONAL RIVER GUIDE. 1981. Single sheet (double-sided). A color map with text describing access, hazards, fishing, etc. Available from: American Canoe Assoc.

631.OUACHITA RIVER FLOAT TRIP. 19?? Guide with a separate map. Available from: Headquarters, Ouachita National Forest, Hot Springs, AR 71901.

California (CA)

632.Cassidy, Jim, and Calhoun, Fryar. FORKS OF THE KERN. 1983. Single sheet, waterproof paper, plastic case. Little Kern confluence to Johnsondale Bridge, Class V, 17 miles. Available from: American Canoe Association; National Org. for River Sports.

633.Cassidy, Jim, and Calhoun, Fryar. LOWER KERN RIVER. 1983. Single sheet, waterproof paper, plastic case. Mail Dam Campground (Isabella Reservoir) to Democrat Picnic Area, Class IV, 18 miles. Available from: ACA; National Org. for River Sports.

634.Cassidy, Jim, and Calhoun, Fryar. SOUTH FORK AMERICAN. 1983. Single sheet, waterproof paper, plastic case. Chili Bar to Salmon Falls Bridge, 20 miles. Available from: ACA; National Org. for River Sports.

635.Cassidy, Jim, and Calhoun, Fryar. TUOLUMNE RIVER. 1983. Single sheet, waterproof paper, plastic case. Lumsden Campground to Ward's Ferry, Class IV, 18 miles. Available from: ACA; National Org. for River Sports.

636.Cassidy, Jim, and Calhoun, Fryar. UPPER KERN RIVER. 1983. Single sheet, waterproof paper, plastic case. Johnsondale Bridge to Kernville, Class II-V, 19 miles. Available from: ACA; National Org. for River Sports.

637.INFORMATION GUIDE TO WHITEWATER BOATING: SOUTH FORK OF THE AMERICAN RIVER. Available from: El Dorado Planning Dept., 360 Fair Ln., Placerville, CA 95667

638.Nealy, William. AMERICAN RIVER, SOUTH FORK. Single sheet, 18 x 35 in. In the Nealy poster style, Chili Bar to Camp Lotus. Available from: Menasha Ridge Press.

639.Nealy, William. AMERICAN RIVER, SOUTH FORK. Single sheet, 18 x 35 in. In the Nealy poster style, Camp Lotus to Folsum Lake. Available from: Menasha Ridge Press.

640.NORTHERN CALIFORNIA ATLAS & GAZETTEER. 198? Topographic road maps (contour interval 100 meters, Scale 1:150,000). The gazetteer has map-keyed descriptions of parks, bicycle routes campgrounds, wineries, hiking, fishing, wildlife, canoe trips, and much more. Available from: DeLorme Mapping Co.

641.SOUTHERN CALIFORNIA ATLAS & GAZETTEER. 198? Topographic road maps (contour interval 100 meters, Scale 1:150,000). The gazetteer has map-keyed descriptions of parks, bicycle routes campgrounds, wineries, hiking, fishing, wildlife, canoe trips, and much more. Available from: DeLorme Mapping Co.

Colorado (CO)

642.Cassady, Jim, and Calhoun, Fryar. LOWER ARKANSAS. 19?? Single sheet (waterproof). Gives descriptions of each rapid from Salida to Canyon City. Available from: Colorado Kayak Supply; National Organization for River Sports.

643.Cassady, Jim, and Calhoun, Fryar. UPPER ARKANSAS. 19?? Single sheet (waterproof). Gives descriptions of each rapid from Granite to Salida. Available from: Colorado Kayak Supply; National Organization for River Sports.

644.Nealy, William. BROWN'S CANYON OF THE ARKANSAS. 19?? Single sheet. 18 x 35 in. In the Nealy poster style. Available from: Menasha Ridge Press.

645.THE UPPER COLORADO RIVER: KREMMLING TO SHOSHONE. 198? A map-guide with the cover subtitle: "River of Changing Landscapes." Available from: the BLM (Superintendent of Documents).

Connecticut (CT)

646.CANOEING IN CONNECTICUT. 19?? Map-guide. Available from: CT Environmental Protection Dept., Parks & Forestry Br.

647.A GUIDE FOR THE CANOEIST ON THE FARMINGTON. 1969. Single sheet. 48 x 39 cm. Scale 1:100,000. Shows points of interest. Relief shown by hachures. Available from: Farmington River Watershed Association

Florida (FL)

648.FLORIDA ATLAS & GAZETTEER. 198? Topographic road maps (contour interval 100 meters, Scale 1:150,000). The gazetteer has map-keyed descriptions of parks, bicycle routes campgrounds, wineries, hiking, fishing, wildlife, canoe trips, and much more. Available from: DeLorme Mapping Co.

649.DeLorge, John O. WEST FLORIDA CANOE TRAIL GUIDE: PERDIDO RIVER, BLACKWATER RIVER AND TRIBUTARIES, YELLOW AND SHOAL RIVERS, ECONFINA RIVER AND HOLMES CREEK. 1978. 3 single sheets. 92 x 61 cm. Scale 1: 125,000. Covers Pensacola region. Relief shown by spot heights. Includes text, index map and color illustrations. Available from: American Canoe Association

650.EVERGLADES NATIONAL PARK CANOE TRAIL GUIDE. 19?? Map-guide. Available from: Everglades National Park, P.O. Box 279, Homestead, FL 33030

651.FLORIDA CANOE TRAIL GUIDE. 19?? Sixteen routes described; a supplement describes eight more. Maps. Available from: FL Natural Resources Dept., Recreation and Parks Div.

652.GUIDE TO FLORIDA CANOEING RIVERS. 19?? Guide to 35 canoe trails. Index map and trail descriptions. Available from: FL Natural Resources Dept.

653.SUWANNEE RIVER CANOE MAP. 19?? Single sheet. 17 x 22 in. Access to the river at 47 points between Fargo, GA and the Gulf. Available from: Suwannee River Water Mgmt. Dist., P.O. Drawer K, White Spring, FL

Georgia (GA)

654.CANOEING THE CHATTOOGA. 19?? Available from: USFS, Sumpter National Forest, Star Route, Walhalla, SC 29691.

655.CHATTOOGA NATIONAL WILD AND SCENIC RIVER. 19?? Available from: USFS, Sumpter National Forest, Star Route, Walhalla, SC 29691.

656.Masters, Bill, and Masters, Judy. RIVER RUNNERS GUIDE TO THE CHATTOOGA. 19?? Single sheet (waterproof). Detailed, annotated map. Available from: American Canoe Association

657.Nealy, William. CHATTAHOOCHEE RIVER, LOWER SECTION. 19?? Single sheet. 18 x 35 in. A poster-map drawn in the inimitable Nealy cartoon manner. Available from: Menasha Ridge Press.

658.Nealy, William. CHATTAHOOCHEE RIVER, UPPER SECTION. 19?? Single sheet. 18 x 35 in. A poster-map drawn in the inimitable Nealy cartoon manner. Available from: Menasha Ridge Press.

659.Nealy, William. CHATTOOGA (SECTION IV). 19?? Single sheet. 18 x 35 in. A poster-map drawn in the inimitable Nealy cartoon manner. Available from: Menasha Ridge Press.

660.Nealy, William. CHATTOOGA (SECTION III). 19?? Single sheet. 18 x 35 in. A poster-map drawn in the inimitable Nealy cartoon manner. Available from: Menasha Ridge Press.

661.Rathnow, Ron. CHATTOOGA RIVER, SECTION 4. 19?? Waterproof flip-map. Available from: Menasha Ridge Press.

662.RIVER RUNNERS GUIDE TO THE CHATTOOGA RIVER. 19?? Waterproof scroll map. Available from: ACA

663.WILDERNESS CANOEING IN OKEFENOKEE NATIONAL WILDLIFE REFUGE. 19?? Map-guide showing 6 trails in the Swamp. Available from: Okefenokee National Wildlife Refuge, Rt. 2 Box 338, Folkston, GA 31537

Idaho (ID)

664.RIVER OF NO RETURN. 19?? Single sheet (waterproof). A Backeddy Books publication covering the Main Salmon. Available from: Backeddy Books; National Organization for River Sports.

665.A RIVER RUNNER'S GUIDE TO IDAHO. 19?? Describes 16 river systems, and gives information on campsites, difficulty, etc. Available from: ID Parks and Recreation Dept.

666.THE SALMON: RIVER OF NO RETURN. 1986. Single sheet. Published by the USFS, Northern and Inter-mountain regions. Available from: Superintendent of Documents.

667.SNAKE RIVER OF HELLS CANYON. 19?? Single sheet (waterproof). 16 x 21 in. Hells Canyon Dam to Heller Bar, 81 miles. A Backeddy Books publication. Available from BackeddyBooks; Westwater Books.

668.WATERWAYS OF THE LOWER COEUR D'ALENE RIVER. 19?? A map-guide of the marshes and lakes of the lower river. May still be available from: Superintendent of Documents.

Iowa (IA)

669.IOWA CANOE TRIPS. 19?? A map-guide to about 20 rivers. Available from IA Natural Resources Dept.

Kansas (KS)

670.ARKANSAS RIVER. 1990. Single sheet. 9 x 16 in. Two maps covering Raymond to Hutchinson. One of a series of mimeographed map-guides. Available from: Kansas Canoe Association, Box 2885, Wichita, KS 67201.

671.FALL RIVER. 1990. Single sheet. 9 x 16 in. Covers Hwy. K-99 bridge to Climax boat ramp. One of a series of mimeographed map-guides. Available from: Kansas Canoe Association, Box 2885, Wichita, KS 67201.

672.GROUSE CREEK. 1990. Single sheet. 9 x 16 in. Covers Silverdale to Arkansas River. One of a series of map-guides. Available from: Kansas Canoe Association, Box 2885, Wichita, KS 67201.

673.KANSAS RIVER. 1990. Single sheet. 9 x 16 in. Three maps covering K-77 bridge to Burcham Park access at Lawrence. One of a series of mimeographed map-guides. Available from: Kansas Canoe Association, Box 2885, Wichita, KS 67201.

674.KANSAS STREAMS. 19?? Map-guide. Available from: KS Wildlife and Parks Dept.

675.LITTLE BLUE & BIG BLUE RIVERS. 1990. Single sheet. 9 x 16 in. Covers Marshall-Washington county line to Irving bridge. One of a series of mimeographed map-guides. Available from: Kansas Canoe Association, Box 2885, Wichita, KS 67201.

676.MARAIS DES CYGNES RIVER. 1990. Single sheet. 9 x 16 in. Two maps covering from Miami County State Lake to Marais des Cygnes Waterfowl Management Area. One of a series of mimeographed map-guides. Available from: Kansas Canoe Association, Box 2885, Wichita, KS 67201.

677.REPUBLICAN RIVER CANOE TRAIL. 1990. Single sheet. 9 x 16 in. From US 81 to the old Burlington bridge. One of a series of mimeographed map-guides. Available from: Kansas Canoe Association, Box 2885, Wichita, KS 67201.

678.SMOKY HILL RIVER. 1990. Single sheet. 9 x 16 in. Covers six miles of the river near Kanopolis, KS. One of a series of mimeographed map-guides. Available from: Kansas Canoe Association, Box 2885, Wichita, KS 67201.

Kentucky (KY)

679.DANIEL BOONE NATIONAL FOREST. 19?? Map-guide. Available from: Daniel Boone Nat. Forest, 100 Vaught Rd., Winchester, KY 40391.

Maine (ME)

680.ALLAGASH AND ST. JOHN. 1984. Single sheet? A DeLorme product showing access, campsites, etc. In color. Available from: American Canoe Association

681.ALLAGASH WILDERNESS WATERWAY. 19?? Illustrated map-guide, with information on access, etc. Available from: ME Conservation Dept., Parks and Recreation Bureau.

682.ESCAPE TO ME. 19?? Map-guide to flatwater canoeing. Available from: ME Economic and Community Development Office.

683.MAINE ATLAS & GAZETTEER. 198? Topographic road maps (contour interval 100 meters, Scale 1:150,000). The gazetteer has map-keyed descriptions of parks, bicycle routes, campgrounds, wineries, hiking, fishing, wildlife, canoe trips, and much more. Available from: DeLorme Mapping Co.

684.WILD ME. 19?? Map-guide to whitewater. Available from: ME Economic and Community Development Office.

Maryland (MD)

685.CHESAPEAKE CANOE TRAILS. 19?? Map-guide outlining access and camping along the Choptank River and Tuckahoe Creek. Available from: Tourism Council of the Upper Chesapeake, P.O. Box 66, Centerville, MD 21617

686.GUIDE TO THE POTOMAC RIVER FALL LINE RAPIDS: SENECA TO WASHINGTON, DC. River Maps Ltd. 1983. Single sheet. Map and paddling guuide to the urban Potomac River; 18 mi. with rapids ranging from Class I/II to VI. Available from: American Canoe Association

687.HIKER'S GUUIDE TO THE C&O CANAL. 19?? A map-guide aimed at walkers, but useful for paddlers. Available from: Mason-Dixon Council of Boy Scouts, 1200 Crestwood Dr., Hagerstown, MD 21740.

688.Nealy, William. SAVAGE RIVER. 19?? Single sheet. 18 x 35 in. A poster-map in the Nealy manner: amusing, yet accurate. Available from: Menasha Ridge Press.

689.THE POTOMAC RIVER AND THE C&O CANAL. 19?? Five strip-maps in color. Available from: Interstate Commission on the Potomac River Basin.

Massachusetts (MA)

690.SOME FLATWATER CANOEING SUGGESTIONS. 19?? Map-guide describing runs on 8 rivers in MA and surrounding states. Available from: Appalachian Mountain Club.

Michigan (MI)

691.MICHIGAN ATLAS & GAZETTEER. 198? Topographic road maps (contour interval 100 meters, Scale 1:150,000). The gazetteer has map-keyed descriptions of parks, bicycle routes, campgrounds, wineries, hiking, fishing, wildlife, canoe trips, and much more. Available from: DeLorme Mapping Co.

692.MICHIGAN CANOE TRAILS. 19?? Map-guide. Available from: MI Natural Resources Dept., Recreation Div.

693.MICHIGAN GUIDE TO EASY CANOEING. 19?? Map-guide. Available from: MI Natural Resources Dept.

694.WEST MICHIGAN CANOE MAP. 19?? Map-guide. Available from: West Michigan Tourist Association, 136 Fulton E., Grand Rapids, MI 49503.

Minnesota (MN)

695.BOUNDARY WATERS CANOE AREA WILDERNESS MAPS. 1982? Single sheet, waterproof ink, printed on polyolefin plastic. Twenty-one BWCAW maps on a scale of 2 in. to 1 mi. (144 sq. mi. per sheet), contours, campsites, portages, and hiking trails. Available from: McKenzie Maps.

696.KETTLE RIVER CANOE ROUTE. 1986. Single sheet. 12 x 16 in. One of a series of small sheet maps of Minnesota waterways giving access, campsites, rapids, etc., on the map and descriptive information on the verso. Available from: Minnesota Dept. of Natural Resources.

697.MAPS OF NORTHERN MINNESOTA AND ONTARIO. 198? Single sheet. SHEET. 10 X 20 IN. A map index to 30 sheet maps of the Superior-Quetico region. Available from: W.A. Fisher Co., Box 1107, Virginia, MN 55792.

698.Miles, Catherine, and Yaeger, Donald. MINNESOTA OUTDOOR ATLAS. 1979. A large spiral-bound work with maps, photographs, and descriptions of the 10,000 lakes and 25,000 miles of rivers. May still be available from: Minnesota Outdoor Atlas, 3790 Northome Rd., Wayzata, MN 55391.

699.ROOT RIVER CANOE & BOATING ROUTE MAP. Single sheet. 18 x 24 in. Section from Chatfield to the Mississippi confluence. Gives access, campsites, etc. on the map, and descriptive text and photographs on the verso. Available from: Minnesota Dept. of Natural Resources.

700.RUM RIVER CANOE ROUTE. 1987. Single sheet. 12 x 16 in. One of a series of small sheet maps of Minnesota waterways giving access, campsites, rapids, etc., on the map and descriptive information on the verso. Available from: Minnesota Dept. of Natural Resources.

701.VERMILION RIVER CANOE ROUTE. 1986. Single sheet. 12 x 16 in. One of a series of small sheet maps of Minnesota waterways giving access, campsites, rapids, etc., on the map and descriptive information on the verso. Available from: Minnesota Dept. of Natural Resources.

Mississippi (MS)

702.MISSISSIPPI RIVERS AND STREAMS. 19?? Map-guide of canoeing waters. Available from: MS Natural Resources Dept.

Missouri (MO)

703.CANOEING IN NORTHERN MISSOURI. 19?? Map-guide. Available from: MO Natural Resources Dept.

704.CURRENT RIVER. 19?? Single sheet? Map of the river. Available from: S.G. Adams Printing.

705.JACKS FORK RIVER. 19?? Single sheet? Map of the river. Available from: S.G. Adams Printing.

706.ST. FRANCIS RIVER. 19?? Single sheet? Available from: Liquid Pleasure Press, 6633 San Bonita Dr., St. Louis, MO 63105.

Montana (MT)

707.BLACKFOOT RIVER GUIDE. 1982? Single sheet. Forest Service map? Available from: Superintendent of Documents.

708.THE FLOATER'S GUIDE. 19?? Map-guide. Available from: Forest Service, P.O. Box 7669, Missoula, MT 59807.

709.MISSOURI RIVER GUIDE. 1982? Single sheet. Forest Service map? From Holter Lake to Great Falls. Available from: Superintendent of Documents.

710.MONTANA AFLOAT: ENJOYING MONTANA'S RIVERS. 1987. Single sheet. 9 x 24 in. A series of color maps of the Big Sky's major floatable streams based on USGS quads. First three published: Bitterroot, Blackfoot, and Madison rivers. Includes river miles, access hazards, etc. Available from: American Canoe Association

711.MONTANA'S POPULAR FLOAT STREAMS. 19?? Map-guide about canoeable parts of 23 rivers. Available from: MT Fish, Wildlife and Parks Dept., Fisheries Div.

712.WILD AND SCENIC MISSOURI RIVER. 19?? Map-guide. Bureau of Land Mgmt., P.O. Box 30157, Billings, MT 59107.

Nebraska (NE)

713.CANOEING IN NEBRASKA. 19?? Map-guide. Available from: NE Game and Parks Comm., Recreation Div.

714.NEBRASKA CANOE TRAILS. 19?? Map-guide describing 7 major river runs on the : Upper Calamus, Republican, Elkhorn, Dismal, Platte, and North Platte rivers. Available from: NE Game and Parks Comm., Recreation Div.

New Hampshire (NH)

715.CANOEING. 19?? Map-guide about 7 rivers. Available from: White Mountain Region Association, 5 Middle St., Lancaster, NH 03584.

716.CANOEING ON THE CONNECTICUT RIVER. 19?? Map-guide on the river and surroundings. Available from: New England Power Co., 9 Court St., Lebanon, NH 03766.

717.NEW HAMPSHIRE ATLAS & GAZETTEER. 198? Topographic road maps (contour interval 100 meters, Scale 1:150,000). The gazetteer has map-keyed descriptions of parks, bicycle routes, campgrounds, wineries, hiking, fishing, wildlife, canoe trips, and much more. Available from: DeLorme Mapping Co.

718.SUMMER CANOEING AND KAYAKING IN THE WHITE MOUNTAINS OF NEW HAMPSHIRE. 19?? Map-guide. Available from: NH Fish and Game Dept.

New Jersey (NJ)

719.CANOEING IN NEW JERSEY. 19?? Map-guide. Available from: NJ Environmental Protection Dept., Green Acres and Recreation Div.

720.CANOEING THE PINELANDS RIVERS. 19?? Fold-out map of 12 runs. Available from: NJ Environmental Protection Dept., Fish, Game & Wildlife Div.

New Mexico (NM)

721.Cassady, Jim, and Calhoun, Fryar. RIO GRANDE RIVER GUIDE. 19?? Single sheet (waterproof). Eight runs from Lobatos bridge to Velarde (including Taos Box). Available from: National Organization for River Sports.

722.Lopez, John. THE RIO GRANDE. 19?? Single sheet? Poster map. Available from: Colorado Kayak Supply, P.O. Box 3059, Buena Vista, CO 81211.

723.RAFTING, KAYAKING AND CANOEING ON THE RIO GRANDE AND CHAMA RIVERS. 19?? Map-guide. Available from: NM Energy, Minerals and Natural Resources Dept., Park and Recreation Div.

724.RIO GRANDE WILD RIVER. 19?? Map-guide. Available from: Bureau of Land Mgmt., P.O. Box 1449, Santa Fe, NM 87501

New York (NY)

725.ADIRONDACK CANOE ROUTES. 19?? Map-guide with planning map. Available from: NY Environmental Conservation Dept., Public Affairs Div.

726.CANOE TRIPS. 19?? Map-guide with brief information on 35 rivers. Available from: NY Environmental Conservation Dept., Public Affairs Div.

727.THE DELAWARE AND OUTDOOR RECREATION. 19?? A map-guide. Available from: American Canoe Association

728.Duffy, Richard. THE DELAWARE RIVER DUFF MAP: A CANOEING GUIDE, A FISHING GUIDE, A CAMPING GUIDE, A SIGHTSEEING GUIDE, A CONSERVATION GUIDE. 1975. Single sheet(s)? A map-guide. Availability unknown.

729.NEW YORK ATLAS & GAZETTEER. 198? Topographic road maps (contour interval 100 meters, Scale 1:150,000). The gazetteer has map-keyed descriptions of parks, bicycle routes, campgrounds, wineries, hiking, fishing, wildlife, canoe trips, and much more. Available from: DeLorme Mapping Co.

730.UPPER DELAWARE SCENIC AND RECREATIONAL RIVER, NEW YORK—PENNSYLVANIA, OFFICIAL MAP AND GUIDE. 1986. Single sheet. Scale 1:177,500. Produced by the National Park Service. Available from: NPS (Superintendent of Documents.)

North Carolina (NC)

(Note: for Chattooga River maps see Georgia.)

731.B. EVERETT JORDAN DAM AND LAKE OF THE HAW. 19?? Single sheet? Map. Available from: US Army Corps of Engineers, B. Everett Jordan Dam and Lake, P.O. Box 144, Moncure, NC 27559

732.GUIDE TO THE FRENCH BROAD GAP RAPIDS. 1984. Single sheet. Covers 7.5 mi. from Rt. 1151 to Hot Springs, NC; 17 major rapids with difficulty ranging from Class I-IV. Published by River Maps Ltd. Available from: American Canoe Association (ACA)

733.GUIDE TO THE NOLICHUCKY GAP RAPIDS. 1984. Single sheet. Covers the 8.5 miles from Poplar, NC to Erwin, TN; rapids difficulty to Class V. published by River Maps Ltd. Available from: ACA

734.Nealy, William. DUKE FOREST. 19?? Single sheet. 18 x 35 in. One of a series of Nealy cartoon poster-maps suitable for boat or wall. Available from: Menasha Ridge Press.

735.Nealy, William. FRENCH BROAD. 19?? Single sheet. 18 x 35 in. One of a series of Nealy cartoon poster-maps suitable for boat or wall. Available from: Menasha Ridge Press.

736.Nealy, William. HAW RIVER, LOWER SECTION. 19?? Single sheet. 18 x 35 in. One of a series of Nealy cartoon poster-maps suitable for boat or wall. Available from: Menasha Ridge Press.

737.Nealy, William. HAW RIVER, UPPER SECTION. 19?? Single sheet. 18 x 35 in. One of a series of Nealy cartoon poster-maps suitable for boat or wall. Available from: Menasha Ridge Press.

738.Nealy, William. NANTAHALA RIVER. 19?? Single sheet. 18 x 35 in. One of a series of Nealy cartoon poster-maps suitable for boat or wall. Available from: Menasha Ridge Press.

739.Nealy, William. NOLICHUCKY RIVER GORGE. 19?? Single sheet. 18 x 35 in. One of a series of Nealy cartoon poster-maps suitable for boat or wall. Available from: Menasha Ridge Press.

740.NEW HOPE RIVER, 19?? Single sheet? Map. Available from: US Army Corps of Engineers, B. Everett Jordan Dam and Lake, P.O. Box 144, Moncure, NC 27559

North Dakota (ND)

741.LITTLE MISSOURI RIVER FLOAT TRIPS. 19?? Map-guide. Available from: Forest Service, Medora Ranger Dist., 1409 W. Villard St., Dickinson, ND 58601.

742.NORTH DAKOTA CANOEING WATERS. 19?? Map-guide on 15 rivers. Available from: Bureau of Land Mgmt., P.O. Box 1220, Dickinson, ND 58601.

Ohio (OH)

743.EXPLORE OHIO BY CANOE. 19?? Map-guide of publically accessible waterways. Available from: OH Natural Resources Dept., Parks and Recreation Div.

744.OHIO ATLAS & GAZETTEER. 198? Topographic road maps (contour interval 100 meters, Scale 1:150,000). The gazetteer has map-keyed descriptions of parks, bicycle routes, campgrounds, wineries, hiking, fishing, wildlife, canoe trips, and much more. Available from: DeLorme Mapping Co.

Oklahoma (OK)

745.FLOATING THE ILLINOIS. 19?? Map-guide. Available from: OK Wildlife Conservation Dept., Fisheries Div.

746.OKLAHOMA CANOE TRAILS. 19?? Map-guide to 7 canoeing river routes. Available from: OK Tourism and Recreation Dept., Marketing Services Div.

Oregon (OR)

747.HELL'S CORNER GORGE. 19?? Map-guide to the Gorge section of the Klamath on the California-Oregon border. Available from: Colorado Kayak Supply.

748.OWYHEE RIVER GUIDE. 198? Waterproof paper. Available from: River Graphics.

749.POPULAR DRIFTING/CANOEING STREAMS IN OREGON. 19?? Brief descriptions of 11 routes with distances, hazards, etc. Available from: OR Transportation Dept.

750.THE ROGUE RIVER. 19?? Descriptive map-guide of the river and surrounding national forest. Available from: Siskiyou National Forest Headquarters, P.O. Box 440, Grants Pass, OR 97526.

Pennsylvania (PA)

751.CANOEING IN DELAWARE AND SUSQUEHANNA WATERSHEDS OF PENNSYLVANIA. 19?? Map-guide. Available from: PA Environmental Resources Dept., Fish Commission.

752.CANOE ROUTES. 19?? Coverage of the Allegheny, Monongahela, Ohio, Susquehanna, and Delaware rivers. Available from: PA Environmental Resources Dept.

753.Gray, Thomas L. CANOEING STREAMS OF THE UPPER OHIO BASIN. 1974. Single sheet. 12 x 21 in. A map of the Allegheny, Ohio, and Monongahela watersheds color-coded to indicate difficulty. Available from: Thomas Gray, 11121 Dewey Rd., Kensington, MD 20895.

754.Harding, Rich. YOUGHIOGHENY RIVER GUIDE. 1975. Single sheet. 25 x 38 in. Drawn to a scale of 2 5/8 in. to 1 mi. Information includes diagrams of major rapids and photographs. Available from: Rich Designs, 481 S. Ashburton, Columbus, OH 43213; American Canoe Association (ACA)

755.Nealy, William. YOUGHIOGHENY RIVER, LOWER SECTION. 19?? Single sheet. 18 x 35 in. One of a series of Nealy cartoon poster-map suitable for boat or wall. Available from: Menasha Ridge Press.

756.PADDLE PENNSYLVANIA. 19?? Map-guide which has river difficulty and aesthetics ratings. Available from: PA Environmental Resources Dept.

757.PENNSYLVANIA ATLAS & GAZETTEER. 198? Topographic road maps (contour interval 100 meters, Scale 1:150,000). The gazetteer has map-keyed descriptions of parks, bicycle routes, campgrounds, wineries, hiking, fishing, wildlife, canoe trips, and much more. Available from: DeLorme Mapping Co.

758.THE SCHUYKILL RIVER. 1982. Eight strip-maps on waterproof paper covering the river from Port Clinton to Philadelphia's Fairmont Dam (102 mi.). Scale: 2 1/2 in. to 1 mi. Published by the Delaware River Commission. Available from: ACA

Rhode Island (RI)

759.PAWCATUCK RIVER AND WOOD RIVER. 19?? Map-guide. Available from: RI Environmental Management Dept., Parks and Recreation Div.

South Carolina (SC)

(Note: for Chattooga River maps see GEORGIA.)

760.FLOATERS GUIDES TO THE TYGE AND ENOREE RIVERS. 19?? Map-guide. Available from: Forest Service, P.O. Box 2227, Columbia, SC 29202.

761.SOUTH CAROLINA RIVER TRAILS. 19?? Map-guide describing 10 major rivers. Available from: Parks, Recreation and Tourism Dept., Recreation Div.

South Dakota (SD)

762.SOUTH DAKOTA CANOEING GUIDE. 19?? Map-guide with information on 11 major routes. Available from: SD Game, Fish and Parks Dept., Parks and Recreation Div.

Tennessee (TN)

763.BIG SOUTH FORK NATIONAL RIVER AND RECREATION AREA MAP. 19?? A map-guide to the Big South Fork National River. Available from: Tennessee Valley Authority, 311 Broad St., Chattanooga, TN 37402-2801.

764.BUFFALO RIVER FLOAT MAP. 19?? Map-guide. Available from: TN Wildlife Resources Agency, Fish Management Div.

765.CANOEING IN TENNESSEE. 19?? Map-guide detailing 22 routes and showing access, difficulty, etc. Available from: TN Wildlife Resources Agency, Fish Management Div.

766.ELK RIVER CANOE TRAILS. 19?? A map-guide. Available from: Tennessee Valley Authority, 311 Broad St., Chattanooga, TN 37402-2801.

767.EMORY RIVER WATERSHED. 19?? A map-guide. Available from: Tennessee Valley Authority, 311 Broad St., Chattanooga, TN 37402-2801.

768.LITTLE BEAR CREEK CANOE TRAILS. 19?? A map-guide. Available from: Tennessee Valley Authority, 311 Broad St., Chattanooga, TN 37402-2801.

769.LITTLE RIVER CANOE TRAIL—LAKE BERKELEY. 19?? Map-guide of canoe routes near Land Between the Lakes, KY. Available from: U.S. Army Corps of Engineers, Nashville, TN 37210

770.LITTLE TENNESSEE VALLEY CANOE TRAILS. 19?? A map-guide. Available from: Tennessee Valley Authority, 311 Broad St., Chattanooga, TN 37402-2801.

771.Nealy, William. HIWASSIE RIVER. 19?? Single sheet. 18 x 35 in. Another in the off the wall series of comic poster-maps suitable for on-the-river use. Available from: Menasha Ridge Press.

772.Nealy, William. OCOEE RIVER. 19?? Single sheet. 18 x 35 in. Another in the off the wall series of comic poster-maps suitable for on-the-river use. Available from: Menasha Ridge Press.

773.Nealy, William. OCOEE RIVER, SQUIRT EDITION. 19?? Single sheet. 18 x 35 in. Another in the off the wall series of comic poster-maps suitable for on-the-river use. Available from: Menasha Ridge Press.

774.OBED-EMORY CANOE TRAILS. 19?? A map-guide. Available from: Tennessee Valley Authority, 400 W. Summit Hill Dr., Knoxville, TN 37902-1499.

775.THE OBED WILD AND SCENIC RIVER. 19?? Map-guide. Available from: TN Tourist Development Dept.

776.TENNESSEE VALLEY CANOE TRAILS. 19?? A map-guide. Available from: Tennessee Valley Authority, 400 W. Summit Hill Dr., Knoxville, TN 37902-1499.

Texas (TX)

777.BIG BEND NATIONAL PARK. 19?? Single sheet? Map. Available from: Big Bend National Park Headquarters, Big Bend, TX 79834.

778.BIG SLOUGH CANOE TRAIL. 19?? Map-guide of a trip in the Davey Crockett National Forest. Available from: Forest Service, 701 N. First St., Lufkin, TX 75901.

779.FLOATING TEXAS WHITEWATER. 19?? Map-guide showing Texas paddling opportunities and including access, flow, etc. Available from: TX Parks and Wildlife Dept., Parks Div.

Vermont (VT)

780.CANOEING ON THE CONNECTICUT RIVER. 19?? Map-guide with 9 maps plus general paddling information. Available from: VT Natural Resources Agency, Forests, Parks and Recreation Dept.

781.CANOE TRIPS IN VERMONT. 19?? Map-guide. Available from: VT Development and Community Affairs Agency, Travel Div.

782.VERMONT ATLAS & GAZETTEER. 198? Topographic road maps (contour interval 100 meters, Scale 1:150,000). The gazetteer has map-keyed descriptions of parks, bicycle routes, campgrounds, wineries, hiking, fishing, wildlife, canoe trips, and much more. Available from: DeLorme Mapping Co.

Virginia (VA)

783.FLOATING THE JAMES RIVER. 19?? Single sheet? Map (including sectional maps of places of note). Available from: VA Game and Inland Fisheries Comm., Fish Div.

784.A GREAT PLACE TO CANOE. 19?? A brief map-guide to routes. Available from: VA Economic Development Dept., Tourism Section.

785.GUIDE TO THE NEW RIVER OF VIRGINIA. 1983. Single sheet. From the mouth of the Wilson to Claytor Lake—78 mi., with difficulty ranging from Class I to IV. Designed for the canoeist and fisherman. Published by River Maps Ltd. Available from: American Canoe Association (ACA)

786.WHERE TO CANOE IN VIRGINIA. 19?? Map-guide briefly describing 11 runs. Available from: Game and Inland Fisheries Comm., Fish Div.

Washington (WA)

787.WASHINGTON ATLAS & GAZETTEER. 1988. 120 p. Topographic road maps (contour interval 100 meters, Scale 1:150,000). The gazetteer has map-keyed descriptions of parks, bicycle routes, campgrounds, wineries, hiking, fishing, wildlife, canoe trips, and much more. Available from: DeLorme Mapping Co.

West Virginia (WV)

788.GUIDE TO HARPER'S FERRY RAPIDS. 1983. Single sheet. Coverage of the confluence of the Shenandoah and the Potomac—including the Shenandoah Staircase—9 mi., with a difficulty from Class I-III. Published by River Maps, Ltd. Available from: American Canoe Association (ACA)

789.GUIDE TO THE GAULEY CANYON RAPIDS: LAKE SOMMERSVILLE TO SWISS. 1983. Single sheet. The 26 mi. of Class III-IV rapids of the Gauley Canyon (43 major rapids described). Includes access points. Published by River Maps, Ltd. Available from: ACA

790.GUIDE TO THE LOWER GORGE OF THE NEW RIVER. 1983. Single sheet. Nineteen miles covered (22 rapids), from Thurmond to Hawk's Nest, with whitewater from Class III+ rapids ranging from Class I/II to VI. Published by River Maps, Ltd. Available from: ACA

791.GUIDE TO THE NEW RIVER. 1981. Single sheet. New River from Claytor Lake to Bluestone Lake, for the canoeist or sportsman. Published by River Maps, Ltd. Available from: ACA

792.Nealy, William. CHEAT RIVER CANYON. 19?? Single sheet. 18 x 35 in. One of a series of Nealy cartoon poster-maps suitable for boat or wall. Available from: Menasha Ridge Press.

793.Nealy, William. GAULEY RIVER. 19?? Single sheet. 18 x 35 in. One of a series of Nealy cartoon poster-maps suitable for boat or wall. Available from: Menasha Ridge Press.

794.Nealy, William. NEW RIVER GORGE. 19?? Single sheet. 18 x 35 in. One of a series of Nealy cartoon poster-maps suitable for boat or wall. Available from: Menasha Ridge Press.

795.Nealy, William. SHENANDOAH RIVER. 19?? Single sheet. 18 x 35 in. One of a series of Nealy cartoon poster-maps suitable for boat or wall. Available from: Menasha Ridge Press.

796.WEST VIRGINIA STREAM MAP. 19?? Available from: WV Natural Resources Div.

Wisconsin (WI)

797.KICKAPOO CANOE TRAIL. 19?? Map-guide. Available from: Kickapoo Valley Association, Inc., Rt. 2 Box 211, La Farge, WI 54639.

798.ST. CROIX NATIONAL SCENIC RIVERWAY. 19?? Guide containing camping and canoeing information. Available from: National Park Service, St. Croix National Scenic Riverway Headquarters, P.O. Box 708, St. Croix Falls, WI 54024.

799.WISCONSIN ATLAS & GAZETTEER. 198? Topographic road maps (contour interval 100 meters, Scale 1:150,000). The gazetteer has map-keyed descriptions of parks, bicycle routes, campgrounds, wineries, hiking, fishing, wildlife, canoe trips, and much more. Available from: DeLorme Mapping Co.

800.WISCONSIN WATER TRAILS. 19?? Map-guide. Available from: WI Natural Resources Dept., Parks and Recreation Bureau.

Wyoming (WY)

801.BRIDGER NATIONAL FOREST. 19?? Single sheet? Map showing BNF section of the Green River. Available from: Bridger National Forest Headquarters, Forest Svc. Bldg., Kemmerer, WY 83101.

802.FLOATING THE SNAKE RIVER. 19?? Single sheet? Map of Upper Snake. Available from: Grand Teton National Park Headquarters, Moose, WY 83012.

803.MEDICINE BOW NATIONAL FOREST. 19?? Single sheet? Map showing MBNF section of the North Platte River. Available from: Medicine Bow National Forest Headquarters, 605 Skyline Dr., Laramie, WY 82070.

804.THE UPPER NORTH PLATTE RIVER IN COLORADO AND WYOMING. 1983. Single sheet (waterproof). Published by the Wyoming Game and Fish Dept. Shows access, rapids, campsites, etc., on 200 miles of river. Avialable from: National Organization for River Sports; American Canoe Association (ACA)

Chapter 2

Technique and Instruction

805.THE AMERICAN CANOE ASSOCIATION RIVER SAFETY REPORT, 1986-1988. Edited by Charles C. Walbridge. Newington, VA: The American Canoe Association (ACA), 1989. 94 p. Illus. Paper. The chapter titles in this book read like tragic headlines in the local newspaper (and, indeed they often are): "Tree Stump Claims Kayaker," "Fast, Cold Water Kills Man on Pine Creek." Walbridge compiles river drowning reports (and some near misses) from a variety of sources every two or three years as a way for clubs, professional outfitters, and individuals to engage in some sobering consciousness-raising on the dangers of whitewater. The 1986-88 compilation contains 61 accident descriptions.

806.Arthur, Michael, and Ackroyd-Stolarz, Stacy. A RESOURCE MANUAL ON CANOEING FOR DISABLED PEOPLE. Hyde Park, ON: Canadian Recreational Canoeing Association, 1983. 44 p. Illus. Bibl. Paper. ***

807.Bechdel, Les, and Ray, Slim. RIVER RESCUE. 2d ed. Boston, MA: Appalachian Mountain Club, 1989. 238 p. Illus. Bibl. Index. Paper. In a new edition of the standard reference on river safety and rescue, the authors address the critical information needs of both beginner and advanced boater in the often neglected areas of safety and rescue. Bechdel is a renown paddler and rescue methods teacher/consultant, while Ray is an equally well-known kayaker, and free-lance writer/photographer. Their collaboration has produced a book containing concise instruction and high-quality drawings and photographs which, in combination, illustrate river characteristics, hazards, rescue techniques, rescue equipment, medical considerations, and actual rescues.

808.Beletz, Al, and Beletz, Syl. CANOE POLING. 1974. Reprint. Photos and sketches by Frank, Syl and Al Beletz. St. Louis, MO: A.C. Mackenzie Press, 1989. [136] p. Illus. Index. Paper. The authors, noted for their proficiency in the specialized art of poling canoes, were chairpersons of the American Canoe Association's National Poling Committee. Poling can be competitive or the technique can be used to provide access to remote areas near the upper reaches of rivers and small streams. Basic and advanced strokes, pole shoes and spikes, double poling, competition, acquiring standing position stability, and small stream travel are six of the topics covered from a total of 22 chapters. This "home-made" book does have unique information on a specialized subject, but at the same time, do not expect felicitous writing, professional editing, or quality typography.

809.Bell, Patricia J. ROUGHING IT ELEGANTLY: A PRACTICAL GUIDE TO CANOE CAMPING. Eden Prairie, MN: Cat's Paw Press, 1987. 159 p. Illus. Bibl. Index. Paper. Canoe camping in the BWCA, Voyageurs NP, and Quetico Provincial Park. How to plan a trip, choose proper apparel, camp, stay healthy and select a camp, by a long-time canoeist and trip leader. Bell's particular focus is on "elegant" camp cookery, including menu planning and nutrition.

810.Birkby, Robert. LEARN HOW TO CANOE IN ONE DAY: QUICKEST WAY TO START PADDLING, TURNING, PORTAGING, AND MAINTAINING. Harrisburg, PA: Stackpole Books, 1990. 103 p. Illus. Index. Paper. "I can assure you that with a little guidance, you can canoe. There is no great mystery to it, no secret art beyond your grasp. In fact, you can become a fairly good quiet-water canoeist in just eight hours," (page 3). This is the premise of Birkby's book—and it may just work. His writing is straight-forward, the type is large, the photographs (by Kate Joost), and drawings (by Barbara Lien) are well-done. Birkby's "how to" chapters are arranged in one or two-hour practice sessions which are preceded by a chapter on canoe history.

811.Boy Scouts of America. WHITEWATER. Boy Scouts of America Merit Badge Series. Irving, TX: Boy Scouts of America, 1988. 70 p. Illus. ***

812.Bridge, Raymond. THE COMPLETE CANOEIST'S GUIDE. New York: Charles Scribner's Sons, 1978. 301 p. Illus. Index. Bridge, author of THE COMPLETE GUIDE TO KAYAKING (see below), and five other outdoors handbooks, addresses virtually every facit of canoeing. The beginning and intermediate reader is instructed in canoeing equipment, transport, construction, paddling technique on lakes and rivers, poling, camping, trip planning, and making accessories. Bridge carefully enunciates the principals which underlie the "how to" practicalities of his material.

813.Bridge, Raymond. THE COMPLETE GUIDE TO KAYAKING. New York: Charles Scribner's Sons, 1978. 312 p. Illus. Index. Bridge is also the author of THE COMPLETE CANOEIST'S GUIDE (see above). His kayaking guide is a comprehensive package covering the whole kayaking scene. Careful study of the technique chapters on learning to paddle and the Eskimo Roll should help beginners progress swiftly to intermediate level. Plentiful illustrations (photographs and drawings) complement the text. Selected chapter headings: Paddles and Other Essentials, River Cruising and White-Water Touring, Touring on Lakes and the Ocean, An Introduction to Slalom and Downriver Racing, and Building Kayaks.

814.Burch, David. FUNDAMENTALS OF KAYAK NAVIGATION. Chester, CT: Globe Pequot Press, 1987. 283 p. Bibl. Index. Paper. A compilation of navigation information prepared for the sea kayaker. Burch coaches the reader in the use of charts, topo maps, compass use, finding and monitoring position, tides and currents, trip planning, reduced visibility navigation, and "Coast Pilots" publications. Arms, fingers, paddles and eyes can substitute for standard navigational tools by following the author's practical tips. The work is illustrated by drawings and reproductions of charts and tables.

815.CANOEING. Prepared by the American National Red Cross. 2d ed., revised. Washington, DC: American National Red Cross, 1985. 452 p. Illus. Bibl. Index. Paper. Revision of the ANRC classic which provides information required for the Red Cross canoeing programs, basic through instructor level. Hundreds of two-color sketches illustrate specific activities. All areas of paddle sports including kayaking and rafting are covered—although mention of kayak and raft technique is limited. Instructions on canoe paddling, poling, carrying, rescue, repair, camping, competition, and sailing are very detailed. Safety is stressed throughout.

816.CANOEING AND KAYAKING. Washington,DC: American National Red Cross, 1981. 219 p. Illus. Index. Paper. Prepared by members of the Red Cross Canoeing Advisory Committee as a revision of the organization's CANOEING textbook, 1977 edition, and with contributions by Robert Jay Evans and Robert Anderson. It is apparent why this instruction manual remains a standard work in its field; it is simply the most clearly-presented basic technique manual on the bookshelf. Mastery of the textual instructions is fostered by hundreds of two-color sequential sketches. Some of the topics addressed: survey of the sport, equipment, trip planning, training drills, river technique, rescue of people, and rescue of equipment. The subject index is sixteen pages long, and provides precise access to the contents.

817.CANOEING INSTRUCTION AND LEADERSHIP MANUAL. Hyde Park, ON: Canadian Recreational Canoeing Association, 19—? 168 p. Illus. Paper. ***

818.A CANOEIST'S MANUAL OF ENVIRONMENTAL AND ETHICAL CONCERNS. Hyde Park, ON: Canadian Recreational Canoeing Association, 19—? 83 p. Illus. Paper. ***

819.CANOE SAFETY RESOURCE MANUAL: A COMPREHENSIVE RESOURCE BOOK ON CANOE SAFETY. Edited by James Raffan. Willowdale, ON: Canoe Ontario, 1984. 151 p. Illus. Bibl. Maps. Paper. "...There are few established instructional programs that concentrate on the one aspect of canoeing that is common to all canoeists—canoe safety. To meet the need for a simple, effective canoe safety program, Canoe Ontario has developed the CANOE SAFETY RESOURCE MANUAL... . The manual has four sections, each devoted to a different aspect of canoeing safety" (introduction). The sections are titled: "A 5-Part Step-by-Step Safety Instruction Program;" "Certification Courses;" "Canoeing Statistics and Accident Case Studies; and, "Canoeing Information." This is a loose leaf manual with the summary pages in section 1 sealed in waterproof plastic laminate. A revised edition is scheduled for publication in 1990.

820.CANOE TRAVEL HANDBOOK. Prepared by the Canadian Recreational Canoeing Association with the assistance of Fitness and Amateur Sport

Canada. Hyde Park, ON: The Association and Fitness and Amateur Sport Canada, 1981. 46 p. Illus. Bibl. Paper. ***

821.Cary, Bob. THE BIG WILDERNESS CANOE MANUAL: A VETERAN GUIDE AND OUTFITTER TELLS YOU ALL ABOUT CAMPING, PADDLING, AND VOYAGING IN THE SPIRIT OF THE NEW OUTDOOR ETHIC. New York: David McKay, 1978. 183 p. Illus. Index. Cary, a long-time BWCA guide, writes about canoe camping in an anecdotal style which is at once entertaining and instructional. The intended readership is beginner-intermediate. (The book is approved for sale in the Boy Scouts official trading posts.) A few of the subjects covered: canoe shopping and customizing, family and group trips, hunting and fishing by canoe, and "reading" rapids. A reprint was published by Arco in 1983.

822.Dowd, John. SEA KAYAKING: A MANUAL FOR LONG-DISTANCE TOURING. Rev. ed. Vancouver, BC: Douglas & McIntyre; Seattle, WA: University of Washington Press, 1988. 303 p. Illus. Bibl. Index. Paper. This third edition of the "classic" offshore kayaking text is "suitable for paddlers of all levels," however Dowd assumes the reader has some background in the areas of navigation, camping and general survival. Emphasis here is on offshore journey technique (out on the bounding main), with little specific information about protected waters coastal tripping for which one might consult Washburne's, THE COASTAL KAYAKER'S MANUAL, (below). The variables of huge seas, low water temperatures, weather changes, rough beach approaches, etc., make Dowd's brand of sea kayaking an awsome paddling experience indeed. Table of contents: equipment, technique, seamanship, navigation, weather, reading the sea, hazards, storms, camping, first aid, survival, expedition planning, and guided tours.

823.Drabik, Harry. HARRY DRABIK'S GUIDE TO WILDERNESS CANOEING. Illustrated by Randall W. Scholes. Minneapolis, MN: Nodin Press, 1987. 143 p. Illus. Paper. Longtime backcountry guide Drabik imparts insightful gems of wilderness canoeing information of potential use to a broad audience ranging from guides and trip leaders to rank beginners. The author shows understanding of human nature and compassion for the urbanized being confronted by nature in the raw. Some of his subjects include: early and late season canoeing, weather, the "wet foot/dry foot" theory of canoe entry and exit, map and compass use, food, knots, and lashings. Some fifty pages of "guide's stories" (and poems) complete the book.

824.Drabik, Harry. THE SPIRIT OF CANOE CAMPING: A HANDBOOK FOR WILDERNESS CANOEISTS. Illustrated by Randall W. Scholes. Minneapolis, MN: Nodin Press, 1981. 127 p. Illus. Paper. Drabik runs an outfitter service in Minnesota's Boundary Waters. This book is based on his experiences with clients which he interweaves with the practical aspects of wilderness canoeing, i.e., clothing, equipment, canoeing skills, and camping basics. His intended audience: a family considering an extended canoe trip. Throughout the work, the author conveys his deep regard for the wilderness and his philosophy of the natural world by means of anecdotal narrative, and poetry. Evocative drawings by Randall Scholes.

825.THE ENTRY LEVEL GUIDE TO CANOEING & KAYAKING. Camden, ME: Canoe Magazine, 1984. Illus. Paper. ***

826.Evans, Eric, and Evans, Jay. THE KAYAKING BOOK. Rev. ed. Lexington, MA: Stephen Greene Press, 1988. 294 p. Illus. A new edition of the definitive work by former national kayak champion, Eric Evans, and his Olympic coach father, Jay. Kayak is spoken here: history, equipment, basic/advanced techniques, competition and additional information sources. Photographs and drawings illustrate everything. Fundamental maneuvers, e.g., the Eskimo roll, are shown in both drawings and photographs, and patiently coached using step-by-step narrative. This book may be as good an all-purpose kayak manual as is currently available.

827.Farmer, Charles J. THE DIGEST BOOK OF CANOEING. Chicago: Follett Publishing, 1979. 96 p. Illus. Bibl. Paper. "Everything you need to know about canoes and canoeing," (cover subtitle). Well, not quite. Farmer's chapters are a scant two or three pages long, and despite numerous illustrative drawings and photographs, there is not much here to sink one's teeth into, even for the most uninformed beginner. Organized in four parts: "How to Choose and Use Your Canoe," "What to Do with Your Canoe," "How and Where to Go," and, "Some Additional Information." This title is no longer in print.

828.Fears, J. Wayne. THE COMPLETE BOOK OF CANOE CAMPING. Tulsa, OK: Winchester Press, 1981. 205 p. Illus. Index. Paper. "A detailed guide to canoeing fundamentals and techniques, canoe equipment, camping equipment, planning, trips, choosing campsites, streamside cooking, preventing emergencies, surviving a stranding, canoe fishing and hunting, outstanding float trips, establishing and maintaining canoe trails, canoe camping with small children, and protecting the environment" (cover subtitle). Clear narrative and good illustrations raise this beginner's manual to a level exceeding most in its genre.

829.Foshee, John H. SOLO CANOEING: A GUIDE TO THE FUNDAMENTALS, EQUIPMENT, AND TECHNIQUES FOR RUNNING RIVERS SOLO IN AN OPEN CANOE. Harrisburg, PA: Stackpole Books, 1988. 235 p. Illus. Index. Paper. The author states in his foreword that the rewards of solo canoeing are freedom from searching for a partner, from the disappointment of missed trips due to partner "no shows," and from the idiosyncrasies of another personality. Moreover, "the canoe itself, being more lightly loaded, is easier to paddle, faster, more maneuverable, and has a shallower draft." Foshee brings twenty years of experience to the task of teaching solo canoe river running. In nine illustrated chapters (photographs and diagrams) of progressively more advanced techniques, he describes the craft, its modifications, necessary equipment, stroke techniques, maneuvers, river reading, safety and rescue. Definitions, rescue rope/bag throwing, shuttles, safety codes, and river and paddler ratings are addressed in an appendix.

830.Foshee, John H. YOU, TOO, CAN CANOE: THE COMPLETE BOOK OF RIVER CANOEING. Huntsville, AL: Strode Publishers, 1977. 435 P. Illus. Bibl. "...The basic techniques and manuevers and paddle strokes of river canoeing [and] many of those other 1,001 things that prove to be often important and always useful to know" (preface). Foshee has organized his book into three main parts ("The Basics," "Techniques, Paddle Strokes, and the River," "Safety, Rescue, Repair, and Logistics"), then subdivided into eighteen chapters including those on equipment selection, canoe transport, river reading, paddle techniques, safety, and rescue. His chapter on repair has particularly good descriptions and illustrations concerning fixing aluminum and fiberglass canoes. Although this work is somewhat dated (most obviously noticeable in the equipment sections), the basic/standard techniques material comprising the bulk of the book has continuing usefulness.

831.Foster, Thomas S. RECREATIONAL WHITE WATER CANOEING: AN ILLUSTRATED GUIDE. Millers Falls, MA: Leisure Enterprises, 1978. 92 p. Illus. Paper. A longtime canoeist and instructor, Foster has written a basic introduction to whitewater canoeing as a purely recreational activity. A mastery of flat water skills is prerequisite. The author teaches "...tandem and solo paddling strokes and their respective applications to maneuvers and tactics on the river" (p. iii). There are dozens of illustrations. "Worksheets" (a series mini-reviews of paddling techniques covered), conclude the work. There is a revised edition (1981), which I was unable to inspect.

832.Gilpatrick, Gil. THE CANOE GUIDE'S HANDBOOK. Yarmouth, ME: DeLorme Publishing, 1983. 153 p. Illus. Index. Paper. "Most trippers today want the [canoe guide or trip leader] to show them how, not do it for them. They want to be participants" (introduction). In a response to this need, Gilpatrick wrote this handbook for individuals already having basic canoeing and woodcraft skills who find themselves thrust into roles of canoe trip leadership, and who must meet the challenge to both teach and guide. Safety is stressed. Other chapter subjects: equipment, provisions, paddling, portaging, wet weather, and appreciation of nature.

833.Gordon, I. Herbert. THE CANOE BOOK. New York: McGraw-Hill, 1978. 238 p. Illus. Bibl. Index. Paper. A comprehensive and readable book on all aspects of canoeing written with the beginning paddler in mind. Gordon has carefully organized his work into three parts: "About Canoeing" (terminology and technique), "Wilderness Canoeing" (choosing a trip, portaging, camping and first aid), and, "Appendixes" (information sources, manufacturers and glossary). Descriptions and instructions are enlivened with anecdotal material and drawings. THE CANOE BOOK is out of print, but there should be copies available in public libraries everywhere.

834.Gullion, Laurie. CANOEING AND KAYAKING INSTRUCTION MANUAL. Newington, VA: American Canoe Association, 1987. 121 p. Illus. Bibl. Paper. "This manual is designed to help paddlers become knowledgeable, effective instructors and to assist experienced instructors in continuing their education. The intent is to present the technical knowledge, paddling skills and teaching methods recommended by the American Canoe Association" (introduction). Techniques are for three types of paddling/craft: solo and tandem open canoe, C1 and C2 (decked canoe), and K1 (kayak). Gullion's manuel has chapters that address: safety, general technical information, specific paddling skills, a variety of teaching methods, elements of paddling lessons, and specific ACA requirements in the instructor certification process. In another chapter, she outlines the ACA's flatwater, moving water and whitewater courses.

835.Harrison, David, and Harrison, Judy. CANOE TRIPPING WITH CHILDREN: UNIQUE ADVICE TO KEEPING KIDS COMFORTABLE. Merrillville, IN: ICS Books, 1990. Bibl. Paper. ***

836.Harrison, David. SPORTS ILLUSTRATED CANOEING: SKILLS FOR THE SERIOUS PADDLER. 1981. Reprint. New York: Sports Illustrated, Winner's Circle Books, 1988. 190 p. Illus. Paper. Comprehensive coverage of the sport, from novice through expert paddler, by an accomplished writer and canoeist. Originally published almost ten years ago, Harrison's book has aged gracefully—the photographs showing craft and gear, which most often give evidence of advancing years, seem fresh. Organization progresses sequentially through twelve chapters: craft, equipment, paddling skills (basic, flat water, moving water, fast water, whitewater), safety, trips, expeditions, competition, and motorized canoes. The author describes a progression of techniques with clarity and economy. His descriptions are linked to sequential photographs and drawings, resulting in effective instructional modules. Photographs by Harrison and Tom Ettinger. Drawings by H. Russell Suiter.

837.Herzog, David Alan. A GUIDE TO BIG WATER CANOEING. Pickering, ON: Beaverbooks; Chicago: Contemporary Books, 1978. 131 p. Illus. Index. Paper. Basic and advanced techniques of canoeing on big lakes and along ocean coasts. The title holds out the promise of a detailed treatment of a narrowly focused topic, however, the level of detail one would expect is too often lacking.

838.Hubbard, Don. THE COMPLETE BOOK OF INFLATABLE BOATS. Vancouver, BC: Gordon Soules Book Publishers; Ventura, CA: Western Marine Enterprises, 1980. 256 p. Illus. Index. Paper. Inflatables of all designs and for all purposes are in common use today. They have long been accepted as "real" boats, and for some purposes, especially that of floating a heavy cargo of people and equipment down a river, they have no equal. Certainly they are the bread and butter machine of river outfitters. Moreover, the inflatable kayak is a matchless fun and forgiving whitewater play boat. Storage space and transportability also favor inflatable use. While Hubbard's book is showing its age, the chapters on selection, care and repair, and technique contain information which remains relevant.

839.Huser, Verne. RIVER CAMPING: TOURING BY CANOE, RAFT, KAYAK, AND DORY. Photographs by R. Valentine Atkinson. New York: Dial Press, Solstice Press Book, 1981. 154 p. Illus. Bibl. Paper. "It is my purpose in writing this book to help inform people of the principles of minimal impact camping and its practical applications" (preface). Huser does so with very brief, often anecdotal explanations of camping and paddling methods which he organizes as subtopics under nine chapter headings: The River, Preparation, Craft, Gear, Technique, At the River, Health and Safety, River Running, and, At Camp. A list of information and equipment sources concludes the work. RIVER CAMPING is an informative, well-illustrated beginners overview of all the basics—a snapshot of the touring scene.

840.Hutchinson, Derek C. DEREK C. HUTCHINSON'S GUIDE TO SEA KAYAKING. Chester, CT: Globe Pequot Press, 1985. 122 p. Illus. Index. Paper. "I have written this book so that it is not simply a book on how to kayak. Rather, it is a book on how to kayak in such a way as to live to kayak another day" (introduction). Much of Hutchinson's book deals with survival kayaking as the introductory passage suggests; he presents chapters on self-rescue, deep-water rescues, special problems afloat, hazardous wildlife, emergency aid, and strategies for survival. The author is a British expert, hence the overall UK (canoeing) approach. There is some additional North American kayaking material doubtless gathered during his extended sojourns in the Great Northwest. The old prints of Eskimo craft add visual interest, while the many technique drawings (and a few photographs) are useful adjuncts to the text.

841.Hutchinson, Derek. ESKIMO ROLLING. Camden, ME: International Marine Publishing, 1988. 152 p. Illus. Index. Paper. If not the last word on the Eskimo roll, Hutchinson's book about this basic kayak skill is the most thorough to date. Through clear description and his own sketches, he covers the areas of instruction, practice, and execution of various roll techniques. Hutchinson is a renown sea kayaker, therefore it is not surprising to find in his book that techniques best suited to the coastal kayaker predominate over those for their river counterparts. However there is much material which is applicable to all waters.

Interspersed with the instructional material are "rolling anecdotes" told by the experts, and some of the history of the sport.

842.INSTRUCTOR CERTIFICATION PROGRAM. Hyde Park, ON: Canadian Recreational Canoeing Association, 19—? 108 p. Illus. Paper. ***

843.Jacobson, Cliff. THE BASIC ESSENTIALS OF CANOEING. Basic Essentials Series. Merrillville, IN: ICS Books, 1988. 64 p. Illus. Index. Paper. An inexpensive introduction to canoeing by an authority on the subject. This is a no-nonsense work with illustrated chapters of six to ten pages giving the basics of canoe construction, choice of a craft, accessories, transport, flat and whitewater paddling techniques, and hazards.

844.Jacobson, Cliff. CANOEING WILD RIVERS. Rev. ed. Merrillville, IN: ICS Books, 1989. 339 p. Illus. Index. Paper. "...This book is not for just those who would tackle the wild rivers of the far north. It is for paddlers everywhere who love wilderness waterways and want to learn some fresh new ideas as well as the nuts and bolts of canoeing remote waters" (introduction). This new edition of a classic has been expanded by more than fifty pages and revised with over 200 updates. The text is a variety of advise and instruction enlivened with anecdotal accounts by Jacobson and other contributors. If one is contemplating a canoe trip above 60 degrees north latitude, this is must reading for arcane, but necessary information, e.g.: finding unmarked portages, "dry places," food preparation/preservation hints, over-reliance on the map, beasts, and bush roads. Appendixes: review of basic strokes; mailing addresses in Canada and Alaska (for information, maps, and supplies), equipment list; medical kit (non-perscription); international river rating scale; and, temperature chart.

845.Jacobson, Cliff. THE NEW WILDERNESS CANOEING & CAMPING. Rev. ed. Merrillville, IN: ICS Books, 1986. 317 p. Illus. Index. Paper. Revised edition of WILDERNESS CANOEING & CAMPING (NY: Dutton, 1977), which "...retains all the solid information and money-saving tips which made its predecessor so popular a decade ago. But now Cliff Jacobson has updated the material and included new procedures, new chapters [5], new photos and ... illustrations [88] by Cliff Moen, noted Minnesota artist" (publisher's note). What may elevate this book above the ordinary introductory work are the scores of tips and experiential vignettes provided. This has the combined effect of holding the attention and building the confidence of the reader. In addition to material on paddling and portaging, Jacobson tells how to choose a canoe and equipment, where to get it, and how to repair and care for it. In other chapters, the author tells how to canoe camp with tots and teens, and advises on customizing canoes, paddles, and equipment.

846.Johnstone, D. Bruce. GUIDE TO CANOE CAMPING. Martinsville, IN: American Camping Association, 198? 52 p. Illus. Bibl. Paper. A concise, inexpensive introduction to canoe technique, waterways camping and trip planning. Descriptions are clear and crisp, further enhanced by nicely-rendered drawings.

847.Keating, Lee. WOODS AND WATER: THE COMMON SENSE BOOK OF CANOEING. Halifax, NS: Nimbus Publishing, 1981. 152 p. Illus. Paper. Keating's background as licenced guide, competitive canoeist, and instructor are ample prerequisites for writing this most comprehensive book on canoe handling technique. He presents material dealing with the full spectrum of the sport, cutting across all levels of expertise. Novices can read about the fundamentals of handling, tripping, portaging, packing, summer canoe camps, informal competition, design, selection, safety, care and repair. For the more skilled, advanced handling, poling, and whitewater techniques are fully explained. The text is literate and the descriptions are clear. The narrative is fortified by numerous photographs and drawings.

848.Kuhne, Cecil. ADVANCED RIVER RAFTING. Mountain View, CA: Anderson World, 1980. 210 p. Illus. Bibl. Paper. "A comprehensive guide to rafting, camping, cookery, and wilderness photography for the river veteran or the serious beginner" (cover subtitle). The material in Kuhne's earlier book, RIVER RAFTING, (see below), has been augmented, expanded, and rearranged to appeal to the advanced rafter. In one sense, this is putting old wine into a new bottle. However, the information on raft modification, river photography, managing river recreation, and an extensive bibliography, are useful additions.

849.Kuhne, Cecil. RIVER RAFTING. Mountain View, CA: World Publications, 1979. 153 p. Illus. Paper. Some of the information in this book is repeated in Kuhne's ADVANCED RIVER RAFTING (see above). In this book, however, there are many more how-to descriptions and illustrations showing paddling or rowing techniques, raft construction, and equipment. Seven chapters: The Raft, Rafting Equipment, Running Rapids, River Camping, River Safety, First Aid, and Equipment Maintenance and Repair.

850.Littledeer, Tom. THE GLIDE: THE THEORY OF GLIDING A CANOE. Edited by Sharron Wall. Chambly, PQ: Leading Edge Designs, 1984. 50 p. Illus. Bibl. Paper. "By drawing on concepts from science and aviation, this manual lays the groundwork for the theory of gliding, and introduces a comprehensive glossary of useful terminology, intended to facilitate understanding of the dynamic forces involved in canoeing" (introduction). Littledeer addresses the seldom asked question of why a canoe works. Illustrations are by the author.

851.McGinnis, William, et al. CLASS V BRIEFING. El Sobrante, CA: Whitewater Voyages/River Exploration Ltd., 1985. 29 p. Paper. Pocket-size overview of state-of-the-art rafting rules and techniques for guides preparing to raft Class V rivers contributed by expert guides/outfitters. There are condensed paragraphs of explanation under headings: preparation; gear packing and rigging; put-in talk; on the river; portages; flips; wraps; emergency evacuation; hoisting signals; and, Class V staffing.

852.McGinnis, William. THE GUIDE'S GUIDE: REFLECTIONS ON GUIDING PROFESSIONAL RIVER TRIPS. El Sobrante, CA: Whitewater Voyages/River Exploration Ltd., 1981. 129 p. Illus. Paper. From the beginning page, it is obvious that McGinnis' manual is a no-nonsense working tool by a professional river guide, for professionals. The book was written to train guides on trips run by McGinnis' outfit, Whitewater Voyages. It should be required reading for commercial boatwo/men on every river. The introduction, under the "Guides and Guests" heading, quickly sets the customer-orientation tone of the book with seldom seen information on diplomacy, customer relations, keeping the "show" on the river despite show-stopping problems, kindness, positive thinking, mingling with guests, group togetherness, alcohol, entertainment, amorous advances, thank-you letters, etc. Main sections on boat handling, safety and food planning are done with equal thoroughness—including dozens of clear illustrations. There is no index, however each paragraph is "indexed" through highlighting key words in the margin. Test questions from the whitewater guide school written exam are given in part 3.

853.McNair, Robert E.; McNair, Matty L.; and Landry, Paul A. BASIC RIVER CANOEING. [New ed.] Martinsville, IN: American Camping Association, 1985. 81 p. Illus. Bibl. Paper. "Complete Instructional Guide to Whitewater Canoeing" (cover subtitle). This latest version of an old standard appears to be a revision of the 3rd edition (1972). It is intended both as a primer for beginners and a guide for polishing intermediate paddling techniques. The co-authors are eminently qualified: Bob was the first National Slalom Chairman of the ACA; daughter, Matty, is a trained outdoorsperson and canoeing instructor, while her husband, Paul, was a canoe racer (marathon) in Ontario for two seasons. The result of this collaboration is a tutorial with concise instructions and clear illustrations concerning equipment, strokes, river reading, maneuvers, strategy, slalom, wilderness canoeing, and becoming a whitewater instructor.

854.Mason, Bill. PATH OF THE PADDLE. Foreword by Pierre Elliott Trudeau. Toronto, ON: Key Porter Books; Minocqua, WI: Northword Press, 1984. 200 p. Illus. Bibl. Index. Paper. The first Canadian edition was published by Van Nostrand Reinhold (1980). Two 54-minute, color video PATH OF THE PADDLE products subtitled: "WHITEWATER," and "QUIETWATER" (Northword Press, 1977) are currently available. The printed manual covers all the basics of canoe handling in all waters. Mason's text is clearly written; his illustrative anecdotes taken from years of canoeing experience insure that the "how-to" information never becomes ponderous. The diagrams, sequential photographs, and whitewater "tests" are extremely well presented, and contribute to making this book one of the very best in its genre. Mason has chapters on solo and double paddling techniques, reading rapids, whitewater maneuvers, wipeouts, rapids-running alternatives, safety, types of canoes, and "no-trace" camping.

855.Mason, Bill. SONG OF THE PADDLE: AN ILLUSTRATED GUIDE TO WILDERNESS CAMPING. Toronto, ON: Key Porter Books; Minocqua, WI: Northword Press, 1988. 186 p. Illus. Bibl. Index. Paper. The paddle's song that Mason heard has the same force and pull as that of the Sirens for Odysseus—not onto the destructive rocks but, rather, away from civilization, to the waterways-studded Canadian outback. Mason spent much of his life as outdoorsman, canoe guide, wilderness artist, and quiet advocate for nature conservation. His wilderness expertise and creative temperament combine in making this book an authoritative yet non-pedagogical canoe camping manual. Illustrated with over 300 photographs and sketches, the book covers paddling, equipment, design of canoes, transport, safety, and first aid.

856.Mead, Robert Douglas. THE CANOER'S BIBLE. Rev. ed. Revised by J. Wayne Fears. Doubleday Outdoor Bibles. New York: Doubleday, 1989. 156 p. Illus. Maps. Bibl. Paper. This Fears' revision updates the Robert Mead edition (1976) of a standard introductory work—one of eighteen titles in the popular Doubleday Outdoor Bibles series. The authors' emphasis is on instructing in the basics of canoeing within the context of family recreation. Their goal is to provide enough information for the novice reader to safely and enjoyably begin overnight canoe tripping. To this end, beginning chapters introduce the sport and give advice on choosing canoes and paddles; in chapter 3 he describes canoe handling; 4 and 5, equipment and tripping gear; 6, planning a trip; 7, emergencies; and, 8 "canoe country" (an overview of North American paddling destinations). Heavily illustrated (black and white photographs and a few diagrams).

857.Narvey, Alex. THE CANADIAN CANOEING COMPANION: AN ILLUSTRATED RESOURCE GUIDE TO PADDLING CANADA'S WILDERNESS. Winnipeg, MB: Thunder Enlightening Press, 1988. 144 p. Illus. Bibl. Index. Paper. Narvey provides a Canadian perspective on canoeing and canoe tripping dedicated to the safety of canoeists and the environment. He reveals "tricks" learned during his years as a canoe trip leader, e.g., "plans for outdoor gear that you can actually use on a canoe trip..." (wannigan, reflector oven, portage pack, throw bag, etc.). Care of the environment is highlighted, and, in fact, a discussion of controlled impact camping constitutes section one. Other sections: "The Skills" (paddling, travelling, portaging, planning, rescues); "The Equipment" (care, construction); and "Resources" (bibliography, organizations, schools, sources).

858.Nealy, William. KAYAK: THE ANIMATED MANUAL OF INTERMEDIATE AND ADVANCED WHITEWATER TECHNIQUE. Birmingham, AL: Menasha Ridge Press, 1986. 171 p. Illus. Paper. Complex and difficult whitewater skills seem to make much more sense when presented in sequential cartoon panels. Nobody writing and illustrating paddling books employs the technique (or the skill and humor) of artist/kayaker Nealy. The result is a unique "adult" comic book about intermediate and advanced kayak paddling. Of particular note are Nealy's sections on self rescue and assisted rescue. Other sections: Paddle Fu ("Ninja kayaking"), Hydro-topography, Air traffic control (hand signals), The Joy of Flood (big water technique), and First Aid (a one-page "chapter" in which Nealy admonishes the reader to take a first aid course because acquisition of these specialized skills is outside the scope of the book).

859.O.R.C.A. CANOE PROGRAM MANUAL. Produced by the Ontario Recreational Canoeing Association. [Willowdale], ON: The Association, 198? Paper. ***

860.Ovington, Ray, and Ovington, Moraima. CANOEING BASICS FOR BEGINNERS. Harrisburg, PA: Stackpole Books, 1984. 224 p. Illus. Paper. Basic instructional material for beginners in flat water and river canoeing. The Ovingtons' book is in two parts: "Basic Equipment" (nomenclature, canoe selection, paddles, repair), and "Mastering the Basics" (techniques for small lakes, large lakes, gentle rivers, fast narrow rivers, whitewater, poling, lining, and portaging). There are 50 "situation" diagrams (a very few of which seem cramped and, therefore unclear) with facing-page explanatory captions.

861.Pulling, Pierre. CANOEING THE INDIAN WAY: STRAIGHT TALK FOR MODERN PADDLERS FROM THE DEAN OF AMERICAN CANOEISTS. 1979. Reprint. Harrisburg, PA: Stackpole Books, 1989. 118 p. Illus. Index. Paper. Pierre (Albert Van Siclen) Pulling has written a thoroughly self-congratulatory manual, e.g., "in writing it, I read nothing essential except what I had written [in 3 earlier works] myself" (preface). The book is a curiosity of the canoe paddling instruction genre—of interest more for Pulling's boldly- expressed opinions, than for practical content. The photographs are muddy and the drawings amateurish.

862.A RESOURCE MANUAL ON CANOEING REGATTAS. Hyde Park, ON: Canadian Recreational Canoeing Association, 198? 90 p. Illus. Paper. ***

863.Riviere, Bill. THE OPEN CANOE. Boston, MA; Toronto: Little, Brown, 1985. 305 p. Illus. Bibl. Index. Paper. Canoeing and outdoors author and former Maine guide, Riviere has written a book which attempts to be, "...a statement for canoeing and canoes in the 1980s" (introduction). His focus is on contemporary canoe innovations, i.e., the new materials, hydrodynamic designs, bent and laminated paddles, new paddling technique, and growth of organized competition. While Riviere's book in some ways constitutes a technological refresher course, it is also a tool for those new to the sport. He therefore gives equal attention to the standard how-to's of craft selection, paddling, reading whitewater, poling, portaging, safety, and camping. Photographs from manufacturers, plus uncluttered drawings by L. Randal Boyd illustrate technique and equipment detail.

864.Ross, Catherine; Hutton, Deborah; and Dunbar, Pamela. WHEN THE WILDERNESS BECONS: A CANOE TRIPPING HANDBOOK. Cobalt, ON: Highway Book Shop, 1981. 105 p. Illus. Paper. ***

865.Rowe, Ray. WHITE WATER KAYAKING. Harrisburg, PA: Stackpole Books, 1988. 127 p. Illus. Bibl. Index. Paper. "A simple guide to the best techniques and equipment for success" (cover). Over 100 step-by-step diagrams (by Ron Brown) and some 70 action photographs are features of this all-color import from Great Britain. Rowe describes kayak technique—basic techniques to competition skills—in an easily-followed style, grouped into short paragraphs, three columns to a page. This is expert advice from a renown kayaker in a very attractive package.

866.Sanders, William. GUIDE TO INFLATABLE CANOES & KAYAKS. Mountain View, CA: World Publications, 1979. 218 p. Illus. Bibl. Paper. Inflatable technology has progressed and paddle gear has improved since publication of Sanders' guide, but his chapters on technique, maintenance, emergencies, tripping and camping have aged well. The author is knowledgable and his writing clear. Illustrations range from amateurish backyard technique sequences to glossy promo shots from manufactrers.

867.Sanders, William. KAYAK TOURING. Harrisburg, PA: Stackpole Books, 1984. 247 p. Illus. Bibl. Index. Paper. As Sanders writes in his opening chapter "this is primarily a book on kayak touring—using the kayak to actually go somewhere... ." Intending to help beginners understand the basics of whitewater and open-water kayak handling, the author also has chapters on essential gear and the selection of the best kayaks for touring. Illustrated with photographs (often manufacturer-supplied) and drawings.

868.Schmidt, Ernest F. CANOEING. 1981. Reprint. Merit Badge Series, no. 3308. Irving, TX: Boy Scouts of America, 1986. 72 p. Illus. Bibl. ***

869.Snyder, James E. THE SQUIRT BOOK: THE ILLUSTRATED MANUEL OF SQUIRT KAYAKING TECHNIQUE. Illustrated by William Nealy. Birmingham, AL: Menasha Ridge Press, 1987. 162 p. Illus. Paper. "Boof: to impact with the hull—a technique for flat landings from vertical drops" (Glossary of Squirterms, p. 157). Pursuing their three-dimensional "subsport" of kayaking, a growing cult of squirt boaters operate a very low-volume craft in half-submerged fashion using special techniques. Snyder teaches squirtology utilizing both practical and philosophical explanations. The result is a very specialized book with an often humorous and off-the-wall quality. Nealy's drawings assist in understanding the most obscure concepts expressed in the text.

870.STANDARD TEST OF ACHIEVEMENT IN CANOEING. 4th ed. Prepared by the Canadian Recreational Canoeing Association. Hyde Park, ON: The Association, 1988. 105 p. Illus. Paper. ***

871.Tejada-Flores, Lito. WILDWATER: THE SIERRA CLUB GUIDE TO KAYAKING AND WHITEWATER BOATING. Drawings by Carol Ingram. San Francisco, CA: Sierra Club Books, 1978. 329 p. Illus. Bibl. Index. Paper. An often-praised book on whitewater technique by a well-known writer and instructor in several outdoor "adrenalin sports." Tejada-Flores' literate style is particularly refreshing. He teaches maneuvers in detailed, step-by-step progression, within the context of the natural and unnatural vagaries of river hydraulics. Psychological problems which may impede mastering the paddlesports are addressed within a positive, supportive framework. In all, the author has produced a carefully organized, thorough, and highly-readable guide for the whitewater kayak (and to a lesser degree, raft and mini-inflatable) beginner and intermediate.

872.Urban, John T., and Williams, T. Walley III. WHITEWATER HANDBOOK. 2d ed. Boston, MA: Appalachian Mountain Club, 1981. 197 p. Illus. Bibl. Index. Paper. An expanded and updated revision of a popular instructional text (over 100,000 copies of the 1965 edition were published). The current edition covers C-1's and C-2's in addition to open canoes and kayaks. Urban's original chapters on paddler interaction with moving water remain, while Williams' "new" chapters include information on strokes, technique, trip organization, equipment, safety and rescue. Leslie Eden contributed the information on kayak paddling. More than 100 photos and drawings facilitate self-instruction.

873.U'Ren, Stephen B. PERFORMANCE KAYAKING. Harrisburg, PA: Stackpole Books, 1990. 184 p. Illus. Bibl. Paper. U'Ren, kayaking instructor and member of the U.S. National Whitewater Slalom teams of the mid 80s, brings this expertise to bear in this instruction manual intended for beginner through advanced paddlers. His goal is to teach how to play and work a river with elegance and safety. The manual begins with the fundamentals and progressively builds on them. U'Ren's emphasis on technique and finesse makes his book a useful tool for good paddlers who are interested in correcting ingrained bad habits. Chapter seven, "Play Paddling," is by Bob McDougall.

874.Washburne, Randel. THE COASTAL KAYAKER'S MANUAL: A COMPLETE GUIDE TO SKILLS, GEAR, AND SEA SENSE. Chester, CT: Globe Pequot Press, 1989. 226 p. Illus. Bibl. Index. Paper. Washburne states in his introduction that "this book is designed to help you make kayaks your own special link to the sea. My frame of reference is the North American paddling environment and boats and equipment commonly available in Canada and the United States. My perspective is that sound equipment, which you know how to use, is critical for safety, but security in sea kayaking depends on skills and knowledge. Learning these occupies most of the space in this book." There are twenty-one chapters, illustrated with photographs, drawings, and charts, covering: kayaks (fiberglass, plastic, single, double, folding); gear (paddles, sprayskirts, life vests, clothing); paddling (stroke cadence, braces, sweeps, draws, launching, landing, surfing); capsize recovery; and, navigation (nautical charts, tidal currents, compasses, dead reckoning, piloting). Equipment checklist in the appendix.

875.Watters, Ron. THE WHITE-WATER RIVER BOOK: A GUIDE TO TECHNIQUES, EQUIPMENT, CAMPING, AND SAFETY. Photographs by Robert Winslow. Seattle, WA: Pacific Search Press, 1982. 204 p. Illus. Index. Paper. The basics of river running in decked boats and rafts. Sequential photographs on kayak paddling and rolling techniques are particularly well done, as are the drawings of oar manuevers in the rafting chapter. Watters presents his material clearly and precisely. Alternatives (e.g., types of paddle craft and equipment), are examined in a non-biased way, allowing the reader to choose based on the facts. Trip planning, "river cuisine," low-impact camping, sample checklist, and information sources chapters conclude the book.

876.Wirth, Bob. OPEN BOAT CANOEING. West Nyack, NY: Parker Publishing, 1985. 271 p. Illus. Index. Paper. ***

Chapter 3

Competition

877. Canadian Canoe Association. SPRINT RACING CANOEING: LEVEL I, COACHING CERTIFICATION. Ottawa, ON: The Association, 1984. 66 p. Illus. Bibl. ***

878. Canadian Canoe Association. Sprint Racing Council. NATIONAL TEAM PROGRAM FOR EXCELLENCE. Vanier, ON: The Council, 198-. ***

879. Dallas, Frank. OLYMPIC KAYAKING. American Canoe Association?, 19—? 101 p. Illus. Paper. ***

880. Endicott, William T. THE DANGER ZONE: DOWNRIVER CANOEING AT THE HIGHEST LEVELS. Bethesda, MD: W.T. Endicott, 1985. 365 p. Paper. ***

881. Endicott, William T. TO WIN THE WORLDS: A TEXTBOOK FOR ELITE SLALOMISTS AND THEIR COACHES. 1981. Reprint. Bethesda, MD: W.T. Endicott, 1986. 294 p. Illus. ***

882. Endicott, William T. THE ULTIMATE RUN: CANOE SLALOM AT THE HIGHEST LEVELS. Bethesda, MD: W.T. Endicott, 1983. 524 p. Illus. Paper. ***

883. Evans, Eric, and Burton, John. WHITEWATER RACING: A COMPREHENSIVE GUIDE TO WHITEWATER SLALOM AND WILDWATER RACING IN CANOES AND KAYAKS. n.p., 1980. 166 p. Illus. Bibl. Paper. Evans and Burton are kayak racing celebrities with world class credentials. A book written about competitive paddling by these two gentlemen instantly becomes required reading for racers considering the "big time," or anyone else who simply wants to become more competitive in recreational races. "Simply stated, whitewater racing means going fast without making errors" (p. 1). The authors show how to be quick and smart through instructional chapters on slalom technique, slalom racing, wildwater technique, physical and mental preparation, and equipment. The book has no publisher imprint, but is available from Nantahala Outdoor Center, Star Rt., Box 68, Bryson City, NC 28713.

884. FLATWATER. Wasco, IL: National Paddling Committee, American Canoe Association, 198? 24 p. Illus. Paper. ***

885. Heese, Fred. CANOE RACING. Pickering, ON: Beaverbooks; Chicago: Contemporary Books, 1979. 223 p. Illus. Index. Paper. With CANOE RACING, Heese, world class canoe competitor and expert instructor, offers readers an unembellished and enthusiastic introduction to this challenging sport of North American origin. His focus is on marathon racing (nine chapters) although information on training, diet, and some paddling techniques have applicability for flat water sprint and whitewater racing. A fairly extensive race directory of reqularly-held North American competitions concludes the book.

886. I.C.F. SLALOM AND WHITEWATER RULES. Produced by the Canadian White Water Association. Surrey, BC: The Association, 1989. Paper. ***

887. Johnston, C. Fred. BOOK OF CHAMPIONS OF THE CANADIAN CANOE ASSOCIATION, 1900-1984. Ottawa, ON: Canadian Canoe Association, 1988. 225 p. Illus. Tables. Paper. An enormous data-base of results of racing activities in which the CCA has been involved since the beginning of the century. Johnston chronologically lists medalists within the various classes (with their club affiliations), and the first place finish times of the following championships: Canadian Canoe Association Championships, Canada Games (1969-81), North American and Pan American Canoe Racing Championships (1953-84), and the Canadian Olympic Canoeing Teams (1924-84). The tabular data are preceded by a CCA chronological history and list of member clubs and officials.

888. NATIONAL CHAMPIONSHIP MANUAL. Compiled by Muzz Lahey. Vanier, ON: Canadian Canoe Association, 1981. 38 p. Diag. Paper. "This document has been developed as a guide to divisions or clubs organizing a National Championship Regatta" (introduction). Lahey explains the duties of the eight required race committees, and the "critical path" of organizing a regatta from inception until final report. Appendixes: A) information and advertising; B) sponsorship; C) the regatta course; and, D) national office responsibilities.

889. Richards, Gordon, and Wade, Paul. THE COMPLETE BOOK OF CANOEING AND KAYAKING. Edited by Ian Dear. London, North Pomfret, VT: Batsford, 1981. 142 p. Illus. Index. An "imported" title in which Richards and Wade present canoe and kayak techniques and the various competitive and recreational aspects of paddle sports from the British/Contenental perspective. Emphasized are racing—marathon, slalom, sprint and wild water. The authors devote considerable attention to fitness. Other contents: the first outing, care and maintenance, safety, first aid, rescue, coaching for competition, other canoe sports (sea, surf, polo, sailing, North American canoeing), and the "international scene."

890. Toro, Andy. CANOEING: AN OLYMPIC SPORT. 1987. 416 p. Paper. ***

Chapter 4

Trip Accounts

891. Bachman, Ben. UPSTREAM: A VOYAGE ON THE CONNECTICUT RIVER. 1985. Reprint. Chester, CT: Globe Pequot Press, 1988. 217 p. Map. Paper. Four hundred miles up the Connecticut, from Long Island Sound to the Canadian border by tug, train, automobile, bicycle, and foot—but mostly by canoe. A keen observer and accomplished writer, Bachman records his experiences among the people of the valley—and its animals: watching a wading (and seemingly unspookable) moose cow in a peaceful headwaters pond; or, submitting to the milk cow as she licked the back of his perspiring neck while he rested streamside after a strenuous paddle. These and many other delightful images by a storyteller-canoeist await the reader of UPSTREAM.

892. Bangs, Richard, and Kallen, Christian. RIVERGODS: EXPLORING THE WORLD'S GREAT WILD RIVERS. San Francisco, CA: Sierra Club Books, Yolla Bolly Press Book, 1985. 210 p. Illus. Index. ***

893. Beer, Bill. WE SWAM THE GRAND CANYON. Seattle, WA: The Mountaineers, 1988. 171 p. Illus. Maps. "The true story of a cheap vacation that got a little out of hand" (dust jacket subtitle). Okay, the book is somewhat outside the scope of this information guide — Beer and his companion John Daggett did not paddle or row through the Grand Canyon — but hey, they did use self-propelled methods. This is an engrossing and often humorous account of an incredible swim of 280 miles the pair took in 1955. Colorado river runners today speculate that while this trip could never be duplicated (Glen Canyon Dam has since been constructed), it could not even be approximated since the release water is simply too frigid to permit constant emersion. Of course, a wet suit could overcome this. (Daggett and Beer wore war surplus rubber gear.) And finally, there is the technical obsticle that swimming the Grand is illegal. Black and white and color illustrations document the trip.

894. Browning, Peter. THE LAST WILDERNESS: 600 MILES BY CANOE AND PORTAGE IN THE NORTHWEST TERRITORIES. 2d ed. Lafayette, CA: Great West Books, 1989. 179 p. Illus. Maps. Bibl. Paper. Between Lake Athabasca and Great Slave Lake is a wilderness of woods and water seldom traversed by man. In the summer of 1964, the author and a companion canoed 600 miles within this area. Their route began at Black Lake, proceeded up the Chipman and Dubawnt rivers, turned westerly down the Talston and Snowdrift rivers, and ultimately, to the eastern arm of Great Slave Lake. An inventory of food and equipment is included. The first edition of this work was published in 1975. Illustrated with fifty-nine photographs.

895. Davis, Norah Deakin. THE FATHER OF WATERS: A MISSISSIPPI RIVER CHRONICLE. Photographs by Joseph Holmes. San Francisco, CA: Sierra Club Books, 1982. 178 p. Illus. Index. ***

896. Dina, James. VOYAGE OF THE ANT: A TRUE STORY OF INGENUITY AND PERSEVERANCE...OF BUILDING A BIRCHBARK CANOE WITH STONE TOOLS AND PADDLING UP THE CONNECTICUT RIVER TO REDISCOVER THE LOST WORLD OF THE INDIANS. Harrisburg, PA: Stackpole Books, 1989. 154 p. Illus. Map. Paper. This is Dina's zen of birchbark canoe paddling—up the Connecticut river from near tidewater to Quebec, working against wind, current, (and reason?). It is the story of a quest, an intelligent, unassuming telling of why (and how) the author fashioned a canoe and paddles from natural materials, using primitive tools; why he went upstream; and, in so doing, what insights he gained about the early native inhabitants of the valley.

897. Dohnal, Karel. YUKON SOLO. Portland, OR: Binford & Mort, 1984. 215 p. Illus. Map. Paper. Journal account of a sixty-six day, 1930-mile trip down the Yukon River during the summer of 1973.

The trip begins at the headwaters of the Salmon River, a Yukon tributary, and concludes at Anakanuk, near Norton Sound. While Dohnal's writing is less than fluid, the river information is detailed and potentially helpful for Yukon trip planners, e.g., his campsite advice: choose the downstream tips of islands with low tundra vegetation allowing evening breezes to keep insects away. A river mileage table, lists of required maps, and a brief trip budget complete the work.

898. Downes, P. G. SLEEPING ISLAND: THE STORY OF ONE MAN'S TRAVELS IN THE GREAT BARREN LANDS OF THE CANADIAN NORTH. 1943. Reprint. Saskatoon, SK: Western Producer Prairie Books, Spectra, 1988. 305 p. Illus. Maps. Paper. First published by Coward-McCann in 1943, this reprint has a forword, notes and a revised photo section by R. H. Cockburn, an academic who, since 1982 has been editing and seeing into print Downes' journals. The book is derived from Downes' diaries and route book of a trip through northern Manitoba and Saskatchewan in 1939. In his forword, Cockburn writes: "As a narrative of an arduous canoe trip, SLEEPING ISLAND has few equals. Downes was fortunate to have travelled when he did into little-known, unmapped country where natives still lived on the land and there remained a tangible aura of wilderness mystery." The author was an accomplished lay-ethnologist and a professional cartographer. These skills are evidenced by his observations about the Indians and the Inuit with whom he lived and "hard" travelled, and the several maps showing the waterways he followed from Lake Winnipeg to Nueltin Lake.

899. DuBois, Eliot. AN INNOCENT ON THE MIDDLE FORK: A WHITEWATER ADVENTURE IN IDAHO'S WILDERNESS. Seattle, WA: The Mountaineers; Vancouver, BC: Douglas & McIntyre, 1987. 187 p. Illus. Map. Paper. Two trip accounts rolled into one—in the main section, DuBois writes of the terrors and triumphs of his solo 1942 Middle Fork trip in a foldboat as a 20-year-old "innocent." The book is noteworthy because of its historical significance as the record of the first solo Middle Fork descent. The brief second section written from the perspective of a raft passenger floating the same river some forty years later, contains the author's update of the river's history, his consideration of the process of change, and an appeal for conservation of this unique recreation resource.

900. Harris, Eddy L. MISSISSIPPI SOLO: A RIVER QUEST. New York: Nick Lyons Books, 1988. 250 p. As any good trip account must, Harris' story of his canoe voyage down the length of the Mississippi combines an account of his adventure with keen and very personal observations. The author's insights on the people he encountered in America's heartland are fresh, revealing, and sometimes extraordinary. To read this entertaining and thought-provoking trip account by a talented professional journalist of African-American heritage is a singular treat, one which provides a unique perspective and understanding of a great river and its people and places.

901. Hildebrand, John. READING THE RIVER: A VOYAGE DOWN THE YUKON. Boston: Houghton Mifflin, 1988. 243 p. Bibl. Paper. A 2,000-mile Yukon canoe journey undertaken as both challenge and balm for the wounded spirit. Hildebrand combines a sharp eye with facile descriptive powers; case in point from chapter seventeen: "It is perfectly bleak terrain [the Yukon below Kaltag], a Euclidean landscape of bald headlands and muskeg swamps, all sharp right angles and planes." Maybe it is the best writing about the Yukon since Jack London," observed Robert Stone.

902. Johnson, Beth. YUKON WILD: THE ADVENTURES OF FOUR WOMEN WHO PADDLED 2,000 MILES THROUGH AMERICA'S LAST FRONTIER: WITH YUKON RIVER GUIDE AND LOGISTICS SUMMARY. Stockbridge, MA: Berkshire Traveller Press, 1984. 400 p. Illus. Map. Bibl. Index. What would lure four Texas women away from their jobs, homes, family and friends for three months to paddle canoes 2,000 miles down the Yukon River? "...To save the earth," (Evelyn Edens, 51), "...the completion of therapy," (Sue Sherrod, 40), ..."more or less to rebel," (Jude Hammett, 27), "...to meet a king salmon, a grizzly bear, an Arctic tern, a moose , an Eskimo, an Athapascan Indian, and maybe a caribou and a whale," (Beth Johnson, 28). Johnson tells her river story, organized into a daily journal, in a plain-spoken, "warts and all" anecdotal style. A 24-page "Yukon River Guide and Logistics Summary, "provides valuable and specific trip log and planning information right down to the number, fabric, weight, and cost of socks to be taken along.

903. Johnston, David, and Nicholson Krista. BLUE WATER SUMMER: A PACIFIC COASTAL KAYAK ADVENTURE. Exeter, England: Orca Publications, 1986. 167 p. Illus. Maps. Paper. ***

904. Kesselheim, Alan S. WATER AND SKY: REFLECTIONS OF A NORTHERN YEAR. Drawings by Marypat Zitzer. Golden, CO: Fulcrum, 1989. 311 p. Illus. Maps. Describes a 416-day canoe journey from Jasper, Alberta, to Baker Lake, Northwest Territories, which the author undertook in 1985-86 with his companion (now wife), artist, Marypat Zitzer. The route is down the Athabasca River to a winter site at the eastern end of Lake Athabasca, and northeast from there via various lakes and the Chipman, Dubawnt, and Kazan Rivers to Baker Lake in the Barrens. Kesselheim's book is a record of an extraordinary wilderness adventure. At the same time, it is an introspective examination of his feelings regarding the journey and his companion.

905. Kaufmann, Paul D. PADDLING THE GATE: A KAYAK TRIP ON SAN FRANCISCO BAY. Illustrated by Jane Oka. Santa Monica, CA: Mara Books, 1978. 78 p. Illus. Paper. Kaufmann is a physician, psychiatrist, Jungian analyst and place-bound kayaker who conveys in PADDLING THE GATE the wonder and excitement he experiences during his regular solo kayak trips on San Francisco Bay; those times when he turns westerly where soon the currents "...agree to cooperate to join forces, building toward the awesome power flowing out the Gate" (p. 25).

906. Klein, Clayton. COLD SUMMER WIND. Fowlerville, MI: Wilderness House Books, 1983. 277 p. Illus. Maps. Bibl. Index. Essays describing five extended canoe trips taken over a period of years by Klein and his son, Darrell on Canada's Arctic and sub-Arctic waterways. The author is a wilderness canoeist with plenty of information to convey, and reading occasionally infelicitous prose is a small price to pay to learn about the following trips: 1) Woolaston Lake (SK), and down the Cochrane River to Reindeer Lake (MB); 2) Snowbird Lake (NT) to Jackpine Narrows in Reindeer Lake; 3) the length of the Kazan River (NT) to Chesterfield Inlet on Hudson Bay; 4) Thelan River (NT) to Chesterfield Inlet; and, 5) down the Back River from Muskox Rapids to the Meadowbank River. Extracts from the diaries of Catholic missionary, Fr. Joseph Buliard, are included in Klein's chapters on the Garry Lake Mission.

907. Klein, Clayton, and Kruger, Verlen. ONE INCREDIBLE JOURNEY. Rev. ed. Fowlerville, MI: Wilderness Adventure Books, 1988. 344 p. Illus. Bibl. Paper. Klein wrote this account of the 1971 "Cross-Continent Canoe Safari" from notes, diaries, photographs and maps supplied by Kruger. Kruger's paddling partner (in the stern) was Clinton Waddell; together they paddled 7,400 miles from Montreal to the Bering Sea in under six months—a record which stands today. The team followed the historic fur trade routes—both French and Russian: up the Ottawa River, across Lake Superior, through the Boundary Waters Canoe Area and the Churchill and Clearwater drainages, down the Mackenzie River, and then, across the Mackenzie Mountains before descending the Yukon River to the Bering Sea. Understandably, we learn far more about the somewhat proud, God-fearing Kruger than his taciturn mate, but so what? The challenge is the thing, and it is the essence of this adventure. Illustrated with thirty-four black and white photographs and eight maps (the cloth edition, published in 1985, has sixteen pages of color plates).

908. Klein, Clayton, ed. A PASSION FOR WILDERNESS: THE CALL OF RIVER AND MOUNTAIN. Fowlerville, MI: Wilderness Adventure Books, 1986. 355 p. Illus. Maps. Bibl. Paper. A collection of eleven trip accounts by five authors of journeys by water and land, spanning the continent from Labrador to Colorado to the Arctic Ocean. Arrangementof the material is by region and author: Elmar Engel (Labrador); Valerie Fons Kruger (Des Moines River, IA); Clayton Klein (Anderson River, NT); Theodor Mellenthin (Nahanni River, NT); and, Richard E. Winslow III (Vermont). Poems conclude the first four sections.

909. Krakel, Dean, II. DOWNRIVER: A YELLOWSTONE JOURNEY. San Francisco, CA: Siera Club Books, 1987. 250 p. Map. *** 910. McGuffin, Gary, and McGuffin, Joanie. WHERE RIVERS RUN. Toronto: Stoddart Publishing; Washington, DC: Stone Wall Press, 1988. 241 p. Illus. Maps. The tale of a young Canadian couple who paddled 6,000 miles on a two-year canoe trek across their country. They travelled from Baie Comeau on the St. Lawrence, following the historic Voyageurs trail northwest to Athabasca and Great Slave lakes, then down the Mackenzie to Inuvik on the Beaufort Sea. The McGuffins make a strong plea for waterways conservation with a number of examples of environmental depredation witnessed along their route. While the polluting residue resulting from "civilization" is a recurring issue, this is not relentlessly pessimistic reading—the authors also thoroughly document the beauty and magic of the north. This is, ultimately, an adventure story featuring appealing and vulnerable co-stars in a beautiful but potentially dangerous natural setting.

911. McKay, John W. ARCTIC ADVENTURE: A KAZAN RIVER JOURNAL, BEING A NARRATIVE, DAY BY DAY, OF A GROUP OF INTREPID ADVENTURERS ON THE KAZAN RIVER, N.W.T. IN THE SUMMER OF 1982. Toronto: Betelgeuse Books, 1983. 189 p. Illus. Paper. An account of a trip organized by David Pelly, who wished to introduce others to the arctic wilderness which he had found so intriguing on an expedition down the Back River in 1977, (see entry 917 below: Pelly, David F., EXPEDITION: AN ARCTIC JOURNEY THROUGH HISTORY ON GEORGE BACK'S RIVER). The diverse group of eight adventurers had what was essentially a relaxing trip on the Kazan—one in which they traveled in harmony with the environment at a leisurely pace. This relaxed tempo enabled ice blockades to be viewed as exciting events rather than frustrating impediments, and permitted extended enjoyment of the scenery, birdlife (over 30 species), whitewater, huge lakes, artifacts of the human history of the region (the Sarvaqtuurmiut), and the exquisite pleasures of super-fresh fish and crowberry jam.

912. May, George W. DOWN ILLINOIS RIVERS, OR FLOAT-PADDLE ADVENTURES. Ann Arbor, MI: Edwards Brothers, 1981. 400 p. Illus. Bibl. In his preface, May writes that he may be guilty of using this book on river trips "...as a vehicle to get off some personal philosophy and reminiscences... ." To be sure, there is enough fanciful digression from the actual experience of floating eighteen "little" Illinois rivers to sufficiently irk the restive reader seeking trip-specific material; however, interspersed, there is a quantity of useful and interesting information on the practicalities of each trip, local history, nature, and ecology. The craft used on these trips (the "Rob Roy,") is a homely, flat -bottomed scow propelled by paddle. May's rivers: Spoon, Sangamon, Vermilion, Kaskaskia, Iroquois, Kankakee, Des Plaines, Mackinaw. Embarras, Rock, Pecatonica, Fox, Green, La Moine, Big Muddy, Little Wabash, Cache, and Saline.

913. Morse, Eric W. FRESHWATER SAGA: MEMOIRS OF A LIFETIME OF WILDERNESS CANOEING IN CANADA. Foreword by Angus C. Scott. Toronto, London; University of Toronto Press, 1987. 189 p. Illus. Maps. Index. Paper. "This book is intended as neither a how-to handbook nor a history of early canoeing. It is a saga, in the sense of being a personal chronicle of events over the sixty-year period 1918-78—memoirs of a lifetime's canoeing which was almost entirely done in my vacations and for no more reason than recreation" (introduction). Most of the vacations were taken in the company of a small group of friends whom the press dubbed the "Voyageurs." During his lifetime, Morse canoed scores of Canada's waterways east of the Rockies. FRESHWATER SAGA is divided into two roughly geographic parts: Part One: Historic Routes (Quetico, the Churchill and Mackenzie Rivers, Lake Superior, etc.), and, Part Two: The Barren Lands and the Sub-Arctic (the Hanbury, Thelon, Dubawnt, Kazan, and Taltson Rivers, and Reindeer, Great Slave and Great Bear Lakes, etc.). A series of maps showing the waterways, routes and years paddled completes Morse's book.

914. Nash, Roderick Frazier. THE BIG DROPS: TEN LEGENDARY RAPIDS OF THE AMERICAN WEST. Rev. ed. Boulder, CO: Johnson Books, 1989. 216 p. Maps. Bibl. Index. Paper. With this revision of the long out of print 1978 edition which he co-authored with Robert O. Collins, Nash pays tribute to some of the great rapids of western rivers and the people who have run them. The author, a conservationist-historian-boatman who has logged more than 40,000 river miles, is well known in both academic and river running circles. The ten big drops he has chosen: Clavey Falls (Tuolumne-CA), Rainie Falls (Rogue-OR), Hell's Half Mile (Green-CO), Warm Springs (Yampa-CO), Satan's Gut (Colorado-UT), Redside (Middle Fork of the Salmon-ID), Big Mallard (Main Salmon-ID), Granite Creek (Snake-ID, OR), Crystal (Colorado-AZ), and Lava Falls (Colorado-AZ).

915. Norment, Christopher. IN THE NORTH OF OUR LIVES: A YEAR IN THE WILDERNESS OF NORTHERN CANADA. Camden, ME: Down East Books, 1989. 248 p. ***

916. O'Connor, Cameron, and Lazenby, John, eds. FIRST DESCENTS: IN SEARCH OF WILD RIVERS. Birmingham, AL: Menasha Ridge Press, 1989. 163 p. Illus. Paper. Twenty stories comprise this anthology of river "firsts." The editors write in their introduction that "...we chose the excellent stories that make up this book because they portray first descents in a broad sense. We chose them for their excitement, but also for their humor and for the insights they provide into why we run rivers. What they have in common is the thrill shared by all who run a river for the first time." The essays range from Andrzej Pietowski's taut account of his squeeze through "the belly of the earth" (the canyon of Peru's raging Rio Colca), to a hilarious run down a rain-swollen suburban storm drain ditch (Polio Creek) by a much younger William (never Bill) Nealy in a plastic K-Mart rowboat. Photographs and drawings illustrate the work.

917. Pelly, David F. EXPEDITION: AN ARCTIC JOURNEY THROUGH HISTORY ON GEORGE BACK'S RIVER. Toronto: Betelgeuse Books, 1981. 172 p. Illus. Bibl. Index. Description of a 1977 Northwest Territories canoe expedition down the Back River to Pelly Lake which partially retraced the original voyage of discovery made by George Back's party in 1833-34. Pelly juxtaposes history with contemporary wilderness canoe adventure. A number of sketches from the Back expedition are reproduced.

918. Perkins, Robert. AGAINST STRAIGHT LINES: ALONE IN LABRADOR. Illustrations by the author. Boston, MA: Little, Brown, Atlantic Monthly Press Book, 1983. 191 p. Illus. Paper. ***

919. Raffan, James. SUMMER NORTH OF SIXTY: BY PADDLE AND PORTAGE ACROSS THE BARREN LANDS. 224 p. Toronto: Key Porter Books, 1990. ***

920. Rennicke, Jeff, ed. RIVER DAYS: TRAVELS ON WESTERN RIVERS. Golden, CO: Fulcrum, 1988. 204 p. Illus. Maps. Call this a book of essays or a collection of trip accounts, either description will suffice. RIVER DAYS is a random assemblage of twenty-seven "campfire" stories (nine previously published) by eight well-known rivermen writing about their favorite runs on western rivers. (Was there never a riverwoman hunkered around the Rennicke campfire with a great tale to tell?) The editor contributes thirteen essays, Verne Huser (4), Brian Clark (3), David Bolling and Paul Hoobyar (2 each), Robert Gildart, Larry Rice, and Bill Stewart (1 each). The storys about the classic runs make absorbing reading; each is preceded by a small map and access data in tabular form. Runs described are on the following rivers: American (CA), Arkansas (CO), Colorado (CO, UT, AZ), Deschutes (OR), Dolores (CO), Flathead (MT), Green (CO, UT), Gunnison (CO), Klamath (CA), Kobuk (AK), Owyhee (OR), Rio Chama (NM), Rio Grande (TX), Rogue, (OR), Salmon (CA), Salmon (ID), Selway (ID), Skykomish (WA), Snake (ID), Tuolumne (CA), and Yampa (CO).

921. Rice, Larry. GATHERING PARADISE: ALASKA WILDERNESS JOURNEYS. Golden, CO: Fulcrum Publishing, 1990. 303 p. Illus. Bibl. ***

922. RIVERS RUNNING FREE: STORIES OF ADVENTUROUS WOMEN. Edited by Judith Niemi and Barbara Wieser. Minneapolis, MN: Bergamot Books, 1987. 287 p. Illus. Maps. Bibl. Paper. "This is a book about adventurous and exploring impulses in women, about travelling in wild places by canoe. Many of these women have travelled great distances, but the real stories are the journeys of mind and spirit" (preface). There are thirty-seven such stories written by women between 1900 and the present. Six are excerpts from previously published works. This is a valuable and fascinating anthology both for its comprehensive and diverse content, and for its feminine perspective on canoeing—most of the trips recounted are by women soloing or part of a group of other women. Trip locations range from Alaska (Yukon River, Porcupine River, Prince William Sound), Labrador (George River), through many other lower Canada and United States waters, to the Sea of Cortez. Illustrated by contemporary photographs, sometimes of the author of the piece, but more often of unidentified women engaged in canoeing activities.

923. Rom, William N. CANOE COUNTRY WILDERNESS: A GUIDE'S CANOE TRAILS THROUGH THE BWCA AND QUETICO. Minneapolis, MN: Voyageur Press, 1987. 212 p. Illus. Paper. Reminiscences about the trips through the canoe trails of the Boundary Waters Canoe Area, Quetico-Superior, Arctic Canada, and more. "[Rom] knows the North both from the perspective of a native son and from that of the many urban voyageurs he has introduced to its charms" (foreword).

924. Salmon, M. H. GILA DESCENDING: A SOUTHWESTERN JOURNEY. 2d ed. San Lorenzo, NM: High-Lonesome Books, 1986. 201 p. Illus. Paper. Armed with rod and revolver and ably assisted by tomcat and hound dog, Salmon takes the reader for an extended ride down the Gila River of New Mexico and Arizona. The trip is 200 miles, mostly in a canoe, sometimes on foot, always interesting. This is not a "chills and thrills" trip account; its pace is mostly relaxed, like that of the river's. The rewards are more subtile. Salmon's observations are as often on scenes passing through his mind as those off the bow of his canoe. He is in the tradition of good storytellers: a keen sense of humor and an eye for the absurd. The Gila, an unremarkable trickle by most navigable waterway standards, is transformed into something far more—a thoroughly delightful stream flowing along with Salmon's canoe and his imagination.

925. Schultz, James Willard. FLOATING ON THE MISSOURI. Edited by Eugene Lee Silliman. Norman, OK; London: University of Oklahoma Press, 1979. 142 p. Maps. Index. Paper. The noted outdoor writer, James Schultz ("Apikuni") and his Indian wife, Natahki, floated the Missouri River in

a flat-bottomed skiff from Fort Benton to the Milk River confluence in the fall of 1901. The description of the trip was serialized in FOREST AND STREAM between February 15, and May 24, 1902; this is its first publication in book form. Schultz writes of the Blackfeet, the passing of the frontier, the game to be hunted, and the river. The turn-of-the-century perspective lends added interest to an intrinsically fascinating account.

926. SEEKERS OF THE HORIZON: SEA KAYAKING VOYAGES FROM AROUND THE WORLD. Edited by Will Nordby. Chester, CT: Globe Pequot Press, 1989. 320 p. Illus. Index. An anthology of eleven stories about salt water kayaking edited by a well-known paddler and author. The essays describe a great range of kayak experiences, from those keen perceptions of Paul Kaufmann as he paddles around San Francisco Bay ("Paddling the Gate"), to the gripping account by Hannes Lindemann ("An Impossible Voyage"), of his solo crossing of the Atlantic in a folding boat. Other stories in this collection: Susan Meredith, "Alaskan Remembrances;" John Bauman, "Icelandic Odyssey;" Will Nordby, "Glacier Bay Discoveries;" Audrey Sutherland, "The Canoe;" Chris Duff, "The Lucky One;" Christopher Cunningham, "Voyage of the Paper Canoe;" Frank Goodman, "Seven Tales for Seven Lives;" Larry Rice, "Rocks, Ice, and White Whales;" Greg Blanchette, "Paddling around Hawaii."

927. Shepardson, Carl. THE FAMILY CANOE TRIP: A UNIQUE APPROACH TO CANOEING. Merrillville, IN: ICS Books, 1985. 299 p. Illus. Paper. Traces a three-year, three-stage, 6000-mile canoe voyage from New Hamphshire to Fort Yukon, Alaska, completed by the Shepardson family (Carl, Margie, Tina [age eight], and five year old Randy). The subtitle notwithstanding, this is a trip account, not instructional material about family canoe camping. The presence of two children on a trip of this magnitude is the perspective but not the centerpiece of this work; the overarching lesson is that a long canoe voyage can be done with kids—not specifically how to do it. The book is a good read simply for the bold adventure that it documents.

928. Steber, Rick, and Taylor, Shell. NEW YORK TO NOME: THE NORTHWEST PASSAGE BY CANOE. Croton-on-Hudson, NY: North River Press, 1987. 168 p. Illus. Maps. The story (as told to Steber) of two young New York clerks, Sheldon Taylor and Geoffrey Pope, who decided one day to take a canoe trip up the Hudson, turn left across Canada and Alaska, and then swing sharp right at the Bearing Sea to Nome—where they arrived some 7800 miles and two summers later. Staked by Taylor's sister, Muriel (after whom they named their canoe) the young men paddled away from the 42nd Street pier one chilly April day in 1936. Upon reaching Canada, they followed the traditional fur trade route west (not the commonly-understood sea route "Northwest Passage" to which the subtitle somewhat misleadingly refers). Taylor and Pope reached Fort Smith, N.W.T. in October and overwintered. In spring they began the second leg down the MacKenzie, up the Rat, finally descending the Yukon to the sea where they paddled coastwise to Nome, arriving on August 11, 1937.

929. Stresau, Marion. CANOEING THE BOUNDARY WATERS: THE ACCOUNT OF ONE FAMILY'S EXPLORATIONS. Edmonds, WA: Signpost Books, 1979. 154 p. Illus. Map. Paper. Stresau writes of the experiences she shared with her family in the BWCA. They begin as greenhorns, and through considerable adventure and misadventure extending over a decade of summers on the water, develop into a crew of seasoned paddlers.

930. Sutherland, Audrey. PADDALING MY OWN CANOE. Honolulu, HI: University Press of Hawaii, 1978. 136 p. Illus. Map. Recounts eight trips the author has made along the northeast coast of Molokai, Hawaii—hiking, swimming, and paddling inflatables. This is a rain forest and water wilderness. Misty waterfalls slip from clifftops, dropping 3,000 feet into the warm Pacific wherein swim fish named uhu, maiko, palani and kihikihi. Sutherland's description of this wild island paradise is interwoven with her views on natural history, Hawaiian culture, gormet camp food, and survival techniques. Drawings by Dorothy Bowles.

931. Tryck, Keith. YUKON PASSAGE: RAFTING 2,000 MILES TO THE BERING SEA. New York: Times Books, 1980. 218 p. Illus. ***

932. Wise, Ken C. CRUISE OF THE 'BLUE FLUJIN.' Fowlerville, MI: Wilderness Adventure Books, 1987. 216 p. Illus. Maps. Bibl. "Cold as blue flujin where sailors say fire freezes," (from Herman Melville's, WHITEJACKET). Blue flujin is also the name of one of the canoes used by four Sea Scouts who may have been the first to paddle the full length of the Inside Passage. Wise, who received the 1988 writer of the year award from the Gem State (Idaho) Writer's Guild for this book, recalls his epic 1936 journey made with Gene Zabriskie, Wilfred Cash and Philip Fallis. Some or all of the group paddled from Seattle to Skagway, climbed

White Pass, and then launched at Lake Bennett, continuing from there down the Yukon River to Circle, Alaska. The tale is told in an unembellished style with some dialogue supplied. Drawings and contemporary photographs illustrate the book.

933. Witmer, Dale E. 3,000 MILES BY CANOE. Mountain View, CA: World Publications, 1979. 154 p. Illus. Paper. An account of a trip down the Missouri-Mississippi Rivers from Three Forks, Montana to New Orleans, undertaken by Witmer and his sons in a custom-designed canoe. The adventures along the way constitute the central theme, but there is also much about the necessities of planning, equipment, and provisioning—practical information for would-be long distance canoe trippers.

Chapter 5

History and Biography

934.Arima, Eugene Y. INUIT KAYAKS IN CANADA: A REVIEW OF HISTORICAL RECORDS AND CONSTRUCTION BASED MAINLY ON THE CANADIAN

MUSEUM OF CIVILIZATION'S COLLECTION. Canadian Ethnology Service Paper, 110. Ottawa, ON: National Museums of Canada, 1987. 235 p. Illus. Bibl. Paper. ***

935.Arman, Florence, and Wooldridge, Glen. THE ROGUE: A RIVER TO RUN. Foreword by Ted Trueblood. Grants Pass, OR: Wildwood Press, 1982. 276 p. Illus. Bibl. Index. Paper. "The story of pioneer whitewater river runner Glen Wooldridge and his first eighty years on the Rogue River" (title page). Wooldridge has excelled in many river-related occupations—guide, outfitter, doryman, boat-builder, fisherman, and hyperbolic story-teller. Arman's is an anecdotal account of the life and good times of a true Oregon original. She leaves Wooldridge's remembrances and tall tales unchanged from the way he related them; these stories are highlighted in boldface throughout the book. The result is an entertaining work about a fabulous character and a fabulous river.

936.Back, Brian. THE KEEWAYDIN WAY, A PORTRAIT: 1893-1983. Temagami, ON: Keewaydin Camp, 1983. 206 p. Illus. Maps. Bibl. Paper. An "oral history" of Keewaydin (youth camp with a wilderness canoe-tripping emphasis), the oldest private camp in North America, which "...celebrates the elusive myths of male camaraderie, friendship, loyalty, courage and unadvertised accomplishment" (introduction).

937.Brower, Kenneth. THE STARSHIP AND THE CANOE. New York: Harper & Row, Perennial Library, 1983, c1978. 270 p. Maps. ***

938.CANEXUS: THE CANOE IN CANADIAN CULTURE. Edited by James Raffan, and Bert Horwood. Illustrations by Bill Mason. Foreword by Kirk Wipper. Toronto: Betelgeuse Books, 1988. 212 p. Illus. Index. Paper. Perhaps more than any other single thing, the canoe joined and molded Canada. It is a singular artifact, beautiful and practical—and sometimes overlooked as a vital element in the development of Canada. "The word `canexus' is a neologism coined to muster images of the canoe as a connection linking people to each other, to culture, and to the land" (introduction). The book, CANEXUS, is a compilation of fourteen essays reflecting different ways of thinking about the canoe—historical, sociological, spiritual, technological, philosophical, and ethnological. The journeys undertaken by the essayists are those of the imagination: the reader may be transported along the mist-shrouded coast of B.C.; ponder the complexities of canoeing and gender roles; bake some bannock; or simply enjoy a good canoe story. "This is a book for paddlers, but more importantly, it is a book for non-paddlers, would-be paddlers, readers, and armchair adventurers of all kinds who have ever wondered about the canoe's place in Canadian culture" (introduction). Some of the contributors: Shelagh Grant, Bruce Hodgins, E.Y. Arima, Philip Chester, Kenneth G. Roberts, Gwyneth Hoyle, Roderick A. Macdonald and C.E.S. Franks.

939.THE CANOE INDIANS OF SHOALWATER BAY: THEIR CANOES AND HOW THEY USED THEM, WITH A BIBLIOGRAPHY. Tokeland, WA: Heritage Committee, Shoalwater Bay Indian Tribe, 1984. 11 leaves. Bibl. Typescript. A capsule history (with a three-page bibliography) of the dugout canoes used by the Shoalwater/Chehalis/ Chinook Indians of coastal Washington State.

940.Carrey, Johnny, and Conley Cort. THE MIDDLE FORK OF THE SALMON RIVER AND THE SHEEPEATER WAR. Cambridge, ID: Backeddy Books, 1977. 152 p. Illus. Bibl. Index. Paper. ***

941.Carrey, Johnny, and Conley, Cort. RIVER OF NO RETURN. Cambridge, ID: Backeddy Books, 1978. 319 p. Illus. Bibl. Index. ***

942.Carrey, Johnny; Conley, Cort, and Barton, Ace. SNAKE RIVER OF HELLS CANYON. Cambridge, ID: Backeddy Books, 1979. 399 p. Illus. Bibl. Index. ***

943.Cassidy, John. A GUIDE TO THREE RIVERS. San Francisco, CA: Friends of the River, 1981. 295 p. Illus. Maps. Paper. ***

944.Clark, Georgie White, and Newcomb, Duane. GEORGIE CLARK: THIRTY YEARS OF RIVER RUNNING. San Francisco: Chronicle Books, 1979. 165 p. Illus. Paper. The legendary "Woman of the Rivers" tells about her life as adventurer, guide and outfitter running the rivers of North America. She was one of the first to use huge triple-rigs — lashed-together surplus bridge pontoons seating two dozen passengers like eggs in a carton and propelled by outboard motor. Clark writes about her early years cycling across America, hiking in the Southwest, and SWIMMING the Grand Canyon. Other river trips on Alaska's Copper, the Fraser, and the Rio Grande de Santiago are some of the later adventures contributing to a full and remarkable life. Another Clark biography (annotated in the first edition of WILDERNESS WATERWAYS): DeRoss, Rose Marie, ADVENTURES OF GEORGIE WHITE, 3d ed., Costa Mesa, CA: Gardner, 1970.

945.Cook, David S. ABOVE THE GRAVEL BAR: THE INDIAN CANOE ROUTES OF MAINE. Milo, ME: Milo Printing, 1985, 111 p. Illus. Bibl. Paper. "Prehistoric people traveled extensively throughout Maine and when they built the first birch bark canoe they had the equivalent of the wheel" (introduction). Cook writes that these early ancestors of the Penobscots and Passamaquoddys developed a network of canoe routes. He has followed many of the routes and reports his observations and related readings from the perspective of lay archaeologist and history teacher.

946.Cook, William. THE WEN, THE BOTANY, AND THE MEXICAN HAT: THE ADVENTURES OF THE FIRST WOMAN THROUGH GRAND CANYON ON THE NEVILLS EXPEDITION. Orangevale, CA: Callisto Books, 1987. 151 p. Illus. Map. Paper. In 1938, two botanists, Elzada Clover and Lois Jotter Cutter, became the first women to successfully run the length of the Grand Canyon. (The first woman to try it, Bessie Hyde in 1928, presumably drowned with her husband Glen near the lower end of the Canyon where their boat was found). The original purpose of the trip was to "botanize" the Canyon, however high public interest concerning the women taking this dangerous journey soon overshadowed the scientific aspects. The 1938 trip, which like that of the Hyde's was to begin in Green River, Utah and continue downstream 660 miles to Boulder Dam, also marked the beginning of commercial floats through the Canyon. Four men and two women comprised the forty-six day expedition guided by the legendary Norm Nevills. The three boats used (the "Wen," "Botany," and Mexican Hat"), were Nevills' custom design—flat-bottomed, oar-driven, and made from marine plywood. Much of the material for Cook's account is from Clover's diary and Nevills' trip log. The book is arranged by date, and illustrated with fourteen contemporary photographs.

947.Cooley, John. THE GREAT UNKNOWN: THE JOURNALS OF THE HISTORIC FIRST EXPEDITION DOWN THE COLORADO RIVER. Flagstaff, AZ: Northland Publishing, 1988. 207 p. Illus. Maps. Bibl. Index. Cooley recounts the 1869 adventure of Major John Wesley Powell in which Powell and nine other men first explored, mapped, and gave names to Colorado River landmarks. This is the first compilation of all the surviving journals, accounts, and letters of Powell and his crew. "Arranged as a continuous narrative from 24 May to 1 September, 1869, they present a richly textured and more colorful story of this amazing adventure into the unknown than could any single account" (introduction). The illustrations are contemporary drawings made from the photographs taken during the second Powell expedition (1871-72).

948.Crowley, William. RUSHTON'S ROWBOATS AND CANOES: THE 1903 CATALOG IN PERSPECTIVE. Blue Mountain Lake, NY: Adirondack Museum; Camden, ME: International Marine Publishing, 1983. 80 p. Illus. Index. Paper. J. Henry Rushton sold his first boat around 1873. Some seven years later his reputation as the preeminent builder of lightweight craft was assured when he built the eighteen pound "Wood Drake" for George Washington Sears (Nessmuk). A touring canoe of that weight was unheard of until then. Nessmuk quickly let the world know of Rushton's skill through his letters published in FOREST AND STREAM magazine. The first Rushton mail-order catalog was published at about the same time Sears and Montgomery Ward started theirs. The 1903 catalog (with drawings of all stock boats and accessories, descriptions, prices, and index) is reproduced in its entirety. Sixteen pages of contemporary photographs, boat drawings, and specifications are included.

949.Davidson, James West, and Rugge, John. GREAT HEART: THE HISTORY OF A LABRADOR ADVENTURE. New York: Viking, 1988. 385 p. Illus. If ever there were a true-life adventure which should become a feature film, this one is it. All the stock Hollywood elements are in place: the wild and beautiful Labrador subarctic setting, Indians, excitement, danger, death, a beautiful woman, a canoe chase... ! Davidson and Rugge, are well-known to canoeists for their classic, THE COMPLETE WILDERNESS PADDLER. In this latest collaboration, they tell the story of the ill-fated Hubbard-Wallace journey across 550 miles of Labrador's unmapped barrens. Three men, Leonidas Hubbard Jr., Dillon Wallace, and George Elson, set out by canoe in July, 1903; three months later two returned. Hubbard, unable to go on, had remained behind where he died of starvation. This is but prelude to part two of the drama in which Hubbard's wife Mina undertakes a new expedition in 1905, intending to finish what her husband started. This becomes a race when Wallace, whom she blames for her husband's death, mounts his own expedition. For a fictionalized biography of Elson, see Clayton Klein's, CHALLENGE THE WILDERNESS, (citation below).

950.Dietz, Lew. THE ALLAGASH. 1968. Reprint. Rivers of America. Illustrated by George Loh. Thorndike, ME: Thorndike Press, 1978. 264 p. Illus. Maps. Bibl. Paper. ***

951.Durham, Bill. CANOES AND KAYAKS OF WESTERN AMERICA. 1960. Reprint. Seattle, WA: Shorey Book Store, 1974. 103 p. Illus. Bibl. ***

952.Dyson, George. BAIDARKA. Foreword by Kenneth Brower. Edmonds, WA: Alaska Northwest Publishing, 1986. 215 p. Illus. Index. Paper. Bai.dar.ka: a portable boat made of skins stretched over wood frames and widely used by Alaskan coastal natives and Aleuts. No longer the philosopher-hermit of Kenneth Brower's THE STARSHIP AND THE CANOE, Dyson emerges in this, his first book, as northwest historian, kayak craftsman, and adventurer. He begins his three part narrative with the first Russian sighting of an Alaskan native kayaker in 1732. This is followed by a recounting of his 1977 "Baidarka Expedition." He concludes the book with a detailed revelation of his latest baidarka designs and finished products. There are scores of color photographs of the expeditions and kayaks under construction, plus a number of contemporary lithographs and photographs illustrating the period 1732-1933. Included is a description and series of photographs of the 48-foot Dyson kayak creation, the "Mt. Fairweather."

953.Endicott, William T. THE RIVER MASTERS: A HISTORY OF THE WORLD CHAMPIONSHIPS OF WHITEWATER CANOEING. Washington, DC: [The author.] 1979. 186 p. Illus. Maps. Paper. "This book is an attempt to record the history of international competition in whitewater canoeing. It begins with the story of how whitewater boats evolved and how racing them became an organized sport. Subsequent chapters relate in a more or less chronological way, highlights of the World Championships of whitewater canoeing, held every odd-numbered year since 1949" (author's note.) Endicott also includes accounts of the 1972 Olympic Games, and the Europa Cup races of 1974, 1976 and 1978. A "photo album" and an extensive list of all World Championship competitors (with country and career record) are other parts of the volume.

954.Flavell, George F. THE LOG OF THE PANTHON: AN ACCOUNT OF AN 1896 RIVER VOYAGE FROM GREEN RIVER, WYOMING TO YUMA, ARIZONA THROUGH THE GRAND CANYON. Edited by Neil B. Carmony and David E. Brown. Foreword by Barry Goldwater. Boulder, CO: Pruett Publishing, 1987. 109 p. Illus. Bibl. Index. Paper. Published for the first time, this is the edited version of Flavell's notebook containing the log of the Panthon, the fifteen-foot wooden boat in which the author and his companion, Ramon Montez, traversed 1,500 miles of the Green and Colorado rivers. The two men were the first to traverse the Grand Canyon who were not paid members of a government or business sponsored expedition—and perhaps may thus be considered the pioneers of whitewater recreational boating on the Colorado.

955.Freeman, Lewis R. THE COLORADO RIVER YESTERDAY, TODAY AND TOMORROW. New York, Dodd, Mead, 1923. 450 p. Illus. As stated in his foreword, Freeman attempts in this book to convey the "flesh-and-blood humanness" of such renown Colorado River explorers and navigators as Alarcon, Escalante, Ashley, Manly, Hardy, Ives, Wheeler, Powell, Dellenbaugh, Stanton, Stone and the Kolb brothers. This is not a history/biography in the detached academic sense, but one laced with opinion and conjecture; it is a history written in the style of the time by an author who admits his discomfort at being a river rat turned writer. Therin lies its charm. Contemporary photographs and sketch maps illustrate the work.

956.Gidmark, David. BIRCHBARK CANOE: THE STORY OF AN APPRENTICESHIP WITH THE INDIANS. Burnstown, ON: General Store Publishing House, 1989. 159 p. Illus. Paper. Gidmark records his experience learning from an Algonquin master craftsman the Indian method of making a birchbark canoe. The building of the craft is central to the book, and construction details are carefully explained and illustrated with photographs. However, the important lessons learned by the author are those of the difficulty of entering another culture and being accepted by its people.

957.Gilpatrick, Gil. ALLAGASH: THE STORY OF MAINE'S LEGENDARY WILDERNESS WATERWAY. Freeport, ME: DeLorme Publishing, 1983.

235 p. Illus. Maps. Bibl. Gilpatrick, registered Maine guide and outdoor resources instructor, mixes fact and fancy into a brew of history, historical fiction and trip account surrounding the legendary Allagash River. There are three parts to the book; the author first examines the folklore of the Wabnaki, the regionally indigenous native American tribe. Part II is an account of Maine's robust lumber industry beginning in the early decades of the 1800s. In the last part, Gilpatrick guides the reader on a contemporary Allagash trip, pointing out the sights along the way. Two maps (Allagash Falls; Allagash River Wilderness Area), and photographs and drawings illustrate the text.

958.Hartsough, Mildred L. FROM CANOE TO STEEL BARGE ON THE UPPER MISSISSIPPI. Minneapolis, MN: Upper Mississippi Waterway Association; University of Minnesota Press, 1934. 308 p. Illus. Maps. Bibl. ***

959.Holmes, Tommy. THE HAWAIIAN CANOE. Hanalei, HI: Editions Limited, 1981. 191 p. Illus. Bibl. Index. Holmes acknowledges the extent and diversity of the help he received throughout the fifteen years this volume was in preparation; there were dozens of people involved including editors, librarians, scholars, photographers, artists, kupuna (wise ones), and just willing friends. The result is indeed an impressive and important work which documents the history of a cultural artifact critical to the lives of a people bounded by a vast ocean. The many illustrations (diagrams, archival and contemporary photographs) are splendid. A sampling of chapter headings: Origins, Voyaging, Materials, Canoe Building, Paddles, Canoeing Skills, Fishing, and Petroglyphs. Holmes' book should long stand as the definitive work on the Hawaiian Canoe.

960.Hubbard, Mina Benson. A WOMAN'S WAY THROUGH UNKNOWN LABRADOR: AN ACCOUNT OF THE EXPLORATION OF THE NASCAUPEE AND GEORGE RIVERS BY MRS. LEONIDAS HUBBARD, JUNIOR. Toronto: William Briggs, 1908. 338 p. Illus. Map. Index. Mina Hubbard's account of her husband Leonidas' exploration along the George River of eastern Labrador which cost his life, and of her own subsequent journey through the regiorn. Most of the trip diary of Leonidas Hubbard has been included in this book. In her wish to clear the many misconceptions surrounding the ill-fated expedition, Hubbard retraced the trip in the company of George Elson, her husband's guide. "She mapped the great Northwest or Nascaupee River, encountered the caribou migration at the Height of Land, observed the primitive Nascaupee Indians of the George, and made her way finally to Ungava Bay on the Hudson Straits" (William B. Cabot's introduction).

961.Huber, J. Parker. THE WILDEST COUNTRY: A GUIDE TO THOREAU'S MAINE. Boston, MA: Appalachian Mountain Club, 1981. 198 p. Index. ***

962.Kerfoot, Justine. WOMAN OF THE BOUNDARY WATERS: CANOEING, GUIDING, MUSHING AND SURVIVING. Foreword by Les Blacklock. Grand Marais, MN: Women's Times Publishing, 1986. 200 p. Illus. Maps. Index. Kerfoot, operator of a hunting lodge on Minnesota's Gunflint Lake since 1928, writes about her life in the Border Lakes country. A degree in zoology was her formal preparation, however it was from the cumulative experience.

Chapter 6

Pictorial Works

985.AMERICA'S WILD AND SCENIC RIVERS. Prepared by the Special Publications Division, National Geographic Society. Washington, DC: The Division, 1983. 199 p. Illus. Bibl. Index. ***

986.BORDER COUNTRY: THE QUETICO-SUPERIOR WILDERNESS. Photographs by Craig Blacklock and Nadine Blacklock. Text by Tom Klein. Introduction by Gaylord Nelson. Minocqua, WI: NorthWord Press, 1988. 168 p. Illus. The political struggle to create the Boundary Waters Canoe Area on the U.S. side of the Quetico-Superior wilderness, was finally ended in 1978 with congressional passage of the B.W.C.A. Wilderness bill. Klein's impassioned essay about the place and the fight for protective legislation notwithstanding, the book is fundamentally a picture album—and what pictures! There are approximately 125 pages of magnificent color photographs by the Blacklocks. The photographs were taken over a two-year period in all seasons. The Blacklocks work evokes a mood of serenity and beauty approaching that of the real thing.

987.BOUNDARY WATERS. Photographs by Jerry Stebbins. Text by Greg Breining. Minneapolis, MN: Nodin Press, 1983. 96 p. Illus. ***

988.Crowley, Kate, and Link, Mike. BOUNDARY WATERS CANOE AREA WILDERNESS. Voyageur Wilderness Books. Stillwater, MN: Voyageur Press, 1987. 96 p. Illus. Paper. A hybrid book having the triple attributes of a coffee table pictorial, natural history, and trip account. Crowley and Link are naturalists who share their expertise and love of the B.W.C.A. in which they live and work. In chapters of four or five pages, each lushly illustrated with large color photographs, the authors take thoughtful note of plants and animals of the region, and of the composite meaning of the Boundary Waters treasure. Photographs by: Daniel J. Cox, Sharon Eaton, Michael Furtman, Peter Hawkins, Steve Kuchera, Ron Miles, Ronald Morreim, Peter Roberts, and Phil and Judy Sublett.

989.Crowley, Kate, and Link, Mike. LAKE SUPERIOR'S NORTH SHORE AND ISLE ROYALE. Stillwater, MN: Voyageur Press, 1989. ***

990.Harrington, Richard. RIVER RAFTING IN CANADA. Edmonds, WA: Alaska Northwest Publishing, 1987. 112 p. Illus. Index. Paper. Short narrative accounts of twenty-two selected Canadian rivers on which trips may be booked with rafting companies. Each essay is illustrated with several color photographs. The book serves as a marketing tool for guides and outfitters, since Harrington gives them virtually equal billing with the waterways on which they conduct their business. A sampling of the rivers covered: Batiscan (PQ), Rouge (PQ), Magnetawan (ON), Ottawa (PQ-ON), Pigeon (MB), Oldman (AB), Highwood (AB), Slave (NT), Coppermine (NT), Firth (YT), Tatshenshini (YT), Kicking Horst (BC), Chilliwack (BC), Chilcotin (BC) and, Toby Creek (BC).

991.Jenkinson, Michael. WILDERNESS RIVERS OF AMERICA. New York: Abrams, Chanticleer Press, 1981. 270 p. Illus. Index. "Coffee table" book containing some 200 sumptuous photographs of eleven canoeable North American waterways selected for their beauty and diversity. The waterway chapters are introduced by a locator map followed with a descriptive narrative by noted writer-paddler, Jenkinson, then the photographs take over—none showing any trace of a human being or artifact. The waterways and the photographers: Noatak- AK (Sam Abell), Fraser-BC (Steve Wilson), Salmon-ID (Boyd Norton), Colorado-CO/UT/AZ (David Muench), Rio Grande-NM/TX (David Muench), B.W.C.A.-WI/ON (Annie Griffiths), Buffalo-AR (George Silk), Atchafalaya-LA (Yva Momatiuk and John Eastcott), Allagash-ME (Charles Steinhacker), Upper Hudson-NY (Dan Budnik), and Suwannee-FL/GA (Wendell Metzen). See this book at your library; it is out of print.

992.Junas, Lil. CADRON CREEK: A PHOTOGRAPHIC NARRATIVE. Little Rock, AR: Ozark Society Foundation, 1979. 96 p. Illus. Maps. Some ninety black and white photographs (and a few in color) dominate this waterway pictorial by an award-winning photojournalist. Junas describes Cadron country in words and pictures which blend into an appealing low-key look at a central Arkansas way of life to be cherished. She concludes her book with descriptions and access maps for four of the most popular runs on the North and East Forks: Iron Bridge to Pinnacle Springs; Pinnacle Springs to Highway 65; Highway 65 to Highway 295; and, Highway 36 to Highway 107.

993.Rennicke, Jeff. THE RIVERS OF COLORADO. Colorado Geographic Series, No. 1. Billings and Helena, MT: Falcon Press, 1985. 111 p. Illus. Bibl. Rennicke's book is hard to categorize—perhaps pictorial geography comes the closest. It is the first in a series which has some resemblance in size and content to the Alaska Geographic Series. The gorgeous color photographs, 120 of them, are on virtually every page. The pictures are a stunning feature of the book, but in narrative sandwiched between, writer-guide Rennicke has plenty to say about Colorado river use, river people, river history, river running, river wildlife, geology, scenery, conservation, and dam building.

994.Stephens, Hal G., and Shoemaker, Eugene M. IN THE FOOTSTEPS OF JOHN WESLEY POWELL: AN ALBUM OF COMPARATIVE PHOTOGRAPHS OF THE GREEN AND COLORADO RIVERS, 1871-72 AND 1968. Boulder, CO: Johnson Books; Denver, CO: The Powell Society, 1987. 286 p. Illus. Maps. Bibl. Index. Paper. One hundred and ten historic pictures taken by the photographic team on the second Powell Expedition were selected by Stephens and Shoemaker for this album. On the facing page of each of the 1871-72 photographs are their 1968 counterparts—taken from virtually the identical camera stations and cropped and scaled to match the originals. The result is an impressive historical and photographic achievement. The comparisons are fascinating, documenting as they do the way man has altered the river environment (impoundments, reduced/regulated flow, introduction of the tamarisk), and the way nature inexorably works over time (rockslides, tributary stream bed changes, movement of massive boulders). Implicit also is the realization that there is a great deal that has remained almost unchanged during the intervening 100 years. Narrative commentary, including geological identification, accompanies each pair of photographs. The book is also available in a cloth-bound edition.

995.TWO OZARK RIVERS: THE CURRENT AND THE JACKS FORK. Photographs by Oliver Schuchard. Text by Steve Kohler. Columbia, MO: University of Missouri Press, 1984. 130 p. Illus. Maps. Bibl. Congress voted national park status for the Current and Jacks Fork rivers in 1964, giving them the name Ozark National Scenic Riverways. Looking at Schuchard's eighty stunning photographs of the clear blue-green waters of the rivers and the lovely region surrounding them, one can easily understand both the desire and the need to preserve these natural wonders through legislation. (With all this recognition resulting from national park status, the increase in the number of summertime visitors to the O.N.S.R. is itself a significant environmental problem; some two million people visit yearly, many of whom may be seen all over the rivers in floating aluminum traffic jams.) In his narrative, Kohler explains the intricate geology of caves and springs, the flora and fauna, and the varied human history of the region from the first interaction of Indians and settlers to the present day.

996.WILD WATERS: CANOEING CANADA'S WILDERNESS RIVERS. Edited by James Raffan. Toronto: Key Porter Books, 1986. 151 p. Illus. Above all, WILD WATERS is a picture book. To be sure, there are descriptions of canoe trips that the editor has taken on each of the featured rivers, but the well-served purpose of his book is to provide an album in which the pictures offer a "...glimpse of that river's personality," as Bill Mason writes in his foreword. The photographs are all in color; many spread across facing pages. Raffin's selection of eight "expedition quality" rivers (nine if you count the Coppermine addressed in the introductory essay) are representative of Canada's geographic vastness and topographic diversity. The rivers: Moisie, Missinaibi, Clearwater, Kazan, Hood, Bonnet Plume, Nahanni, and Liard.

Chapter 7, Section 1

Periodicals and Paddlesports Magazines

997.ACA COMPETITOR'S NEWSLETTER. Newington, VA: American Canoe Association. National Paddling Committee. National Slalom & Wildwater Committee, vol. 1-, 1982-? Monthly? This typescript newsletter is possibly defunct. The last issue inspected is dated March, 1983. Contents include competition rules, race registration entry deadlines, yearly race calendar, race results, and several pages of NPC news items. Source: American Canoe Association, P.O. Box 1190, Newington, VA 22122-1190.

998.ACA DOWNEAST SAILOR. American Canoe Association. National Sailing Committee, vol. 1-, 198?-. Bi-monthly? The typescript newsletter issue which was inspected is dated February, 1984. This ACA—affiliated group is composed of individuals interested in sailing canoes. Newsletter contents include notes of the affiliate meeting held at the ACA Congress in Madison, directories of Committee officers and members, "for sale" items, and plans for a canoe conversion sailing rig. Source: American Canoe Association, P.O. Box 1190, Newington, VA 22122-1190.

999.THE AMERICAN CANOEIST. Lafayette, IN: American Canoe Association, vol. 1-, 1979-. Bi-monthly. Contains several feature articles per issue. The December, 1989 issue includes articles reporting events at the ACA Congress in Savannah, accessability (of physically impaired) to canoesport, a club profile, a biography of Ray Boessel, a history of boat construction materials, and an article on paddling technique. Regular departments: editorial, news notes, safety, competition, recreation, conservation, accent on youth, reviews, and classified. Source: The American Canoeist, P.O. Box 5483, Lafayette, IN 47903.

1000.AMERICAN WHITEWATER: JOURNAL OF THE AMERICAN WHITEWATER AFFILIATION. Palatine, IL: American Whitewater Affiliation, vol. 1-, 1967-. Bi-monthly. Running title: WHITEWATER. Intended primarily for decked boat paddlers (although open canoeists and rafters are not totally ignored). This is a "labor-of-love" periodical by enthusiasts for enthusiasts. Regular departments: news briefs, conservation news, and safety reports (by Charles Walbridge). Recent issues examined had "themes," e.g., International Boating Issue, and Gauley Festival Issue. A subscription to AW is automatic with AWA membership. Indexed by SPORTSEARCH, and "self-indexed" since 1969 (this is a separately published author-subject-title index to articles). Source: American Whitewater Affiliation, 146 North Brockway, Palatine, IL 60067.

1001.CANOE. Kirkland, WA: Canoe America Associates, vol. 1-, 1973-. Six times yearly (March, May, July, August, October, December). "North America's #1 Resource for Canoeing & Kayaking" (subtitle from cover). This slick, four-color magazine has a circulation of about 55,000, making it the largest paddling publication in Canada or the U.S.A. The October, 1989 issue might be considered typical, with the following feature articles: 1989 World Whitewater Championships; special boat building section (3 articles); trip journal (Costa Rica); "World Enough and Time" (trip-planning); and a destinations article, "Winter's Paddling Getaways." Regular departments: editorial, letters, news notes, reviews, technique, etc. Publishes an annual canoe and accessories buying guide in the December issue. If time or pocketbook dictate subscribing to one all-round paddling publication, CANOE should probably be it. Accepts display advertising. Indexed by PHYSICAL EDUCATION INDEX; SPORTSEARCH; and "self indexed" since volume 1 (computer-accessible author, title subject index to articles). Source: CANOE, P.O. Box 3146, Kirkland, WA 98083.

1002.CANOE AND KAYAK RACING NEWS: JOURNAL OF NORTH AMERICAN COMPETITION PADDLING. Kirkland, WA: Canoe America

Associates, vol. 1-, 1989-. Six times yearly. Premier issue of this tabloid-size newspaper was published in October, 1989. "Although each issue will emphasize an event of national or international significance in a discipline, we will try to include in each issue event coverage, schedules and results for all branches of canoe and kayak racing" (editorial, Oct., 1989). Events covered: marathon, whitewater (slalom, wildwater, open canoes), flatwater sprint, outrigger, canoe triathlon, rodeos, squirt contests, ocean racing (kayaks, surf skis), canoe poling, sailing, and orienteering. Accepts display advertising. Source: CANOE, P.O. Box 3146, Kirkland, WA 98083.

1003.THE CANOEIST JOURNAL: A NEWSLETTER FOR CONTEMPORARY CANOEISTS FROM PAT MOORE. Stoughton, WI: Moore Canoes, vol. 1-, 1984-. Bi-monthly? This publication has possibly ceased, although its parent company, Moore Canoes, is still very much in business. The May, 1984 issue inspected contained this statement: "This is not a newsletter in the sense of relating current events but, rather, in the profession of new ideas and the understanding of the products of those ideas" (page 1). Source: Moore Canoes, P.O. Box 242, Stoughton, WI 53589.

1004.CANOE NEWS. Dayton, OH: United States Canoe Association, vol. 1-, 1968-. Bi-monthly? Included with membership in the USCA, whose "5-C" slogan is: cruising, conservation, camping, competition, and camaraderie. Some of the articles in the January/February, 1984 issue inspected: association president's letter; river training for the marathon canoe racer; USCA race calendar; Pontiac Triathalon; conservation news; and, the 1984 Nationals results. Source: US Canoe Association, 4169 Middlebrook Dr., Dayton, OH 45440-3311.

1005.CANOESPORT JOURNAL. Oscoda, MI: American Canoesport Inc., vol. 1-, 1987-. Quarterly. "North America's Magazine of the Open Canoe" (cover subtitle). "Slick" magazine format with four or five illustrated feature articles per issue intended for an audience of serious canoeists. In the most recent issue inspected (late season, 1989), there are articles on the physics of paddle strokes, paddle construction principles, a Merrimack River trip, and the theory and practice of switching sides. Regular columns: editorial, nature, camping, wildwater, equipment reviews, book reviews, etc. Accepts display advertising. Source: Canoesport Journal, P.O. Box 635, Oscoda, MI 48750.

1006.CCA TODAY. Gloucester, ON: Canadian Canoe Association, vol. 1-, 1989-. Monthly? "Official Bulletin of the Canadian Canoe Association," (cover). Supersedes the Association's three previous periodicals: CANOE (1976-1979?); [CCA] NEWSLETTER (1980-1982?); and, PADDLES UP (1983-1989?). "Each issue will highlight a cover feature [e.g.,"Best Canadian Finish at Junior Worlds"], together with regular columns on news from the C.C.A. office, discipline/club news, summary of competitive results, domestic sport, coaching/officials articles, upcoming events, and general `bits and pieces' on the canoeing world" (Commodore's Message, August, 1989, p. 5). Source: Canadian Canoe Association, 1600 Prom. James Naismith Drive, Gloucester, ON, K1B 5N4.

1007.CHE-MUN. Toronto: Che-Mun, vol. 1-, 19—?-. "Newsletter of wilderness canoeing" (subtitle). Unable to examine an issue due to "address change." Source: Che-Mun, Box 548, Sta. O, Toronto, ON M4A 2P1; alternate source: Michael Peak, c/o PADDLER, 157 Silver Birch Ave., Toronto, ON M4E 3L3.

1008.CKI NEWS: CANOE AND KAYAK INDUSTRY NEWSLETTER. Kirkland, WA: Canoe America Associates, vol. 1-, 1989?-. Quarterly. "A quarterly publication for paddlesports retailers and manufacturers..." (subtitle from cover). The issue inspected (Fall, 1989) is a 12-page no-nonsense marketing tool aimed directly at the people engaged in some facit of the business of paddlesports. A sampling of the articles: "Positioning Paddlesports for 1992" (marketing article); calendar of shows/events; speakers listing; tips for better press coverage; and advice about press releases. Accepts display advertising. Source: Canoe America Associates, P.O. Box 3146, Kirkland, WA 98083.

1009.CURRENTS. Colorado Springs, CO: National Organization for River Sports, vol. 1-, 1979-. Bi-monthly. "Voice of the National Organization for River Sports," (cover subtitle). Contains news and informative pieces on river access, conservation, technique, equipment, events, and other aspects of river running. Several recent issues examined have articles under the standardized headings: "River Access," "River Conservation," "River Technique," "River People," and "River Profiles." Accepts display advertising. Source: NORS, P.O. Box 6847, Colorado Springs, CO 80904.

1010.EASTERN PROFESSIONAL RIVER OUTFITTERS ASSOCIATION. NEWSLETTER. Knoxville, TN: The Association, vol. 1-, 1975?-.

Quarterly. Fifty-three eastern river outfitters (including 3 from Canada) who run whitewater float trips, plus 22 other commercial vendors comprise the association membership. They receive subscriptions to this newsletter which is concerned with: safety; trip quality; and, conserving the wilderness/wildlife of the eastern U.S. The newsletter was not examined. Source: 530 S. Gay St., Suite 222, Knoxville, TN 37902.

1011.EDDY LINE CANOE NEWS. Tunkhannock, PA: no. 1-, 198-? Bi-monthly? May have ceased publication. Regional focus on canoeing in eastern Pennsylvania and surroundings (Delaware River, Lehigh River, etc.). The issue inspected (no. 8, June/July, 198?) has articles on constructing knee pads, canoe camping, regional recreational paddling events, and PFD's. Accepts display advertising. (Possible) source: Eddy Line, R.D. 6 Box 313 A, Tunkhannock, PA 18657.

1012.FORCE 10. Elk, CA: Ocean White Water Tours, vol. 1-, 198-? Semi-annual? May have ceased publication. This is a typed and stapled newsletter published by an ocean kayaking instruction/guiding outfit which contains stories, techniques and pointers on unprotected shorline ocean cruising. (Possible) source: P.O. Box 167, Elk, CA 95432.

1013.KANAWA. Hyde Park, ON: Canadian Recreational Canoeing Association, vol. 1-, 19—? Quarterly. "The national newsmagazine for recreational canoeing in Canada" (cover subtitle). Selected articles in the issue inspected (Winter, 1989): report of the annual CRCA meeting in Winnipeg; "How to Keep the Wild in Wilderness;" Bill Mason Scholarship Fund; Nikon/CRCA photograph contest; and, "Oriental Odyssey" (a brief history of paddling in the Orient) Accepts display advertising. Source: C.R.C.A., P.O. Box 500, Hyde Park, ON N0M 1Z0.

1014.KANAWA JOURNAL. Toronto: Kanawa International Museum of Canoes, Kayaks and Rowing Craft, vol. 1-, 1985-. Annual. Subscriptions for members of the museum. Upon selection of a site, a national campaign is planned to raise money for the construction of a museum. Kirk Wipper, physical educator and former Director of Camp Kandalore, has built the collection to over 600 craft and 1000 related artifacts. Although KANAWA JOURNAL issues were unexamined, they were to contain technical articles on the entire Kanawa collection. Source: address inquiry to: Paddler, 157 Silver Birch Ave., Toronto, ON M4E 3L3.

1015.LETTRE A LA POSTE. Montreal, PQ: Federation quebecoise de Canoe-Kayak D'eau Vive, vol. 1-, 1983-. 5-6 issues per year. Official newsletter of the Quebec Canoe-Kayak Federation. The issue inspected (Nov., 1984) was dedicated to Rene Guillemette for his 12 years of dedication to Quebec paddlesport. Selected contents: president's message; article about Guillemette; report of the Federation annual meeting; and, general and affiliate news. Source: F.Q.C.K., 4545 Ave. Pierre-de-Coubertin, C.P. 1000, Succ. M., Montreal, PQ H1V 3R2.

1016.NACLO NEWS. Murdock, FL: National Association of Canoe Liveries and Outfitters, vol. 1-, 19—? Bi-monthly. Newsletter publishing articles of (mostly) economic interest to canoe, kayak, raft renters/outfitters, and manufacturers and distributors of related products. Sample of material in one of the issues examined (Jan., 1990): economic survey (paddler visitation data); tax planning; report of the annual meeting; and, Pennsylvania livery regulations. Accepts display advertising. Source: NACLO, P.O. Box 1149, Murdock, FL 33938-1148.

1017.NASTAWGAN: QUARTERLY JOURNAL OF THE WILDERNESS CANOE ASSOCIATION. Toronto: The Association, vol. 1-, 1974?-. Quarterly. Name changed from THE WILDERNESS CANOEIST with vol. 9, 1982. Illustrated articles of canoe trips into Canada's wilderness, usually contributed by association members. Association news briefs, trip dates, and conservation/ environmental articles are regular features. Among others, the Autumn, 1989 issue has articles on: a Coppermine River trip, Spanish River trip, Little Sturgeon River trip, the Yukon Teritory (history), conservation, deer mating season, and Algonquin Park. Accepts display advertising. Source: W.C.A., P.O. Box 496, Postal Sta. K, Toronto, ON M4P 2G9.

1018.NEW RIVER CURRENTS. Hinton, WV: New River Scenic Whitewater Tours, Inc., vol. 1-, 1983?- . Bi-annual? Strictly a vehicle to promote the publisher's West Virginia paddle touring business. The information about facilities and accommodations for those interested in running the New, Gauley, and Bluestone Rivers may be useful. Accepts display advertising. Source: New River Scenic Whitewater Tours, Inc., P.O. Box 637, Hinton, WV 25951.

1019.OCEAN KAYAK NEWS. Ferndale, WA: Ocean Kayak, Inc., vol. 1-, 1988-. Quarterly. This tabloid-size periodical is a free-distribution marketing tool published by Ocean Kayak

(Scupper). The Summer, 1989 issue examined has: letters to the editor; a Chesapeake Bay guide article; "Chincoteague Outing;" a camping gear article; and, a Sea Anemone article, among others. Editorial policy seems to be that the material has to deal with Scuppers or mention the "S" word somewhere within. Accepts display advertising. Source: Ocean Kayak, Inc., 1920 Main St., Ferndale, WA 98248.

1020.PADDLER: FOR CANOEISTS AND KAYAKERS. Toronto: Paddler, vol. 1-, 1986-. Quarterly. A mass-circulation (23,000), four-color periodical for the Canadian canoeist or kayaker which includes trip accounts, heritage, environment, technique, and equipment. Some articles/sections in the Spring, 1990 issue examined: Subenacadie Canal trip; excerpt from James Raffin's SUMMER NORTH OF SIXTY; "Vive la Difference" (between whitewater canoeists and kayakers); canoe and kayak buyer's guide; and, a Bowron Lakes trip description. Accepts display advertising. Source: Paddler, 157 Silver Birch Ave., Toronto, ON M4E 3L3.

1021.RIVER RUNNER. Fallbrook, CA: Tanis Group, vol. 1-, 1981-. 7 issues yearly (Feb., Apr., May, Jun., Aug., Oct., Dec.). Previous title until 1984: RIVER RUNNER MAGAZINE. A major (19,000 circulation), commercial, four-color periodical providing information on equipment, technique, conservation, destinations, and related swift water paddling matters. Contents of the May, 1990 issue examined: "Dream rivers" (annual world-wide top ten selection); "Five Fundamentals" (basic kayak techniques); "Kayak Kinematics;" "Paddling the Pecos;" "Paddling Wear;" and "Departments." Accepts display advertising. Source: River Runner, P.O. Box 697, Fallbrook, CA 92028.

1022.SEA KAYAKER. Seattle, WA: Sea Kayaker, Inc., vol. 1-, 1984-. Quarterly. A specialized, paddlesport publication (circulation 9,000) covering the sea and lake kayaking scene. Material is organized by section/topic, of which there were 12 in the issue examined (Winter, 1989/90). A sampling of articles from that issue: "Boston's North Shore;" "Sea of the Amazon" (part III of a trip report from Turkey); an article on mangroves; surf techniques; a kayak drowning report; and, pumps and bailers. Departments: book reviews, trade news, club listing, calendar, and advertiser's index. Accepts display advertising. Source: Sea Kayaker, Inc., 6327 Seaview Ave., N.W., Seattle, WA 98107.

1023.WESTERN CANOER: NEWS FROM CLIPPER CANOES. Abbotsford, BC: Western Canoeing, Inc., vol. 1-, 1978?-. Annual. A tabloid, free-distribution marketing annual published by the manufacturers of Clipper canoes. The Spring, 1989 issue inspected contains articles describing trips; hints on paddling technique; wilderness and family canoeing; and, the omnipresent pictures and specifications of 40 Clipper models. Source: Western Canoeing, INc., Box 115, Abbotsford, BC V2S 4N8.

1024.WESTERN RIVER GUIDES ASSOCIATION. NEWSLETTER. Denver, CO: The Association, vol. 1-, 19—?-. Quarterly. Distributed to approximately 600 professional river outfitter members. Sample of the contents of issues inspected (August and October, 1989): WRGA joins with BLM to support Wild and Scenic designation for Westwater Canyon; report of Glen Canyon Dam environmental impact study order; western water flow report; news from California, Idaho and Oregon outfitters; speakers at Confluence "89 (annual meeting); Forest Service outfitter and guide policy consolidation; and, an update on WRGA activities. Accepts display advertising. Source: WRGA, 360 S. Monroe, Suite 300, Denver, CO 80209.

1025.WIDE WORLD OF CANOEING. Point Pleasant, NJ: Aqua-Field Publications, vol. 1-, 198?-. Other title: CANOEING (1980-). Unable to obtain a copy of this periodical for review. Source: Aqua-Field Publications, 728 Beaver Dam Rd., Point Pleasant, NJ 08742.

1026.WOODEN CANOE. Blue Mountain Lake, NY: Wooden Canoe Heritage Association, vol. 1-, 1979-. Quarterly. A "museum" journal devoted to disseminating information on preserving, studying, building, restoring, and using wooden and birchbark canoes. Subscriptions are included with membership in the WCHA. The "Tenth Anniversary Issue" examined (issue 36) contains excerpts from the best of previous numbers of WOODEN CANOE. A selection of contents: historical sketches of six canoe manufacturers; 7 building/repair articles; and, the "outdoor" section with articles on tumplines, camp cooking, and wilderness trip preparation. Accepts classified advertisements. Source: WCHA, P.O. Box 226, Blue Mountain Lake, NY 12812.

Chapter 7, Section 2

Periodicals and Club Newsletters

1027. ANorAK. Hopewell, NJ: Association of North Atlantic Kayakers, 1981?-. Bi-monthly. The association is a network of salt water paddlers located on the eastern seaboard. The typescript newsletter issue (supplement #1) which was inspected is dated October, 1983. Issue contents: a kayaking safety introduction followed by five coastal trip accounts, a book review, and, a listing of sources for further information. Source: ANorAK, 46 Princeton Rd., Hopewell, NJ 08525.

1028.BY-WAYS. Chicago: American Youth Hostels, Metropolitan Chicago Council, vol. 1-, 19—?-. Irregular. Unable to either inspect a copy of this newsletter, or verify the source address. Source: AYH, Metro Chicago Council, 3712 N. Clark St., Chicago, IL 60613.

1029.CANEWS [CSBC]. Vancouver, BC: Canoe Sport BC, vol. 1-, 1985?-. Monthly. Possibly defunct. Unable to verify current address. This is a typescript newsletter containing news and feature articles from the four separate British Columbia paddling groups under the umbrella of Canoe Sport BC: The BC Olympic Canoe and Kayak Association, BC Recreational Canoeing Association, Whitewater Canoeing Association of BC, and BC Marathon Canoe Racing Association. Accepts display advertising. Last known source: 1200 Hornby St., Vancouver, BC V6Z 2E2.

1030.CANEWS [ORCA]. Willowdale, ON: Ontario Recreational Canoeing Association, vol. 1-, 1981-. Quarterly. ORCA is the recreational canoeing affiliate of Canoe Ontario. Newsletter contents from the Spring, 1985 issue: editorial, news notes, book review, and short (illustrated) articles on life preservers, "canoe birding," racing, stroke technique, etc. Accepts display advertising. Source: c/o Canoe Ontario, 1220 Sheppard Ave. East, Willowdale, ON M2K 2X1.

1031.COASTAL CA:NEWS. Portsmouth, VA: Coastal Canoeists, Inc., 19—? Bi-monthly. "Dedicated to the Preservation and Enjoyment of Wilderness Waterways" (cover). A tightly-edited newsletter reporting club news and events in Virginia and adjacent regions. Conservation and safety articles are also prominent features in the several issues inspected. Some articles are reprints from other club newsletters. Accepts display advertising. Source: Coastal Canoeists, Inc., 2008 Charleston Ave., Portsmouth, VA 23704.

1032.CONFLUENCE. Palatine, IL: vol. 1-, 1989-. Quarterly. A new quarterly with an interesting concept—publication of a selection of photo-reproduced articles from about 100 club newsletters from throughout the U.S. The editor/publisher is Marge Cline, longtime editor of THE GRADIENT, newsletter of the Chicago Whitewater Association. Issues are about twenty pages in length and have a distinctly home-made character. Source: Confluence, 1343 North Portage, Palatine, IL 60067.

1033.THE GRADIENT. Chicago: Chicago Whitewater Association, vol. 1- 19—? Monthly. "A news letter by, for, and about Chicago Whitewater Association" (cover subtitle). The subtitle describes the general contents of this typed and stapled club newsletter compiled by long-time editor, Marge Cline. Source: The Gradient, 1343 North Portage, Palatine, IL 60067.

1034.HUT. Minneapolis, MN: Minnesota Canoe Association, vol. 1-, 19—?-. Bi-monthly. Unable to inspect a copy of this newsletter, or verify the source address. Source: MCA, P.O. Box 14207 Univ. Sta., Minneapolis, MN 55414.

1035.ILLINOIS PADDLING COUNCIL. NEWSLETTER. Lemont, IL: The Council, vol. 1-, 19—?-. Monthly. Unable to inspect a copy of this newsletter, or verify the source address. Source: 9 Pfeiffer St., Lemont, IL 60439.

1036.KANSAS CANOE ASSOCIATION. NEWSLETTER. Wicheta, KS: The Association, vol. 1-, 1975-. Bi-monthly. Word-processed club newsletter containing news, events, and general interest canoeing and kayaking articles. Nov./Dec., 1989 contents sample: statement of association purpose, activities calendar, meeting announcement, trip reports, chapter news, and, general news. Accepts display advertising. Source: K.C.A., P.O. Box 2885, Wicheta, KS 67201.

1037.NEW YORK-NEW JERSEY RIVER CONFERENCE. NEWSLETTER. Bound Brook, NJ: The Conference, vol. 1-, 19—?-. Quarterly. Unable to inspect a copy of this newsletter, or verify the source address. Source: NY-NJRC, 52 W. Union Ave., Bound Brook, NJ 08805.

1038.NWRA NEWSLETTER. Portland, OR: North West Rafters Association, vol. 1-, 1982?-. Monthly? Current address unverified. A club newsletter (typed format) with a membership of predominantly Oregon rafting enthusiasts. The Dec., 1984 issue had an extensive listing of western permit rivers giving state, river, permit required, runnable season, and agency address. Other contents: news notes, trip dates, various meeting reports, classified ads, and, an article on running the Upper Clackamas in highwater. Accepts display advertising. Source: NWRA, P.O. Box 19008, Portland, OR 97219.

1039.OCEANLETTER. Victoria, BC: Ocean Kayaking Association of B.C., vol. 1-, 1981-. Bi-monthly ? Current address unverified. Typewritten ten-pager on "legal-size" paper. The issue inspected (Mar., 1985), has the following sections/articles: editoria,; South Moresby Island wilderness logging update, "The Dangers of Not Wearing a Spraydeck," training and certification poll, "The Joys of Winter Paddling," classified ads, and letter(s) to the editor. (Possible) source: O.K.A.B.C., P.O. Box 1574, Victoria, BC V8W 2X7.

1040.THE RECREATIONAL CANOEIST. Brooklyn, NY: Metropolitan Canoe & Kayak Club, Inc., vol. 1-, 1976-. Quarterly. One of the most professionally-polished club newsletters, and at 1,000 circulation certainly one of the largest. Articles are arranged by topic, e.g., the Jan./Feb./Mar., 1990 issue has: travel (outside the NY area), travel (within the NY area), calendar, instruction, conservation, membership, and, classifieds. Accepts display advertising. Source: MC&KC, P.O. Box 021868, Brooklyn, NY 11202-0040.

1041.SPLASHES. South Charleston, WV: West Virginia Wildwater Association, vol. 1-, 19—?-. Irregular. Word-processed newsletter of club news and paddling articles (often reprints from other club publications). The January, 1990 issue has four pages on the drowning of kayaker, Ken Kajiwara. Other items: activities calendar, editorial on safety, notice of the Seventh Annual National Paddling Film Festival, and, a river gradient and flow graph. Source: WVWA, P.O. Box 8413, South Charleston, WV 25303.

1042.TVCC NEWSLETTER. Chattanooga, TN: Tennessee Valley Canoe Club, vol. 1-, 1979?-. Bi-monthly. Typewritten club news organ. One of the issues examined (Jan./Feb., 1990) had the following material: dues reminder, annual meeting report, trip calendar, Tellico River trip report, backpack trip report, Conasauga River USFS study, overnight cruise on the Toccoa River, river safety, and, Ocoee recreation schedule. Source: TVCC, P.O. Box 11125, Chattanooga, TN 37401.

1043.WISCONSIN CANOE ASSOCIATION. NEWSLETTER. Mosinee, WI: The Association, vol. 1-, 19—?-. Irregular. Unable to inspect a copy of this newsletter, or verify the source address. Source: WCA, 100 West Ln., Mosinee, WI 54455.

Chapter 7, Section 3

Watersports and Boating Magazines

1044. AMERICAN RIVERS. Washington, DC: American Rivers Conservation Council, vol. 1-, 1973-. Quarterly. This newsletter is received by members of American Rivers (formerly the American Rivers Conservation Council). Unable to inspect a sample copy for review. Source: American Rivers, 800 Pennsylvania Ave. SE, Suite 303, Washington, DC 20003.

1045. THE ASH BREEZE: JOURNAL OF THE TRADITIONAL SMALL CRAFT ASSOCIATION. Mystic, CT: The Association, vol. 1-, 1979-. Quarterly. "Museum" periodical received by members of TSCA, an organization dedicated to activities connected with pleasure watercraft which were constructed before the marine gasoline engine. Some contents of the Winter, 1986 issue: chapter news, an article on building a Cajun pirogue, another on restoring a St. Lawrence River skiff, and yet another on traditional small boats in Kansas. Accepts display and classified advertisements. Source: Traditional Small Craft Assocoation, P.O. Box 350, Mystic, CT 06355.

1046. BOUNDARY WATERS JOURNAL. Ely, MN: Boundary Waters Journal, vol. 1-, 1987-. Quarterly. Covers the natural history and recreation of the BWCA, Quetico Park, and Superior National Forest region. Source: Boundary Waters Journal, Rte. 1, Box 1740, Ely, MN 55731.

1047. HEADWATERS. San Francisco, CA: Friends of the River, vol. 1-, 1977-. Bi-monthly. Tabloid-size periodical with a California/western river conservation focus, and supported by contributions. The most recent issue examined (May/June, 1990) includes articles on a nationwide "manifesto" for rivers; fluctuating water levels on the Colorado River; "most endangered" status for the American and Klamath Rivers; a "wrap kit" for disengaging rafts from boulders; and, mining operations threatening the Tatshenshini River in British Columbia. Accepts display advertising. Source: Friends of the River, Bldg. C, Fort Mason Center, San Francisco, CA 94123.

1048. ISLANDS: AN INTERNATIONAL MAGAZINE. Santa Barbara, CA: Islands Publishing Co., vol. 1-, 1981-. Bi-monthly. Very sumptuous, upscale, four-color publication about, yes, islands—populated or un, but mostly the former if the issue inspected (May/June, 1990) is any indication. Sampling of articles: Cuba; Dalmatian Coast (and outlying islands); and, Hawaii. Accepts display advertising. Source: Islands Publishing Co., 3886 State St., Santa Barbara, CA 93105.

1049. MESSING ABOUT IN BOATS. Wenham, MA: vol. 1-, 1983-. Bi-weekly. Small boats of every description: canoes, kayaks, rowboats, sailboats, or motorboats are the special provence of this "fanzine." The emphasis seems to be on hands-on building and repair projects, and small boat trip reports. Selected articles in the issue of Dec. 1, 1989: "About this Kayak Safety...;" a north-central California canoe trip account; ST. Lawrence inboard engine boat; "The San Francisco Pelican" (sailing a heavy weather dingy); designs and projects (for 5 or 6 boats); and, a kayak trip account (Baffin Island). Accepts display advertising. Source: Messing About in Boats, 29 Burley St., Wenham, MA 01984.

1050. OCEANS. Stamford, CT: Oceans Magazine Associates, Inc., vol. 1-, 1969-. Bi-monthly. Indexed: BIOLOGICAL & AGRICULTURAL INDEX; READERS' GUIDE TO PERIODICAL LITERATURE; GENERAL SCIENCE INDEX; and, MAGAZINE INDEX. Source: Oceans Magazine, 2001 W. Marin St., Stamford, CT 06902.

1051. OCEANSPORTS INTERNATIONAL. Soquel, CA: Ocean Sports International, vol. 1-, 1984-. Quarterly. A slick "waterplay" periodical which covers the windsurfing, diving, sailing, and kayaking scene in (predominantly) North America and the Caribbean. The magazine uses some articles with a resort promotion tie-in—two out of eight in the vol. 6, no. 4 issue examined. Selected articles: Bay Islands dive guide; bareboating in the B.V.I.; windsurfing Aruba and Baja; and, kayaking the Bahamas. Accepts display advertising. Source: Ocean Sports International, P.O. Box 1388, Soquel, CA 95073.

1052. SHAVINGS. Seattle, WA: The Center for Wooden Boats, vol. 1-, 1979-. Bi-monthly. Published for members of the Center for Wooden Boats. A "museum" newsletter, circulation 3,000, for the devotee of self-propelled or powered wooden boats. Selected contents of one issue examined (July/Aug. 1989): report on the Thirteenth Annual Wooden Boat Festival (Seattle); a wooden boat "saga"; an historical sketch on delivering the Davis Boats in 1938; events calendar; and, classifieds. Accepts display advertising. Source: C.W.B., 1010 Valley St.

1053. SMALL BOAT JOURNAL. Atlanta, GA: Small Boat Journal, vol. 1-, 1979-. Bi-monthly. A mass-circulation (58,000), four-color, slick stock magazine which publishes canoeing, kayaking, or dorying articles occasionally. All small boats (no "yacht" types) are covered to some degree, but sail and power are emphasized. Issue inspected (January, 1990), has the article: "In Satan's Gut: Modern Dorymen Follow Powell's Path down the Colorado." Accepts display advertising. Source: Small Boat Journal, 2100 Powers Ferry Rd., Atlanta, GA 30339.

1054. WOODENBOAT. Brooklin, ME: WoodenBoat Publications, Inc., vol. 1-, 1974-. Bi-monthly. "The magazine for wooden boat owners, builders and designers" cover subtitle). The operative word here is definately "wooden." This is a 105,000-circulation, glossy stock, four-color magazine in which articles on sail and rowed boats predominate, with only occasional stories about paddle-powered craft (two on canoes for 1989). Self-indexed (the January/February number has an index for the previous year). Accepts display advertising. Source: WoodenBoat Publications, Inc., P.O. Box 78, Brooklin, ME, 04616.

Chapter 7, Section 4

General Sports, Conservation, and Nature Magazines

1055.ADVENTURE TRAVEL. Emmaus, PA: Rodale Press, vol. 1-, 1987-. Annual. Continues a semi-annual serial with the same title formerly published in New York. Contains whitewater articles usually as a promotional vehicle for outfitters. Source: Rodale Press, 33 E. Minor St., Emmaus, PA 18049.

1056.AMERICAN FORESTS. Washington, DC: American Forestry Association, vol. 1-, 1895-. Bi-monthly. The logging industry advocacy purpose of this periodical should not diminish its potential as a source for the wilderness waterways paddler. Indexed: AGRICULTURAL INDEX; GENERAL SCIENCE INDEX; MAGAZINE INDEX; and, READERS' GUIDE TO PERIODICAL LITERATURE. Source: AFA, 1319 Eighteenth St., N.W., Washington, DC 20036.

1057.APPALACHIA. BULLETIN ISSUE. Boston, MA: Appalachian Mountain Club, vol. 1 n.s.-, 1934-. Monthly. Continues APPALACHIA BULLETIN, and APPALACHIA. Subscribers are members of the AMC. Hiking, mountaineering, paddling, conservation, and the natural world are dominant themes. Indexed: ARTS AND HUMANITIES CITATION INDEX; BIOLOGICAL ABSTRACTS; and, P.A.I.S. Source: AMC, 5 Joy St., Boston, MA 02108.

1058.AUDUBON. New York: National Audubon Society, vol. 1-, 1899-. Bi-monthly. Subscribers are members of the NAS. Not for birdwatchers only, but everyone interested in the full spectrum of information about the natural world. Indexed: BIOLOGICAL ABSTRACTS; GENERAL SCIENCE INDEX; MAGAZINE INDEX; and, READERS' GUIDE TO PERIODICAL LITERATURE. Source: NAS, 950 Third Ave., New York, NY 10022.

1059.BACKPACKER. Emmaus, PA: Rodale Press, vol. 1-, 1973-. Bi-monthly. Absorbed WILDERNESS CAMPING. An occasional wilderness waterways article. Indexed: MAGAZINE INDEX; and SPORTSEARCH. Source: Rodale Press, 33 E. Minor St., Emmaus, PA 18049.

1060.BC OUTDOORS. Surrey, BC: Northwest Digest Ltd., vol. 1-, 1945-. Monthly. Western Canada's largest outdoor publication. Almost every issue has an article on wilderness waterways in British Columbia or the Yukon Teritory. Indexed: CANADIAN PERIODICALS INDEX. Source: Northwest Digest Ltd., 202-1132 Hamilton St., Vancouver, BC V6B 2S2.

1061.THE BEAVER: A MAGAZINE OF THE NORTH. Winnipeg, MB: Hudson's Bay Co., vol. 1-, 1920-. Bi-monthly. Paddling enthusiasts will be interested in the features on modern-day canoe voyages and Canadian geography as well as those of exploration and the fur trade days. Indexed: CANADIAN PERIODICAL INDEX; and, MAGAZINE INDEX. Source: Hudson's Bay Co., 77 Main St., Winnipeg, MB R3C 2R1.

1062.BROWN'S GUIDE TO GEORGIA. Atlanta, GA: Brown's Guide Ltd., vol. 1-, 19—?-. Monthly. Almost every issue has an article on some Peach State paddling stream. Source: Brown's Guide Ltd., 3765 Main St., College Park, GA 30337.

1063.CAMPING CANADA. Mississagua, ON: CRV Oublishing Co., vol. 1-, 1971-. 7 times yearly. Large circulation (50,000) general camping magazine. Indexed: SPORTSEARCH. Source: CRV Publishing Co. Ltd., 2077 Dundas St. E., Suite 202, Mississauga, ON L4X 1M2.

1064.CAMPING JOURNAL. New York: Davis Publications, vol. 1-, 19—?-. 9 times yearly. Camping and outdoor recreation. Indexed: ACCESS. Source: Davis Publications, 380 Lexington Ave., New York, NY 10017.

1065.CAMPING MAGAZINE. Martinsville, IN: American Camping Association, vol. 1-, 1926-. 7 times yearly. Subscriptions to members of the association. Indexed: READERS' GUIDE TO PERIODICAL LITERATURE; MAGAZINE INDEX; SPORTS PERIODICALS INDEX; and, SPORTSEARCH. Source: ACA, Bradford Woods, Marinssville, IN 46151.

1066.CANADIAN GEOGRAPHIC. Ottawa, ON: Royal Canadian Geographical Society, vol. 1-, 1930-. 11 times yearly. Former title: CANADIAN GEOGRAPHICAL JOURNAL. Subscriptions to members of the society. Indexed: CANADIAN PERIODICAL INDEX; and, SOCIAL SCIENCES INDEX. RCGS, 488 Wilbrod St., Ottawa, ON K1N 6M8.

1067.DUCKS UNLIMITED. Long Grove, IL: Ducks Unlimited, vol. 1-, 1937-. Bi-monthly. Articles on wetlands conservation and preservation throughout North America. Subscriptions to members of the group. Source: Ducks Unlimited, 1 Waterfowl Way at Gilmer Rd., Long Grove, IL 60047.

1068.EXPLORE. Calgary, AB: Explore Publishing Ltd., no. 1-, 1981-. Bi-monthly. Former title: EXPLORE ALBERTA! MAGAZINE. For outdoor enthusiasts interested in self-propelled activities. Source: Explore Publishing Ltd., 301 14th St. NW, #470, Calgary, AB T2N 2A1.

1069.FIELD AND STREAM. New York: Times Mirror Magazines, vol. 1-, 1895-. Monthly. Absorbed FOREST AND STREAM (Aug., 1930). Split into regional editions in May, 1984. Indexed: MAGAZINE INDEX; READER'S GUIDE TO PERIODICAL LITERATURE; and, SPORTS PERIODICALS INDEX. Source: Times Mirror Magazines, 2 Park Ave., New York, NY 10016.

1070.INUKTITUT. Ottawa, ON: Indian and Northern Affairs, vol. 1-, 1959-. Cover title: INUTTITUN AND INUTTITUUT. Text in English and Inuit (romanized): some issues include text in French. Indexed: ASTIS BIBLIOGRAPHY. Source: Indian and Northern Affairs, 400 Laurier, W., Ottawa, ON K1A 0H4.

1071.KNAPSACK. Washington, DC: American Youth Hostels, vol. 1-, 1988-. Semi-annual. "The semi-annual travel journal of American Youth Hostels" (cover subtitle). Subscription through youth hostel membership. Source: AYH, P.O. Box 37613, Washington, DC 20013-7613.

1072.NATIONAL GEOGRAPHIC. Washington, DC: National Geographic Society, vol. 1-, 1888-. Monthly. Subscriptions for members of the society. Indexed: CANADIAN PEIODICAL INDEX; MAGAZINE INDEX; and, READERS' GUIDE TO PERIODICAL LITERATURE. Source: NGS, 17 & "M" Sts. N.W., Washington, DC 20036.

1073.NATIONAL PARKS. Washington, DC: National Parks & Conservation Association, vol. 1-, 1927-. Bi-monthly. Continues NATIONAL PARKS & CONSERVATION MAGAZINE. Subscriptions for members of NPCA. Indexed: MAGAZINE INDEX; READERS' GUIDE TO PERIODICAL LITERATURE. Source: NPCA, 1015 31st St. N.W., Washington, DC 20007.

1074.NATURE CANADA. Ottawa, ON: Canadian Nature Federation, vol. 1-, 1972-. Quarterly.Concerned with Canada's natural history and the conservation of her resources. Source: CNF, 453 Sussex Dr., Ottawa, ON K1N 6Z4.

1075.NORTHEAST OUTDOORS. Waterbury, CT: Northeast Outdoors, Inc., vol. 1-, 1968-. Monthly. Primarily for family campers, with descriptions of campgrounds and touring regions. Source: Northeast Outdoors, Inc., Box 2180, Waterbury, CT 06722.

1076.OUTDOOR CANADA. Toronto: Outdoor Canada Publishing, Ltd., 1-, 1972-. 9 times yearly. Intended for families and individuals who love the Canadian outdoors. Publishes a number of paddling articles, sometimes two per issue. Indexed: CANADIAN PERIODICAL INDEX; and, SPORTSEARCH. Source: Outdoor Canada Publishing, Ltd., 801 York Mills Rd., Suite 301, Toronto, ON M3B1X7.

1077.OUTDOOR JOURNAL. Hubbard, OH: Outdoor journal, 1-, 1963-. Monthly. Covers sports and outdoor life in Ohio and Pennsylvania. Source: Outdoor Journal, Box 8, Hubbard, OH 44425.

1078.OUTDOOR LIFE. New York: Times Mirror Magazines, vol. 1-, 1897-. Monthly. "The national outdoor magazine with regional news" (cover). Absorbed OUTDOOR RECREATION, and FISHERMAN. Indexed: MAGAZINE INDEX; and, READERS' GUIDE TO PERIODICAL LITERATURE. Source: Times Mirror Magazine Div., 380 Madison Ave., New York, NY 10017.

1079.OUTSIDE. Chicago: Mariah Publishing Corp., vol. 1-, 1976-. Monthly. OUTSIDE and MARIAH merged to become MARIAH/OUTSIDE in 1979, only to drop the "MARIAH" in 1980. Has a readership of affluent young North Americans interested in high-energy outdoor pursuits.

Indexed: ACCESS; POPULAR MAGAZINE REVIEW; and, SPORTSEARCH. Source: Mariah Publ. Corp., 1165 N. Clark St., Chicago, IL 60610.

1080.OUTSIDE BUSINESS MAGAZINE. Chicago: Mariah Publications Corp., vol. 1-, 1976-. Monthly. "The business magazine for the outdoor recreation market" (subtitle). Formerly OUTSIDE MAGAZINE, and NATIONAL OUTDOOR OUTFITTERS NEWS. Distributed free to "qualified" personnel. Source: 1165 N. Clark St., 7th Fl., Chicago, IL 60610-2845.

1081.PRAIRIE CLUB BULLETIN. Chicago: Prairie Club of Chicago, vol. 1-, 1915-. Monthly. "Organized for the promotion of outdoor recreation in the form of walks, outings, camping and canoeing" (subtitle). Source: PCC, 10 S. Wabash St. 603A, Chicago, IL 60603.

1082.REAL TRAVEL. Calgary, AB: Real Travel Communications, vol. 1-, 1987-. Quarterly. "The magazine for adventure travellers" (cover). Source: Real Travel Comm., 301 14th St. N.W., Calgary, AB T2N 2A1.

1083.SIERRA. San Francisco, CA: Sierra Club, vol. 1-, 1911-. Bi-monthly. "Outings Directory" (including paddle trips) annually in the Jan./Feb. issue. Indexed: MAGAZINE INDEX; READERS' GUIDE TO PERIODICAL LITERATURE; and, GENERAL SCIENCE INDEX. Source: Sierra Club, 730 Polk St., San Francisco, CA 94109.

1084.SPORTS GUIDE: OUTDOOR RECREATION, FITNESS & TRAVEL FOR THE WEST. Salt Lake City, UT: Mills Publishing, Inc., vol. 1-, 1983-. Monthly. Action outdoor sports, e.g., skiing, snowboarding in winter; rafting, cycling in the summer—no golf, tennis, etc. Distributed free by western outdoor sports retailers. Source: Mills Publishing, Inc., 2010 South 1000 East, Salt Lake City, UT 84105.

1085.SPORTS ILLUSTRATED. New York: Time Inc., vol. 1- 1954-. Weekly. Deals with the totality of the sports scene—from women's bathing attire to sport franchise litigation. Very occasional "outdoors" articles. Two imitative clones are: INSIDE SPORTS, and SPORT. Indexed: MAGAZINE INDEX; READERS' GUIDE TO PERIODICAL LITERATURE; and, MAGAZINE ARTICLE SUMMARIES. Source: Time Inc., Time & Life Bldg., Rockefeller Center, New York, NY 10020-1393.

1086.SPORTS 'N SPOKES. Phoenix, AZ: Sports 'n Spokes, vol. 1-, 1976-. Bimonthly? Publishes an occasional paddlesports article, e.g., a kyaking piece in the March/April, 1990 issue. Indexed: SPORTSEARCH. Sports 'n Spokes, 5201 N. 19th Ave, Suite 111, Phoenix, AZ 85015.

1087.SUNSET. Menlo Park, CA: Lane Publishing, vol. 1-, 1898-. Monthly. "The magazine of western living" (subtitle). Issued in regional and special editions. Has occasional articles on self-propelled travel including waterways trips. Indexed: MAGAZINE INDEX; and, READERS' GUIDE TO PERIODICAL LITERATURE. Source: Lane Publishing, 80 Willow Rd., Menlo Park, CA 94025-3691.

1088.WESTERN OUTDOORS. Costa Mesa, CA: Western Outdoors Publications, vol. 1- 1953-. 9 times yearly. Coverage on where to go in the West for fishing, hunting, camping, and pleasure boating. Indexed: POPULAR MAGAZINE REVIEW. Source: Western Outdoors Pub., 3197-E Airport Loop Dr., Costa Mesa, CA 92626.

1089.WILDERNESS. Washington, DC: Wilderness Society, vol. 1-, 1935-. Quarterly. Publishes articles on wilderness areas, natural history, and conservation. Subscriptions for society members. Indexed: GENERAL SCIENCE INDEX; MAGAZINE INDEX; and, READERS' GUIDE TO PERIODICAL LITERATURE. Source: Wilderness Society, 1400 Eye St. N.W., Washington, DC 20005.

1090.WILDERNESS ALBERTA. Calgary, AB: Alberta Wilderness Association, vol. 1-, 1968-. Quarterly. Formerly ALBERTA WILDERNESS ASSOCIATION. NEWSLETTER. Tabloid format. Subscriptions for members of the association. Indexed: SPORTSEARCH. Source: AWA, Box 6398, Sta. D, Calgary, AB T2P 2E1.

1091.WILDERNESS ARTS AND RECREATION. Edson, AB: Big Bear Wilderness Services, vol. 1-, 1976-. Bi-monthly.Outdoor life and recreation in Alberta. Source: Big Bear Wilderness Services, P.O. Box 2640, Edson, AB T0E 0P0.

1092.WISCONSIN TRAILS. Madison, WI: Wisconsin Tales and Trails, vol. 1-, 1959-. Bi-monthly. Continues WISCONSIN TALES AND TRAILS. Publishes an average of two articles yearly on some aspect of wilderness waterways. Source: Wisconsin Tales and Trails, P.O. Box 5650, Madison, WI 53705.

Chapter 8

Videorecordings

1093. ADVANCED CANOE HANDLING. Mastering the Wilderness Series. Checkmate Productions, 198? One videocassette, 25 min., sd., col., Beta, VHS. Summary: Part I: stroke review; rough water paddling. Part II: capsize, righting, re-entry and rescue procedures; whitewater technique. Source: Canadian Recreational Canoeing Association, Box 500, Hyde Park, ON N0M 1Z0.

1094. ARKANSAS RIVER BLOOPERS. Englewood, CO: Photographic Expeditions, 1986? 1 videocassette, 25 min., sd., col., VHS. Summary: The Arkansas River equivalent of the "dumb plays" videos from professional team sports—raft flips, kayak crashes, et al. Features Seidel's Suckhole, Reefer Madness and Sunshine rapids. Source: Westwater Books, Box 2560, Evergreen, CO 80439.

1095. BASHKAUS: HARD LABOR IN SIBERIA. Filmed by John Armstrong. Venice, CA: 1989? 1 videocassette, 47 min., sd., col, VHS. Summary: Descent of the very hairy Bashkaus River in Siberia by a Sobek-sponsored combined U. S. and Russian kayak group. The U. S. members of the party were the first non-Russians to attempt the Bashkaus. Source: John Armstrong, 34 1/2 Wavecrest Ave., Venice CA: 90291.

1096. BASIC SOLO TECHNIQUE. Produced, written and directed by Patrick Moore. Stoughton, WI: Moore Canoes, 1989. 1 videocassette, 40 min., sd., col., VHS. Summary: Moore cuts through paddling theory to teach the basics by example. This is an unpretentious video in which Moore demonstrates the necessary strokes for beginners. Camera work by Cindy Hanson. Source: Moore Canoes, P. O. Box 242, Stoughton, WI 53589.

1097. THE BIRCH CANOE BUILDER. Produced by Frank Palco. Directed by Craig Hinde. Van Nuys, CA: AIMS Media, 198? 1 videocassette, 23 min., sd., col., Beta, VHS?, Study guide. Summary: Recollections from the life of Bill Hafeman and his wife, Violet from when they first settled in the Minnesota woods in the 1920s until 1972. This is combined with materials and processes for building a birch bark canoe, using no metal fasteners. Shows how the Hafeman's lives are tied to the natural cycles around them, and ways they can see that human activities have begun to disrupt even their deep woods environment.

1098. BLASTING INTO THE THIRD DIMENSION. Directed by John Davis. Liberty, SC: Perception, Inc., 1985. 1 videocassette, 14 min., sd., col., Beta, VHS. Summary: Produced by Perception as a marketing tool for the "Sabre" squirt boat. Davis' video contains footage of expert squirt boating action with Jesse Whittimore, whose explanations give insight into squirt technique. Source: Nantahala Outdoor Center, US 19 W, Box 41, Bryson City, NC 28713.

1099. CANOE BASICS. 198? 1 videocassette. 40 min., sd., col., VHS. Summary: Production techniques (freeze frame, on-screen text), and close attention to the detailed components of strokes are employed to instruct the canoeing novice. Source: Northwest River Supplies, P. O. Box 9186, Moscow, ID 83843-9186.

1100. CANOEING IS FOR EVERYONE. Directed by Kathy Taylor. Rick Kizuk Video Productions, 198? 1 videocassette, 30 min., sd., col., Beta, VHS. Summary: Illustrates how persons with a disability can be integrated into mainstream canoeing programs. The RESOURCE MANUAL ON CANOEING FOR DISABLED PERSONS (see entry in another chapter above) serves as a printed reference guide. Canadian Recreational Canoeing Association, Box 500, Hyde Park, ON N0M 1Z0.

1101. CANOEING WORLD (ICF). 198? 1 videocassette, 18 min., sd., col., Beta?, VHS? Source: Canadian Canoe Association, 1600 Prom., James Naismith Dr., Gloucester, ON K1B 5N4.

1102. CANOE ONTARIO AND AFFILIATES. Willowdale, ON: Canoe Ontario, 198? 1 videocassette, 30 min., sd., col., VHS. Summary: A promotional overview of Canoe Ontario and each of its four affiliations: Ontario Canoe Sprint Racing Affiliation; Ontario Recreational Canoeing Association; Ontario Marathon Canoe Racing Association; and, Ontario Wild Water Affiliation. Source: Canoe Ontario, 1220 Sheppard Ave. East, Willowdale, ON M2K 2X1.

1103. CESAR'S BARK CANOE. 198? 1 videocassette, 58 min., sd., col., VHS. Summary: Cesar Newashish, a 67 year old Cree Indian, builds a birch bark canoe using traditional materials and tools. Subtitles in English, French and Cree. Source: National Film Board of Canada, 1251 Ave. of the Americas, New York, NY 10020.

1104. CHILIBAR/SNAKEDANCE. Jersey City, NJ: Gravity Sports Films, 1985? 2 segments on 1 videocassette, sd., col., Beta?, VHS? Summary: The 1985 Chilibar Whitewater Rodeo and the Wyoming Surfing Safari share action footage on this videocassette. Source: Gravity Sports Films, 100 Broadway, Jersey City, NJ 07306.

1105. THE CHILKO RIVER ACCIDENT: WHAT HAPPENED AND WHY. Colorado Springs, CO: National Organization for River Sports, 1989? 1 videocassette, 35 min., sd., col., VHS Summary: Five men wearing life jackets drowned in the rapids of the Chilko River (BC) in 1987. Diagrams, illustrations, and river footage show how this and other river accidents could have been prevented. Source: NORS, Box 6847 Colorado Springs, CO 80904.

1106. THE CITIZEN RACERS WORKSHOP. 198? 1 videocassette, sd., col., Beta?, VHS. Summary: World class kayaking and C-boating, including gate technique, is scrutinized. Coverage shows training, mental preparation, boat positioning, and paddle placement. Source: Nantahala Outdoor Center, US 19W, Box 41, Bryson City, NC 28713.

1107. COLD, WET & ALIVE. Nichols Productions, 1989. 1 videocassette, 23 min., sd., col., VHS. Summary: Focuses on how a person gets hypothermia in a recreational setting, and what to do about it. Computer animation is used to show the effects of hypothermia. Source: American Canoe Association Film Library, Audio Visual Services, Special Services Bldg., University Park, PA 16802.

1108. COMING BACK ALIVE. Produced by National Film Board of Canada. Chicago, IL: International Film Bureau, 1982. 1 videocassette, 23 min., sd., col., Beta, VHS. Summary: The lake scenery near Thunder Bay, Ontario, and advice from Don Johnston, a representative from the Lakehead Search and Rescue Unit, combine in a practical discussion of recreational boating safety. Issued also as a motion picture. Source: Canadian Video Factory, 820 28 St. N. E., Calgary, AB T2A 6K1.

1109. THE C-1 CHALLENGE, WITH KENT FORD. Directed by John C. Davis. Lexington, KY: Video Lab, 1989. 1 videocassette, 30 min., sd., col., VHS. Summary: Extolls the virtues of C-1 paddling to the open canoe and kayak audience. Ford demonstrates technique: kneeling rather than sitting; single blade paddle; easy rolling. Source: NOC Outfitters, US 19W, Box 41, Bryson City, NC 28713.

1110. COSMETIC GELCOAT AND FIBERGLASS REPAIR, VOL. 1: BASIC GELCOAT DAMAGE; VOL. 2: STRESS CRACKS, AIR VOIDS AND FRACTURES. 198? 2 videocassettes of 75 min. and 110 min., sd., col., VHS? Summary: Step-by-step process of doing non-structural fiberglass repair is demonstrated by Jerry Swartz of Precision Fiberglass. Source: Bennett Marine Video, 730 Washington St., Marina Del Rey, CA 90292.

1111. COSTA RICA. Englewood, CO: Photographic Expeditions, 198? 1 videocassette, 30 min., sd., col., VHS. Summary: Footage of Class V whitewater paddling on five Costa Rican rivers. Hosted by world class kayaker, Rafael Gallo. Source: Wyoming River Raiders, 601 Wyoming Blvd., Casper, WY 82609.

1112. DARE THE WILDEST RIVER. Produced and directed by Joe Munroe. Santa Monica, CA: Pyramid Film and Video, 1977. 1 videocassette, 19 min., sd., col., Beta?, VHS. Summary: Thrills and spills footage, and side-canyon excursions of a group of dorymen and rafters as they run the length of the Grand Canyon. Source: Pyramid Film and Video, Box 1048, Santa Monica, CA 90406.

1113. DETERMINING THE WEATHER. Mastering the Wilderness Series. Checkmate Productions, 198? 1 videocassette, 25 min., sd., col., Beta, VHS Summary: Part I: environmental signs of weather change; moisture, pressure, stable and unstable conditions. Part II: cloud formations; cold and warm air masses; precipitation, thunder and lightning. Source: Canadian Recreational Canoeing Association, Box 500, Hyde Park, ON N0M 1Z0.

1114. DEVIL'S CANYON: STEVE MAHAY'S WHITEWATER CHALLENGE. Produced by Evan Swenson. Directed by Tom Christensen. Anchorage, AK: Alaska Outdoors, 1986. 1 videocassette, 25 min., sd., col., VHS. Summary: River-adventurer Mahay's first-ever navigation of the whitewater of Devil's Canyon of the Susitna River, Alaska. Source: Alaska Outdoors, P. O. Box 190324, Anchorage, AK 99519-0324.

1115. DIRECTION FINDING. Mastering the Wilderness Series. Checkmate Productions, 198? 1 videocassette, 25 min., sd., col., Beta, VHS Summary: Part I: map types, latitude and longitude determination; map contours, symbols, distances, declination, and Agonic Line. Part II: compass use, and its use with maps; route charting; determining direction without a compass; sun and wristwatch. Source: Canadian Recreational Canoeing Association, Box 500, Hyde Park, ON N0M 1Z0.

1116. DOLORES RIVER: SNAGGLETOOTH 1983. Photographic Expeditions, 1983? 1 videocassette, sd., col., Beta, VHS. Summary: Features kayakers and rafters running the best rapids at normal flow and the record high levels in May, 1983. Source: National Organization for River Sports, P. O. Box 6847, Colorado Springs, CO 80904.

1117. DOROTHY MOLTER: LIVING IN THE BOUNDARY WATERS. Filmed by Judith Handel and Wade Black. Minneapolis, MN: Jade Films, 1986? 1 videocassette, 42 min., sd., col., VHS. Summary: Handel and Black's film explores who Molter was; why she lived in the BWCA for 50 years—mostly alone; what she thought of "ordinary" life and of her own lifestyle; and how her life changed from season to season. Source: Jade Films, P. O. Box 8913, Minneapolis, MN 55408.

1118. DOUBLES BASIC. See: PATH OF THE PADDLE: QUIET WATER (below).

1119. DOUBLES WHITE WATER. See: PATH OF THE PADDLE: WHITE WATER (below).

1120. THE DROWNING MACHINE. State College, PA: Filmspace, 1981? 1 videocassette, 20 min., sd., col., Beta?, VHS? Summary: Shows its intended audience of emergency rescue personnel two ways to rescue victims trapped in the hydraulics at low head dams. Combines on-the-scene, "live" reports, interviews with survivors and rescue professionals, and simulated rescues to demonstrate techniques. Source: Canoe Onterio, 1220 Sheppard Ave. East, Willowdale, ON M2K 2X1.

1121. FAST AND CLEAN. Produced and directed by Russ Nichols. Cheverly, MD: Nichols Productions, 1980. 1 videocassette, 37 min., sd., col., Beta? VHS? Summary: Nichols follows World Champions Cathy Hearn and Jon Lugbill, and other world class paddling competitors as they prepare for the 1979 Worlds in Quebec. Source: American Canoe Association Film Library, Audio Visual Services, Special Services Bldg., University Park, PA 16802.

1122. FUNDAMENTALS OF THE CANOE: BASIC CANOE HANDLING. Mastering the Wilderness Series. Checkmate Productions, 198? 1 videocassette, 25 min., sd., col., Beta, VHS. Summary: Part I: canoe configuration and its effect; review of canoe parts; type of construction/ materials. Part II: pre-travel check; entering; occupant location; paddle parts; basic strokes; safety. Source: Canadian Recreational Canoeing Association, Box 500, Hyde Park, ON N0M 1Z0.

1123. FUNDAMENTALS OF WHITEWATER RAFTING. Produced by R. W. Miskimins. Grants Pass, OR: Environmental Images, 1989? 1 videocassette, sd., col., VHS?. Summary: Reading the river and rowing techniques are presented and discussed both in the classroom and on the river. Source: Environmental Images, 575 South Espey Rd., Grants Pass, OR 97527.

1124. FUN FOREVER. Filmed by Paul Marshall. Albright, WV: Preferred Modes, 1988. 1 videocassette, 30 min., sd., col., VHS. Summary: This video is intended for experienced whitewater paddlers who are interested in getting into the world of "squirting. " The performance capabilities of squirt boats (and their expert paddlers) are fully explored. Source: Preferred Modes, Rt. 1, Box 30, Albright, WV 26519.

1125. GETTIN' DOWN UNDER. Jersey City, NJ: Gravity Sports Films, 198? 1 videocassette, sd., col., Beta?, VHS? Summary: Jesse Whittemore and Jeff Snyder demonstrate their squirtboating skills. Source: Gravity Sports Films, 100 Broadway, Jersey City, NJ 07306.

1126. GRAND CANYON '85. Jersey City, NJ: Gravity Sports Films, 1985? 1 videocassette, sd., col., Beta?, VHS? Summary: Running the Colorado River in Grand Canyon in rafts and kayaks. Source: Gravity Sports Films, 100 Broadway, Jersey City, NJ 07306.

1127. A GRAND EXPERIENCE. Englewood, CO: Photographic Expeditions, 198? 1 videocassette, 40 min., sd., col., VHS? Summary: An 18-day trip on this classic western river through fabled Grand Canyon. Also shows side hikes and the major rapids, including the infamous Crystal and Lava Falls. Source: Wyoming River Raiders, 601 Wyoming Blvd., Casper, WY 82609.

1128. THE GREAT OUTDOORS, PROGRAM 8, HANG GLIDING AND FLATWATER CANOES. Produced by WGBH Television. Deerfield, IL: MTI Teleprograms, 1984. 1 videocassette, 30 min., sd., col., VHS. Summary: Host and sportsman Jim Tabor soars up any away on a hang glider, followed by a visit to the tropic of wild flowers and game birds located fourteen miles from downtown Boston. He is also featured flatwater canoeing, and shares tips on how to cope with insects. WGBH, 125 Western Ave., Boston, MA 02134.

1129. THE GREAT OUTDOORS, PROGRAM 13, KAYAKING AND HIKING FUN. Produced by WGBH Television. Deerfield, IL: MTI Teleprograms, 1984. 1 videocassette, 30 min., sd. col., VHS. Summary: Host and sportsman Jim Tabor takes a refresher course on strokes and paddles used in kayak cruising. He also hikes along the Appalachian Trail in Georgia, and is seen rafting down the Trisuli River rapids. WGBH, 125 Western Ave., Boston, MA 02134.

1130. THE GREAT WHITE HUNTERS. Englewood, CO: Photographic Expeditions, 198? 1 videorecording, 47 min., sd., col., VHS. Summary: Action/humor scenes of paddlers searching for the "unrunnable" river—Toulumne (CA), Trinity (CA), Wenatchee (WA), Colorado (Gore Canyon, CO), Clear Creek (CO), South Fork Clearwater (ID), and North Fork Payette (ID)— backed up by an appropriate musical soundtrack. Source: Wyoming River Raiders, 601 Wyoming Blvd., Casper, WY 82609.

1131. GUIDE TO CANOEING. Produced and directed by William Morris. The L. L. Bean Video Library. Freeport, ME: L. L. Bean, Inc., 1986. 1 videocassette, 105 min., sd., col., VHS. Summary: Ken Stone informs and demonstrates techniques for prospective canoers, including selecting the proper craft for your intended purpose, canoe accessories, strokes and canoe handling, solo and tandem. There is an extended section on practical handling of canoes in various situations, including whitewater. Source: L.L. Bean, Freeport, ME 04033.

1132. HARDBOATING: EAST MEETS WEST. 198? 1 videocassette, sd., col., VHS. Summary: A three-part video beginning with Jess Whittemore, Jeff Snyder and others squirtboating in West Virginia. This is followed by Nolan Whitesell open canoeing on California's Cherry Creek, and action from the Western rodeo circuit. Source: Gravity Sports Films, 100 Broadway, Jersey City, NJ 07306.

1133. HYPOTHERMIA: THE CHILL THAT NEED NOT KILL. Directed by Greg Bowler. Orono, ME: University of Maine/ University of New Hampshire Sea Grant Program, 1983. 1 videocassette, 18 min., sd., col., VHS. Summary: Paddlers can ignore the survival suit portion of this video. However, they will find other instruction valuable, e. g., footage on Heat Escape Lessening Posture (HELP). Source: Marine Advisory Program, 30 Osburn Hall, University of Maine, Orono, ME 04469.

1134. HYPOTHERMIA: THINK SURVIVAL, NOT RESCUE. Directed by Greg Bowler. Orono, ME: University of Maine/ University of New Hampshire Sea Grant Program, 1983. 1 videocassette, 28 min., sd., col., VHS. Summary: Intended primarily as a training film for commercial fishermen, but has accurate and universally applicable information on survival in cold water. Source: Marine Advisory Program, 30 Osburn Hall, University of Maine, Orono, ME 04469.

1135. JOE SELIGA, WOOD AND CANVAS CANOE CRAFTSMAN. 198? 1 videocassette, 52 min., sd., col., VHS. Summary: Follows the details of canoe construction from the sawmill to the final coat of varnish, demonstrated by a master builder in a folksy and informative fashion. Source: Piragis Northwoods Co. 105 N. Central Ave. Ely, MN 55731.

1136. KAYAK. Juneau, AK: Alaska State Museum, 1986. 1 videocassette, 28 min., sd., col., Beta, VHS. Summary: The role the kayak has played in Alaska history. Source: Alaska State Museum, 395 Whittier St., Juneau, AK 99801.

1137. KAYAK. Produced by Len Aitken and Bill Snider. Santa Monica, CA: Pyramid Film and Video, 198? 1 videocassette, 9 min., sd., col., VHS. Summary: This is a preview copy demonstrating the joy and poetry of kayaking by means of slow motion, underwater shots, flatwater reflections, bow-mount camera work, and appropriate "mood" music. Source: Pyramid Film and Video, Box 1048, Santa Monica, CA 90406.

1138. KAYAK BASICS. Liberty, SC: Perception Inc., 198? 1 videocassette, sd., col., Beta, VHS. Summary: A close look at the Eskimo roll, with both the "C to C" and the "screw roll" taught poolside by Olympian Chris Spelius. Source: Nantahala Outdoor Center, US 19 W, Box 41, Bryson City, NC 28713.

1139. KAYAK HANDLING: THE BASIC STROKES. 198? 1 videocassette, 43 min., sd., col., VHS. Summary: World slalom champion, Richard Fox demonstrates kayak paddling techniques and their whitewater uses. Fox provides insights on how to roll, and attempts to answer the novice kayaker's question, "just how do you make this thing go straight?" Source: Northwest River Supplies, P. O. Box 9186, Moscow, ID 83843-9186.

1140. KAYAK PADDLING WITH BOB MCDOUGALL. Jersey City, NJ: Gravity Sports Films, 198? 1 videocassette, 24 min., sd., col., VHS. Summary: "How-to" footage presenting whitewater kayaking as a learned series of skills, furthering any intermediate/advanced paddler's understanding of some of the more enjoyable and elusive moves. Source: Gravity Sports Films, 100 Broadway, Jersey City, NJ 07306.

1141. KAYAK TOURING, BASIC SKILLS; SEA KAYAK RESCUES. Produced and written by Christine Robinson. Directed and edited by Helen Rezanowich. Vancouver, BC: Ecomarine Ocean Kayak Centre; LunaSea Video Productions, 1985. 1 videocassette with 2 titles of 32 and 20 min., sd., col., Beta, VHS. Summary: Basic instruction in sea kayaking and ocean rescue techniques, shot on location in Vancouver and Sookie, BC, and narrated by Sher Morgan. KAYAK TOURING is available seprately. Source: Ecomarine Ocean Kayak Centre, 1668 Duranleau St., Vancouver, BC V6H 3S4.

1142. LOON COUNTRY BY CANOE. Produced by Dan Gibson. Toronto: Dan Gibson Productions, 1987. 1 videocassette, 30 min., sd., col., VHS. Summary: A visual wilderness experience with natural sounds—nomusic or narrative. D. Gibson, 128 Pears, Toronto, ON M5R 1T2.

1143. A MARGIN FOR ERROR. Washington, DC: American National Red Cross, 1979. 1 videocassette, 22 min., sd., col., VHS. Summary: Stresses safety preparation and trip planning by comparing two ill-prepared canoeists with a group of properly prepared paddlers. Source: American Canoe Association, Audio Visual Services, Special Services Bldg., University Park, PA 16802.

1144. THE MIDDLE FORK OF THE SALMON. Englewood, CO: Photographic Expeditions, 1989. 1 videocassette, 28 min., sd., col., VHS. Summary: A "guidebook" video with: access and permit information, rapids, hot springs galore, and pristine scenery. Source: Wyoming River Raiders, 601 Wyoming Blvd., Casper, WY 82609.

1145. NEVER BEFORE, NEVER AGAIN. 1990? 1 videocassette, 92 min., sd., col., VHS. Summary: Video converted from film of the "incredible journey" (see Trip Accounts chapter) of Verlen Kruger and Cliff Waddell as they crossed 7,000 miles of North American waterways in 176 days. Source: Verlen Kruger, 2906 Meister Lane, Lansing, MI 48906.

1146. 1984 OLYMPIC CANOEING EVENTS. 1984? 1 videocassette, 60 min., sd., col., Beta?, VHS? Source: Canadian Canoe Association, 1600 Prom., James Naismith Dr., Gloucester, ON K1B 5N4.

1147. 1984 OLYMPIC CANOEING MEDAL WINNERS. 1984? 30 min., sd., col., Beta?, VHS. Summary: Focuses on the six medal winning races at the 1984 Olympics. One athlete from each crew is interviewed. Source: Canadian Canoe Association, 1600 Prom., James Naismith Dr., Gloucester, ON K1B 5N4.

1148. 1989 WORLD CUP WHITEWATER SLALOM RACE. 1989. 1 videocassette, 60 min., sd., col., VHS. Summary: The world's best whitewater paddlers race against the clock at the Minden (Ontario) Wild Water Preserve. This footage captures thc cxcitement of the events, highlighting the top competitors in: K-1 Men, K-1 Women, C-1 Men, and C-2 Men. Source: Canoe Ontario, 1220 Sheppard Ave. East, Willowdale, ON M2K 2X1.

1149. 1981 INTERNATIONAL 10 2M CANOE WORLD CHAMPIONSHIPS. Bay Cable TV, 1981? 1 videocassette, 40 min., sd., col., VHS, 3/4 in. U-matic. Source: American Canoe Association Film Library, Audio Visual Services, Special Services Bldg., University Park, PA 16802.

1150. 1986 WORLD CHAMPIONSHIPS. 1986? 1 videocassette, 58 min., col., Beta?, VHS? Source: Canadian Canoe Association, 1600 Prom., James Naismith Dr., Gloucester, ON K1B 5N4.

1151. OCEAN KAYAKING. Produced and directed by Earl Blue. Ferndale, WA: Ocean Kayak, 1989. 1 videocassette, 39 min., sd., col., VHS? Summary: Kayak surfing in California; exploration of Catalina Island coves and caves; kayak testing session on Puget Sound. Source: Ocean Kayak, 1920 Main ST., Ferndale, WA 98248.

1152. ONLY NOLAN. Produced and directed by Clinton La Tourrette. Boise, ID: Outdoor Videos, 1988. 1 videocassette, 24 min., sd., col., VHS. Summary: On Idaho's rock n' roll North Fork of the Payette, Nolan Whitesell demonstrates expert techniques of whitewater open canoe paddling in a craft manufactured by the company bearing his name. The video concludes with a combination Whitesell interview and "soft sell. " Source: Outdoor Videos, 1317 E. Jefferson, Boise, ID 83712.

1153. ON TO THE POLAR SEA. Produced by William B. Hoyt. Directed by Peter Raymont. Atlanta, GA: WTBS/PBS, 1984? 1 videocassette, (approx.) 50 min., sd., col., 1/2 in., VHS? Summary: The Bonnet Plume and Peel Rivers (YT/NT) are the setting for this 16-day canoe expedition through the far northwest to the Arctic Circle. TBS, 100 International Blvd., Atlanta, GA 30348.

1154. PADDLE OUT OF PERIL. Produced and filmed by Dan Gibson and Omar Stringer. Amherst, NY: A. V. Explorations, 1979. 1 videocassette, 25 min., sd., col., Beta, VHS. Summary: Intended to instruct on potential canoeing hazards, and offer common-sense ways to employ preventative safety measures for accident avoidance. Source: Canadian Recreational Canoeing Association, Box 500, Hyde Park, ON N0M 1Z0.

1155. PADDLES UP. Wolf Ruck Productions, 1977. 1 videocassette, 19 min., sd., col., VHS. Summary: Olympic (sprint) style paddling, showing the beauty and action of C-1 (with Olympic silver medalist John Woods), K-1, K-2, K-4, and 15-person war canoe racing. Source: Canoe Ontario, 1220 Sheppard Ave. East, Willowdale, ON M2K 2X1.

1156. PADDLE TO THE SEA. Produced by Julian Biggs. Directed and filmed by Bill Mason. National Film Board of Canada, 1966. 1 videocassette, 28 min., sd., col., Beta, VHS. Summary: A children's odyssey about the journey of a hand-carved toy canoeman making its way from Canada's northern forest downstream to the distant sea. Source: National Film Board of Canada, 1251 Ave. of the Americas, New York, NY 10020.

1157. PATH OF THE PADDLE: QUIET WATER. New York: National Film Board of Canada, 1984. 1 videocassette, 54 min., sd., col., VHS. Summary: The legendary Bill Mason demonstrates basic paddling strokes for nascent solo and double canoers. He shows how to combine these strokes to maneuver the canoe at will. There is some whitewater footage. Filmed in the Canadian Shield country. Incorporates two videos: SOLO BASIC, and DOUBLES BASIC. See also Mason's companion video on whitewater, cited immediately below. Source: Northword Press, Box 1360, Minocqua, WI 54548.

1158. PATH OF THE PADDLE: WHITE WATER. New York: National Film Board of Canada, 1984. 1 videocassette, 54 min., sd., col., VHS. Summary: Award-winning filmmaker, Bill Mason, demonstrates how to read rapids and apply that knowledge using appropriate paddling strokes in maneuvering a canoe safely through whitewater. A complete course in solo or double whitewater canoeing incorporates wilderness visual appeal. Combines two videos: SOLO WHITE WATER, and DOUBLES WHITE WATER. See also Mason's companion video on quiet water, cited immediately above. Source: Northword Press, Box 1360, Minocqua, WI 54548.

1159. PAUCARTAMBO: INCA RIVER [1 Videocassette]. Filmed by John Armstrong. New York: Wombat Film & Video, 1986. 1 videocassette, 41 min., sd., col., VHS. Summary: Follows five American kayakers as they run the Paucartambo River in Peru during the 1985 rainy season. A sequel, PAUCARTAMBO: THE REST OF THE RIVER, is cited below. Source: Armstrong Pictures, 34 1/2 Wavecrest Ave., Venice, CA 90291.

1160. PAUCARTAMBO: THE REST OF THE RIVER [1 Videocassette]. Filmed by John Armstrong. Venice, CA: Armstrong Pictures, 1987. 1 Videocassette, 58 min., sd., col., VHS. Summary: Armstrong films the very impressive river rapids, and the people and the culture of the Paucartambo in the high Andes of Peru. This video is a sequel to PAUCARTAMBO: INCA RIVER, (above). Source: Armstrong Pictures, 34 1/2 Wavecrest Ave., Venice, CA 90291.

1161. PERSPECTIVES ON PADDLING. 1988. 1 videocassette, 13 min., sd., col., Beta, VHS. Summary: Kayaking footage. Source: Ocean River Sports, 1437 Store St., Victoria, BC V8W 3J6.

1162. PIVOT POINT. Bryson City, NC: Nantahala Outdoor Center, 198? 1 videocassette, 30 min., sd., col., VHS. Summary: Based on the NOC's canoe instruction classes. Shows the correct technique for the intermediate to advanced paddler. Source: Nantahala Outdoor Center, US 19 W, Box 41, Bryson City, NC 28713.

1163. QAJAQ KLUBBEN. 1987. 1 videocassette, 80 min., sd., col., Beta, VHS. Summary: Showcases the paddling skills of Greenland kayakers. Source: Heath Services Inc., Rt. 1 Box 125, Damon, TX 77430.

1164. REGATTA SAFETY. 198? 1 videocassette, 18 min., sd., col., VHS? Source: Canadian Canoe Association, 1600 Prom., James Naismith Dr., Gloucester, ON K1B 5N4.

1165. RESCUE FOR RIVER RUNNERS. Calgary, AB: University of Calgary, 1981. 1 videocassette, 28 min., sd., col., Beta, VHS. Summary: Demonstrates fastwater canoe, kayak and raft rescue techniques. Source: National Film Board of Canada, 1251 Ave. of the Americas, New York, NY 10020.

1166. RIVER HOUSE ROCKS & ROLLS. Erwin, TN: River House Productions, 1990? 1 videocassette, sd., col., Beta?, VHS? Summary: Features a rock n' roll soundtrack, and dynamic footage of hot runs and wipeouts on the Ocoee, Nolichucky, and Russell Fork. Source: River House Prod., P. O. Box 415, Irwin, TN, 37650.

1167. RIVER OF THE GRAND CANYON. Written and directed by W. L. Rusho. Sun Time Productions, 1987. 1 videocassette, 40 min., sd., col., VHS. Summary: Discusses the history of exploration of the Grand Canyon and the Colorado River. Use of old stills (dating from 1872) and motion picture footage of past and present-day river trips affords some interesting viewing. Source: Westwater Books, Box 2560, Evergreen, CO 80439.

1168. RIVER OF THE RED APE. San Francisco, CA: River World/One Pass Home Video, 1986. 1 videocassette, 56 min., sd., col., VHS. Summary: Footage of the first attempt to navigate the Alas River on the equatorial island of Sumatra. Stunning scenes of whitewater, tropical forest, and one of the world's great populations of Orangutans. Source: Sobek Expeditions Inc., P. O. Box 1089, Angels Camp, CA 95222.

1169. RIVER RESCUE. Produced in cooperation with Les Bechdel. Jersey City, NJ: Gravity Sports Films, 198? 1 videocassette, 55 min., sd., col., VHS. Summary: Bechdel and Anne R. Ford demonstrate the techniques from Bechdel and Slim Ray's book, RIVER RESCUE (cited in chapter 1). Actual and simulated rescues involving canoes, kayaks, rafts, and duckies. Source: Northwest River Supplies, P. O. Box 9186, Moscow, ID 83843-9186.

1170. RIVER RUNNER WORKOUT. Produced by Arthur Rouse and Amy Schenck. Lexington, KY: Video Editing Services, 1988. 1 videocassette, 40 min., sd., col., VHS. Summary: Schenck (M. S. Physical Education) has designed an in-home exercise circuit for competitive paddlers which concentrates on strengthening the upper body. The exercises utilize common objects such as brooms and chairs. Some river footage of kayaking and canoeing is intercut with the exercise workout. Source: Video Editing Services, 327 Old East Vine St., Lexington, KY 40507.

1171. RIVER SCAPES. Englewood, CO: Photographic Expeditions, 198? 1 videocassette, 30 min., sd., col., VHS. Summary: A visual and aural tone poem featuring several desert and alpine rivers. Source: Wyoming River Raiders, 601 Wyoming Blvd., Casper, WY 82609.

1172. RIVERS OF CHILE. Sport International, 198? 1 videocassette, sd., col., VHS? Summary: Video footage of the Bio-Bio and other Chilean rivers. Source: National Organization for River Sports, P. O. Box 6847, Colorado Springs, CO 80904.

1173. RIVER SONG: A NATURAL HISTORY OF THE COLORADO RIVER IN GRAND CANYON. Produced, directed and photographed by Don Briggs. Grand Canyon, AZ: Grand Canyon Natural History Association, 1987. 1 videocassette, 40 min., sd., col., VHS. Summary: The Colorado River and its course through the Grand Canyon, showing the animals, plants, and geology. Music by Arnold Black and narration by Richard Chamberlain. Source: Westwater Books, Box 2560, Evergreen, CO 80439.

1174. ROCKY'S ROLLING LESSON. Produced and directed by Rocky Rossi. Jersey City, NJ: Gravity Sports Films, 1984. 1 videocassette, 15 min., sd., col., VHS. Summary: Part of a three-film series teaching Eskimo roll techniques. Source: Gravity Sports Films, 100 Broadway, Jersey City, NJ 07306.

1175. RUBBERBOATING DOWN EAST. Jersey City, NJ: Gravity Sports Films, 198? 1 videocassette, sd., col., Beta?, VHS. Summary: Footage of rafts and duckies frolicking in five classic whitewater rivers of the eastern U. S. : New, Cheat, Tyart, Upper Youghiogheny, and Gaully. Source: Gravity Sports Films, 100 Broadway, Jersey City, NJ 07306.

1176. A SECOND HELPING. Bryson City, NC: Nantahala Outdoor Center, 198? 1 videocassette, 30 min., sd., col., Beta?, VHS. Summary: Shows all the basic strokes and brief review of rolling. Produced by the instruction department at NOS, and intended for beginners or as a refresher course for those needing to review their strokes. Source: Nantahala Outdoor Center, US 19 W, Box 41, Bryson City, NC 28713.

1177. THE SELWAY AND LOCHSA RIVERS. Englewood, CO: Photographic Expeditions, 198? 1 videocassette, 42 min., sd., col., VHS. Summary: Shows what to expect, shuttle information, campsites, put-ins, take-outs, and so forth, for two scenic wilderness rivers in north-central Idaho. Source: National Organization for River Sports, P. O. Box 6847, Colorado Springs, CO 80904.

1178. SHOWCASE OF THE AGES. Joe Munroe Visual Productions, 1989? 1 videocassette, 40 min., sd., col., VHS. Summary: Geological history of the Grand Canyon from the air, rim, side canyons, and the Colorado river. This video combines art and graphics to show the formation of the canyon over millions of years. Source: National Organization for River Sports, P. O. Box 6847, Colorado Springs, CO 80904.

1179. SLAMMIN' SALMON WHITEWATER BLOOPERS. Ashland, OR: Gayle Wilson Productions, 198? 1 videocassette, 40 min., sd., col., Beta?, VHS? Summary: A "crash tape" of kayak and raft pratfalls filmed on California's Salmon River. Source: Gayle Wilson Productions, 265 Alta, Ashland, OR 97520.

1180. SOLITUDES, EPISODE ONE: LOON COUNTRY BY CANOE. Toronto: Dan Gibson Productions, 1985. 1 videcocasette, 30 min., sd., col., Beta, VHS. Summary: Listen to the sounds of nature; a visual experience that contains only the natural sounds of the environment explored. Source: Holborne Records, P.O. Box 3095, Mt. Albert, ON L0G 1M0.

1181. SOLO BASIC. See: PATH OF THE PADDLE: QUIET WATER (above).

1182. SOLO WHITEWATER. See: PATH OF THE PADDLE: WHITE WATER (above).

1183. SOMEWHERE IN IDAHO. A WEEK IN COLORADO. Jersey City, NJ: Gravity Sports Films, 1985? 2 segments on 1 videocassette, sd., col., Beta?, VHS? Summary: The first segment features paddling action on the South Fork of the Salmon (ID); the second segment affords a quick paddle tour of four Colorado rivers, plus the 1985 Animas Rodeo. Source: Gravity Sports Films, 100 Broadway, Jersey City, NJ 07306.

1184. SONG OF THE PADDLE. Produced by Bill Brind and Marrin Canell. Directed by Bill Mason. New York: National Film Board of Canada, 1978. 1 videocassette, 41 min., sd., col., Beta, VHS. Summary: Follows a family canoeing across the waterways of Canada. Source: National Film Board of Canada, 1251 Ave. of the Americas, New York, NY 10020.

1185. SOUTH FORK OF THE SALMON AND THE NORTH FORK OF THE PAYETTE. Englewood, CO: Photographic Expeditions, 198? 1 videocassette, 32 min., sd., col., VHS. Summary: Catarafts running some very technical Idaho whitewater. Includes footage of the first complete descent (including the first 12 miles) of the North Fork of the Payette. Source: Northwest River Supplies, P. O. Box 9186, Moscow, ID 83843-9186.

1186. SPRINT CANOEING LEVEL 3 TECHNICAL-STARTS. 198? 1 videocassette, 8 min., sd., col, Beta?, VHS? Source: Canadian Canoe Association, 1600 Prom., James Naismith Dr., Gloucester, ON K1B 5N4.

1187. SUSITNA. Knik Kanoers & Kayakers, Inc., 198? 1 videocassette, 10 min., sd., col., VHS, 3/4 in. U-matic. Summary: A local production which combines still and moving photography to describe this challenging Alaska river from the standpoint of an expert whitewater paddler. Source: American Canoe Association Film Library, Audio Visual Services, Special Services Bldg., University Park, PA 16802.

1188. TICKET TO FREEDOM: A LOOK AT KAYAK TOURING IN THE 80'S. Produced by Paul Sharpe. Easley, SC: Aquaterra, 1985. 1 videocassette, 25 min., sd., col., Beta, VHS. Summary: Introductory video on sea kayak touring showing this activity from the earler days of use by the Eskimo until the present. Source: Aquaterra, P. O. Box 1357-S, Easley, SC 29641.

1189. TO KAYAK. Bodacious Film, 1975. 1 videocassette, 33 min., sd., col., VHS. Summary: Introduction to all aspects of kayaking: equipment, safety, basic paddling techniques, cruising, and racing. Source: Canoe Ontario, 1220 Sheppard Ave. East, Willowdale, ON M2K 2X1.

1190. THE ULTIMATE CANOE VIDEO. Filmed by Nolan Whitesell. Whitesell, 198? 1 videocassette, 60 min., sd., col., Beta?, VHS? Summary: Footage of an open canoe descent of Niagara Gorge, the Upper Yough, Gauley, Cherry Creek (CA), and the Colorado in Grand Canyon. Source: Menasha Ridge Press, P. O. Box 59257, Birmingham, AL 35259-9257.

1191. THE UNCALCULATED RISK. American Red Cross, 1978. 1 videocassette, 15 min., sd., col., VHS. Summary: Instruction in accident prevention through showing what could go dangerously wrong in whitewater paddling situations. Source: Canoe Ontario, 1220 Sheppard Ave. East, Willowdale, ON M2K 2X1.

1192. UPPER TAOS BOX OF THE RIO GRANDE—FIRST DESCENT. Englewood, CO: Photographic Expeditions, 198? 1 videocassette, 60 min., sd., col., VHS. Summary: First successful raft descent of this very difficult New Mexico whitewater. Shows six rafters in a demonstration of team effort. Source: National Organization for River Sports, P. O. Box 6847, Colorado Springs, CO 80904.

1193. VIDEO GUIDE TO THE ROGUE RIVER. 198? 1 videorecording, sd., col., VHS? Summary: Video "guidebook" to Oregon's Rogue including: put-ins and take-outs, and shuttle information. Source: Wyoming River Raiders, 601 Wyoming Blvd., Casper, WY 82609.

1194. VOICES FROM THE STONE. Produced by Art Vitarelli. Reel Orange, Inc., 1989? 1 videocassette, 60 min., sd., col., VHS? Summary: Reviews the river running history and present day activities on the Colorado River in Grand Canyon, answering the questions: who was first to run the canyon, and who should have that privilege today? Source: National Organization for River Sports, P. O. Box 6847, Colorado Springs, CO 80904.

1195. WATERMARKS. Tallahassee, FL: WFSU Television, 198? 1 videocassette, 30 min., sd., col., Beta?, VHS? Summary: Examines the politics involved in trying to preserve one of Florida's last natural rivers now threatened by dams and dredging. Source: WFSU-TV, 202 Dodd Hall, Tallahassee, FL 32306.

1196. WATERWALKER. New York: National Film Board of Canada, 1984. 1 videocassette, 90 min., sd., col., Beta, VHS. Summary: This video reverently records ten years of canoe trips on and around the north shore of Lake Superior by filmmaker/artist, Bill Mason. The video is in three segments: Mason canoeing along Superior's shore; his poling, sailing and portaging upriver; and, a final segment of fast-paced downriver run. Interspersed throughout are shots of Mason working on his landscape paintings. Source: Northword Press, Box 1360, Minocqua, WI 54548.

1197. WESTERN BOATING PACKAGE. Jersey City, NJ: Gravity Sports Films, 198? 1 videocassette, 100 min., sd., col., Beta?, VHS. Summary: A bundle of three videos featuring "Liquid Madness" (Colorado River), "Urban Kayak" (hole-playing sequences), and "Five Idaho Classics" (a video guidebook to famous Idaho runs). Source: Gravity Sports Films, 100 Broadway, Jersey City, NJ 07306.

1198. WHITEWATER. Angels Camp, CA: Sobek, 198? 5 segments on 1 videocassette, 120 min., sd., col., Beta, VHS. Summary: A whitewater package featuring five "exotic" rivers: Bio-Bio (Chile), Omo (Africa), Rogue (Oregon), Tatshenshini (Alaska), and the Colorado in Grand Canyon. Source: Sobek, Box 7007, Angels Camp, CA 95222.

1199. WHITEWATER CANOEING. 198? 1 videocassette, 28 min., sd., col., Beta?, VHS. Summary: An introduction to the sport of whitewater canoeing. Source: American Canoe Association Film Library, c/o Audio Visual Services, Special Services Bldg., University Park, PA 16802.

1200. WHITEWATER CANOEING, SKETCHING CANADIAN WOODS. The Great Outdoors, program 9. Produced and directed by Christopher Gilbert. WGBH-Outside, Appalachian Mountain Club; Northbrook, IL: MTI Teleprograms, 1984. 1 videocassette, (approx.) 50 min., sd., col., VHS. Credits: presenter, Jim Tabor; photography, Bill Charette; editor, Bob Burns. Summary: Exhibits gear and demonstrates paddling techniques for whitewater canoeing. Also visits the Canadian woods with a sketch artist, and offers baking recipes for backpackers. Finally goes to Angel Island in San Francisco Bay for off-road running. Source: WGBH Television, 125 Western Ave., Boston, MA 02134.

1201. WHITEWATER GREY HAIR [Videorecording?]. Produced by Bill Briggs. Directed by Mark Davis. Tucson, AZ: Ray Manley Films, 1983. sd., col., Beta?, VHS? Summary: Documents a raft trip down the Colorado River and through the Grand Canyon taken by a group of senior citizens— the rapids, camp life, and canyon beauty with a classical music soundtrack.

1202. WHITEWATER PRIMER. Washington, DC: Boating Education Branch, U. S. Coast Guard, 1984. 1 videocassette, 17 min., sd., col., Beta, VHS, 3/4 in. U-matic. Summary: Demonstrates the right and wrong approaches to whitewater canoeing. Source: National Audio Visual Center, General Services Administration, Washington, DC 20409.

1203. WHITEWATER SELF DEFENSE: THE ESKIMO ROLL, THE EDDY TURN & PORTAGE. Nichols Productions, 1977. 1 videocassette, 14 min. sd., col., Beta, VHS. Summary: An instructional video for beginning decked boat paddlers. Depicts both a C-1 and kayak roll using slow motion, stop action, line drawings, and above and underwater angles. Source: American Canoe Association Film Library, Audio Visual Services, Special Services Bldg., University Park, PA 16802.

1204. WHITEWATER SURVIVAL. Produced by Bill Ward. Denver, CO: KUSA Television, 198? 1 videocassette, (approx.) 50 min., sd., col., Beta?, VHS? Summary: River safety video acclaimed for its authority and impact. Source: National Organization for River Sports, P. O. Box 6847, Colorado Springs, CO 80904.

1205. THE WILD & SCENIC ROGUE RIVER. Ashland, OR: Gayle Wilson Productions, 1990? 1 videocassette, 30 min., sd., col., VHS? Summary: A river runners view of one of the classic whitewater rivers in the United States. Shows the rapids, wildlife, campsites, and side hikes. Source: Gayle Wilson Prod., 265 Alta, Ashland, OR 97520.

1206. WILDERNESS RIVERS. Camera One, 198? 1 videocassette, ? min., sd., col., Beta?, VHS. Summary: A look at the best wilderness and whitewater rivers in the U. S., from the Chattooga to the Rogue. Source: Nantahala Outdoor Center, US 19 W, Box 41, Bryson City, NC 28713.

1207. WILDERNESS SURVIVAL. Mastering the Wilderness Series. Checkmate Productions, 198? 1 videocassette, 25 min., sd., col., Beta, VHS. Summary: Part I: review of preventive measures; coping with emergencies; meeting essential physical requirements; emergency items; movement under emergency conditions; shelters; signaling. Part II: sunstroke; hypothermia, heat exhaustion/cramp/fatigue; dehydration, sunburn, blisters, and trenchfoot. Source: Canadian Recreational Canoeing Association, Box 500, Hyde Park, ON N0M 1Z0.

1208. WILDERNESS TRIPPING. Mastering the Wilderness Series. Checkmate Productions, 198? 1 videocassette, 25 min., sd., col., Beta, VHS. Summary: Part I: basic planning considerations of distance, duration and terrain; clothing, sleeping gear, layering (clothing); shelter and menues; equipment check; packing gear; preparing participants. Part II: selecting and establishing campsites; fires; camp cooking; review of minimal impact or no-trace camping. Source: Canadian Recreational Canoeing Association, Box 500, Hyde Park, ON N0M 1Z0.

1209. THE WILDERNESS WORLD OF SIGURD OLSON. Produced by Ray Christensen and Steve Kahlenbeck. Minneapolis, MN: Filmedia, 1980. 1 videocassette, 28 min., sd., col., Beta, VHS. Summary: A profile of writer/canoeist/ecologist/ naturalist, Sigurd F. Olson and his Quetico-Superior wilderness world filmed about two years before he died. Filmedia, Inc., 221 S. River Ridge Cir., Minneapolis, MN 55425.

1210. YAKITY YAK. Englewood, CO: Photographic Expeditions, 198? 1 videocassette, 30 min., sd., col., VHS. Summary: Action kayaking footage shot on over 15 western rivers—and in Costa Rica. Contains a humorous sketch on the origin of the kayak. Source: Wyoming River Raiders, 601 Wyoming Blvd., Casper, WY 82609.

1211. YELLOWSTONE CONCERTO [Videorecording?] Helena, MT: Montana Department of Fish and Game, 1977. 1 videocassette?, 32 min., sd., col., VHS? Summary: Follows the course of the Yellowstone River from its many mountain tributaries. Shows the diversity of life which depends on the river and makes a plea for preservation. Source: Montana Dept. of Fish and Game, Conservation Education Bureau, Sam W. Mitchell Bldg., Helena, MT 59601.

Chapter 9

Indexes and Computerized Sources

1212. THE AMERICAN WHITEWATER AFFILIATION NATIONWIDE WHITEWATER INVENTORY: A LIVING DATABASE OF SIGNIFICANT WHITEWATER RIVER SEGMENTS. Edited by Pope Barrow. Palatine, IL: AWA, vol. 1-, 1989-. Computer-accessible database. A computerized database containing a listing of each significant whitewater river segment (2,200 segments, 36,000 miles of whitewater) in the United States. A print version with the same title (180 pages, with maps and bibliography) was published in 1989. The data were assembled from existing state and regional databases, whitewater guidebooks, and reports from individual river runners. The first edition (both electronic and print formats) was made available in 1989 and is "updated frequently." It covers 39 states (accurate data was unavailable for FL, HI, IN, IA, KS, LA, NE, ND, OK, MS, and SD). No Class I, artificial courses, ocean surf, tidal areas, impoundments, or bypassed reaches are included. Listings in the printed database give river name, state, county, segment mileage, and whitewater difficulty (ISRD). The computerized version (available on a 5-1/4-inch floppy diskette) is compatible with IBM-compatible computers with a hard drive and dBase III or dBase III+ software. Contact: AWA Whitewater Inventory, 136 13th St. S.E., Washington, DC, 20003.

1213. AMERICAN WHITEWATER ARTICLE INDEX. Palatine, IL: American Whitewater Affiliation, vol. 1-, 1967?-. Computer-accessible database. The American Whitewater Affiliation has recently completed an index containing some 1,300 entries which provides access to articles in its bimonthly journal, AMERICAN WHITEWATER. The index covers materials beginning with its early issues of the 1960s. Access is by subject or author. Printouts available on request. Contact: AWA, c/o Pope Barrow, 146 N. Brockway, Palatine, IL 60067.

1214. CANOE MAGAZINE DATABASE. Kirkland, WA: Canoe America Associates, vol 1-, 1973-. Computer-accessible database organized by subject. Computerized index (dBase III+) to the contents of the CANOE magazine from its beginnings in 1973. Photocopies of articles available. Contact: CANOE, P.O. Box 3146, Kirkland, WA 98083 (206)827-6363.

1215. PHYSICAL EDUCATION INDEX. Cape Gerardeau, MO: BenOak Publishing, vol. 1-, 1978-. Quarterly. Printed subject index to articles in almost 200 periodicals covering health, physical education, physical therapy, dance, recreation, sports, and sports medicine. PEI is quarterly, with the fourth issue an annual cumulation. Contact: BenOak, P.O. Box 474, Cape Gerardeau, MO 63702-0474 (314)334-8789.

1216. SEA KAYAKER [INDEX]. Seattle, WA: Sea Kayaker, vol. 1-, 1984-. Cumulative index of all articles published since its start in 1984, organized by broad subject category and listed in reverse chronological order. The index is published as a special supplement to SEA KAYAKER. Some issues of the magazine ("Resources" section) contain an extensive index to paddling articles in a number of different paddlesports periodicals. Contact: SEA KAYAKER, 6327 Seaview Ave. N.W., Seattle, WA 98107.

1217. SPORT. Ottawa, ON: Sport Information Resource Centre (SIRC). vol. 1-, 19??-. Computer-accessible database. A large, computerized bibliographic database (230,000 citations) available through commercial vendors (BRS, BRS After Dark, CISTI, DIALOG, and Knowledge Index). Cites scientific and practical literature from books (since 1949) and journal and magazine articles (since 1975) in the areas of individual and team sports, recreation, sports medicine, and physical education. Not a prime source for practical articles on paddlesports, but it should be consulted for any comprehensive literature-searching project. Many larger libraries provide professional searching of this database for their clientele. SIRC will also run searches on request. Printed counterparts to SPORT are: SPORT BIBLIOGRAPHY (8 volumes, plus annual issues) and SPORTSEARCH (vol. 1-, 1985-, monthly), a current awareness index for nearly 300 sport and physical education periodicals published in English and French. SPORT DISCUS is another CD-ROM product that will run on an IBM-compatible or Apple Macintosh computer. Coverage of articles found through SPORT DISCUS begins with 1975, and its search capabilities are comparable to SPORT. Contact: Sport Information Resource Centre, 1600 Promenade, James Naismith Dr., Gloucester, ON K1B 5N4 (613)748-5704.

1218. SPORTS PERIODICALS INDEX. Ann Arbor, MI: National Information Systems, vol. 1-, 1985-. Monthly. Printed subject index to 85 popular North American sport and recreation periodicals. SPI has annotated entries and is updated monthly. Contact: National Information Systems Inc., 2750 S. State St., Ann Arbor, MI 48104-6738.

Chapter 10, Section 1

Maps and Charts

Federal Agencies Sources

CANADA

ENERGY, MINES, AND RESOURCES CANADA, EARTH PHYSICS BRANCH, 580 Booth St., Ottawa, ON K1A 0E4 (613)996-3355 The EPB has an inventory of specialized maps: gravity, magnetic, seismic, and topographic.

ENERGY, MINES, AND RESOURCES CANADA, FEDERAL SURVEYS AND MAPPING BRANCH, Surveys, Mapping and Cartographic Centre, 615 Booth St., Ottawa, ON K1A 0E9 (613)995-4321 The Branch publishes a booklet listing index maps for the available topographic series: scales of 1:125,000; 1:500,000; and 1:1,000,000. Also included is a master index map to the regional index maps in the 1:50,000 series. For index maps and the individual national topographic series maps, address orders and payment to the centre. Lists of maps: CATALOGUE OF PUBLISHED MAPS; and NEW AND REVISED MAPS.

ENVIRONMENT CANADA, CANADIAN HYDROGRAPHIC SERVICE, Institute of Ocean Sciences, P.O. Box 8080, Ottawa, K1G 3H6 (613)998-4931 Charts for all the Great Lakes and Canadian coastal waters are sold through this office.

ENVIRONMENT CANADA, Public Service Centre, Rm. 1640, Whitney Block, Queen's Park, Toronto, ON M7A 1W3 (416)965-6511 (maps); (416)965-1123 (photographs). Both topographic maps and aerial photographs are available.

NATIONAL ARCHIVES OF CANADA, 395 Wellington St., Ottawa, ON K1A 0N3 (613)995-8094 Maintains a departmental library housing the national map collection. The collection is open to the public with no referrals needed for patrons beyond high school age.

NATIONAL LIBRARY OF CANADA, 395 Wellington St., Ottawa, ON K1A 0N4 (613)995-9481 Extensive holdings of Canadian public documents.

UNITED STATES

TENNESSEE VALLEY AUTHORITY, Maps and Surveys Dept., 311 Broad St. Chattanooga, TN 37402-2801 (615)751-2133 The TVA is a government-owned corporation which has recreation as one subsidiary mission. Various waterways maps covering its territories are available. TVA publishes two useful reference lists: TVA MAPS PRICE CATALOG; and, INDEX TO TOPOGRAPHIC MAPS CURRENTLY AVAILABLE THROUGH TVA (in the agency's AL, MS, KY, VA, NC, SC, and TN jurisdiction).

U.S. DEPT. OF AGRICULTURE, FOREST SERVICE, Information Office, P.O. Box 2417, Washington, DC 20013 (202)447-3760 For maps of waterways within national forest boundaries, inquire at the regional office nearest the area of your interest (NATIONAL FOREST VISITOR MAPS, approximate cost is $1.00). See Chapter 11, Section 1 for regional office addresses.

U.S. DEPT. OF COMMERCE, NATIONAL OCEANIC AND ATMOSPHERIC ADMINISTRATION, National Ocean Service, Distribution Branch, Riverside, MD 20737-1199 (301)436-6990 Publishes charts for waters surrounding the United States and its possessions. A free index shows coverage of: the Atlantic and Gulf coasts, Puerto Rico, and the Virgin Islands; Pacific coast including Hawaii, Guam, and Samoa; Alaska including the Aleutian Islands and the Great Lakes and adjacent waterways. Smaller, lighter charts (a kayak convenience) are available for some areas. NOAA also publishes a series of UNITED STATES COAST PILOTS.

U.S. DEPT. OF DEFENSE, DEFENSE MAPPING AGENCY, Distribution Services, 6500 Brooks Lane, Washington DC 20315-0010 (202)227-2495; (800)826-0342 The DMA has combined military map and charting responsibilities. The agency has extensive inventories of topographic and other types of maps from virtually every place in the world. Many larger libraries maintain a collection of these maps. Ordering publications: DMA CATALOG OF MAPS, CHARTS, AND RELATED PRODUCTS, VOLS. I-X; MISCELLANEOUS AND SPECIAL PURPOSE NAVIGATIONAL CHARTS, SHEETS AND TABLES (nautical charts); and, DEFENSE MAPPING AGENCY PUBLIC SALE CATALOG (topographic maps).

U.S. DEPT. OF THE ARMY, UNITED STATES ARMY CORPS OF ENGINEERS, 20 Massachusetts Ave. N.W., Washington, DC 20314 (202)272-0660 The Corps has wide-ranging responsibilities for design, construction, and operation of civil works projects related to rivers, harbors and waterways, and for the preservation of navigable waters and related resources such as wetlands. Some maps of waterways within its jurisdiction are distributed by the Corps. See Chapter 11, Section 1 for addresses of Corps divisions.

U.S. DEPT. OF THE INTERIOR, BUREAU OF LAND MANAGEMENT, Office of Public Affairs, Interior Bldg., Washington, DC 20240 (202)343-9435 The BLM offers surface ownership status maps based on the USGS 1:100,000 metric series. The maps are referenced by the same names using the (USGS)INDEX TO TOPOGRAPHIC AND OTHER MAP COVERAGE, or the CATALOG OF TOPOGRAPHIC AND OTHER PUBLISHED MAPS. The BLM also has specialized map-guides of popular recreational rivers within its jurisdiction. Address all inquiries to the relevant state office. See Chapter 11, Section 1 for field office addresses.

U.S. DEPT. OF THE INTERIOR, UNITED STATES GEOLOGICAL SURVEY, National Mapping Div., National Center, 12201 Sunrise Valley Dr., Reston, VA 22092 (703)648-6131

The USGS publishes index maps by state (INDEX TO TOPOGRAPHIC AND OTHER MAP COVERAGE, and the CATALOG OF TOPOGRAPHIC AND OTHER PUBLISHED MAPS) which show maps available for ordering in a variety of series including the standard 7 1/2 minute quadrangle series (1:24,000; 2 5/8 inches to the mile). The indexes also indicate locations of map dealers and map libraries in various states. Moreover, the Geological Survey has information on aerial photographs available from various agencies through its publication, STATUS OF AERIAL PHOTOGRAPHY.

General list of USGS publications: NEW PUBLICATIONS OF THE U.S. GEOLOGICAL SURVEY (monthly, with yearly supplements); MAP DATA CATALOG; and, U.S. GEOLOGICAL SURVEY MAP SALES CATALOG (loose-leaf).

A network of 13 Earth Science Information Centers responds to requests that are made in person, by mail, or by telephone and assists in the selection and ordering of all Geological Survey products. EARTH SCIENCE INFORMATION CENTERS: ALASKA: 4230 University Dr., Rm. 101, Anchorage, AK 99508-4664 (907)561-5555 ALASKA: U.S. Courthouse, Rm. 113, 222 W. 7th Ave., Box 53, Anchorage, AK 99513-7546 (907)271-4307 CALIFORNIA: 7638 Federal Bldg., 300 N. Los Angeles St., Los Angeles, CA 90012 (213)894-2850 CALIFORNIA: Bldg. 3, Rm 3128 (MS 532), 345 Middlefield Rd., Menlo Park, CA 94025 (415)329-4390 CALIFORNIA: 504 Custom House, 555 Battery St., San Francisco, CA 94111 (415)556-5627 COLORADO: 169 Federal Bldg., 1961 Stout St., Denver, CO 80294 (303)844-4169 COLORADO: Box 25046, Federal Center, Denver, CO 80225 (303)236-5829 DISTRICT OF COLUMBIA: Dept. of the Interior Bldg., 18th and C Sts. NW, Rm. 2650, Washington, DC 20240 (202)343-8073 MISSISSIPPI: Bldg. 3101, Stennis Space Center, MS 39529 (601)688-3544 MISSOURI: 1400 Independence Rd., Rolla, MO 65401 (314)341-0851 UTAH: 8105 Federal Bldg., 125 S. State St., Salt Lake City, UT 84138 (801)524-5652 VIRGINIA (NATIONAL CENTER): 507 National Center, Rm. 1C402, 12201 Sunrise Valley Dr., Reston, VA 22092 (703)860-6045 WASHINGTON: 678 U.S. Courthouse, W. 920 Riverside Ave., Spokane, WA 99201 (509)456-2524

U.S. DEPT. OF THE INTERIOR, NATIONAL PARK SERVICE, Office of Public Affairs, P.O. Box 37127, Washington, DC 20013-7127 (202)343-7394 The NPS provides visitor maps for selected recreational waterways within national park boundaries. Inquiries should be directed to the appropriate regional office (see Chapter 11, Section 1 for regional addresses). The NPS also does the planning and technical assistance work for the National Wild and Scenic Rivers System.

Chapt r 10, Section 2

Maps and Charts

Provincial and State Agencies Sources, Canada and the United States

ALABAMA: Geological Survey, P.O. Box O, Tuscaloosa, AL 35486-9780 (205)349-2852 Highway Dept., 1409 Coliseum Blvd., Montgomery, AL 36130 (205)242-6356

ALASKA: Geological and Geophysical Surveys Div., 3700 Airport Way, Fairbanks, AK 99709 (907)474-7147 Transportation and Public Facilities Dept., P.O. Box Z, Juneau, AK 99811-2500 (907)465-3900

ALBERTA: Alberta Geological Survey, Alberta Research Council, P.O. Box 8330, Station F, Edmonton, AB T6H 5X2 (403)438-7676 Transportation and Utilities, Twin Atria, 4999 98th Ave., Edmonton, AB T6B 2X3 (403)427-2731

ARIZONA: Transportation Dept., Highway Div., 206 S. 17th Ave., Phoenix, AZ 85007 (602)255-7391

ARKANSAS: Geology Commission, 3815 W. Roosevelt Rd., Little Rock, AR 72204 (501)371-1488 Highway and Transportation Dept., P.O. Box 2261, Little Rock, AR 72203 (501)569-2227

BRITISH COLUMBIA: Min. of Energy, Mines and Petroleum Resources, Geological Survey Bureau, 756 Fort St. #200 Victoria, BC V8V 1X4 (604)356-2818 Min. of Transportation and Highways, 940 Blanchard St., Victoria, BC V8V 3E6 (604)387-3198

CALIFORNIA: Dept. of Conservation, Div. of Mines and Geology,1416 9th St., Rm. 1320, P.O. Box 2980, Sacramento, CA 95814 (916)445-1923 Transportation Dept., 1120 N St., Sacramento, CA 95814 (916)445-5937

COLORADO: Natural Resources Dept., Geological Survey Div., 1313 Sherman St., Denver, CO 80203 (303)866-2611 Highways Dept., 4201 E. Arkansas Ave., Rm. 262, Denver, CO 80222 (303)757-9483

CONNECTICUT: Environmental Protection Dept., State Geologist, 165Capitol Ave., Hartford, CT 06106 (203)566-3540 Dept. of Transportation, P.O. Drawer A, Wethersfield, CT 06109-0801 (203)566-3010

DELAWARE: Geological Survey, Univ. of Delaware, DGS Bldg., Newark, DE 19716 (302)451-2833 Dept. of Transportation, Div. of Highways, P.O. Box 778, Dover, DE 19903 (302)736-4303

FLORIDA: Dept. of Natural Resources, State Lands Div., Survey and Mapping Bureau, 3900 Commonwealth Blvd., Tallahassee, FL32399 (904)488-2427 Transportation Dept., 605 Suwannee St., Tallahassee, FL 32399-0450 (904)488-8984

GEORGIA: Natural Resources Dept., State Geologist, 205 Butler St. S.E., Suite 1252, Atlanta, GA 30334 (404)656-3214 Transportation Dept., 2 Capitol Sq., Rm. 10, Atlanta, GA 30334-1002 (404)656-5267

HAWAII: Survey Div., P.O. Box 119, Honolulu, HI 96810 (808)548-7422 Transportation Dept., 869 Punchbowl St., Honolulu, HI 96813 (808)548-2268

IDAHO: Geological Survey, Univ. of Idaho, 332 Morrill Hall, Moscow, ID 83832 (208)885-7991 Transportation Dept., 3311 W. State St., Box 7129, Boise, ID 83707 (208)334-8818

ILLINOIS: Energy and Natural Resources Dept., Geographical Information Office, 325 W. Adams St., Rm. 300, Springfield, IL 62704 (217)785-2800 Transportation Dept., Highways Div., 2300 S. Dirksen Pkwy., Springfield, IL 62764 (217)782-2151

INDIANA: Dept. of Natural Resources, Geological Survey Div., 611 N. Walnut Grove, Bloomington, IN 47405 (812)855-9350 Transportation Dept., 100 N. Senate Ave., Indianapolis, IN 46204 (317)232-5518

IOWA: Natural Resources Dept., Geological Survey Bureau, Wallace State Office Bldg., Des Moines, IA 50319 (319)338-1173 Transportation Dept., Highways Div., 800 Lincoln Way, Ames, IA 50010 (515)239-1124

KANSAS: Geological Survey, 1930 Constant Ave., Campus West, Topeka, KS 66047 (913)864-3965 Transportation Dept., Docking State Office Bldg., Topeka, KS 66612 (913)296-3585

KENTUCKY: Geological Survey, 228 Mining and Minerals Resources Bldg., 120 Graham Ave., Lexington, KY 40506-0107 (606)257-5863 Economic Development Cabinet, Map Sales Services, Capitol Plaza Twr., 24th Fl., Frankfort, KY 40601 (502)564-4886

LOUISIANA: Geological Survey, Box G, Univ. Station, Baton Rouge, LA 70803 (504)342-6754 Transportation and Development Dept., P.O. Box 94245, Baton Rouge, LA 70804-9245 (504)379-1210

MAINE: Geological Survey, State House Station 22, Augusta, ME 04333 (207)289-2801 Transportation Dept., State House Station 16, Augusta, ME 04333-0016 (207)289-2551

MANITOBA: Energy and Mines, 330 Graham Ave., #555, Winnipeg, MB R3C4E3 (204)945-4154 Highways and Transportation, 215 Garry St., Winnipeg, MB R3C 3Z1 (204)945-2004

MARYLAND: Natural Resources Dept., Geological Survey, 2300 St. Paul St., Baltimore, MD 21218 (301)554-5503 Dept. of Transportation, State Highway Admin., 707 N. Calvert St., Baltimore, MD 21202 (301)333-1111

MASSACHUSETTS: Dept. of Public Works, 10 Park Plaza, Rm. 4150, Boston, MA 02116 (617)973-7800

MICHIGAN: Dept. of Natural Resources, Geological Survey Div., Box 30028, Lansing, MI 48926 (517)334-6907 Transportation Dept., Travel Information Office, Box 30050, Lansing, MI 48909 (517)373-8700

MINNESOTA: Geological Survey, 2624 University Ave. W., St. Paul, MN 55114-1057 (612)627-4780 Transportation Dept., Transportation Bldg., Rm. B-20, St. Paul, MN 55155 (612)296-7968

MISSISSIPPI: Geological Bureau, Drawer 4915, Jackson, MS 39216 (601)359-6228 Highway Dept., P.O. Box 1850, Jackson, MS 39215-1850 (601)359-1209

MISSOURI: Geology and Land Survey Div., P.O. Box 250, 111 Fairgrounds Rd., Rolla, MO 65401 (314)364-1752 Highway and Transportation Dept., Capitol and Jefferson Sts., Jefferson City, MO 65102 (314)751-2840

MONTANA: Natural Resources and Conservation Dept., Cartographic Bureau, 1520 E. 6th Ave., Helena, MT 59620 (406)444-6739 Highways Dept., 2701 Prospect Ave., Helena, MT 59620 (406)444-6200

NEBRASKA: Conservation and Survey Div., Univ. of Nebraska, 113 Nebraska Hall, Lincoln, NE 68508 Roads Dept., P.O. Box 94759, Lincoln, NE 68509 (402)479-4512

NEVADA: Bureau of Mines, Univ. of Nevada, Reno, NV 89557 (702)784-6596 Transportation Dept., 1263 S. Stewart St., Carson City, NV 89712 (702)687-5440

NEW BRUNSWICK: Dept. of Natural Resources and Energy, P.O. Box 6000, Fredericton, NB E3B 5H1 (506)453-2206 Dept. of Transportation, P.O. Box 6000, Fredericton, NB E3B 5H1 (506)453-2663

NEW FOUNDLAND: Dept. of Mines and Energy, Geological Survey, P.O. Box 8700, St. John's, NF A1B 4J6 (709)576-2763 Dept. of Works, Services and Transportation, Confederation Bldg., P.O. Box 8700, St. John's, NF A1B 4J6 (709)576-3278

NEW HAMPSHIRE: Geologic Bureau, Dept. of Geology, Univ. of New Hampshire, Durham, NH 03824 Transportation Dept., P.O. Box 483, Concord, NH 03301 (603)271-3736

NEW JERSEY: Bureau of Geology and Topography, John Fitch Plaza, P.O. Box 1889, Trenton, NJ 08625 Transportation Dept., CN 600, 1035 Parkway Ave., Trenton, NJ 08625 (609)530-3535

NEW MEXICO: Energy, Minerals and Natural Resources Dept., 2040 S. Pacheo St., Santa Fe, NM 87505 (505)827-5804 Highway and Transportation Dept., P.O. Box 1149, Santa Fe, NM 87504 (505)827-5134

NEW YORK: Geological Survey, Education Bldg., Rm. 973, Albany, NY 12224 Transportation Dept., Mapping Services Bureau, State Campus Bldg. 5, Albany, NY 12232 (518)457-4408

NORTH CAROLINA: Div. of Mineral Resources, P.O. Box 27687, Raleigh, NC 27611 Transportation Dept., Div. of Highways, Box 25201, 1 S. Wilmington St., Raleigh, NC 27611 (919)733-7384

NORTH DAKOTA: Geological Survey, P.O. Box 8213, Univ. Station, Grand Forks, ND 58202 (701)777-5132 Transportation Dept., 608 E. Boulevard Ave., Bismark, ND 58505-0700 (701)224-2581

NOVA SCOTIA: Dept. of Mines and Energy, Geological Surveys Div., 1701 Hollis St., P.O. Box 1087, Halifax, NS B3J 2X1 (902)424-4162 Dept. of Transportation and Communications, P.O. Box 186, Halifax, NS B3J 2N2 (902)424-4036

OHIO: Natural Resources Dept., Geological Surveys Div., 1207 Grandview Ave., Columbus, OH 43212 (614)265-6576 Transportation Dept., 25 S. Front St., Columbus, OH 43215 (614)466-2448

OKLAHOMA: Geological Survey, Univ. of Oklahoma, Norman, OK 73069 Transportation Dept., 200 N.E. 21st St., Oklahoma City, OK 73105 (405)521-2631

ONTARIO: Min. of Northern Development and Mines, Ontario Geological Survey, 77 Grenville St., Toronto, ON M5S 1B3 (416)965-1283 Min. of Transportation, 1201 Wilson Ave., 1st Fl. West Twr., Downsview, ON M3M 1J8 (416)235-2771

OREGON: Dept. of Geology and Mineral Industries, 910 State Office Bldg., Portland, OR 97201 (503)229-5580 Dept. of Transportation, Map Distribution Unit, Transportation Bldg., Rm. 17, Salem, OR 97310 (503)378-6388

PENNSYLVANIA: Environmental Resources Dept., Geologic Survey, P.O. Box 2357, Harrisburg, PA 17120 (717)787-2169 Dept. of Transportation, Publications Sales Unit, Transportation and Safety Bldg., Rm. 110, Harrisburg, PA 17120 (717)783-8800

PRINCE EDWARD ISLAND: Dept. of Energy and Forestry, Shaw Bldg., 3rd Fl., P.O. Box 2000, Charlottetown, PE C1A 7N8 (902)368-5010 Dept. of Transportation and Public Works, P.O. Box 2000, Charlottetown, PE C1A 7N8 (902)368-5161

QUEBEC: Min. de l'Energie et des Ressources, Direction generale de l'Exploration Geologique et Minerale, 1620 bou de l'Entente, 2e Et., Quebec, PQ G1S 4N6 (418)643-4617 Min. des Transports, 700 boul. Saint-Cyrille est, Quebec, PQ G1R 5H1 (418)643-6860

RHODE ISLAND: Transportation Dept., 210 State Bldg., Providence, RI 02903 (401)277-2508

SASKATCHEWAN: Dept. of Energy and Mines, 1914 Hamilton St., Regina, SK S4P 4V4 (306)787-2528 Dept. of Highways and Transportation, 1855 Victoria Ave., Regina, SK S4P 3V5 (306)787-4032

SOUTH CAROLINA: Div. of Geology, P.O. Box 927, Columbia, SC 29202 (803)734-9100 Highways and Public Transportation Dept., P.O. Box 191, Columbia, SC 29202 (803)737-1270

SOUTH DAKOTA: Water and Natural Resources Dept., Geological Survey, Joe Foss Bldg., 523 E. Capitol Ave., Pierre, SD 57501 (605)677-5227 Transportation Dept., 700 Broadway Ave. E., Pierre, SD 57501-2586 (605)773-3265

TENNESSEE: Conservation Dept., Div. of Geology, G-5 State Office Bldg., 701 Broadway, Nashville, TN 37219-5237 (615)742-6691 Transportation Dept., Map Sales Office, James K. Polk Bldg., 505 Deaderick St., Rm. 1000, Nashville, TN 37219 (615)741-2208

TEXAS: Economic Geology Bureau, Univ. of Texas, P.O. Box X, Austin, TX 78713-7508 (512)471-1534 Highways and Public Transportation Dept., 11th and Brazos, P.O. Box 5051, West Austin Station, Austin, TX 78763-5051 (512)463-8601

UTAH: Natural Resources Dept., Geological and Mineralogical Survey Div., 1606 Black Hawk Way, Salt Lake City, UT 84108-1280 (801)581-6831 Transportation Dept., Community Relations Div., 4501 S. 2700 West, Salt Lake City, UT 84119 (801)965-4390

VERMONT: Natural Resources Agency, State Geologist, 103 S. Main St., Waterbury, VT 05676 (802)244-5164 Transportation Agency, 133 State St., Montpelier, VT 05602 (802)828-2657

VIRGINIA: Mines, Minerals and Energy Dept., Mineral Resources Div., P.O. Box 3667, Charlottesville, VA 22903 (804)293-5121 Transportation Dept., 1221 E. Broad St., Richmond, VA 23219 (804)786-2715

WASHINGTON: Natural Resources Dept., Geology and Earth Resources Div., 201 John A. Cherberg Bldg., MS QW-21, Olympia, WA 98504 (206)459-6372 Transportation Dept., Transportation Bldg., MS KF-01, Olympia, WA 98504 (206)753-2150

WEST VIRGINIA: Geological and Economic Survey, P.O. Box 879, Morgantown, WV 26507 (304)594-2331 Transportation Dept., Highways Div., Map Sales Unit, 1900 Washington St. E., Charleston, WV 25305 (304)348-0103

WISCONSIN: Geological and Natural History Survey, Univ. of Wisconsin, 1815 University Ave., Madison, WI 53706 (608)262-8956 Transportation Dept., 3617 Pierstorff St., P.O. Box 7910, Madison, WI 53707-7910 (608)266-2910

WYOMING: Geological Survey, P.O. Box 3008 Univ. Station, Univ. of Wyoming, Laramie, WY 82071 (307)766-2286 Highway Dept., P.O. Box 1708, Cheyenne, WY 82002 (307)777-4010

Chapter 10, Section 3

Maps and Charts

Non-Government Sources

Canada

Bovey Marine Ltd., 375 Water St., Vancouver, BC V6B 3J5 (604)685-8216 Chart dealer.

Canada Map Co., 211 Yonge St., Toronto, ON M5B 1M4 (416)362-9297 Mapmaker, map dealer.

Dominion Map Ltd., 541 Howe St., Vancouver, BCV 6C2 Mapmaker, map dealer.

Gabriel Aero Marine Instruments, 1490 Lower Water St., Halifax, NS B3J 2R7 (902)423-7252; 351 St. Paul St. W., Montreal, PQ H2Y 2A7 (514)845-8342 Chart dealer.

McGill Maritime Services, 369 Place d'Youville, Montreal, PQ H2Y 2G2 (514)849-1125 Chart dealer.

Maritime Services Ltd., 3440 Bridgewater St., Vancouver, BC V5K 1B6 (604)294-4444 Chart dealer.

Ocean River Sports, 1437 Store St., Victoria, BC V8W 3J6 (604)381-4233 Chart dealer.

United States

S.G. Adams Printing and Stationery Co., 10th and Olive Streets, St. Louis, MO 63101 Mapmaker.

American Canoe Association, P.O. Box 1190, Newington, VA 22122-1190 (703)550-7523 Map dealer.

American Geographical Society, Broadway and 156th St., New York, NY 10017 (212)242-0214 Mapmaker.

American Nautical Services Navigation Center, 514 Biscayne Blvd., Miami, FL 33132 (305)358-1414 Chart dealer.

Backcountry Bookstore, P.O. Box 191, Snohomish, WA 98290 (206)568-8722 Map dealer.

Backeddy Books, P.O. Box 301, Cambridge, ID 83610 Map dealer.

Bahia Mar Marine Store, 801 Seabreeze Blvd., Fort Lauderdale, FL 33316 (305)764-8831 Chart dealer.

Baker, Lyman and Co., 3220 1-10 Service Rd. W., Metairie, LA 70001 (504)831-3685; 8876 Gulf Fwy. Suite 110, Houston, TX 77007 (713)943-7032 Chart dealer.

Boxells Chandlery, 68 Long Wharf, Boston, MA 02110 (617)523-5678 Chart dealer.

W.T Brownley Co., 118 W. Plume St., Norfolk, VA 23510 (804)622-7589 Chart dealer.

Captains Nautical Supplies, 138 N.W. 10th St., Portland, OR 97209 (503)227-1648; 1914 Fourth Ave., Seattle, WA 98101 (800)448-2278 Chart dealer.

Chatham Laminating Co., P.O. Box 5171 Sta. A, Savannah, GA 31403 Chart maker.

Colorado Kayak Supply, P.O. Box 291, Buena Vista, CO 81211 Mapdealer.

Compass Maps Inc., P.O. Box 4369, Modesto, CA 95352 (209)529-5017 Mapmaker.

County Maps, 50 Puetz Pl., Lyndon Station, WI 53944 (608)666-3331 Map dealer.

Creative Consultants (McKenzie Maps), 37 Providence Bldg, 334 W. Superior St., Duluth, MN 55802 (800)232-0069 (in MN), and (800)346-0089 (elsewhere) Mapmaker.

DeLorme Mapping Co., P.O. Box 298-6000, Freeport, ME 04032 (207)865-4171, or (800)227-1656 Mapmaker.

Educational Adventures (Quinn Maps), P.O. Box 4190, Sunriver, OR 97707 (503)593-3545 Mapmaker.

Erickson Maps, 337 17th St., Oakland, CA 94612 (415)893-3685 Mapmaker.

Geoscience Resources, P.O. Box 2096, (2990 Anthony Rd.), Burlington, NC 27215 (800)742-2677 Map dealer.

Hammond Inc., 515 Valley St., Maplewood, NJ 07040 (201)763-6000 Mapmaker.

High Sierra Outdoor Center, 100 E. Sierra Ave., Suite 3102, Fresno, CA 93710 Map dealer.

Hubbard Scientific Co., 1946 Raymond St., P.O. Box 105, Northbrook, IL 60062 (312)272-7810 Mapmaker.

R.H. John Chart Agency, 518 23rd St., Galveston, TX 77550 (409)763-6762 Chart dealer.

(Les) Jones Maps, Star Route, Box 13A, Heber City, UT 84032 Mapmaker.

K.D.B. Enterprises (Big Sky Maps), P.O. Box 33, Nampa, ID 83651 (208)466-1592 Mapmaker.

Kistler Graphics Inc., P.O. Box 5467, Denver, CO 80217 Mapmaker.

McCurnin Nautical Charts Co., 2318 Woodlawn Ave., Metairie, LA 70001 (504)888-4500 Chart dealer.

McKenzie Maps, c/o Creative Consultants, 37 Providence Bldg, 334 W. Superior St., Duluth, MN 55802 (800)232-0069 (in MN), and (800)346-0089 (elsewhere) Mapmaker.

Manasha Ridge Press, P.O. Box 59257, Birmingham, AL 35259-9257 (205)991-0373 Map dealer.

Marshall Penn York Inc., 1538 Erie Blvd., West Syracuse, NY 13204 (315)422-2162 Map dealer.

Maryland Nautical Sales, 1143 Hull St., Baltimore, MD 21230 (301)752-4268 Chart dealer.

Metsker Maps, 111 S. 10th St., Tacoma, WA 98402 (206)383-5557; 1008 2nd Ave., Seattle, WA 98104 (206)623-8747 Mapmaker.

National Geographic Society, 17th and M Streets N.W., Washington, DC 20036 (202)857-7000 Mapmaker.

National Organization for River Sports, Box 6847, Colorado Springs, CO 80904 (719)473-2466 Map dealer.

The National Survey, Chester, VT 05143 (802)875-2121 Mapmaker.

New York Nautical Instrument and Service Corp., 140 W. Broadway, New York, NY 10013 (212)962-4522 Chart dealer.

A.J. Nystom and Co., 3333N. Elston Ave., Chicago, IL 60618 Mapmaker.

Pacific Map Center, 647 Auahi St., Honolulu, HI 96813 (808)531-3800 Chart dealer.

Pic-Tour Guide Maps, P.O. Box 3042, Federal Way, WA 98003

Pittman Map Co., 930 S.E. Sandy Blvd., Portland, OR 97214 (503)232-1161 Mapmaker.

Quinn Maps, c/o Educational Adventures, P.O. Box 4190, Sunriver, OR 97707 (503)593-3545 Mapmakers.

Rand McNally, P.O. Box 7600, Chicago, IL 60680 (312)673-9100 Mapmaker.

River Graphics, Box 783, Nederland, CO 80466 Mapmaker.

Safe Navigation Inc., 107 E. 8th St., Long Beach, CA 90813 (213)590-8744 Chart dealer.

Southwest Instruments Co., 235 W. 7th St., San Pedro, CA 90731 (213)519-7800 Chart dealer.

Tradewind Instruments Ltd., 2540 Blanding Ave., Alameda, CA 94501 (415)523-5726 Chart dealer.

Westwater Books, Box 2560, Evergreen, CO 80439 (303)670-0586 Map dealer.

The Wilderness Press, 2440 Bancroft Way, Berkeley, CA 94704 (415)843-8080 Mapmaker.

Wild Rose Guidebooks, Box 240047, Anchorage, AK 99524 Mapdealer.

Chapter 10, Section 4

Maps and Charts

Bibliographies and Other Lists

11219. American Geographical Society of New York. Map Dept. INDEX TO MAPS IN BOOKS AND PERIODICALS. Boston: G.K. Hall, 1971-, supplement no. 1-. Annual? ***

1220. BIBLIOGAPHIC GUIDE TO MAPS AND ATLASES. Boston, MA: G.K. Hall, 1980-. Annual *** This guide is designed to "bring together publications cataloged by the Research Libraries of the New York Public Library and the Library of Congress." (preface).

1221. Canada. Surveys and Mapping Branch. CATALOGUE OFPUBLISHED MAPS/ CATALOGUE DES CARTES PUBLIEES. Ottawa: Dept. of Energy, Mines and Resources. 1974?-. Annual? ***

1222. Carrington, David K., and Stephenson, Richard W., eds. MAP COLLECTIONS IN THE UNITED STATES AND CANADA, A DIRECTORY. 4th ed. New York: Special Libraries Association, 1985. 178 p. Index. Paper. Extensive list of 804 special map libraries in North America. A typical library entry gives: name, address, telephone, contact person, size of collection, annual accessions, specialization, depository status, clientele served, loan availability, and reproduction facilities.

1223. Cobb, David A., Comp. GUIDE TO U.S. MAP RESOURCES. Chicago, London: American Library Association, 1986. 196 p. Index. Comprehensive guide to 919 map collections found in all types of U.S. libraries, excluding company libraries. Descriptions are regularized to give: name, address, telephone, hours, supervisor, special strengths, holdings size, chronological coverage, catalog access, clientele served, depository status, loan availability, and copy facilities.

1224. Cooper, Bernard. MAPS TO ANYWHERE. Athens: Univ. of Georgia Press, 1990. ***

1225. Field, Lance. MAP USER'S SOURCEBOOK. London, Rome, New York: Oceana Publications, 1982. 194 p. Maps. Bibl. "This book brings together, in a single volume, a compendium of maps sources which can be used as a practical aid to those who enjoy being about in the outdoors world ... fishermen, botanists, campers, hikers, mountaineers, backpackers, airplane pilots, hunters, snowshoers, cross country skiers, sailors, canoeists, bikers..." (preface). Chapter 1: A brief Review of Cartography Worldwide; Chapter 2: Map Facts; Chapter 3: "Map Sources" (an extensive, state-by-state directory of retail outlets and libraries).

1226. GEOSCIENCE RESOURCES: MAP CATALOG. Burlington, NC: Geoscience Resources, 198-? Annual? Map sales catalog listing hundreds of maps and charts from public and private mapmakers. Some of the map types offered: geological, geothermal, metamorphic, physiography, raised relief, soils, topographic, and water resources.

1227. INTERNATIONAL MAPS AND ATLASES IN PRINT. Edited by Kenneth L. Winch. 2nd ed. New York: Bowker Publishing, 1976. 866 p. Illus. Index. Information on more than 8,000 maps and atlases. Comprehensive data on maps available from existing bibliographies, publisher catalogs, library accession lists, and other sources. Aeronautical and nautical navigation charts and those maps produced for advertising use have been excluded. Arrangement is by world region and country. Within a country designation, the materials are divided into map and atlas categories and are further subdivided into 20 types. Cited information includes title, scale, publisher, year of publication, and general description.

1228. THE MAP CATALOG: EVERY KIND OF MAP AND CHART ON EARTH AND EVEN SOME ABOVE IT. Edited by Joel Makower and Laura Bergheim. New York: Vantage Books, Tilden House Book,1986. 252 p. Illus. Index. Paper. ***

1229. MAPS AND ATLASES (UNITED STATES AND FOREIGN). Subject bibliography, SB-102. Washington, DC: U.S. Government Printing Office, Superintendent of Documents, 198-? Irregular *** Title in 1983: MAPS (UNITED STATES AND FOREIGN).

1230. MAPS TO ANYWHERE: 10,000 MAP AND TRAVEL PUBLICATIONS REFERENCE CATALOG. Hollywood, CA?: Travel Centers of the World,1974- . (Annual?) Illus. Maps. Paper. Sales catalog. Information is presented in five columns: name of map, order number, publisher, wholesale price, and suggested retail price. Of the 3,772 entries, about 75 percent represent road and topographic maps.

1231. National Cartographic Information Center. MAP DATA CATALOG. 2d ed. Reston, VA: National Cartographic Information Center, 1984. 48 p. Illus. Maps. ***

1232. NEW AND REVISED MAPS/NOUVELLES CARTES ET CARTES REVISEES. Ottawa: Canada Map Office, 19??-. Monthly ***

1233. OFFICIAL EASTERN NORTH AMERICA MAP AND CHART INDEX CATALOG. Neenah, WI: U.S.-Canadian Map Service Bureau, 1975. 186 p. Maps. Paper. Eastern and western volumes (see entry 1234). Despite the "official" name, these volumes are published by a commercial firm which sells the more than 200,000 maps and charts listed. Each volume contains reproduced USGS national and state topographic index maps, National Ocean Survey national chart indexes, and indexes for Canadian topographic maps and nautical charts. The geographical boundary separating coverage in the two books is the Mississippi River north to Hudson Bay. The volumes are out of print and obviously dated.

1234. OFFICIAL WESTERN NORTH AMERICA MAP AND CHART INDEXCATALOG. Neenah, WI: U.S.-Canadian Map Service Bureau, 1975. 226 p. Maps. Paper. See entry 1223 for general description.

1235. U.S. GEOLOGICAL SURVEY MAP SALES CATALOG. Rev. ed. Reston, VA: Dept. of the Interior, U.S. Geological Survey, National Mapping Program, 1987-. Loose-leaf. *** Running title: USGS MAP SALES CATALOG.

1236. THE WORLD MAP DIRECTORY. Santa Barbara, CA: Map Link, 1988-. Annual ***

Chapter 11, Section 1

Government Agencies and Private Organizations

Federal Agencies

CANADA

CANADIAN NATIONAL RAILWAY COMPANY, P.O. Box 8100, Montreal, PQ H3C 3N4 (514)399-5430 The CNR is a federal corporation charged with running the national railway freight services, and managing the real estate within its jurisdiction.

ENERGY, MINES AND RESOURCES CANADA, Communications Officer, 580Booth St., Ottawa, ON K1A 0E4 (613)996-3355 Develops resources, protects producers and consumers, encourages mining, and conducts surveying and mapping programs.

ENERGY, MINES AND RESOURCES CANADA, GEOLOGICAL SURVEY OF CANADA, Surveys, Mapping and Remote Sensing Sector, 580 Booth St., Ottawa, ON K1A 0E4 (613)995-4449 REGIONAL OFFICES: ATLANTIC: 40 Havelock St., P.O. Box 368, Amherst, NS B4H 3Z5 (902)667-7249 QUEBEC: 2144 rue King Ouest, #020, Sherbrooke, PQ J1J 2E8 (819)564-5781 ONTARIO: 25 St. Clair Ave. E., Toronto, ON M4T 1M2 (416)973-7503 MANITOBA: 275 Portage Ave., Winnipeg, MB R3B 2B3 (204)983-4954 SASKATCHEWAN: 2221 Cornwall St., #1000, Regina, SK S4P 2L1 (306)780-5401 ALBERTA: 9942 108 St., Edmonton, AB T5K 2J5 (403)420-2496 BRITISH COLUMBIA: 1550 Alberni St., Vancouver, BC V6G 1A5 (604)666-5320 YUKON: 204 Range Rd., Whitehorse, YT Y1A 3V1 (403)668-2636 NORTHWEST TERRITORY: 50th St., Bellanca Bldg., 8th Fl., P.O. Box668, Yellowknife, NT X1A 2N5 (403)920-8295

ENVIRONMENT CANADA, Communication Directorate, Ottawa, ON K1A 0H3 (819)997-6820 Administers various environmental acts including those for wildlife, national parks, weather modification, Arctic waters pollution, fisheries, international boundary waters treaty, navigable waters protection, and northern inland waters.

ENVIRONMENT CANADA, CONSERVATION AND PROTECTION, Headquarters, Place Vincent Massey, Hull, PQ (mailing: Ottawa, ON K1A 0H3) (819)997-1298 INLAND WATERS REGIONAL DIRECTORATES: ATLANTIC: 45 Alderney Dr., Dartmouth, NS B2Y 2N6 (902)426-6050 QUEBEC: 1141 rue de l'Eglise, 8e etage, P.O. Box 10, 100, Ste-Foy, PQ G1V 4H5 (418)648-3921 ONTARIO: 867 Lakeshore Rd., Burlington, ON L7R 4A6 (416)336-4532 PRAIRIE: 1901 Victoria Ave., 1st Fl., Motherwell Bldg., Regina, SK S4P 3R4 (306)780-5319 WESTERN: 1001 W. Pender St., #502, Vancouver, BC V6E 2M9 (604)666-3357

ENVIRONMENT CANADA, PARKS, Communications Directorate, Les Terrasses de la Chaudiere, Hull, PQ (mailing: Ottawa, ON K1A 0H3) (819)997-3736 REGIONAL OFFICES: ATLANTIC: Historic Properties Bldg., Upper Water St., Halifax, NS B3J 1S9 (902)426-3457 QUEBEC: 3 rue Buade, Quebec, PQ G1R 4V7 (418)648-4177 ONTARIO: 111 Water St. E., Cornwall, ON K6H 5S3 (613)938-5866 PRAIRIE: 457 Main St., Winnipeg, MB R3B 3E8 (204)949-2120 WESTERN: P.O. Box 2989, Sta. M, Calgary, AB T2P 3H8 (403)292-4401

FISHERIES AND OCEANS, Communications Branch, 200 Kent St., Ottawa, ON K1A 0E6 (613)993-0989 REGIONAL OFFICES: NEWFOUNDLAND: P.O. Box 5667, St. John's, NF A1C 5X1 (709)772-2022 GULF: P.O. Box 5030, Moncton, NB E1C 9B6 (506)857-6264 SCOTIA-FUNDY: 1649 Hollis St., P.O. Box 550, Halifax, NS B3J 2S7 (902)426-6266 QUEBEC: Gare Maritime, C.P. 15, 500, Cap Diamant, PQ G1K 7Y7 (418)648-2519 CENTRAL AND ARCTIC: 501 University Cres., Winnipeg, MB R3T 2N6 (204)983-5000 PACIFIC: 555 W. Hastings St., Vancouver, BC V6E 5G3 (604)666-6097

FITNESS AND AMATEUR SPORT CANADA, 265 Laurier Ave. W., So. Twr., Journal Bldg., Ottawa, ON K1A 0X6 (613)994-2424 Includes Sport Canada and Fitness Canada programs.

INDIAN AND NORTHERN AFFAIRS CANADA, Les Terrasses de la Chaudiere (mailing: Ottawa, ON K1A 0H4) (819)997-1587 REGIONAL OFFICES, NORTHERN AFFAIRS: NORTHWEST TERRITORIES: P.O. Box 1500, Yellowknife, NT X1A 2R3 (403)920-8111 YUKON TERRITORY: 200 Range Rd., Whitehorse, YT Y1A 3V1 (403)667-3121

TOURISM CANADA, 235 Queen St., Ottawa, ON K1A 0H5 (613)954-3980 This agency is responsible for visitation promotion and support nationwide.

TRANSPORT CANADA, Public Affairs, Transport Canada Bldg., Place de Ville, Tower C, 21st Fl., Ottawa, ON K1A 0N5 (613)990-2309 Oversees marine and surface transportation, Arctic transportation, the Coast Guard, and various pilotage authorities.

TRANSPORT CANADA, MARINE GROUP, Canadian Coast Guard, Canada Bldg., 344 Slater St., Ottawa, ON K1A 0N7 (613)998-1571 COAST GUARD REGIONAL OFFICES: NEWFOUNDLAND: P.O. Box 1300, St. John's, NF A1C 6H8 (709)772-5150 MARITIMES: P.O. Box 1013, Dartmouth, NS B2Y 4K2 (902)426-5182 LAURENTIAN: 104 rue Dalhousie, Quebec, PQ G1K 4B8 (418)648-4158 CENTRAL: One Yonge St., 20th Fl., Toronto, ON M5E 1E5 (416)973-3635 WESTERN: 224 W. Esplande, North Vancouver, BC V7M 3J7 (604)984-3700

UNITED STATES

TENNESSEE VALLEY AUTHORITY, Public Affairs Office, 400 W. Summit Hill Dr., Knoxville, TN 37902-1499 (615)632-8000; Capitol Hill Office Bldg., 412 First St. S.E., Washington, DC 20444-2003 (202)479-4412

U.S. CONGRESS, GOVERNMENT PRINTING OFFICE, SUPERINTENDENT OFDOCUMENTS, Publications Office, Washington, DC 20402 (202)783-3238 GPO bibliographies of government publications: THE GPO SALES PUBLICATIONS REFERENCE FILE (PRF) (bi-monthly); MONTHLY CATALOG OF U.S. GOVERNMENT PUBLICATIONS; U.S. GOVERNMENT BOOKS; and NEW BOOKS (bi-monthly). GPO operates 24 bookstores throughout the United States; a list of these outlets and of depository libraries is available from the superintendent of documents.

U.S. CONGRESS, LIBRARY OF CONGRESS, 101 Independence Ave. S.E., Washington, DC 20540 (202)707-5000 The national library of the United States contains a massive collection with diverse materials of every type, including books (loan division), audio visual materials, prints, manuscripts, and maps (geography and map division).

U.S. DEPT. OF AGRICULTURE, FOREST SERVICE, Information Office, P.O. Box 2417, Washington, DC 20013 (202)447-3760 REGIONAL OFFICES: REGION 1 (northern ID, MT): Northern Regional Forester, Federal Bldg., P.O. Box 7669, Missoula, MT 59807 (406)329-3011 REGION 2 (CO, NE, SD, WY): Rocky Mountain Regional Forester, 11177 W. 8th Ave., Lakewood, CO 80225 (303)234-4185 REGION 3 (AZ, NM) Southwestern Regional Forester, 517 Gold Ave. S.W., Albuquerque, NM 87102 (505)766-2444 REGION 4 (southern ID, NV, UT, WY): Intermountain Regional Forester, Federal Bldg., 324 25th St., Ogden, UT 84401 (801)625-5182 REGION 5 (CA): Pacific Southwest Regional Forester, 630 Sansome St., San Francisco, CA 94111 (415)556-0122 REGION 6 (OR, WA): Pacific Northwest Regional Forester, 319 S.W. Pine St., Portland, OR 97208 (503)221-2877 REGION 8 (AL, AR, FL, GA, KY, LA, MS, NC, TN, TX, VA): Southern Regional Forester, 1720 Peachtree Rd. N.W., Atlanta, GA 30367 (404)347-2384 REGION 9 (MO, PA, WV, WI): Eastern Regional Forester, 310 W. Wisconsin Ave., Milwaukee, WI 53203 (414)291-3693 REGION 10 (AK): Alaska Forester, Federal Office Bldg., P.O. Box 21628, Juneau, AK 99801 (907)586-7263

U.S. DEPT. OF AGRICULTURE, SOIL CONSERVATION SERVICE, Public Information Staff, P.O. Box 2890, Washington, DC 20013 (202)447-4543

U.S. DEPT. OF COMMERCE, NATIONAL OCEANIC AND ATMOSPHERIC ADMINISTRATION, Office of Public Affairs, Washington, DC 20230 (202)377-4190

U.S. DEPT. OF COMMERCE, NATIONAL OCEANIC AND ATMOSPHERIC ADMINISTRATION, NATIONAL OCEAN SERVICE, Atlantic Marine Center, 439 W. York St., Norfolk, VA 23510; Pacific Marine Center, 1801 Fairview Ave. E., Seattle, WA 98102

U.S. DEPT. OF COMMERCE, NATIONAL OCEANIC AND ATMOSPHERICADMINISTRATION, NATIONAL WEATHER SERVICE, National Meteorological Center, 5200 Auth Rd., Camp Springs, MD 20233

ALASKA REGION: Box 21668, 701 C St., Anchorage, AK 99513 (907)271-5136 CENTRAL REGION: 601 E. 12th St., Kansas City, MO 64106 (816)374-5464 EASTERN REGION: 585 Stewart Ave., Garden City, Long Island, NY 11530 (516)222-1616 PACIFIC REGION: 300 Ala Moana Blvd., Rm. 4110, Honolulu, HI 96850 (808)546-5680 SOUTHERN REGION: 819 Taylor St., Ft. Worth, TX 76102 (817)334-2668 WESTERN REGION: 125 S. State St., Salt Lake City, UT 84147 (801)524-5122

U.S. DEPT. OF THE ARMY, UNITED STATES ARMY CORPS OF ENGINEERS, 1000 Independence Ave. S.W., Washington, DC 20314 (202)272-0001 DIVISIONS: LOWER MISSISSIPPI VALLEY: P.O. Box 80, Vicksburg, MS 39180 (601)634-5750 MISSOURI RIVER: P.O. Box 103, Downtown Sta., Omaha, NE 68101 (402)221-3207 NEW ENGLAND: 424 Trapelo Rd., Waltham, MA 02154 (617)894-2400, Ext. 200 NORTH ATLANTIC: 90 Church St., New York, NY 10007 (212)264-7101 NORTH CENTRAL: 536 S. Clark St., Chicago, IL 60605 (312)353-6310 NORTH PACIFIC: P.O. Box 2870, Portland, OR 97208 (503)221-3700 OHIO RIVER: P.O. Box 1159, Cincinnati, OH 45201 (513)684-3002 PACIFIC OCEAN: Bldg. 230, Ft. Schafter, HI 96858 (808)438-1500 SOUTH ATLANTIC: 30 Pryor St. S.W., Atlanta, GA 30303 (404)221-6711 SOUTH PACIFIC: 630 Sansome St., Rm. 1216, San Francisco, CA 94111 (415)556-0914 SOUTHWESTERN: 1114 Commerce St., Dallas, TX 75242 (214)767-2500

U.S. DEPT. OF THE INTERIOR, BUREAU OF LAND MANAGEMENT, Office of Public Affairs, Interior Bldg., Washington, DC 20240 (202)343-9435 FIELD OFFICES, WESTERN STATES: ALASKA: 701 C St., Box 13, Anchorage, AK 99513 (907)271-5076 ARIZONA: 3707 N. 7th St., P.O. Box 16563, Phoenix, AZ 85011 (602)241-5501 CALIFORNIA: Federal Bldg., E-2841, 2800 Cottage Way, Sacramento, CA 95825 (916)978-4743 COLORADO: 2850 Youngfield St., Denver, CO 80215 (303)236-1721 IDAHO: Federal Bldg., Room 398, 3380 Americana Terrace, Boise, ID 83706 (208)334-1401 MONTANA: 222 N. 32nd St., P.O. Box 36800, Billings, MT 59107 (406)255-2904 NEVADA: 4765 Vegas Dr., P.O. Box 26569, Reno, NV 89520 (702)328-6390 NEW MEXICO: Federal Bldg., P.O. Box 1449, S. Federal Pl., Santa Fe, NM 87501-1449 (505)988-6030 NORTH DAKOTA: (contact Montana regional office) OKLAHOMA: (contact New Mexico regional office) OREGON: 825 N.E. Multnomah St., P.O. Box 2965, Portland, OR 97208 (503)231-6251 SOUTH DAKOTA: (contact Montana regional office) TEXAS: (contact New Mexico regional office) UTAH: 324 S. State St., Suite 301, Salt Lake City, UT 84111-2303 (801)539-4010 WASHINGTON: (contact Oregon regional office) WYOMING: 2515 Warren Ave., P.O. Box 1828, Cheyenne, WY 82003 (307)772-2326 EASTERN REGION FIELD OFFICE (for states bordering on or east of the Mississippi River): 350 South Pickett St., Alexandria, VA 22304 (703)461-1400

U.S. DEPT. OF THE INTERIOR, BUREAU OF RECLAMATION, Office of Public Affairs, Interior Bldg., Washington, DC 20240-0001 (202)343-4662 MAJOR REGIONAL OFFICES: GREAT PLAINS REGION: Box 36900, 316 N. 26th St., Billings, MT 59107 (406)657-6218 LOWER COLORADO REGION: Box 427, Nevada Hwy. and Park St., Boulder City, NV (702)293-8420 MID-PACIFIC REGION: 2800 Cottage Way, Sacramento, CA 95825 (916)978-4919 PACIFIC NORTHWEST REGION: Box 043, 550 W. Fort St., Boise, ID 83724 (208)334-1938 UPPER COLORADO REGION: Box 11568, 125 S. State, Salt Lake City, UT 84147 (801)524-5403

U.S. DEPT. OF THE INTERIOR, GEOLOGICAL SURVEY, National Center, 12201 Sunrise Valley Dr., Reston, VA 22092 (703)648-6131 EARTH SCIENCE INFORMATION CENTERS: ALASKA: 4230 University Dr., Rm. 101, Anchorage, AK 99508-4664 (907)561-5555 ALASKA: U.S. Courthouse, Rm. 113, 222 W. 7th Ave., Box 53, Anchorage, AK 99513-7546 (907)271-4307 CALIFORNIA: 7638 Federal Bldg., 300 N. Los Angeles St., Los Angeles, CA 90012 (213)894-2850 CALIFORNIA: Bldg. 3, Rm 3128 (MS 532), 345 Middlefield Rd., Menlo Park, CA 94025 (415)329-4390 CALIFORNIA: 504 Custom House, 555 Battery St., San Francisco, CA 94111 (415)556-5627 COLORADO: 169 Federal Bldg., 1961 Stout St., Denver, CO 80294 (303)844-4169 COLORADO: Box 25046, Federal Center, Denver, CO 80225 (303)236-5829 DISTRICT OF COLUMBIA: Interior Bldg., 18th and C Sts. N.W., Rm. 2650, Washington, DC 20240 (202)343-8073 MISSISSIPPI: Bldg. 3101, Stennis Space Center, MS 39529 (601)688-3544 MISSOURI: 1400 Independence Rd., Rolla, MO 65401 (314)341-0851 UTAH: 8105 Federal Bldg., 125 S. State St., Salt Lake City, UT 84138 (801)524-5652 VIRGINIA (NATIONAL CENTER): 507 National Center, Rm. 1C402, 12201 Sunrise Valley Dr., Reston, VA 22092 (703)860-6045 WASHINGTON: 678 U.S. Courthouse, W. 920 Riverside Ave., Spokane, WA 99201 (509)456-2524

U.S. DEPT. OF THE INTERIOR, NATIONAL PARK SERVICE, Office of Public Affairs, P.O. Box 37127, Washington, DC 20013-7127 (202)343-7394

REGIONAL OFFICES: ALASKA: 2525 Gambell St., Anchorage, AK 99503 (907)276-8166, Ext. 230 MID-ATLANTIC (DE, MD, PA, VA, WV): 143 S. 3rd St., Philadelphia, PA 19106 (215)597-7013 MIDWEST (IL, IN, IA, KS, MI, MN, MO, NE, OH, WI): 1709 Jackson St., Omaha, NE 68102 (402)864-3431 NATIONAL CAPITAL (DC and nearby MD and VA): 1100 Ohio Dr. S.W., Washington, DC 20242 (202)426-6612 NORTH ATLANTIC (CT, ME, NH, MA, NJ, NY, RI, VT): 15 State St., Boston, MA 02109 (617)223-3769 PACIFIC NORTHWEST (ID, OR, WA): 83 S. King St., Suite 212, Seattle, WA 98104 (206)399-5565 ROCKY MOUNTAIN (CO, MT, ND, SD, UT, WY): P.O. Box 25287, Denver, CO 80225 (303)234-2500 SOUTHEAST (AL, FL, GA, KY, MI, NC, PR, SC, TN, VI): 75 Spring St. S.W., Atlanta, GA 30303 (404)242-5185 SOUTHWEST (AR, LA, NM, OK, TX): Box 728 Santa Fe, NM 87504 (505)476-3388 WESTERN (AZ, CA, GU, HI, NV, Northern Mariana Islands): Box 36063, 450 Golden Gate Ave., San Francisco, CA 94102 (415)556-4196

U.S. DEPT. OF THE INTERIOR, UNITED STATES FISH AND WILDLIFE SERVICE, Office of Public Affairs, Interior Bldg., Washington, DC 20240 (202)343-5634; Publications Unit, Washington, DC 20240 (703)358-1711 REGIONAL OFFICES: NORTHWEST: 500 N.E. Multnomah St., Portland, OR 97232 (503)231-6118 SOUTHWEST: 500 Gold Ave. S.W., Albuquerque, NM 87103 (505)474-2321 MIDWEST: Federal Bldg., Twin Cities, MN 55111 (612)725-3500 SOUTHEAST: 17 Executive Park Dr. N.E., Atlanta, GA 30347 (404)881-4671 NORTHEAST: 1 Gateway Center, Suite 700, Newton Corner, MA 02158 (617)829-9200 MOUNTAIN: Denver Federal Center, P.O. Box 25486, Denver, CO 80225 (303)234-2209 ALASKA: 1011 E. Tudor Rd., Anchorage, AK 99507 (907)276-3800

U.S. DEPT. OF TRANSPORTATION, UNITED STATES COAST GUARD, Information Office, 2100 2nd St. S.W., Washington, DC 20593 (202)267-1587 DISTRICT AND FIELD ORGANIZATIONS: ATLANTIC AREA: Governors Island, New York, NY 10004-5098 (212)668-7196 1st DISTRICT (CT, ME, MA, NH, norhtern NJ, eastern NY, RI, VT): 408 Atlantic Ave., Boston, MA 02210-2209 (617)223-8480 2nd DISTRICT (AR, CO, IL, IN, IA, KS, KY, MN, MO, NE, ND, OH, OK, western PA, SD, TN, WV, WI, WY): 1430 Olive St., St. Louis, MO 63101-2378 (314)425-460 15th DISTRICT (DC, DE, MD, southern NJ, NC, eastern PA, VA): 431 Crawford St., Portsmouth, VA 23704-5004 (804)398-6000 7th DISTRICT (FL, GA, PR, SC, VI): 909 S.E. 1st Ave., Miami, FL 33131-3050 (305)350-565 48th DISTRICT (AL, LA, MS, NM, TX): 500 Camp St., New Orleans, LA 70130-3396 (504)589-6298 9th DISTRICT (Great Lakes area): 1240 E. 9th St., Cleveland, OH 44199-2060 (216)522-3910 PACIFIC AREA: Coast Guard Island, Alameda, CA 94501-5100 (415)437-3196 11th DISTRICT (AZ, CA, NV, UT): 400 Oceangate Blvd., Long Beach, CA 90882-5399 (213)499-5201 13th DISTRICT (ID, MT, OR, WA): 915 2nd Ave., Seattle, WA 98174-1067 (206)442-5078 14th DISTRICT (American Samoa, GU, HI, Pacific Islands): 300 Ala Moana Blvd., 9th Fl., Honolulu, HI 96850-4982 (808)541-2051 17th DISTRICT (AK): P.O. Box 3-5000, Juneau, AK 99802-1217 (907)586-2680

Chapter 11, Section 2

Government Agencies and Private Organizations

Provincial and State Agencies

Canada and the United States

ALABAMA: Environmental Management Dept., 1751 W.L. Dickinson Dr., Montgomery, AL 36130 (205)271-7700 Conservation and Natural Resources Dept., Game and Fish Div., 64 N. Union St., Rm. 702, Montgomery, AL 36130-1901 (205)242-3465 Conservation and Natural Resources Dept., 64 N. Union St., Rm. 702, Montgomery, AL 36130-1901 (205)242-3151 Conservation and Natural Resources Dept., Parks Div., 64 N. Union St., Rm. 702, Montgomery, AL 36130-1901 (205)242-3334 Tourism and Travel Dept., 532 S. Perry St. Montgomery, AL 36193 (205)242-4169

ALASKA: Environmental Conservation Dept., P.O. Box O, Juneau, AK 99811-1800 (907)465-2606 Fish and Game Dept., P.O. Box 3-2000, Juneau, AK 99802-2000 (907)465-4113 Natural Resources Dept., 400 Willoughby Ave., Juneau, AK 99801 (907)465-2400 Parks and Outdoor Recreation Div., 225-A Cordova St., Anchorage, AK 99501 (907)762-4505 Commerce and Economic Development Dept., Tourism Div., P.O. Box E, Juneau, AK 99811 (907)465-2010

ALBERTA: Alberta Environment, Oxbridge Pl., 9820 106th St., Edmonton, AB T5K 2J6 (403)427-6267 Alberta Forestry, Lands and Wildlife, Fish and Wildlife Div., Petroleum Plaza, No. Tower, 9945 108th St., Edmonton, AB T5K 2G6 (403)427-8580 Alberta Forestry, Lands and Wildlife, Petroleum Plaza, So. Tower, 9915 108th St., Edmonton, AB T5K 2C9 (403)427-3590 Alberta Research Council, Natural Resources Div., P.O. Box 8330, Station F, Edmonton, AB T6H 5X2 (403)450-5111 Alberta Recreation and Parks, Standard Life Centre, 10405 Jasper Ave., Edmonton, AB T5J 3N4 (403)427-2008 Alberta Tourism, 10025 Jasper Ave., 18th Fl., Edmonton, AB T5J3Z3 (403)427-2280

ARIZONA: Game and Fish Dept., P.O. Box 9099, Phoenix, AZ 85068-9099 (602)942-3000 Outdoor Recreation Coordinator, 800 W. Washington, Suite 415, Phoenix, AZ 85007 (602)542-1996

ARKANSAS: Pollution Control and Ecology Dept., P.O. Box 9583, Little Rock, AR 72219 (501)562-7444 Game and Fish Commission, 2 Natural Resources Dr., Little Rock, AR 72205 (501)223-6305 Parks and Tourism Dept., State Parks Div., 1 Capitol Mall, Little Rock, AR 72201 (501)682-7743 Parks and Tourism Dept., Tourism Div., 1 Capitol Mall, Little Rock, AR 72201 (501)682-1765

BRITISH COLUMBIA: Ministry of Environment, 810 Blanshard St., Victoria, BC V8V 1X5 (604)387-9419 Ministry of Forests, 595 Pandora Ave., 1st Fl., Victoria, BC V8V1X4 (604)387-5255 Ministry of Environment, Wildlife Br., Parliament Bldgs., Victoria, BC V8V 1X5 (604)387-9731 Ministry of Parks, Parliament Bldgs., Victoria, BC V8V 1X5 (604)387-5002 Ministry of Municipal Affairs, Recreation and Culture, 747 Fort St., Victoria, BC V8V 1X4 (604)387-7973 Ministry of Tourism and Provincial Secretary, Parliament Bldgs., Victoria, BC V8V 1X4 (604)387-1311

CALIFORNIA: Environmental Affairs Agency, P.O. Box 2815, Sacramento, CA 95812 (916)322-5840 Resources Agency, Conservation Dept., 1416 9th St., Rm. 1320, Sacramento, CA 95814 (916)322-1080 Resources Agency, Fish and Game Dept., 1416 9th St., 12th Fl., Sacramento, CA 95814 (916)445-7613 Parks and Recreation Dept., P.O. Box 942896, Sacramento, CA 94296-0001 (916)445-2358 Resources Agency, Boating and Waterways Dept., 1629 S St., Sacramento, CA 95814 (916)445-6281

COLORADO: Natural Resources Dept., 1313 Sherman St., Rm. 718, Denver, CO 80203 (303)866-3311 Natural Resources Dept., Wildlife Div., 6060 Broadway, Denver, CO 80216 (303)291-7208 Natural Resources Div., Parks and Outdoor Recreation Div., 1313 Sherman St., Denver, CO 80203 (303)866-3437

CONNECTICUT: Environmental Protection Dept., 165 Capitol Ave., Hartford, CT 06106 (203)566-2110 Environmental Protection Dept., Wildlife Bureau, 165 Capitol Ave., Hartford, CT 06106 (203)566-4683 Environmental Protection Dept., Natural Resources Bureau, 165 Capitol Ave., Hartford, CT 06106 (203)566-2287 Environmental Protection Dept., Parks and Forestry Bureau, 165 Capitol Ave., Hartford, CT 06106 (203)566-2304 Economic Development Dept., Tourism and Travel Promotion Services Div., 865 Brook St., Rocky Hill, CT 06067-3405 (203)258-4286

DELAWARE: Natural Resources and Environmental Control Dept., 89 Kings Hwy., P.O. Box 1401, Dover, DE 19903 (302)736-4403 Natural Resources and Environmental Control Dept., Fish and Wildlife Div., 89 Kings Hwy., P.O. Box 1401, Dover, DE 19903 (302)736-5295 Natural Resources and Environmental Control Dept., Parks and Recreation Div., 89 Kings Hwy., P.O. Box 1401, Dover, DE 19903 (302)736-4401

FLORIDA: Environmental Regulation Dept., 2600 Blairstone Rd., Tallahassee, FL 32399-2400 (904)488-4805 Game and Fresh Water Fish Commission, 620 S. Meridian St., Tallahassee, FL 32399-1600 (904)488-4676 Natural Resources Dept., 3900 Commonwealth Blvd., Tallahassee, FL 32399 (904)487-1841 Natural Resources Dept., Recreation and Parks Div., 3900 Commonwealth Blvd., Tallahassee, FL 32399 (904)488-6131 Commerce Dept., Tourism Div., Collins Bldg. Suite 510C, Tallahassee, FL 32399-2000 (904)488-9447

GEORGIA: Natural Resources Dept., Environmental Protection Div., 205 Butler St. S.E., Suite 1252, Atlanta, GA 30334 (404)656-4713 Natural Resources Dept., Game and Fish Div., 205 Butler St. S.E., Suite 1252, Atlanta, GA 30334 (404)656-3523 Natural Resources Dept., 205 Butler St. S.E., Suite 1252, Atlanta, GA 30334 (404)656-3500 Natural Resources Dept., Parks and Distoric Sites Div., 205 Butler St. S.E., Suite 1252, Atlanta, GA 30334 (404)656-2753 Industry, Trade and Tourism Dept., P.O. Box 1776, Atlanta, GA 30301 (404)656-3056

HAWAII: Land and Natural Resources Dept., Conservation and Resources Enforcement Div., P.O. Box 621, Honolulu, HI 96809 (808)548-5919 Land and Natural Resources Dept., Aquatic Resources Div., P.O. Box 621, Honolulu, HI 96809 (808)548-4000 Land and Natural Resources Dept., P.O. Box 621, Honolulu, HI 96809 (808)548-6550 Land and Natural Resources Dept., State Parks, Outdoor Recreation and Historic Sites Div., P.O. Box 621, Honolulu, HI 96809 (808)548-6550 Business and Economic Development Dept., Tourism Bur., P.O. Box 2359, Honolulu, HI 96804 (808)548-4618

IDAHO: Lands Dept., State House, Rm. 121, Boise, ID 83720 (208)334-2080 Fish and Game Dept., P.O. Box 25, 600 S. Walnut, Boise, ID 83707 (208)334-3746 Water Resources Dept., Water Management Div., State House, Boise, ID 83720 (208)327-7900 Commerce Dept., Travel Promotion Div., 700 W. State St., Boise, ID 83720 (208)334-2470 Parks and Recreation Dept., State House Mall, Boise, ID 83720 (208)334-2154

ILLINOIS: Environmental Protection Agency, P.O. Box 19276, Springfield, IL 62794 (217)782-3397 Conservation Dept., Resource Management Office, Fish Div. 524 S. 2nd St., Springfield, IL 62706 (217)782-6424 Conservation Dept., Resource Management Office, Wildlife Div., 524 S. 2nd St., Springfield, IL 62706 (217)785-2511 Energy and Natural Resources Dept., 325 W. Adams St., Rm. 300, Springfield, IL 62704 (217)785-2500 Conservation Dept., Public Information Office (Parks), 524 S. 2nd St., Springfield, IL 62706 (217)782-7454 Commerce and Community Affairs Dept., Marketing Bureau, Tourism Div., 100 W. Randolph St., Suite 3-400, Chicago, IL 60601 (312)814-4732

INDIANA: Environmental Management Dept., P.O. Box 6015, 105 S. Meridian St., Indianapolis, IN 46206-6015 (317)232-8162 Natural Resources Dept., Fish and Wildlife Div., State Office Bldg., Indianapolis, IN 46204 (317)232-4080 Natural Resources Dept., State Office Bldg., Indianapolis, IN 46204 (317)232-4020 Natural Resources Dept., Outdoor Recreation Div., State Office Bldg., Indianapolis, IN 46204 (317)232-4070 Natural Resources Dept., State Parks Div., State Office Bldg., Indianapolis, IN 46204 (317)232-4124 Commerce Dept., Tourism and Film Development Div., 1 N. Capitol, Suite 700, Indianapolis, IN 46204-2248 (317)232-8864

IOWA: Natural Resources Dept., Environmental Protection Div., Wallace State Office Bldg., Des Moines, IA 50319 (515)281-6284 Natural Resources Dept., Fish and Wildlife Div., Wallace State Office Bldg., Des Moines, IA 50319 (515)281-5154 Natural Resources Dept., Wallace State Office Bldg., Des Moines, IA 50319 (515)281-5385 Natural Resources Dept., Parks, Recreation and Preservation Div., Park and Recreation Bureau, Wallace State Office Bldg., Des Moines, IA 50319 (515)281-5886 Economic Development Dept., Tourism and Visitors Div., 200 E. Grand Ave., Des Moines, IA 50309 (515)281-3100

KANSAS: Health and Environment Dept., Environment Div., Landon State Office Bldg., 901 S.W. Jackson St., Topeka, KS 66612 (913)296-1535 Wildlife and Parks Dept., Landon State Office Bldg., 901 S.W. Jackson St., Topeka, KS 66612 (913)296-2281 Commerce Dept., Tourism Div., 400 S.W. 8th St. 5th Fl., Topeka, KS 66603 (913)296-7091

KENTUCKY: Natural Resources and Environmental Protection Cabinet, Capitol Plaza Tower, 5th Fl., Frankfort, KY 40601 (502)564-3350 Tourism Cabinet, Fish and Wildlife Resources Dept., 1 Game Farm Rd., Frankfort, KY 40601 (502)564-4336 Natural Resources and Environmental Protection Cabinet, Natural Resources Dept., 691 Teton Terrace, Frankfort, KY 40601 (502)564-2184 Tourism Cabinet, Parks Dept., Recreation Div., Capitol Plaza Tower, 10th Fl., Frankfort, KY 40601 (502)564-2172 Tourism Cabinet, Travel Development Dept., Tourism Services Div., Capitol Plaza Tower, 22nd Fl., Frankfort, KY 40601 (502)564-4930

LABRADOR: Atlantic Provinces Transportation Commission, 236 St. George St., #210, P.O. Box 577, Moncton, NB E1C 8L9 (506)857-2820 Atlantic Provinces Economic Council, 5121 Sackville St., #500, Halifax, NS B3J 1K1 (902)422-6516

LOUISIANA: Environmental Quality Dept., Water Resources Div., P.O. Box 44066, Baton Rouge, LA 70804 (504)342-6363 Wildlife and Fisheries Dept., P.O. Box 98000, Baton Rouge, LA 70898 (504)765-2803 Natural Resources Dept., P.O. Box 94396, Baton Rouge, LA 70804-9396 (504)342-4500 Culture, Recreation and Tourism Dept., State Parks Office, P.O. Box 44426, Baton Rouge, LA 70804-4426 (504)342-8111 Culture, Recreation and Tourism Dept., Tourism Office, P.O. Box 94291, Baton Rouge, LA 70804-9291 (504)342-8100

MAINE: Environmental Protection Dept., State House Station 17, Augusta, ME 04333 (207)289-2811 Inland Fisheries and Wildlife Dept., State House Station 41, Augusta, ME 04333 (207)289-2871 Conservation Dept., Parks and Recreation Bureau, State House Station 22, Augusta, ME 04333 (207)289-3821 Conservation Dept., Public Lands Bureau, Recreation Div., State House Station 22, Augusta, ME 04333 (207)289-3061 Economic and Community Development Office, Tourism Office, State House Station 130, Augusta, ME 04333 (207)289-5710

MANITOBA: Manitoba Environment, Community Relations, 330 St. Mary Ave., #960, Winnipeg, MB R3C 3Z5 (204)945-5763 Manitoba Natural Resources, Fisheries Br., 1495 St. James St. Winnipeg, MB R3H 0W9 (204)945-7814 Manitoba Natural Resources, Wildlife Br., 1495 St. James St. Winnipeg, MB R3H 0W9 (204)945-7761 Manitoba Natural Resources, 1495 St. James St., P.O. Box 22, Winnipeg, MB R3H 0W9 (204)945-6784 Manitoba Culture, Heritage and Recreation, 177 Lombard Ave., Winnipeg, MB R3B 0W5 (204)945-2782 Manitoba Natural Resources, Parks Br., 258 Portage Ave. Winnipeg, MB R3C 0B6 (204)945-4362 Manitoba Industry, Trade and Tourism, 155 Carlton St., Winnipeg, MB R3C 3H8 (204)945-2423

MARYLAND: Environment Dept., 2500 Broening Hwy., Baltimore, MD 21224 (301)631-3084 Natural Resources Dept., Public Affairs Office, Tawes State Office Bldg., Annapolis, MD 21401 (301)974-3987 Natural Resources Dept., Forest, Park and Wildlife, Tawes State Office Bldg., Annapolis, MD 21401 (301)974-2240 Economic and Employment Development Dept., Tourism and Promotion Div., 217 E. Redwood St., Baltimore, MD 21202 (301)333-6604

MASSACHUSETTS: Environmental Affairs Executive Office, Environmental Management Dept., Waterways Div., 100 Cambridge St., 19th Fl., Boston, MA 02202 (617)740-1600 Fisheries, Wildlife and Environmental Law Enforcement Dept., Fisheries and Wildlife Div., 100 Cambridge St., Rm. 1901, Boston, MA 02202 (617)727-3151 Environmental Affairs Executive Office, Environmental Management Dept., Forests and Parks Div., 100 Cambridge St., 19th Fl., Boston, MA 02202 (617)727-3180 Economic Affairs Executive Office, Travel and Tourism Office, 100 Cambridge St., 13th Fl., Boston, MA 02114 (617)727-3205

MICHIGAN: Natural Resources Dept., Environmental Protection Div., Box 30028, Lansing, MI 48909 (517)373-7917 Natural Resources Dept., Fisheries Div., Box 30028, Lansing, MI 48909 (517)373-1280 Natural Resources Dept., Wildlife Div., Box 30028, Lansing, MI 48909 (517)373-1263 Natural Resources Dept., Box 30028, Lansing, MI 48909 (517)373-2329 Natural Resources Dept., Recreation Div., Box 30028, Lansing, MI 48909 (517)373-9900 Commerce Dept., Travel Bureau, 333 S. Capitol, Box 30226, Lansing, MI 48909 (517)335-1870

MINNESOTA: Pollution Control Agency, 520 Lafayette Rd. N., St. Paul, MN 55155 (612)296-7283 Natural Resources Dept., Fish and Wildlife Div., 500 Lafayette Rd., St. Paul, MN 55155-4001 (612)297-1308 Natural Resources Dept., 500 Lafayette Rd. St. Paul, MN 55155-4001 (612)296-

3336 Natural Resources Dept., Parks and Recreation Div., 500 Lafayette Rd., St. Paul, MN 55155-4001 (612)296-2270 Natural Resources Dept., Trails and Waterways Div., 500 Lafayette Rd., St. Paul, MN 55155-4001 (612)296-4822 Trade and Economic Development Dept., Tourism Div., 150 E. Kellog Blvd., Rm. 900, St. Paul, MN 55101 (612)296-2755

MISSISSIPPI: Pollution Control Bureau, P.O. Box 10385, Jackson, MS 39289-0385 (601)961-5100 Wildlife, Fisheries and Parks Dept., Fisheries and Wildlife Bureau, P.O. Box 451, Jackson, MS 39205 (601)987-4899 Natural Resources Dept., P.O. Box 20305, Jackson, MS 39209 (601)961-5015 Wildlife, Fisheries and Parks Dept., Recreation and Parks Bureau, P.O. Box 451, Jackson, MS 39205 (601)987-4899 Economic and Community Development Dept., Tourism Div., P.O. Box 849, Jackson, MS 39205 (601)359-3297

MISSOURI: Natural Resources Dept., Environmental Quality Div., P.O. Box176, Jefferson City, MO 65102 (601)751-4810 Conservation Dept., Fisheries Div., 2901 W. Truman Blvd., P.O. Box 180, Jefferson City, MO 65102 (601)751-4115 Conservation Dept., Wildlife Div., 2901 W. Truman Blvd., P.O. Box 180, Jefferson City, MO 65102 (601)751-4115 Natural Resources Dept. P.O. Box 176, Jefferson City, MO 65102 (601)751-3443 Natural Resources Dept. Parks, Recreation and Historical Preservation Div., P.O. Box 176, Jefferson City, MO 65102 (601)751-3443 Economic Development Dept., Tourism Div., P.O. Box 1055, 301 W. High St., Jefferson City, MO 65102 (601)751-3051

MONTANA: Agriculture Dept., Environmental Management Div., Agricultural and Livestock Bldg., Capitol Sta., Helena, MT 59620-0201 (406)444-2944 Fish, Wildlife and Parks Dept., Fisheries Div., 1420 E. 6th Ave., Helena, MT 59620 (406)444-2449 Fish, Wildlife and Parks Dept., Wildlife Div., 1420 E. 6th Ave., Helena, MT 59620 (406)444-2612 Natural Resources and Conservation Dept., 1520 E. 6th Ave., Helena, MT 59620 (406)444-6743 Fish, Wildlife and Parks Dept., Parks Div., 1420 E. 6th Ave., Helena, MT 59620 (406)444-3750 Commerce Dept., Montana Promotion Div., 1424 9th Ave., Helena, MT 59620 (406)444-2654

NEBRASKA: Environmental Control Dept., P.O. Box 98922, Lincoln, NE 68509-8922 (402)471-2186 Game and Parks Comm., Fisheries Div., P.O. Box 30370, 2200 N. 33rd, Lincoln, NE 68503 (402)464-0641 Game and Parks Comm., Wildlife Div., P.O. Box 30370, 2200 N. 33rd, Lincoln, NE 68503 (402)464-0641 Natural Resources Commission, P.O. Box 94876, 301 Centennial Mall S., Lincoln, NE 68509 (402)471-2081 Game and Parks Comm., Parks Div., P.O. Box 30370, 2200 N. 33rd, Lincoln, NE 68503 (402)464-0641 Game and Parks Comm., Recreation Div., P.O. Box 30370, 2200 N. 33rd, Lincoln, NE 68503 (402)464-0641 Economic Development Dept., Travel and Tourism Div., P.O. Box 94666, Lincoln, NE 68509 (402)471-3794

NEVADA: Conservation and Natural Resources Dept., Environmental Protection Div., 123 W. Nye Lane, Carson City, NV 89710 (702)687-4670 Wildlife Dept., Fisheries Div., P.O. Box 10678, Reno, NV 89520 (702)687-0500 Wildlife Dept., Game Div., P.O. Box 10678, Reno, NV 89520 (702)687-0500 Conservation and Natural Resources Dept., State Parks Div., 123 W. Nye Ln., Carson City, NV 89710 (702)687-4370 Tourism Commission, 5151 S. Carson St., Carson City, NV 89710 (702)687-4322

NEW BRUNSWICK: Dept. of the Environment, P.O. Box 6000, Fredericton, NB E3B 5H1 (506)453-3700 Dept. of Natural Resources and Energy, Fish and Wildlife Div., P.O. Box 6000, Fredericton, NB E3B 5H1 (506)453-2433 Dept. of Natural Resources and Energy, P.O. Box 6000, Fredericton, NB E3B 5H1 (506)453-2614 Dept. of Tourism, Recreation and Heritage, Sport and Recreation, Div., P.O. Box 12345, Fredericton, NB E3B 5C3 (506)453-2550 Dept. of Tourism, Recreation and Heritage, Tourism Div., P.O. Box 12345, Fredericton, NB E3B 5C3 (506)453-2377; (800)561-0123

NEWFOUNDLAND: Dept. of Environment and Lands, Environment Div., P.O. Box 8700, St. John's, NF A1B 4J6 (709)576-3394 Dept. of Environment and Lands, Wildlife Div., P.O. Box 8700, St. John's, NF A1B 4J6 (709)576-2817 Dept. of Environment and Lands, Parks Div., P.O. Box 8700, St. John's, NF A1B 4J6 (709)576-2424 Dept. of Culture, Recreation and Youth, Community Recreation, Sport and Fitness, P.O. Box 4750, St. John's, NF A1C 5T7 (709)576-5250 Dept. of Development, Tourism and Rural Development Div., Confederation Annex, 4th Fl., P.O. Box 8700, St. John's, NF A1B 4J6 (709)576-2821

NEW HAMPSHIRE: Fish and Game Dept., 2 Hazen Dr., Concord, NH 03301 (603)271-3512 Resources and Economic Development Dept., Parks and Recreation Div., 105 Loudon Rd., Box 856, Concord, NH 03301 (603)271-3254 Resources and Economic Development Dept., Vacation Travel Promotion Office, 105 Loudon Rd., Box 856, Concord, NH 03301 (603)271-2666

NEW JERSEY: Environmental Protection Dept., Environmental Quality Div., 401 E. State St., Trenton, NJ 08625 (609)292-5383 Environmental Protection Dept., Fish, Game and Wildlife Div., 401 E. State St., Trenton, NJ 08625 (609)292-9410 Environmental Protection Dept., Natural Resources, 401 E. State St., Trenton, NJ 08625 (609)292-3541 Environmental Protection Dept., Parks and Forestry Div., 401 E. State St., Trenton, NJ 08625 (609)292-2733 Environmental Protection Dept., Green Acres and Recreation Div., 401 E. State St., Trenton, NJ 08625 (609)588-3457 Commerce and Economic Development Dept., Travel and Tourism Div., CN 384, 20 W. State St., Trenton, NJ 08625 (609)292-2496

NEW MEXICO: Agriculture Dept., Agricultural and Environmental Services Div., Dept. 3150, Box 30005, Las Cruces, NM 88003 (505)646-3208 Game and Fish Dept., Villagra Bldg., Santa Fe, NM 87503 (505)827-7911 Energy, Minerals and Natural Resources Dept., 2040 S. Pacheo St., Santa Fe, NM 87505 (505)827-5950 Energy, Minerals and Natural Resources Dept., Park and Recreation Div., 2040 S. Pacheo St., Santa Fe, NM 87505 (505)827-7465 Economic Development and Tourism Dept., Tourism and Travel Div., 1100 St. Francis Dr., Santa Fe, NM 87503 (505)827-0295

NEW YORK: Environmental Conservation Dept., Public Affairs Div., 50 Wolf Rd., Albany, NY 12233 (518)457-2390 Environmental Conservation Dept., Fish and Wildlife Div., 50 Wolf Rd., Albany, NY 12233 (518)457-5690 Environmental Conservation Dept., Natural Resources Div., 50 Wolf Rd., Albany, NY 12233 (518)457-0975 Parks, Recreation, and Historic Preservation Office, Bldg. 1, Empire State Plaza, Albany, NY 12238 (518)474-0456 Economic Development Dept., Tourism Div., Twin Towers, 1 Commerce Plaza, Albany, NY 12245 (518)473-0715

NORTH CAROLINA: Environment, Health and Natural Resources Dept., Public Affairs Div., P.O. Box 27687. Raleigh, NC 27611 (919)733-4984 Environment, Health and Natural Resources Dept., Marine Fisheries Div., P.O. Box 27687. Raleigh, NC 27611 (919)726-7021 Environment, Health and Natural Resources Dept., Wildlife Resources Commission, P.O. Box 27687, Raleigh, NC 27611, (919)733-3391 Environment, Health, and Natural Resources Dept., Parks and Recreation Div., P.O. Box 27687, Raleigh, NC 27611, (919)733-4181 Economic and Community Development Dept., Travel and Tourism Development Div., 430 N. Salisbury St., Raleigh, NC 27611 (919)733-4171

NORTH DAKOTA: Environmental Health Section, 1200 Missouri Ave., Bismark, ND 58505 (701)224-2374 Game and Fish Dept., 100 N. Bismark Expressway, Bismark, ND 58501 (701)221-6300 Parks and Recreation Dept., Natural and Recreational Resources Div., 1424 W. Century Ave., Suite 202, Bismark, ND 58501 (701)224-4887 Economic Development Commission, Travel and Tourism Div., 604 E. Boulevard, Bismark, ND 58505 (701)224-2527

NORTHWEST TERRITORIES: Dept. of Renewable Resources, Environment Planning and Assessment Div., Yellowknife, NT X1A 2L9 (403)920-8046 Fisheries and Oceans, Western Arctic Office, P.O Box 1871, Inuvik, NT X0E 0T0 (403)979-3314 South/Central Arctic Office, P.O. Box 2310, Yellowknife, NT X1A 2P7 (403)920-6640 Eastern Arctic Office, P.O. Box 358, Iqaluit, NT X0A 0H0 (819)979-6274 Dept. of Renewable Resources, Wildlife Management Div., Yellowknife, NT X1A 2L9 (403)873-7411 Dept. of Municipal and Community Affairs, Sport and Recreation Div., Yellowknife, NT X1A 2L9 (403)873-7245 TravelArctic, Yellowknife, NT X1A 2L9 (403)873-7200 or (800)661-0788

NOVA SCOTIA: Dept. of the Environment, P.O. Box 2107, Halifax, NS B3J 3B7 (902)424-5300 Dept. of Fisheries, P.O. Box 2223, 1959 Upper Water St., Purdy's Wharf, 3rd Fl., Halifax, NS B3J 3C4 (902)424-5300 Dept. of Lands and Forests, Wildlife, P.O. Box 698, Founder's Sq., Hollis St., Halifax, NS B3J 2T9 (902)678-8921 Dept. of Lands and Forests, Land Resources, P.O. Box 698, Founder's Sq., Hollis St., Halifax, NS B3J 2T9 (902)424-6694 Dept. of Lands and Forests, Parks and Recreation, P.O. Box 698, Founder's Sq., Hollis St., Halifax, NS B3J 2T9 (902)662-3030 Sport and Recreation Commission, 5151 Terminal Rd., 8th Fl., P.O. Box 864, Halifax, NS B3J 2V2 (902)424-7512 Dept. of Tourism and Culture, P.O. Box 456, Halifax, NS B3J 2R5 (902)424-5000

OHIO: Environmental Protection Agency, 1800 Watermark, Box 1049, Columbus, OH 43266-0149 (614)644-2160 Natural Resources Dept., Wildlife Div., Fountain Sq., Columbus, OH 43224 (614)265-6305 Natural Resources Dept., Natural Areas and Preserves Div., Fountain Sq., Columbus, OH 43224 (614)265-6453 Natural Resources Dept., Watercraft Div., Fountain Sq., Columbus, OH 43224 (614)265-6476 Natural Resources Dept., Parks and Recreation Div., Fountain Sq., Columbus, OH 43224 (614)265-6561 Development Dept., Travel and Tourism Div., 77 S. High St., Box 1001, Columbus, OH 43266-0101 (614)466-8844

OKLAHOMA: Health Dept., Environmental Health Services Dept., 1000 NE 10th St., P.O. Box 53551, Oklahoma City, OK 73152 (405)271-8056 Wildlife Conservation Dept., Fisheries Div., P.O. Box 53465 Oklahoma City, OK 73152 (405)521-3721 Wildlife Conservation Dept., Game Div., P.O. Box 53465 Oklahoma City, OK 73152 (405)521-2739 Water Resources Board, P.O. Box 53585, Oklahoma City, OK 73152 (405)271-2523 Tourism and Recreation Dept., Park Div., 500 Will Rogers Bldg., Oklahoma City, OK 73105 (405)521-3411 Tourism and Recreation Dept., Marketing Services Div., 500 Will Rogers Bldg., Oklahoma City, OK 73105 (405)521-3981

ONTARIO: Ministry of the Environment, 135 St. Clair Ave. W., Toronto, ON M4V 1P5 (416)323-4324 Ministry of Natural Resources, Outdoor Recreation, Fisheries Br., Whitney Block, 99 Wellesley St. W., Toronto, ON M7A 1W3 (416)965-5947 Ministry of Natural Resources, Outdoor Recreation, Wildlife Br., Whitney Block, 99 Wellesley St. W., Toronto, ON M7A 1W3 (416)965-4252 Ministry of Natural Resources, Outdoor Recreation, Office of Recreational Boating, Whitney Block, 99 Wellesley St., W., Toronto, ON M7A 1W3 (416)965-3238 Ministry of Natural Resources, Outdoor Recreation, Parks and Recreational Areas Br., Whitney Block, 99 Wellesley St. W., Toronto, ON M7A 1W3 (416)965-5160 Ministry of Tourism and Recreation, Recreation Div., 77 Bloor St. W., Toronto, ON M7A 2R9 (416)965-0898 Ministry of Tourism and Recreation, Tourism Div., 77 Bloor St. W., Toronto, ON M7A 2R9 (416)965-4024

OREGON: Environmental Quality Dept., 811 SW 6th Ave., Portland, OR 97204 (503)229-6271 Fish and Wildlife Dept., Fish Div., P.O. Box 59 Portland, OR 97207 (503)229-5440 Fish and Wildlife Dept., Wildlife Div., P.O. Box 59 Portland, OR 97207 (503)229-5454 Parks and Recreation Div., 525 Trade St. S.E., Salem, OR 97310 (503)378-2796 Economic Development Dept., Tourism Div., 595 Cottage St. N.E., Salem OR 97310 (503)373-1270

PENNSYLVANIA: Environmental Resources Dept., P.O. Box 2063, Harrisburg, PA 17120 (717)787-9580 Environmental Resources Dept., Fish Commission, P.O. Box 1673, Harrisburg, PA 17105-1673 (717)657-4518 Environmental Resources Dept., Game Commission, 2001 Elmerton Ave., Harrisburg, PA 17110-9797 (717)787-6286 Environmental Resources Dept., Resources Management, State Parks Bureau, P.O. Box 1467, Harrisburg, PA 17120 (717)787-6640 Commerce Dept., Travel Development Bur., 433 Forum Bldg., Harrisburg, PA 17120 (717)787-5453

PRINCE EDWARD ISLAND: Dept. of the Environment, P.O. Box 2000, Charlottetown, PE C1A 7N8 (902)368-5320 Dept. of the Environment, Fish and Wildlife, P.O. Box 2000, Charlottetown, PE C1A 7N8 (902)368-4684 Dept. of Tourism and Parks, Parks Br., P.O. Box 2000, Charlottetown, PE C1A 7N8 (902)368-5540 Dept. of Community and Cultural Affairs, Youth, Fitness and Recreation Div., P.O. Box 2000, Charlottetown, PE C1A 7N8 (902)892-0311 Dept. of Tourism and Parks, Tourism Marketing Br., P.O. Box 2000, Charlottetown, PE C1A 7N8 (902)368-4150

QUEBEC: Ministry de l'Environment, 3900 rue Marly, Ste-Foy, PQ G1X 4E4 (418)643-6071 Ministry du Loisir, de la Chasse et de la Peche, Wildlife Resources Directorate, 150 boul. St.-Cyrille Est, Quebec, PQ G1R4Y1 (418)643-2207 Ministry du Loisir, de la Chasse et de la Peche, Recreation, Sports, and Parks Directorate, 150 boul. St.-Cyrille Est, Quebec, PQ G1R 4Y1 (418)643-2207 Ministry du Tourisme, Tourisme Quebec, C.P. 20,000, Quebec, PQ GIK 7X2 (418)873-2015 (Montral area) (800)361-5405 (elsewhere in PQ); (800)361-6490 (ON and the Atlantic provinces); (800)443-7000 (eastern U.S.)

RHODE ISLAND: Environmental Management Dept., 9 Hayes St., Providence, RI 02908 (401)277-6800 Environmental Management Dept., Fish and Wildlife Div., Washington County Govt. Center, Wakefield, RI 02879 (401)789-3094 Environmental Management Dept., Parks and Recreation Div., 9 Hayes St., Providence, RI 02908 (401)277-2632 Economic Development, Promotion and Tourism Div., 7 Jackson Walkway, Providence, RI 02901 (401)277-2601

SASKATCHEWAN: Dept. of Environment and Public Safety, 3085 Albert St., Regina, SK S4S 0B1 (306)787-0197 Dept. of Parks, Recreation and Culture, Fisheries Br., 3211 Albert St., Regina, SK S4S 5W6 (306)787-2884 Dept. of Culture, Multiculturalism and Recreation, 3211 Albert St., Regina, SK S4S 5W6 (306)787-2322 Dept. of Parks and Renewable Resources, 3211 Albert St., Regina, SK S4S 5W6 (306)787-2322 Dept. of Economic Development and Tourism, 1919 Saskatchewan Dr., Regina, SK S4P 3V7 (306)787-4069

SOUTH CAROLINA: Health and Environmental Control Dept., Environmental Quality Control Div., 2600 Bull St., Columbia, SC 29201 (803)734-5360 Wildlife and Marine Resources Dept., Wildlife and Freshwater Fisheries Div., P.O. Box 167 Columbia, SC 29202 (803)734-3886 Parks, Recreation, and Tourism Dept., 1205 Pendleton St., Suite 248, Columbia, SC 29201 (803)734-0159

SOUTH DAKOTA: Game, Fish and Parks Dept., Wildlife Div., 445 E. Capitol, Pierre, SD 57501 (605)773-3381 Water and Natural Resources Dept., Joe Foss Bldg., 523 E. Capitol Ave., Pierre, SD 57501 (605)773-3151 Game, Fish, and Parks Dept., Parks and Recreation Div., 445 E. Capitol, Pierre, SD 57501 (605)773-3392 Economic Development and Tourism Office, 711 Wells Ave., Pierre, SD 57501 (605)773-3301

TENNESSEE: Health and Environment Dept., Environmental Health Services Bureau, 313 Cordell Hull Bldg., Nashville, TN 37219 (615)741-3657 Wildlife Resources Agency, Fish Management Div., P.O. Box 40747, Nashville, TN 37204 (615)781-6575 Wildlife Resources Agency, Wildlife Management Div., P.O. Box 40747, Nashville, TN 37204 (615)781-6610 Conservation Dept., Recreational Services Div., 701 Broadway, Nashville, TN 37219-5237 (615)742-6560 Tourist Development Dept., P.O. Box 23170, Nashville, TN 37202 (615)741-7994

TEXAS: Health Dept., Environmental Programs Div., 1100 W. 49th St., Austin, TX 78756 (512)835-7000 Parks and Wildlife Dept. Fisheries Div., 4200 Smith School Rd., Austin, TX 78744 (512)389-4855 Parks and Wildlife Dept., 4200 Smith School Rd., Austin, TX 78744 (512)389-4971 Agriculture Dept. Natural Resources Office, P.O. Box 12847, Austin, TX 78711 (512)463-7505 Commerce Dept., Capitol Sta., Box 12728, Austin, TX 78711 (512)472-5059

UTAH: Health Dept., Environmental Health Div., P.O. Box 16700, Salt Lake City, UT 84116-0700 (801)538-6121 Natural Resources Dept., Wildlife Resources Div., Fisheries Management, 1596 W. North Temple, Salt Lake City, UT 84116 (801)533-9333 Natural Resources Dept., Wildlife Resources Div., Game Management, 1596 W. North Temple, Salt Lake City, UT 84116 (801)533-9333 Natural Resources Dept., 1636 W. North Temple, Salt Lake City, UT 84116-3156 (801)538-7200 Community and Economic Development Dept., Travel Development Div., Council Hall, Capitol Hill, Salt Lake City, UT 84114 (801)538-1030

VERMONT: Natural Resources Agency, Environmental Conservation Dept., 103 S. Main St., Waterbury, VT 05676 (802)244-8755 Natural Resources Agency, Fish and Wildlife Dept., 103 S. Main St., Waterbury, VT 05676 (802)244-7331 Natural Resources Agency, Forests, Parks and Recreation Dept., 103 S. Main St., Waterbury, VT 05676 (802)244-8711 Development and Community Affairs Agency, Travel Div., 134 State St., Montpelier, VT 05602 (802)828-3236

VIRGINIA: Game and Inland Fisheries Commission, 4010 W. Broad St., Richmond, VA 23230 (206)367-1000 Natural Resources Office, 9th St. Office Bldg., Richmond, VA 23219 (206)786-0044 Economic Development Dept., Tourism Section, 9th St. Office Bldg, 5th Fl, Richmond, VA 23219 (804)786-2051

WASHINGTON: Ecology Dept., MS PV-11, Olympia, WA 98504 (206)459-6168 Natural Resources Dept., 201 John A. Cherberg Bldg., MS QW-21, Olympia, WA 98504 (206)753-1308 Fisheries Dept., 115 General Admin. Bldg., MS AX-11, Olympia, WA 98504 (206)753-6537 Wildlife Dept., 600 N. Capitol Way, MS GJ-11 Olympia, WA 98504 (206)753-5707 State Parks and Recreation Comm, 7150 Cleanwater Lane, KY-11, Olympia, WA 98504 (206)753-2027 Trade and Economic Development Dept., Tourist Promotion Div., 101 General Admin. Bldg., AX-13, Olympia, WA 98504 (206)753-5600

WEST VIRGINIA: Natural Resources Div., Environmental and Regulatory Affairs, Capitol Complex, Bldg. 3, Charleston, WV 25305 (304)348-2761 Natural Resources Div., Wildlife Resources Div., Capitol Complex, Bldg. 3, Charleston, WV 25305 (304)348-2771 Natural Resources Div., Capitol Complex, Bldg. 3, Charleston, WV 25305 (304)348-2754 Economic Development Authority, Capitol Complex, 525 Bldg. 6, Charleston, WV 25305 (304)348-3650

WISCONSIN: Natural Resources Dept., P.O. Box 7921, Madison, WI 53707 (608)266-1099 Development Dept., Tourism Div., P.O. Box 7970, Madison, WI 53707 (608)266-2345

WYOMING: Environmental Quality Dept., Herschler Bldg., 4th Fl. W., Cheyenne, WY 82002 (307)777-7938 Game and Fish Dept., 5400 Bishop Blvd., Cheyenne, WY 82006 (307)777-4601 Agriculture Dept., Natural Resources Div., 2219 Carey Ave., Cheyenne, WY 82002-0100 (307)777-6576 Travel Commission, 25th and College Dr., Cheyenne, WY 82002 (307)777-7777

YUKON TERRITORY: Dept. of Fisheries and Oceans, 122 Industrial Rd., Whitehorse, YT Y1A 2T9 (403)667-2235 Dept. of Renewable Resources, Parks, Resources and Regional Planning, P.O. Box 2703, Whitehorse, YT Y1A 2C6 (403)667-5905 Community and Transportation Services, Recreation, P.O. Box 2703, Whitehorse, YT Y1A 2C6 (403)667-5254 Tourism Yukon, P.O. Box 2703, Whitehorse, YT Y1A 2C6 (403)667-5340

Chapter 11, Section 3

Government Agencies and Private Organizations

Non-Government Organizations

National

CANADA

BOY SCOUTS OF CANADA, National Council, P.O. Box 5151, Station F, Ottawa, ON K2C 3G7 (613)224-5131 Provides an educational, outdoor-oriented program for Canadian youth. PROVINCIAL EXECUTIVE DIRECTORS: ALBERTA: D.A. Dick, 14205 109th Ave., Edmonton, AB T5N 1H5 (403)454-8561 BRITISH COLUMBIA: J.B. Pettifer, 250 Willingdon St., North Burnaby, BC V5C 5Z1 (604)293-1961 MANITOBA: L. Wilcox, 883 Notre Dame Ave., Winnipeg, MB R3E 0M4 (204)786-6661 NEW BRUNSWICK: John Hallett, 55 Rothesay Ave., Saint John, NB E2J 2B2 (506)657-2290 NOVA SCOTIA: Philip S. Newsome, Boy Scout Bldg., 6232 Quinpool Rd., Halifax, NS B3L 1A3 (902)423-9227 NEWFOUNDLAND: F.J. Kavanaugh, 15 Terra Nova Rd., St. John's, NF A1B 1E7 (709)722-0931 ONTARIO: F. Spence, 9 Jackes Ave., Toronto, ON M4T 1E2 (416)923-2461 PRINCE EDWARD ISLAND: William J. O'Doherty, P.O. Box 533, Charlottetown, PE C1A 7L1 (902)894-4777 QUEBEC: S. Breen, 2001 Trans-Canada Hwy., Dorval, PQ H9P 1J1 (514)683-3004 SASKATCHEWAN: (See ALBERTA) YUKON: (See BRITISH COLUMBIA)

CANADIAN ASSOCIATION FOR HEALTH, PHYSICAL EDUCATION AND RECREATION. 1600 James Naismith Dr., Gloucester, ON K1B 5N4 (613)748-5622

CANADIAN CAMPING ASSOCIATION, 1806 Ave. Rd. #2, Toronto, ON M5M3Z1 (416)781-4717 Dedicated to promoting and enhancing the Canadian camping experience. (Provincial affiliates [associations] are listed in Chapter 11, Section 4).

CANADIAN CANOE ASSOCIATION, 1600 James Naismith Dr., Gloucester, ON K1B 5N4 (613)748-5623 Strong orientation toward competitive paddling. Publication: CCA TODAY. Members: 5,000. (Provincial affiliates [associations] are listed in Chapter 11, Section 4)

CANADIAN HOSTELLING ASSOCIATION, 1600 James Naismith Dr., Gloucester, ON K1B 5N4 (613)748-5638 Supervisory body for the individual hostels across Canada.

CANADIAN PARKS AND WILDERNESS SOCIETY, 160 Bloor St. E. #1150, Toronto, ON M4W 1B9 (416)972-0868 Has an abiding interest in conservation issues. Publication: PARK NEWS. CHAPTERS: Algonquin, 69 Sherbourne St., #313, Toronto, ON M5A 3X7 British Columbia, P.O. Box 6007, Station C, Victoria, BC V8P 5L4 Calgary/Banff, P.O. Box 608, Univ. of Calgary, Calgary, AB T4N1N4 Edmonton, 11044 82nd Ave., Edmonton, AB T6G 0T2 Ottawa/Hull, P.O. Box 3072, Station D, Ottawa, ON K1P 6H6 Saskatchewan, P.O. Box 914, Saskatoon, SK S7K 3M4

CANADIAN RECREATIONAL CANOEING ASSOCIATION, P.O. Box 500, Hyde Park, ON N0M 1Z0 (519)473-2109 Dedicated to increasing knowledge of canoeing activities, routes to paddle, and government lobby. Publication: KANAWA. (Provincial affiliates [associations] are listed in Chapter 11, Section 4.)

CANADIAN RED CROSS SOCIETY, 1800 Alta Vista Dr., Ottawa, ON K1G 4J5 (613)739-3000 Provides humanitarian and relief services and has an extensive water safety program. Members: 2,500,000 volunteers, 6,000 staff. DIVISIONS: ALBERTA/NORTHWEST TERRITORIES: 737 13th Ave. S.W., Calgary, AB T2R 1J1 (403)228-2169 BRITISH COLUMBIA/YUKON: 4750 Oak St., Vancouver, BC V6H 2N9 (604)879-7551 MANITOBA: 226 Osborne St. N., Winnipeg, MB R3C 1V4 (204)772-2551 NEW BRUNSWICK: 405 University Ave., P.O. Box 39, St. John, NB E2L 3X3 (506)648-5000 NEWFOUNDLAND: 7 Wicklow St., St. John's, NF A1B 4A4 (709)754-0461 NOVA

SCOTIA: 1940 Gottingen St., P.O. Box 366, Halifax, NS B3J 2H2 (902)423-9181 ONTARIO: 5700 Cancross Ct., Mississauga, ON L5R 3E9 (416)890-1000 PRINCE EDWARD ISLAND: 62 Prince St., Charlottetown, PE C1A 4R2 (902)894-8551 QUEBEC: 2170 Rene-Levesque Blvd. W., Montreal, PQ H3H 1R6 (514)937-7761 SASKATCHEWAN: 2571 Broad St., P.O. Box 1185, Regina, SK S4P 3B4 (306)352-4601

CANADIAN WHITEWATER ASSOCIATION, 12843 Crescent Rd., Surrey, BC V4A 2V7 (604)531-8205 Promotes exploration, enjoyment, and preservation of Canadian rivers. Distributes paddling information. (Provincial affiliates [associations] are listed in Chapter 11, Section 4.)

GIRL GUIDES OF CANADA, 50 Merton St., Toronto, ON M4S 1A3 (416)487-5281 Provides an educational experience for Canadian youth of which outdoor activities are an integral part. Members: 268,000. Publication: CANADIAN GUIDER. PROVINCIAL/TERRITORIAL COMMISSIONERS: ALBERTA: R. Schmidt, 10665 Jasper Ave. #1330, Edmonton, AB T5J 3S9 BRITISH COLUMBIA: Delores Racine, 1462 W. 8th Ave., Vancouver, BC V6H 1E1 MANITOBA: Evelyn Williams, 872 St. James St., Winnipeg, MB R3G 3K2 NEW BRUNSWICK: Ruby Henry, 70 Crown St. #215, St. John, NB E2L 2X6 NEWFOUNDLAND: Susan Patten, Bldg. 566, St. John's Pl., Pleasantville St., St. John's, NF A1A 1S3 NORTHWEST TERRITORIES: Judy McLinton, P.O. Box 2835, Yellowknife, NT X1A 2R2 NOVA SCOTIA: Margaret Masson, 1871 Granville St., Halifax, NS B3J 1Y1 ONTARIO: Marguerite Rogers, 50 Merton St., Toronto, ON M4S 1A3 PRINCE EDWARD ISLAND: Irene Gallant, 100 Upper Prince St., Charlottetown, PE C1A 4S3 QUEBEC: Phyllis Brickwood, 1939 Maisonneuve Blvd. W., Montreal, PQ H3H 1K3 SASKATCHEWAN: Lois Morrison, 1362-A Lorne St., Regina, SK S4R 2K1 YUKON: Pat Nickel, P.O. Box 5133, Whitehorse, YT Y1A 4S3

INTERNATIONAL CANOE FEDERATION OF CANADA, c/o ICF, G. Massaia 59, Florence, Italy Forty-two national canoe federations joined to promote high-level competition in flat racing, slalom, marathon, etc. Offers technical help in Olympic competition. Publication: CANOEING INTERNATIONAL (bimonthly).

KANAWA INTERNATIONAL MUSEUM OF CANOES, KAYAKS AND ROWING CRAFT, c/o Kirk A.W. Wipper, director, Camp Kandalore, Minden, ON (416)978-6095 Prof. Wipper and the Directors of the museum are re-establishing the museum in two separate Ontario locations away from Camp Kandelore.

ROYAL CANADIAN GEOGRAPHICAL SOCIETY, 39 McArthur Ave., Vanier, ÓN KIL 8L7 (613)745-4629 Members: 195,000. Publication: CANADIAN GEOGRAPHIC.

ROYAL LIFE SAVING SOCIETY OF CANADA, 191 Church St., Toronto, ON M5B 1Y7 (416)364-3881 Members: 25,000 individuals, 2,200 affiliated organizations. BRANCHES: ALBERTA/ NORTHWEST TERRITORIES: 11759 Groat Rd., Edmonton, AB T5M 3K6 (403)453-8638 BRITISH COLUMBIA/YUKON: 1235 W. Pender St., Vancouver, BC V6E 2V6 (604)684-6368 MANITOBA: 207 Fort St. #314, Winnipeg, MB R3C 1E2 (204)956-2124 NEW BRUNSWICK: P.O. Box 39 St. John, NB E2L 3X3 (506)648-5010 NEWFOUNDLAND/LABRADOR: Aquahouse, 15 Westerland Rd., St. John's, NF A1B 3R7 (709)576-1953 NOVA SCOTIA: P.O. Box 3010 So., Halifax, NS B3J 3G6 (902)425-5450 ONTARIO: 43 Coldwater Rd., Don Mills, ON M3B 1Y8 (416)447-7276 PRINCE EDWARD ISLAND: P.O. Box 2411, Charlottetown, PE C1A 4A0 (902)892-8381 QUEBEC: C.P. 1000, Succ. M., Montreal, PQ H1V 3R2 (514)252-3000 SASKATCHEWAN: 2205 Victoria Ave., Regina, SK S7P 0S4 (306)522-3651

SPORTS FEDERATION OF CANADA, 1600 James Naismith Dr., Gloucester, ON K1B 5N4 (613)748-5670 Fosters the pursuit of excellence and the development of national pride through sport. 70 member associations. (Provincial affiliates [federations] are listed in Chapter 11, Section 4.)

WILDERNESS CANOE ASSOCIATION, P.O. Box 496 Station K, Toronto, ON M4P 2G9 (416)637-7632 Active in wilderness preservation. Sponsors club outings. Members: 600, primarily in southern Ontario. Publication: NASTAWGAN (quarterly).

UNITED STATES

AMERICAN ALLIANCE FOR HEALTH, PHYSICAL EDUCATION, RECREATION AND DANCE, 1900 Association Dr., Reston, VA 22091 (703)476-3400 Purpose is to improve its fields (physical education, dance, health, athletics, safety education, recreation and outdoor education) through leadership, research, publications, and standards. Members: 42,000; staff 54. Publications: JOURNAL OF PHYSICAL EDUCATION RECREATION AND DANCE; LEISURE TODAY.

AMERICAN CANOE ASSOCIATION, 8580 Cinderbed Rd., Suite 1900, P.O. Box 1190, Newington, VA 22122-1190 (703)550-7523 Promotes canoesport in the United States through instructor certification, safety, and education. The national governing body for Olympic canoeing and kayaking. Members: 5,000 in 12 regional affiliates and 200 state clubs. Publication: THE AMERICAN CANOEIST (bimonthly).

AMERICAN CANOE MANUFACTURERS UNION, 439 E. 51st St., New York, NY 10022 (212)421-5220 Six manufacturer-members who promote the sport through publications and events. Publications: THE CANOEING BOOKLIST; LEARN CANOEING!

AMERICAN GUIDES ASSOCIATION, P.O. Box 935, Woodland, CA 95695 (916)662-6824 An association serving trained and licensed guides and others interested in wilderness travel for personal pleasure. Purpose is to train qualified guides and improve the professional and ethical standards of the profession. Members: 3,000; staff: 15. Maintains National Whitewater Hall of Fame and Library. Publication: EBB AND FLOW.

AMERICAN RAFTING ASSOCIATION, 519 S. Battleground, Kings Mountain, NC 28086 (704)739-0437 Presently inactive. For individuals interested in riverine recreation and ecology. Seeks to develop, operate, and perpetuate river rafting regattas. Maintains a Hall of Fame. Publication: RAFTER.

AMERICAN RED CROSS, 17th and D Streets N.W., Washington, DC 20006 (202)737-8300 Red Cross activities include small craft schools, basic canoeing/kayaking courses, instructor-training rescue operations, and first aid. Chapters: 2,889; staff: 20,201. Publications: RED CROSS NEWS (monthly) and many service-related materials.

AMERICAN RIVERS, 801 Pennsylvania Ave, S.E., Suite 303, Washington, DC 20003 (202)547-6900 A public interest organization with 9,000 members dedicated to protecting free-flowing rivers. Formerly American Rivers Conservation Council. Publication: AMERICAN RIVERS (quarterly).

AMERICAN RIVER TOURING ASSOCIATION, Star Rt. 73, Groveland, CA 95321 (209)962-7873

THE AMERICAN WHITEWATER AFFILIATION, 146 N. Brockway, Palatine, IL 60067 (704)483-5049 More than 1,500 whitewater boating enthusiasts and 50 club affiliates comprise this group interested in protecting whitewater rivers and enhancing the enjoyment of whitewater sports. Sponsors the annual Gauley River Festival. Publication: AMERICAN WHITEWATER (bimonthly).

AMERICAN WILDERNESS ALLIANCE, 7600 E. Arapahoe Rd., Suite 114, Englewood, CO 80112 (303)771-0380 Four thousand members dedicated to conserving wilderness resources. Sponsors American Wilderness Adventures, a group which annually conducts some 80 wildland trips — including canoeing or rafting. These trips are announced in the AWA publication: AMERICAN WILDERNESS ADVENTURES.

AMERICAN YOUTH HOSTELS, P.O. Box 37613, Washington, DC 20013 (202)783-6161 A worldwide nonprofit organization which provides low-cost accommodations in scenic, historic or cultural areas. AYH has over 250 hostels and sponsors bicycle, hiking, skiing, and canoe trips throughout the U.S. One of the most notable "canoe hostels" is the Spirit of the Land Hostel at the group's Wilderness Canoe Base in the Boundary Waters Canoe Area, MN. Publications: AYH HANDBOOK (annual); KNAPSACK (semiannual).

APPALACHIAN MOUNTAIN CLUB, 5 Joy St., Boston, MA 02108 (617)523-0636 Promotes public knowledge and enjoyment of the outdoors, particularly in New England. Maintains trails and huts/shelters. Publishes a series of northeastern river guides (see: AMC RIVER GUIDE, MAINE, etc., in Chapter 1, Section 1). AMC has a large mountaineering library including a map collection. Publication: APPALACHIA BULLETIN (monthly).

BOY SCOUTS OF AMERICA, 1325 Walnut Hill Lane, P.O. Box 152079, Irving, TX 75015 (214)580-2000 The Boy Scouts provide an educational program for the development, citizenship training, and mental and physical fitness of youth. Special focus on outdoor activities. Members: 4,750,000; staff: 3850. Publication: BOYS' LIFE (monthly).

CAMP FIRE INC., 4601 Madison Ave., Kansas City, MO 64112 (816)756-1950 A group for girls and boys up to 21 years of age providing opportunities through informal education for young people to realize their potential. Formerly: Camp Fire Girls. Members: 450,000; staff: 50. Publication: CAMP FIRE MANAGEMENT (quarterly).

DUCKS UNLIMITED, 1 Waterfowl Way, Long Grove, IL 60047 (312)438-4300 Interested in migratory waterfowl and conserving wetlands. Members: 600,000; staff: 210. Publication: DUCKS UNLIMITED MAGAZINE (bimonthly).

EASTERN PROFESSIONAL RIVER OUTFITTERS ASSOCIATION, 531 S. Gay St., Suite 600, Knoxville, TN 37902 (615)524-1045 An association of about 75 outfitting companies promoting commercial canoeing, kayaking and rafting, river conservation and safety. Merged with Western River Guides Association to become America Outdoors.

ENVIRONMENTAL DEFENSE FUND, 257 Park Ave. S., New York, NY 10010 (212)505-2100 Uses its legal resources to reform law and poligy governing the environment. Members: 75,000. Publication: EDF LETTER (bimonthly).

FRIENDS OF THE EVERGLADES, 202 Park St., Miami Springs, FL 33166 (305)888-1230 Scientists and lay-members fostering public awareness and action on the threatened environment of Florida's Everglades. Members: 3,800. Publications: EIS NEWSLETTER; and EVERGLADES REPORT.

FRIENDS OF THE RIVER, Fort Mason Center, Bldg. C, San Francisco, CA 94123 (415)771-0400 Groups and individuals (9,500 members) united to preserve free-flowing rivers, primarily in the West. Campaigns to achieve Wild and Scenic River designation for unprotected wild rivers. Publication: HEADWATERS (bimonthly).

GIRL SCOUTS OF THE U.S.A., 830 3rd Ave at 51st St., New York, NY 10022 (212)940-7500 Encourage personal development through a variety of projects in social action, environmental action, youth leadership, community service, etc. Members: 3,000,000; staff: 500. Publications: GIRL SCOUT LEADER (quarterly for adult leaders).

INTERCOLLEGIATE OUTING CLUB ASSOCIATION, c/o Outing Club, RPI Student Union, Box 26, Rensselaer Polytechnic Institute, Troy, NY 12180 (518)273-8602 Composed of about 4,000 present members (or graduates) of college outing clubs who are interested in enjoying and preserving the wilderness. Sponsors trips, including canoeing, kayaking and rafting. Publications: IOCA NEWS (monthly; and BULLETIN (quarterly).

INTERNATIONAL CANOE FEDERATION — UNITED STATES, c/o ICF, G. Massaia 59, Florence, Italy Forty-two national canoe federations joined to promote high-level competition in flatwater racing, slalom, marathon, etc. Offers technical help in Olympic competition. Publication: CANOEING INTERNATIONAL (bimonthly).

NATIONAL ASSOCIATION FOR STATE RIVER CONSERVATION PROGRAMS, P.O. Box 1467, Harrisburg, PA 17120 (717)787-6816 Promotes cooperation among the 50 managers of state river conservation programs to further the goals of educating the public and creating a national river conservation policy.

NATIONAL ASSOCIATION OF CANOE LIVERIES AND OUTFITTERS, P.O. Box 1149, Murdoch, FL 33938 (813)743-7278 Committed to providing the public with a safe, quality, on-water experience, and protecting the nation's waterways. Members: 300 professional liveries/outfitters. Publications: NACLO NEWS (bimonthly); and LET'S GO PADDLING (annual directory).

NATIONAL AUDUBON SOCIETY, 950 3rd Ave., New York, NY 10022 (212)832-3200 Members: 550,000. Interested in preservation of wildlands and wildlife. Sponsors summer camps and trips. Publications: AMERICAN BIRDS; AUDUBON.

NATIONAL GEOGRAPHIC SOCIETY, 17th and M Streets N.W., Washington, DC 20036 (202)857-7000 A membership of more than 10,000,000 interested in the geography of the world. Sponsors expeditions and research. Library contains some 70,000 volumes and 100,000 maps. Publication: NATIONAL GEOGRAPHIC (monthly).

NATIONAL MARINE MANUFACTURERS ASSOCIATION, 401 N. Michigan Ave., Chicago, IL 60611 (312)836-4747 Promotes the sale and enjoyment of pleasure boats and accessories. Members: 1,500. Publication: INTER/PORT (weekly newsletter).

NATIONAL ORGANIZATION FOR RIVER SPORTS, P.O. Box 6847, 314 N. 20th St., Colorado Springs, CO 80904 (719)473-2466 Dedicated to education and awareness about rivers and river running. Members: 10,000. Publication: CURRENTS (bimonthly).

NATIONAL PADDLING COMMITTEE, 1750 E. Boulder St., Colorado Springs, CO 80909

NATIONAL PARKS AND CONSERVATION ASSOCIATION, 1015 31st St. N.W., Washington, DC 20007 (202)944-8530 Interested in the expansion, conservation, and improvement of national parks and related preserves. Members: 100,000. Publication: NATIONAL PARKS (bimonthly).

THE NATURE CONSERVANCY, 1815 N. Lynn St., Arlington, VA 22209 (703)841-5300 Through gift or purchase, preserves and protects significant lands in perpetuity. Members: 450,000. Publication: THE NATURE CONSERVANCY MAGAZINE (bimonthly).

NORTH AMERICAN BIRCH BARK CANOE ASSOCIATION, 3016 Neola St., Cedar Falls, IA 50613 Inactive.

NORTH AMERICAN LOON FUND, R.R. 4, Box 240-C, Meridith, NH 03253 (603)279-6163 Dedicated to protecting the common loon. Computer database: ANNOTATED LOON BIBLIOGRAPHICAL DATABASE. Members: 6,000; staff: 4. Publication: LOON CALL (quarterly).

NORTH AMERICAN PADDLESPORTS ASSOCIATION, 715 Boylston St., Boston, MA 02116 (617)266-6800

OUTWARD BOUND, 384 Field Point Rd., Greenwich, CT 06830 (203)661-0797 Operates five schools and an urban center to teach self-reliance/awareness in young people through challenging outdoor experiences including canoeing, kayaking, and rafting. Publication: OB NEWSLETTER.

RIVER SAFETY TASK FORCE, 230 Penllyn Pike, Penllyn, PA 19422

RIVER WATCH, c/o AMERICAN RIVERS, 801 Pennsylvania Ave. S.E., Suite 303, Washington, DC 20003 (202)547-6900

SIERRA CLUB, 730 Polk St., San Francisco, CA 94109 (415)776-2211 Protects and conserves threatened natural areas worldwide. Represents 400,000 members with a staff of 250. Has a collection of 5,000 volumes on mountaineering and conservation. Publication: SIERRA (bimonthly).

SOBEK'S INTERNATIONAL EXPLORER'S SOCIETY, 1 Sobek Tower, Angels Camp, CA 95222 (209)736-4524 A for-profit company booking international adventure trips and explorations. Has a collection of some 500 books on international river running. Produces videos on exotic rivers. Publications: ADVENTURE BOOK (annual) and CROCODILE (quarterly).

TRADE ASSOCIATION OF SEA KAYAKING, P.O. Box 84144, Seattle, WA 98124 Association of sea kayak manufacturers, outfitters, media, and other interested parties.

TRADITIONAL SMALL CRAFT ASSOCIATION, P.O. Box 350, Mystic, CT 06355 (203)536-6342 Individuals and institutions interested in traditional small rowing and sailing craft. Members: 600. Publication: THE ASH BREEZE (quarterly).

UNITED STATES CANOE AND KAYAK TEAM, c/o AMERICAN CANOE ASSOCIATION, 8580 Cinderbed Rd., Suite 1900, P.O. Box 1190, Newington, VA 22122-1190 (703)550-7523 Affiliated with the ACA and responsible for managing the U.S. Olympic program.

UNITED STATES CANOE ASSOCIATION, P.O. Box 5743, Lafayette, IN 47903 (317)474-9391 Promotes all types of paddling activities, safety, and waterways preservation. Sponsors National Marathon Canoe and Kayak Championship. Members: 2,000. Publication: CANOE NEWS (bimonthly).

WESTERN RIVER GUIDES ASSOCIATION, 360 S. Monroe, Suite 300, Denver, CO 80209 (303)377-4811 River outfitter-members who seek to promote commercial river touring, preserve and protect the free-flowing sections of western rivers, and increase safety and professionalism in the business. Members 550. Regectly merged with the Eastern Professional Rafting Organization to become America Outdoors.

WOODEN CANOE HERITAGE ASSOCIATION, P.O. Box 226, Blue Mountain Lake, NY 12812 (716)669-2376 Non-profit group (1,000 members) devoted to preserving, studying, communicating, building, restoring, and using wooden and birchbark canoes. Publication: WOODEN CANOE (quarterly).

Chapter 11, Section 4

Government Agencies and Private Organizations

Non-Government Organizations

Provincial and State

ALBERTA Alberta Camping Association, 101 3rd St. S.W., Calgary, AB 2TP4G6 (403)269-6156 Alberta Flatwater Canoe Association, c/o Janet Davies, 5607 Ladbrooke Dr. S.W., Calgary, AB T3E 5Y2 (403)283-3643 Alberta Sport Council, 101 6th Ave. S.W. #450, Calgary, AB T2P 3P4 (403)297-2503 Alberta Whitewater Association, P.O. Box 200, 11044 82nd Ave., Edmonton, AB T6H 0T3

ARKANSAS Ozark Society, P.O. Box 2914, Little Rock, AR 72203

BRITISH COLUMBIA British Columbia Camping Association, 1367 W. Broadway, Vancouver, BC V6H 4A7 (604)737-3000 Friends of the Stikine, 1405 Doran Rd., North Vancouver, BC V7K 1N1 (604)685-5953; (604)932-4818 Outdoor Recreation Council of British Columbia, 1367 W. Broadway, Vancouver, BC V6H 4A9 (604)737-3000 Outward Bound British Columbia, 530 Drake St., Vancouver, BC V6B 2H3 Recreational Canoeing Association of British Columbia, 1367 W. Broadway, Vancouver, BC V6H 4A9 River Outfitters Association of British Columbia, Wilderness Tourism Council, P.O. Box 46132 Station G, Vancouver, BC V6R 4G5 (604)736-9366 Sea Kayak Association of British Columbia, 16064 80th Ave., Surrey, BC B3S 2J7 (604)597-1122 Sport B.C., 1367 W. Broadway, Vancouver, BC V6H 4A9 (604)737-3000 White Water Canoeing Association of British Columbia, 1367 W. Broadway, Vancouver, BC V6H 4A9 (604)737-3000

COLORADO Colorado River Outfitters Association, P.O. Box 502, Westminister, CO 80030 (303)220-8640

CONNECTICUT Farmington River Watershed Association, 749 Hopmeadow St., Simsbury, CT 06070 (203)658-4442

GEORGIA Coastal Plains Area Tourism Council, P.O. Box 1223, Valdosta, GA 31601 Georgia Mountains Planning and Development Commission, P.O. Box 1294, Gainesville, GA 30501 Slash Pine Area Planning and Development Commission, 120 6th St., Atlanta, GA 30313

IDAHO Idaho Outfitters and Guides Association Inc., P.O. Box 95, Boise, ID 83701 (208)342-1438

ILLINOIS American Youth Hostels, Chicago Council, 3712 N. Clark St., Chicago, IL 60613 (312)327-8114 Illinois Paddling Council, 9 Pfeiffer St., Lemont, IL 60439

KANSAS Kansas Canoe Association, P.O. Box 2885, Wichita, KS 67201

LOUISIANA Lafayette Natural History Museum and Planetarium, 637 Girard Park Dr., Lafayette, LA 70503

MANITOBA Manitoba Camping Association, 1495 St. Matthews Ave., Winnipeg, MB R3G 3L3 (204)985-4166 Manitoba Paddling Association Inc., c/o M. Tipples, 1700 Elice Ave., Winnipeg, MB R3H 0B1 (204)985-4000 Manitoba Recreational Canoeing Association, 31 Stanford Bay, Winnipeg, MB R3P 0T5 Manitoba Sports Federation, 1700 Elice Ave., Winnipeg, MB R3H 0B1

MAINE Whitewater Outfitters Association of Maine Inc., P.O. Box 80, West Forks, ME 04985

MASSACHUSETTS Connecticut River Watershed Council, 125 Combs Rd., Easthampton, MA 01027 (413)584-0057 Westfield River Watershed Association, P.O. Box 114, Middlefield, MA 02143

MINNESOTA Spirit of the Land Youth Hostel, Wilderness Canoe Base, Gunflint Trail, HC 64-Box 940, Grand Marais, MN 55604 (218)388-2241

MONTANA Montana Outfitters and Guides Association, P.O. Box 631, Hot Springs, MT 59845

NEW BRUNSWICK Canoe New Brunswick, 36 Mitchner St., Moncton, NB E1C 6L7 New Brunswick Camping Association, P.O. Box 263,

Moncton, NB E1C8K9 (506)857-0203 New Brunswick Sports Federation, Competitive Canoeing, c/o Angus Birse, 109 Gordon St., Moncton, NB E1C 1M5 (902)389-8942 Sport New Brunswick, 65 Brunswick St., Fredericton, NB E3B 1G5 (506)455-3685

NEWFOUNDLAND Newfoundland and Labrador Camping Association, P.O. Box 261, Corner Brook, NF A2H 6C9 (709)639-7279 Newfoundland Canoeing Association, c/o Kevin Redmond, P.O. Box 5961, St. John's, NF A1C 5X4 (709)895-6766

NEW HAMPSHIRE White Mountain Region Association, Box K, Lancaster, NH 03584

NEW JERSEY Delaware River Basin Commission, 25 Scotch Rd., P.O. Box 360, Trenton, NJ 08603

NEW YORK Adirondack Historical Association, Blue Mountain Lake, NY 12812 New York-New Jersey River Conference, 1 Red Cross Pl., Brooklyn, NY 11201 Northeast Sea Kayakers Alliance, c/o C. Sutherland, P.O. Box 444, Tuckahoe, NY 10707

NOVA SCOTIA Canoe Nova Scotia, P.O. Box 3010, S. Halifax, NS B3J 3G6 (902)463-9000 Nova Scotia Camping Association, P.O. Box 3243, S. Halifax, NS B3J 3H5 (902)865-3523 Sport Nova Scotia, 5516 Spring Garden Rd., P.O. Box 3010, S. Halifax, NS B3J 3G6 (902)425-5450

NORTHWEST TERRITORIES Northwest Territories Canoeing Association, P.O. Box 2763, Yellowknife, NT X1A 2R1 Sport North Federation, P.O. Box 336, Yellowknife, NT X1A 2N3 (403)873-3032; (800)661-0797

ONTARIO Canoe Ontario, 1220 Sheppard Ave. E., Willowdale, ON M2K 2X1 (416)495-4180 The Friends of Algonquin Park, P.O. Box 248, Whitney, ON K0J 2M0 Ontario Camping Association, 1806 Avenue Rd. #2, Toronto, ON M5M 3Z1 (416)781-0525 Ontario Canoe Sprint Racing Affiliation, c/o Canoe Ontario, 1220 Sheppard Ave. E., Willowdale, ON M2K 2X1 (416)495-4180 Ontario Marathon Canoe Racing Association, c/o Canoe Ontario, 1220 Sheppard Ave. E., Willowdale, ON M2K 2X1 (416)495-4180 Ontario Parks Association, 1220 Sheppard Ave. E., North York, ON M2K 2X1 (416)495-4088 Ontario Recreational Canoeing Association c/o Canoe Ontario, 1220 Sheppard Ave. E., Willowdale, ON M2K 2X1 (416)495-4180 Ontario Wild Water Affiliation, c/o Canoe Ontario, 1220 Sheppard Ave. E., Willowdale, ON M2K 2X1 (416)495-4180 Sport Ontario, 1220 Sheppard Ave. E., Willowdale, ON M2K 2X1 (416)495-4088

OREGON Northwest Rafters Association, P.O. Box 19008, Portland, OR 97219 Oregon Guides and Packers Inc., P.O. Box 132, Sublimity, OR 93785

PRINCE EDWARD ISLAND P.E.I. Recreational Canoeing Association, P.O. Box 2000, Charlottetown, PE C1A 7N8 Sport P.E.I., Inc., P.O. Box 302, Charlottetown, PE C1A 7K7 (902)368-4110

QUEBEC Association des Camps du Quebec, 4545 ave. Pierre-de-Coubertin, Montreal, PQ H1V 3R2 (514)252-3113 Association Quebecoise de Canoe-Kayak de Vitesse, 4545 ave. Pierre-de-Coubertin, C.P. 1000, Succ. M, Montreal, PQ H1V 3R2 (514)252-3000 Federation Quebecoise de Canot-Camping Inc., 4545 ave. Pierre-de-Coubertin, C.P. 1000, Succ. M, Montreal, PQ H1V 3R2 Sports-Quebec, 4545 ave. Pierre-de-Coubertin, C.P. 1000, Succ. M, Montreal, PQ H1V 3R2 (514)252-3114

SASKATCHEWAN Saskatchewan Camping Association, c/o Saskatoon YMCA, 25 22nd St. E., Saskatoon, SK S7K 0C7 (306)652-7515 Saskatchewan Canoe Association, 1870 Lorne St., Regina, SK S4P2L7 (306)780-9200 Sask Sport Inc., 1870 Lorne St., Regina, SK S4P 2L7 (306)780-9300

TEXAS Brazos River Authority, 4400 Cobbs Dr., P.O. Box 7555, Waco, TX 76710 Guadelupe-Blanco River Authority, 933 E. Court St., P.O. Box 271, Seguin, TX 78155 Sabine River Authority, 118 Bridgeway, 4th Fl., San Antonio, TX 78205

UTAH Canyonlands Natural History Association, 125 W. 200th St., Moab, UT 84532 (801)259-8163 Utah Guides and Outfitters, c/o Western River Guides Association, 360 S. Monroe, Suite 300, Denver, CO 80209 (303)377-4811

WEST VIRGINIA West Virginia Wildwater Association, P.O. Box 8413, South Charleston, WV 25303 (304)965-5602

YUKON TERRITORY Sport Yukon, P.O. Box 4502, Whitehorse, YT Y1A 2R8 (403)668-4236

Chapter 11, Section 5

Government Agencies and Private Organizations

Clubs

ALASKA

Knik Kanoers and Kayakers Inc., c/o Jeanne Molitor, P.O. Box 101935, Anchorage, AK 99510 (907)272-9351

Nova River Runners of Alaska, SRC Box 8337, Palmer AK 99645

Valdez Alpine Club, P.O. Box 1889, Valdez, AK 99686

ALABAMA

Birmingham Canoe Club, c/o James Brown, P.O. Box 951, Birmingham, AL 35201

Gunwale Grabbers, P.O. Box 19913, Birmingham, AL 35219 (205)979-3064

Huntsville Canoe Club, 1000 Airport Rd., 1000 Airport Rd., H 26, Huntsville, AL 35802 (205)634-4510

ALBERTA

Alberta Canoe Association, P.O. Box 4571, Edmonton, AB T6E 5G4

Alberta Recreational Canoe Association, 2714-46 St. S.E., Calgary, AB T2B 2N8

ARIZONA

Arizona Canoe Club, Box 742, Fayetteville, AZ 72701

Arizona Whitewater, 3080 W. Monmouth, Tuscon, AZ 85741 (602)742-3592

Central Arizona Paddlers Club, P.O. Box 1224, Flagstaff, AZ 86002 (602)969-7122

Northern Arizona Paddler's Club, c/o Michael E. Baron, 611 N. San Francisco St., Flagstaff, AZ 86001 (602)774-0844

ARKANSAS

Arkansas Canoe Club, c/o Carol Nelson, 1221 Reservoir Rd. #257, Little Rock, AR 72207

Arkansas Canoe Club/Central AR, 102 Buddenberg Lane, North Little Rock, AR 72118

BRITISH COLUMBIA

British Columbia Kayak and Canoe Club, 1606 W. Broadway, Vancouver, BC V6J 1X6 Canoe B.C., 4022 W. 27th Ave., Vancouver, BC V6S1S8

Canoe Sport B.C. a.k.a. Recreational Canoeing Association of B.C., 1200 Hornby St., Vancouver, BC V6Z 2E2

Olympic Canoe and Kayak Association, of British Columbia, 1200 Hornby St., Vancouver, BC V6Z 1W2

White Water Canoeing Association (of B.C.), 2807 McKenzie Ave., Surrey, BC V4A 3H5

CALIFORNIA

Bay Area Sea Kayakers, c/o Penny Wells, 229 Courtright Rd., San Rafael, CA 94901 (415)457-6094

California Canoe and Kayak, 249 Teksbury Ave., Pt. Richmond, CA 94801 (415)234-0929

California Canoe Association, c/o Norm Malin, 8665 Nagle Ave., Panorama City, CA 91402

California National Olympic Canoe Club, c/o William Quale Jr., P.O. Box 21845, Sacramento, CA (916)391-6912

CSUS Aquatic Center, California State Univ., 6000 J St., Sacramento, CA 95819

Dana Outrigger Canoe Club, c/o Cecelia Harrison, 33751 Cam., Capistrano, San Juan Capistrano, CA 92675 (714)496-5239

Handhand Outrigger Canoe Club, c/o Wade Seeley, 4864 Cape May Ave., San Diego, CA 92109 (619)223-8675

Hokuloa Outrigger Club, c/o Teresa Reynolds, 303 Oakwood, Ventura, CA 93001 (805)653-2456

Hoomau Outrigger Canoe Club, c/o Susann Butterfield, 7780 Brower Lane, Kelseyville, CA 95451 (707)263-3192

Hui O Hawaii of Sacramento, c/o Bob Steele, 9249 Cherry Ave., Orangeville, CA 95662 (916)988-2419

Hui Wa'A O San Jose, c/o Jeffrey Sylva, 1623 Trieste Ct., San Jose, CA 95122 (408)295-7952

Imua Outrigger Club, c/o Derek Harrison, 20102 Imperial Cove, Huntington Beach, CA 92646 (714)963-0116

Kahakai Outrigger Canoe Club, c/o Bruce Anderson, P.O. Box 134, Seal Beach, CA 90740 (213)596-2521

Kahekili O Ke Kai Outrigger Canoe Club, c/o Spencer La Vea, P.O. Box 25364, San Mateo, CA 94402 (415)573-5230

Kai Elua Outrigger Canoe Club, c/o Wendy Dewitt, 2915-F Cowley Way, San Diego, CA 92117 (619)231-9400

Kai Nalu Outrigger Canoe Association, c/o David Smith, 12714 Matteson Ave., #9, Los Angeles, CA 90066 (213)398-0574

Kaimanu Outrigger Canoe Club, c/o Debbie Green, 14275 Rose Dr., San Leandro, CA 94578 (415)895-0435

Kalanikai Outriggers, c/o Patti Lenoto, 4112 Littleworth Way, San Jose, CA 95135 (408)223-8141

Ka Mai'A Outrigger Canoe Club, c/o Elizabeth Mazzetti, 53 Sonoma Ave., Goleta, Ca 93117

Kamalii 'O Ke Kai Canoe Club, c/o Tennyson Heen, 619 Kiowa Cir., San Jose, Ca 95123

Ke Anuenue Outrigger Canoe Club, c/o Arma K.P. Fonseca, 39410 Stratton Common, Fremont, CA 94538 (415)498-5923

Ke Kai O'Uhane Outrigger Canoe Club, c/o Julian Avilla Jr., 643 Cornell Ave., Salinas, CA 93901 (408)758-0033

Kilo Hama Outrigger Club, c/o Brad Saguindel, 1250 Norman Ave., Santa Clara, CA 95054

Koa Kai Outrigger Canoe Club, c/o Herbert Huihui, 227 Carriage Dr., Salinas, CA 93905 (408)753-2263

Lanakila Outrigger Canoe Club, c/o Al Ching, 53 9th St., Hermosa Beach, CA 90254 (213)374-8109

Loma Prieta Paddlers, c/o Ken Brunton, 525 Bonnie View Ct., Morgan Hill, CA 95037 (408)779-2867

Marina Del Rey Outrigger Canoe Club, c/o Nancy Lynne Dopp, 214 Market St., #4, Venice, CA 90291 (213)392-2888

Monarch Bay Canoe Club, c/o Terry Mc Cann, 24371 Barbados Dr., Dana Point, CA 92629 (714)496-7792

Nahoa Athletic Association, c/o Robert J. Crase, 2301 Graham Ave., Redondo Beach, CA 90277 (213)371-5635

Na Mea Wa'A Outrigger Canoe Club, c/o Cheri A. Mendieta, 1059 Plymouth Ave., San Francisco, CA 94112 (415)333-3525

National Outdoor College, c/o Ronald D. Hilbert, P.O. Box 962, Fair Oaks, CA 95628 (916)633-7900

Newport Aquatic Center, c/o Jim Terrell, 1 Whitecliffs Dr., Newport Beach, CA 92660 (714)646-7725

Newport Ourtrigger Canoe Club, c/o James Kauhi Hookano, P.O. Box 3342, Newport Beach, CA 92663 (714)645-6517

Offshore Canoe Club, c/o Kim Hicks, 3857 Birch St., Suite #333, Newport Beach, CA 92660 (714)548-5726

O'Kalani Outrigger of Alameda, c/o Walter Wright Jr., 2704 Central Ave., Alameda, CA 94501 (415)522-6003

Paradise Outrigger Canoe Club, c/o William E. Poulis, 1307A State St., Santa Barbara, CA 93101 (805)963-3797

Popular Outdoor Sport Trips, c/o Bill Hitchings, 7675 Surrey Lane, Oakland, CA 94605 (415)635-4051

Pu Pu O'Hawaii Outrigger Canoe Club, c/o Linda Dresbach, 355 Sheffield Ct., San Jose, CA 95125 (408)371-0136

Redwood Paddlers, 6794 Clara Lane, Forestville, CA 95436 River City Paddlers, c/o John Holland, 428 J St., Suite 400, Sacramento, CA 95814 (916)965-3380

San Diego Outrigger Canoe Club, c/o Julie Robison, 13362 Tiverton Rd., San Diego, CA 92130 (619)422-5995

Santa Barbara Outrigger Canoe Club, c/o Ronald L. Harrig, P.O. Box 92043, Santa Barbara, CA 93190 (805)966-6457

Sequoia Canoe Club, c/o Tom Meldau, P.O. Box 1164, Windsor, CA 95492 (707)526-0940

Sierra Club River Touring Section, c/o John De Paoli, 7015 Fairmount Ave., El Cerrito, CA 94530 (415)527-3578

Uhame Outrigger Canoe Club, c/o Victor Di Novi, 318 C State St., Santa Barbara, CA 93101 (805)962-3585

Venice Outrigger Canoe Club, c/o Bradley Micheal Storms, 11614 Regent St., Mar-Vista, CA 90066 (213)391-5859

Ventura Olympic Canoe Club, c/o Susan L. Bragg, 3427 Gloria Dr., Newbury Park, CA 91320 (805)498-6954

Western Waters Canoe Club, c/o Rich Burchby, 840 Town and Country Village, San Jose, CA 95128-2032 (408)298-6300

COLORADO

Colorado Rocky Mountain School, c/o Bob Campbell, 1493 County Rd, Carbondale, CO 81623 (303)963-2562

Colorado Whitewater Association, c/o Doug Ragan, 7500 E. Arapahoe Rd, Englewood, CO 80112 (303)770-0515

The Confluence Club, P.O. Box 4167, Aspen, CO 81612 (303)925-1796 Fibark Boat Races Inc., c/o Mike Perschbacher, P.O. Box 762, Salida, CO 81201 (303)539-3555

High Country River Rafters Club, 772 Urban Ct., Golden, CO 80401 (303)232-6616

Pikes Peak Whitewater Club, c/o. Kathleen M. Laurin, 1814 W. Boulder, Colorado Springs, CO 80904 (719)471-2640

Rocky Mountain Canoe Club, c/o Ken Ramsay, P.O. Box 729, Broomfield, CO 80038 (303)466-5518

Telluride Navy, P.O. Box 888, Telluride, CO 81435

CONNECTICUT

Appalachian Mtn Club/Ct Chapter, 6 Jay St., Box 443, Forestville, CT 06010

Columbia Canoe Club, c/o Charles A. Herrick, 38 Hunt Rd., Columbia, CT 06237

Connecticut Canoe Racing Association, c/o Earle Roberts, 785 Bow Lane, Middletown, CT 06457 (203)346-0068

CT Chapter AMC, 2 Volovski Rd., Avon, CT 06001

Farmington River Club, c/o William K. Cole, P.O. Box 475, Canton, CT 06019

Farmington River Watershed Association, c/o David Simish, 749 Hopmeadow, Simsbury, CT 06070

Housatonic Area Canoe and Kayak Squad, c/o Douglas Gordon, R.R. Box 307, W. Cornwall, CT 067796 (203)672-0293

Quinnipiac River Watershed Association, c/o Stephen M. Theriault, 99 Colony St., Suite 9, Meridan, CT 06450 (203)272-7494

DELAWARE

Wilmington Trail Club, c/o Lawrence Auspos, P.O. Box 1184, Wilmington, DE 19899 (302)999-9924

DISTRICT OF COLUMBIA

Blue Ridge Voyageurs, 3231 Beech St., N.W. Washington, DC 20015 (202)362-5568; (202)543-1300

Canoe Cruisers/Conservation Club, 322 10th St. S.E., Washington, DC 20003 (202)245-6306

Washington Canoe Club, 333 S. Glebe Rd., Arlington, VA 22204

FLORIDA

Florida Canoe and Kayak Association, c/o Butch Horn, P.O. Box 837, Tallahassee, FL 32302 (904)422-1566

Florida Competition Paddlers Association, 5719 14th Ave., St. Petersburg, FL 33710 (813)381-5707

Florida Sea Kayaking Association, c/o George Ellis, 3095 67th Ave. S., St. Petersburg, FL 33172 (813)864-2651

Peninsula Paddling Club, c/o Lou Glaros, 8751 Shady Glen Dr., Orlando, FL 32819 (407)352-1711

Seminole Canoe and Yacht Club, c/o John Blois, 4619 Oriega Farms Cir., Jacksonville, FL 332205 (904)388-6734

West Florida Canoe Club, 807 Lagoon Dr., Pensacola, FL 32505 (904)434-6619

GEORGIA

Atlanta Whitewater Club, c/o Steve Thomas, P.O. Box 33, Clarkston, GA 30021 (404)299-3752

Central Georgia River Runners, P.O. Box 5509, Macon, GA 31207

Coastal Georgia Paddling Club, c/o Katie Goodwin, 505 Herb River Drive, Savannah, GA 31406

Georgia Canoeing Association, c/o Gwen Bergen, P.O. Box 7023, Atlanta, GA 30357 (404)266-3734

HAWAII

Anuenue Canoe Club, c/o Joseph Nappy Napoleon, P.O. Box 90547, Honolulu, HI 96835 (808)737-1930

Hanalei Canoe Club, c/o Jerry Lefkowitz, P.O. Box 814, Hanalei, HI 96714 (808)826-6803

Hawaiian Sailing Canoe Association, c/o James Kincaid, 155 Kainake Loop, Kalua, HI 96734 (808)261-6728

Hawaii Canoe/Kayak Team, c/o Billy Whitford, 4614 Kilauea Ave., #450, Honolulu, HI 96816 (808)737-4451

Healani Canoe Club, c/o Clement D. Paiaina, 3455 Campbell Ave., Honolulu, HI 96815 (918)787-5647

Hilo Bay Canoe Club, c/o Momi Mauhili, P.O. Box 11420, Hilo, HI 96721-6421 (808)959-6633

Honolulu Canoe Club, c/o John D. Keaulana, P.O. Box 2125, Pearl City, HI 96782

Hui Lanakila Canoe Club, c/o Catherine Y. M. Kam-Ho, P.O. Box 62121, Honolulu, HI 96839-2121 (808)942-0419

Hui Nalu Canoe Club, c/o Diane Warncke, P.O. Box 26342, Honolulu, HI 96825 (808)396-6588

Hui-O-Ikaika Canoe Club, c/o Alika Akau, 84-1065 Kaulawaha Rd., Waianae, HI 96792 (808)695-9001

Kailua Canoe Club, c/o Mary Moore, P.O. Box 177, Kailua, HI 96734 (808)262-8512

Kaiola Canoe Club, c/o Pomaikai Kane, P.O. Box 3502, Lihue, HI 96766 (808)245-4618

Kai Oni Canoe Club, c/o Shirleyann Kalama, 355 Auwinala Rd., Kailua, HI 96734 (808)523-2146

Kai Opua Canoe Club, c/o Mary A. Green, P.O. Box 3079, Kailua-Kona, HI 96745 (808)329-6163

Kamehameha Canoe Club, c/o John Kekua, 158 Alohalani St., Hilo, HI 96720 (808)959-9423

Kanaka Ikaika Inc., Kayak Club, c/o Mike Cripps, P.O. Box 438, Kaneohe, HI 96744 (808)239-9803

Kaneohe Outrigger Canoe Club, 46-241 Heeia St., Kaneohe, HI Kawaihae Canoe Club, c/o Manny Veincent, P.O. Box 856, Kamuela, HI 967434 (808)885-4498 96744

Keauhou Canoe Club, c/o Peter Lasich, P.O. Box 0399755, Kealekekua-Kona, HI 96739 (808)329-3752

Keaukaha Canoe Club, c/o Luana Kawelu, 10 Makani Circle, Hilo, HI 96720 (808)935-7258

Keoua Canoe Club, c/o Kurtis Yaumauchi, P.O. Box 592, Honaunau, HI 96726 (808)328-2354

Koa Kai Canoe Club, c/o George Waikoloa, 3227 Alani Dr., Honolulu, HI 96822 (808)988-3401

Koloa Outrigger Canoe Club, c/o Ruth Potts, P.O. Box 1254, Koloa, HI 96756 (808)742-1343

Kumulokahi Canoe Club, c/o Elmer Cathcart, 2933 Kalakaua Ave., Honolulu, HI 96816

Lanikai Canoe Club, c/o John Foti, 1343 Mokulua Drive, Kailua, HI 96734 (808)261-5550

Leeward Kai Canoe Club Inc., c/o Edith K. Van Gieson, 89-889 Nanakuli Ave., Waianae, HI 96792 (808)668-8635

Lokahi Canoe Club, c/o Susan Trent, 574 Lauiki St., #3, Honolulu, HI 96826 (808)946-4746

Makaha Canoe Club, c/o Luisa Titworth, 87-266 Laulele St., Waianae, HI 96792 (808)668-4031

Mana'E Canoe Club, c/o Kathleen Callahan, Star Rt. 356, Kaunakakai, HI 96748 (808)558-8922

Manu O Ke Kai Canoe Club, c/o Randolph Sanborn, Sr., 278 B Karsten Dr., Wahiawa, HI 96786 (808)621-7240

Na Holo Kai Inc., c/o Warren C.R. Perry, P.O. Box 687, Lawai, HI 96765 (808)245-3688

Na Keiki O Ka Mo'I Canoe Club, c/o Shannon Kaaekuahiwi, 85-128-A Maiuu Rd., Wai'anae, HI 96792 (808)696-4164

Na Wahine O Ke Kai Outrigger Canoe Club, c/o Hannie Anderson, 423 Aulima Loop, Kailua, HI 96734 (808)262-2567

Outrigger Canoe Club, c/o Ray Ludwig, 2909 Kalakaua Ave., Honolulu, HI 96815

Pai'Ea Canoe Club, c/o Lyle Cabacungan, P.O. Box 1629, Kailua-Kona, HI 96745 (808)329-7986

Puna Canoe Club, c/o Michael O'Shaughnessey, P.O. Box 728, Pahoa, Puna, HI 96778 (808)965-7769

Surfsport Canoe Club, c/o Paul Gay, 818 Kainui Dr., Kailua, HI 96734 (808)262-9964

Waikiki Beachboys Canoe Club, c/o Francis 'Blackie' Kalua, 488 Kalamaku St., Honolulu, HI 96813 (808)922-1551

Waikiki Surf Club, c/o Alice K. Froiseth, 791 Sunset Ave., Honolulu, HI 96816 (808)732-2719

Waikiki Yacht Club-Canoe Club, c/o Ralph Hanalei, 1599 Ala Moana Blvd., Honolulu, HI 96815 (808)955-4405

Waikoloa Canoe Club, c/o Louise Knop, P.O. Box 3281 W.U.S., Kamuela, HI 96743 (808)883-9192

Wailani Canoe Club, c/o Maile Mauhili, 395 Todd Ave., Hilo, HI 96720 (808)935-5195

IDAHO

H.P. River Runners, Hewlett Packard Boise Dr., Box 15, Boise, ID 83807 (208)387-1290; (208)323-3437

Idaho Whitewater Association, 3380 Americana Terrace, Boise, ID 83706 (208)384-1244; (208)334-1927

Snake River Whitewater Project, c/o Paul Reep, 550 Shoup Ave., Idaho Falls 83402 (208)524-0282

ILLINOIS

Central Illinois Whitewater, 2502 Willow St., Pekin, IL 61554

Chicago Land Canoe Base, 4019 Narraganett Ave., Chicago, IL 60603

Chicago Whitewater Association, c/o Marge Cline, 1343 N. Portage, Palatine, IL 60067 (312)359-5047

G.L.O.P., P.O. Box 2576, Chicago, IL 60690

Henderson County Tourism Council, c/o Thomas R. Clapp, P.O. Box 278, Oquawka, IL 61469 (309)867-2045

Illinois Paddling Council, 9 Peiffer, Lemont, IL 60439

Lincoln Park Boat Club, c/o Bill Thompson, 2631 N. Richmond, Chicago, IL 60647 (312)278-5539

Mackinaw Canoe Club of Central Illinois, 711 First National Bank Bldg., Peoria, IL 61602 (309)676-6113

Middle Fork Paddling Group, c/o C.E. Wilson, P.O. Box 8, Urbana, IL 61801 (217)328-6666

Northwest Passage Outing Club, c/o Richard Sweitzer, 1130 Greenleaf Avenue, Wilmette, IL 60091 (708)256-4409

Prairie State Canoeists, c/o Ken Beck, 570 Webford, Des Plaines, IL 60016-3317 (708)299-3977

INDIANA

Hoosier Canoe Club, c/o Donnis Kirkman, 6212 Furnas Rd. Indianapolis, IN 46241 (317)856-6356

Indianapolis Canoe Racing Council, 4919 N. Meridian, Indianapolis, IN 46208 (317)255-4900

Kekionga Voyageurs, 3211 Convington, Fort Wayne, IN 46802

North Central Indiana Canoe Club, 57749 8th St., Elkhart, IN 46517 (219)293-7949

Ohio Valley Canoe Club, Rt. 1, Box 252, Tennyson, IN 47637

St. Joe Valley Canoe and Kayak Club, 609 N. Division, Bristol, IN 46507 (219)848-4279

South Bend Moving Water Club, c/o Jim Wagner, 3220 E. Jefferson Blvd., South Bend, IN 46615 (219)234-0191

U.S. Canoe and Kayak Team, 201 S. Capitol Ave., Indianapolis, IN 46225 (317)237-5690

Viking Canoe Club, 1615 Corydon, New Albany, IN 47150 Wildcat Canoe Club, c/o Lance Shelby, P.O. Box 6232, Kokomo, IN 46904-6232

IOWA

North Central Boat Club, R.R. 1, Box 64M, Humbolt, IA 50548 (515)332-2940

KANSAS

Kansas Canoe Association, P.O. Box 2885, Wichita, KS 67201

Kayak Chapter, 3119 Amherst Ave., Manhattan, KS 66502

KENTUCKY

Bluegrass Wildwater Association, c/o Mike Clark, 453 Becky Pl., Lexington, KY 40502

Elkhorn Paddlers, 232 Greenbrier Rd., Lexington, KY 40503 (606)277-0656

Four Rivers Canoe Association, 523 Alben Barkley Dr., Paducah, KY 42001

Southern Kentucky Paddlers Society, P.O. Box 265, Bowling Green, KY 42101

Viking Canoe Club, 6016 Apex Dr., Louisville, KY 40219

MAINE

Bangor Parks and Recreation Dept., c/o Dale W. Theriault, 100 Dutton St., Bangor, ME 04401 (207)942-9000

Maine Canoe/Kayak Racing Org., c/o Earl H. Baldwin, R.F.D.2, Box 268, Orrington, ME 04474 (207)825-4439

Penobscott Paddle and Chowder Society, c/o Diana Laing, R.F.D.2, Box 840, Pittsfield, ME 04967

UMM Outing Club, c/o Richard Scribner, 9 O'Brien Ave., Machias, ME 04654 (207)255-3312

MANITOBA

Canoe Manitoba, 1700 Ellice Ave., Winnipeg, MB R3H 0B1

MARYLAND

Canoe Cruisers/Conservation, 322 10th St. S.E., Washington, DC 20003 (202)245-6306

Greater Baltimore Canoe Club, P.O. Box 235, Riderwood, MD 21139 (301)391-2817

Mason-Dixon Canoe Crusiers, 222 Pleasant Trail, Hagerstown, MD Monocacy Canoe Club, Box 1083, Fredrick, MD 21701

World Championships Inc., c/o Mike Fetchero, P.O. Box 689, Mc Henry, MD 21541 (301)724-5541

MASSACHUSETTS

Appalachian Mountain Club, 5 Joy St., Boston, MA 02108 (617)628-0275; (617)523-0636

Appalachian Mountain Club-Berkshire, c/o William T. Cushwa, 63 Silver St., South Hadley, MA 01075 (413)536-1347

Charles River Watershed Association, c/o Thomas Benton, 2391 Commonwealth Ave., Auburnedale, MA 02166 (617)527-2799

Kayak and Canoe Club of Boston, P.O. 526, Bridge St., Hennier, NH 03242

Outdoor Centre of N.E., 8 Pleasant St., Millers Falls, MA 01349 (413)659-3926

Westfield River Wild Club, c/o J. Defeo, Ingell Rd., Chester, MA 01011 (413)354-9684

MICHIGAN

Lansing Oar and Paddle Club, c/o Bobby Adams, P.O. Box 26254, Lansing, MI 48909

Recreational Canoeing Association, P.O. Box 296, Mantaque, MI 49437 (517)653-2644

RSandC Kayak Club, 1230 Astor Dr., B2022, Ann Arbor, MI 48104

MINNESOTA

Cascaders Canoe and Kayak Club, c/o Secretary/ Treasurer, P.O. Box 61, Minneapolis, MN 55458

Minnesota Canoe Association, c/o Venice Barsness, Box 13567, Dinkytown Station, Minneapolis, MN 55414 (612)725-3478

MISSOURI

Devils Elbow River Team, P.O. Box 338, Devils Elbow, MO 65457

James Creek Team, Rt. 1, Bopx 110H, Odessa, MO 64076

Kansas City Whitewater Club, c/o Bob Behrends, 3727 Jefferson, Kansas City, MO 64111 (816)753-5297

Maremec River Canoe Club, 26 Lake Rd., Fenston, MO 63026 (314)458-3688

Missouri Whitewater Association, c/o Stan Stoy, 2305 White Ash Ct., Florissant, MO 63031 (314)521-4003

Ozark Wilderness Waterways, P.O. Box 16032, Kansas City, MO 64112

MONTANA

Headwater Paddling Association, c/o Doug Habermann, Box 1392, Bozeman, MT 59715 (406)586-0072

Medicine River Canoe Club, 3805 4th Ave. So., Bozeman, MT 59405 (406)761-0303

NEW BRUNSWICK

Canoe New Brunswick, C.P. 220, Kedgwick, NB E0K 1C0

NEWFOUNDLAND

Newfoundland Canoeing Association, P.O. Box 5961, St. John's, NF A1C5X4

NEW HAMPSHIRE

Ledyard Canoe Club, c/o Cynthia Lynch, P.O. Box 9, Hanover, NH 03755 (603)646-2753

Merrimack Valley Paddlers, 51 Christian Hill Rd., Amherst, NH 03031

NEW JERSEY

Appalachian Mountain Club, c/o Donald R. Getzin, 19 Raritan Ave., Apt.7, Highland Park, NJ 08904 (201)249-7898

Canoe Committe/App.Mtn Club/NJ, 64 Lupine Way, Stirling, NJ 07980

Hunterdon County Canoe Club, Hunterdon County Park System, Hwy., 31, Lebanon, NJ 08833

Inwood Canoe Club, c/o Elizabeth E. Sheppard, 186 Hackensack St., E. Rutherford, NJ 07073 (201)935-1353

Mohawk Canoe Club, c/o James M. Howie, Rd. 2, Lebanon, NJ 08833 (201)832-2570

Monoco Canoe Club, c/o Dr. Frank Cancellieri, 861 Colis Neck Rd., Freehold, NJ 07728 (201)431-5678

NEW MEXICO

Adobe Whitewater Club, 3209 Baker Villa, Los Alamos, NM 87544 (505)662-5413

NEW YORK

Adirondack Mtn. Club, 4029 Georgetown Sq., Schenectady, NY 12303 (518)372-7946; (518)385-7206

Adirondack Mtn. Club Schenectady, 722 Rankin Ave., Schenectady, NY 12308

Appalachain Mtn Club/NY Chapter, 6 Jay St, Box 443, Bardonia, NY 10954

Biltmore Beach Club, c/o Joseph Studley, P.O. Box 395, Massapequa, NY 11758 (516)795-9097

Heuvelton Canoe Club, c/o Howard Friot, 7 York St., Heuvelton, NY 13654 (315)344-7744

Hilltop Hoppers Canoe/Kayak Club, c/o Jill Morray, 2323 Pleasant Valley Rd., Berne, NY 12023

Hudson River Whitewater Derby, c/o Janet Palmer, Thirteenth Lake Rd., Box 23, NOrth River, NY 12856

Inland Surfing Association, c/o Steve Busch, 204A Gordon Dr., Binghamton, NY 13901 (607)648-8511

Internatl Canoe and Kayak Club of Oneonta, c/o Gerhard G. Stoeger, P.O. Box 163, Davenport, NY 13750 (607)278-5990

Ka-Na-Wa-Ke Canoe Club, c/o Ronadl Schlie, 6011 Misty Ridge Lane, Clay, NY 13041

Kayak and Canoe Club - New York, c/o Phyllis Horowitz, P.O. Box 329, Phoenicia, NY 12464

Metropolitan Canoe and Kayak Club, c/o Jane Ahlquist, P.O. Box 021868, Brooklyn, NY 11202-0040 (516)482-2752

Niagara Gorge Kayak Club, 66 Deer Run, Glenwood, NY 14069 (716)856-3351

Nissequogue River Canoe Club, c/o Lou Schneider, 3920 Mill Rd., Seaford, NY 11783 (516)221-5614

New York State Canoe Racing Association, c/o Roberta Shapiro, 18 Cheriton Dr., Whitesboro, NY 13492 (315)736-0511

Northern Canoe and Kayak Club, R.D. #2, Potsdam, NY 13676

Sebago Canoe Club, c/o Richard Schneider, 1751 67th St., Brooklyn, NY 11204 (718)241-3683

Sons of the Legion, c/o Art Cacciola, Arden Kelsey Post 907, Candor, NY 13743

The Tenandeho Canoe Association Inc., c/o John F. Erano, 718 Bruno Rd., Clifton Park, NY 12065 (518)877-6277

Tupper Lake Chamber of Commerce, c/o Ginny Shouten, 60 Park St., Tupper Lake, NY 12986 (518)359-3328

NORTH CAROLINA

Carolina Canoe Club, P.O. Box 12932, Raleigh, NC 27605

Catawba Valley Outing Club, c/o Jay Bajorek, 774 4th Street Dr. SW, Hickory, NC 28602 (704)322-2297

Nantahala Racing Club, c/o Mike Hipsher, U.S. 19W, Box 41, Bryson City, NC 28713 (704)488-9017

Triad River Runners, P.O. Box 11283, Bethabara Station, Winston Salem, NC 27116-1283

Triangle Paddlers Inc., c/o Thomas Anderson, P.O. Box 20902, Raleigh, NC 27619

Upper Delaware NS and RR, Box C, Narrowsburg, NY 12764

Whitewater/Syracuse Outing, Ski Lodge, Skytop Road, Syracuse, NY 13210

The Wilderness Center, c/o Lacy C. Starr, P.O.Box 2194, Greensboro, N.C. 27402 (919)299-5811

Yonkers Canoe Club, Alexander and Wells St., Yonkers, NY 10701

NORTHWEST TERRITORIES

NWT CANOE Association, P.O. Box 2763, Yellowknife, NWT X1A 2R1

NOVA SCOTIA

Canoe Nova Scotia Association, P.O. Box 3010 S., Halifax, NS B3J 3G6

OHIO

Antioch Kayak Club, PE Dept, Antioch College, Yellow Springs, OH 45387

Dayton Canoe Club Inc., c/o Robert Aldredge, 1020 Riverside Dr., Dayton, OH 45405 (513)222-9392

Keel Haulers Canoe Club, c/o John Kobak, 1649 Allen Dr., Westlake, OH 44145 (216)871-1758

Mad Hatter Canoe Club, 185 Buckey Rd., Painesville, OH 44077

Toledo River Gang, c/o Mike Sidell, 626 Lousiana Ave., Perrysburg, OH 43551 (419)874-9782

University of Akron Canoe Club, c/o Mary Kay Warner, Ocasek Natatorium, Akron, OH 44325-6301 (216)375-5984

OKLAHOMA

OK Canoers, 1616, Caddell, Norman, OK 73064 (405)360-1892

ONTARIO

Canoe Ontario, 1220 Sheperd Ave. E., Suite 315, Willowdale, ON M2K 2X1

The Hide Away Canoe Club, Box 548, Station "O", Toronto, ON M4A2P1

Marathon Racing Canoe Asssn., P.O. Box 601, Trenton, ON K8V 5R7

Ontario Wild Water Affiliation, 1679 Applewood Rd., MIssiauga, ON L5E 2M2

Wilderness Canoe Association, P.O. Box 496, Station K, Toronto, ON M4P 2G9

OREGON

Lower Columbia Canoe Club, c/o Janice Stuart, 14490 N.W. Hunters Dr., Beaverton, OR 97006 (503)629-8124

Oregon Kayak and Canoe Club, c/o Brian Colony, P.O. Box 692, Portland, OR 97207 (503)629-1863

South Oregon Association of Kayakers, c/o Richard B. Haynes, 5168 Glen Echo Way, Central Point, OR (503)664-5669

Willamette Kayak and Canoe Club, 3050 NW Taylor, Corvallis, OR 97330

PENNSYLVANIA

Allegheny Canoe Club, 755 Spring St., Titusville, PA 16534

Benscreek Canoe Club, c/o Bruce Penrod, P.O. Box 2, Johnstown, PA 15907

Bottoms Up Canoe Club, RD #2, Box 266, Pittsfield, PA 16340

Buck Ridge Ski Club, c/o Pete Bergquist, P.O. Box 179, Bala Cynwyd, PA 19004

Canoe Club Greater Harrisburg, c/o John Ressler, 180 Andersontown Rd., Dover, PA 17315

Conewago Canoe Club, c/o Penny H. Snyder, 670 B Trolley Dr., Dallastown, PA 17313 (717)244-8440

Fox Chapel Canoe Club, 610 Squaw Rd., Pittsburgh, PA 15238

Keystone Canoe Club, c/o Daniel L. Fick, P.O. Box 377, Blandon, PA 19510 (215)670-0829

Keystone River Runners, c/o Donald B. Frew, RD 6, Box 359, Indiana, PA 15701 (412)349-2805

Lancaster Canoe Club, c/o Michelle Mc Cann, 339 N. George St., Millersville, PA 17551 (717)872-4413

Lehigh Gorge Outdoor Club, c/o Larry D. Skinner, 243 Main St., White Haven, PA 18661 (717)443-8075

Lehigh Valley Canoe Club, c/o Eugene Gallagher, 42 N. Canal St., Walnutport, PA 18088 (215)559-9595

Oil City Canoe Club, Rt. 62, Rd. 2, Oil City, PA 16301

PACK, c/o Ray F. Garman, 113 Edward St., Athens, PA 18810 (717)888-5858

Penn Hills Canoe Club, 12200 Garland Dr., Pittsburgh, PA 15235

Philadelphia Canoe Club, c/o David Dannenburg, 4900 Ridge Ave., Philadelphia, PA 19128 (215)844-6727

Raystown Canoe Club, Box 112, Evertt, PA 15537

Sylvan Canoe Club, 132 Arch St., Verona, PA 15231

Three Rivers Paddling Club, c/o Paul Kammer, 400 6th St., Patterson Heights, Beaver Falls, PA 15010 (412)843-5152

Western PA Paddle Sport Association, c/o Rebekah A. Sheeler, P.O. Box 8857, Pittsburgh, PA 16003

PRINCE EDWARD ISLAND

P.E.I. Recreational Canoeing Association, P.O. Box 2000, Charlottetown, PE C1A 7N8

QUEBEC

Federation quebecoise de canot-kayak, 4545 Ave. Pierre-de-Coubertin, C.P. 1000, Succ. M., Montreal, PQ H1V 3R2

Federation quebecoise d'eau vive, 4545 Av. Pierre-de Coubertin, C.P. 1000, Succ. M., Montreal, PQ H1V 3R2

Federation quebecoise du canot-camping, inc., 4545 Ave Pierre-de-Coubertin, C.P. 1000, Succ. M., Montreal, PQ H1V 3R2

RHODE ISLAND

Baer's River Workshop, R.R. 1, 136 Arcadia Rd., Hope Valley, RI 02832

Rhode Island Canoe Association, c/o David Wilson, 193 Pettaconsett Ave., Warwick, RI 02888 (401)781-5187

Rhode Island Canoe Club, 20 Knowles St., Lincoln, RI 02865

Westerly YMCA Canoe and Kayak Club, c/o Scott McLeod, 95 High St., Westerly, RI 02871 (401)596-2894

SASKATCHEWAN

Sakatchewan Canoeing Association, P.O. Box 6064, Saskatoon, SK S7K 4E5

Saskatoon Canoeing Club, P.O. Box 7764, Saskatoon, SK S7K 4J1

SOUTH CAROLINA

Edisto River Canoe and Kayak Club, P.O. Box 1763, Walterboro, SC 29488 (803)549-9595

Foothills Canoe Club, c/o Alice Cole, P.O. Box 6331, Greenville, SC 29606 (803)233-4472

Palmetto Paddlers Inc., c/o Rembert Milligan, 5938 Woodville Rd., Columbia, SC 29206 (803)787-7999

SOUTH DAKOTA

South Dakota Canoe Association, P.O. Box 403, Sioux Falls, SD 57101

TENNESSEE

Bluff City Canoe Club, P.O. Box 40523, Memphis, TN 38104

Chota Canoe Club, c/o James W. Lucas, 1407 Woodcrest Dr., Knoxville, TN 37918 (615)698-2664

City Canoe Club, c/o Lanier Fogg, Box 40523, Memphis, TN 38104 (901)795-3988

E. Tenn. Whitewater Club, P.O. Box 3074, Oak Ridge, TN 37830 Jackson Canoe Club, P.O. Box 3034, Jackson, TN 38301

Tennessee Eastman Hiking and Canoeing Club, Eastman's Employee Ctr., Kingsport, TN 37662 (615)229-2005

Tennessee Scenic River Association, c/o Helen Gibson, 4414 Leland Lane, Nashville, TN 37204 (615)329-3563

Tennesee Valley Canoe Club, P.O. Box 11125, Chatanooga, TN 37401

TEXAS

Alamo Rivermen, P.O. Box 171194, San Antonio, TX 78217 (512)493-7058

Bayou City Whitewater Club, c/o Nancy Martin, P.O. Box 980782, Houston, TX 77098 (713)224-7554

Dallas Downriver Canoe Club, 3124 Caribbean, Mesquite, TX 75150

Heart of Texas Pack and Paddle Club, P.O. Box 164, Killeen, TX 76540

Houston Canoe Club, c/o Bob Arthur, P.O. Box 500582, Houston, TX 77250 (713)467-8857

North Texas River Runners, c/o Billie Mc Callon, 215 Lakeshore Dr., Waxahachie, TX 75165 (214)937-8835

Seadrift Canoe Club, P.O. Box 736, Seadrift, TX 77983

Texas Canoe Racing Association, c/o Kevin Bradley, 9706 Brookshire, Houston, TX 77041 (713)939-7159

Texas River Recreation Association, Rt 1, Box 55R, Martindale, TX 78655 (512)357-6113

Texas Whitewater Association, Box 5429, Austin, TX 78763

United States Canoe Association, Texas Div., Houston, TX 77092

Victoria Canoe Club, Rt. 1, Box 143A, Victoria, TX 77901

VERMONT

Northern Vermont Canoe Cruise, c/o Sheri Larsen, 11 Discovery Rd., Essex Junction, VT 05452 (802)878-6828

VIRGINIA

Blue Ridge River Runners, P.O. Box 315, Monroe, VA 24574

Boaters out of Control, 4807 N. 2nd St., Arlington, VA 22203

Canoe Cruisers Association, c/o Ed Grove, 2420 N. George Mason Dr., Arlington, VA 22207 (703)533-8334

Chesapeake Association of Sea Kayakers, c/o Roger Gathright, 400 Mohican Dr., Portsmouth, VA 23701 (804)461-4483

Coastal Canoeists, c/o Chris Leonard, Box 566, Richmond, VA 23204 (804)282-2634

Mid Atlantic Paddlers Association, c/o Kirk Havens, 154 Pacific Dr., Hampton, VA 23666 (804)838-8998

WASHINGTON

Boeing Alpine Society, 17327 158th St., N.E., Renton, WA 98058 (206)228-3786; (206)655-1141

Puget Sound Paddle Club, 14603 29th Ave., E. Tacoma, WA 98445

Seattle Canoe Club, c/o Dan Henderson, 5900 W. Green Lake Way N., Seattle, WA 98115 (206)522-1774

University Kayak Club, c/o John Hokanson, Intramural Act. Bldg., GD-10, Seattle, WA 98195 (206)524-7426

Washington Kayak Club, c/o Fran Troje, 4257 123rd Ave. S.E., Bellevue, WA 98006 (206)746-6726

Whatcom Association of Kayak Enthusiasts, P.O. Box 1952, Bellingham, WA 08227 (206)676-1529

WEST VIRGINIA

West Virgina Wildwater Club, Rt. 2, Box 29C, Fayetteville, WV 25840

WISCONSIN

Green Bay Paddlers United, c/o Greg Gauthier, 13601 Marshek Rd., Maribel, WI 54227 (414)863-8458

Hoofers Outing Club, c/o Jon Mc Anulty, Wisconsin Memorial Union, Madison, WI 53706 (608)262-1630

Wausau Area Canoe and Kayak Org., P.O. Box 14, Wausau, WI 54402

Wausau Kayak and Canoe Corp., c/o Richard Olsen, P.O. Box 6190, Wausau, WI 54402-6190 (715)845-6231

WYOMING

New Wavers Kayak Club, 5330 S. Elm, Casper, WY 82601

YUKON TERRITORY

White Water Association.-Yukon, 13 Firth Rd., Whitehorse, YT Y1A 2N7

Yukon Voyageurs Canoe Club, 5131 5th Ave., Whitehorse, YT Y1A1L8

WATERWAYS AND GEOGRAPHIC AREA INDEX

Note: Entries included in this index are primarily to guidebooks and other descriptive guide sources intended for the use of paddlers, and to some other sources describing inland and coastal waterways in North America navigable with paddle craft. Streams, lakes, swamps, estuaries, and coastal areas, etc. are listed individually as are provinces, states, regions, parks and refuges and islands. Numbers refer to citation numbers, not page numbers. The citation numbers are keyed with symbols indicating type of material, as shown in the following example for the Alaska entry:

Alaska 110-121, 505-511*, 620-623**, (897), (901-902), (921), (926), (928), (931), 1114v, 1187v

110-121	**No symbol:** description found in a guidebook
505-511*	**Asterisk:** description found in a guide article
620-623**	**Double asterisk:** description found in a map or map-guide
(897), (901-902), etc.	**Parenthesis:** description found in a trip account or pictorial work
1114v, 1187v	**Lower case v:** description found in a videorecording

A

B

C

D

E

F

G

H

M

N

O

P

Q

R

S

T

U

V

W

Y

Z

NAME, TITLE, SUBJECT INDEX

Note: Entries in this index include personal and corporate authors, titles (of books, periodicals, videorecordings) and subjects. Access to brief or ephemeral materials (articles, maps, and map-guides) is by waterway or area in the Waterways Index, above. Numbers refer to citation numbers, not page numbers. The bracketed word [Video] indicates a videorecording title.

A

B

C

D

E

F

H

I

J

K

L

M

N

O

P

Q

R

S

T

U

V

W

Y

Z